TWIN SPICA

3

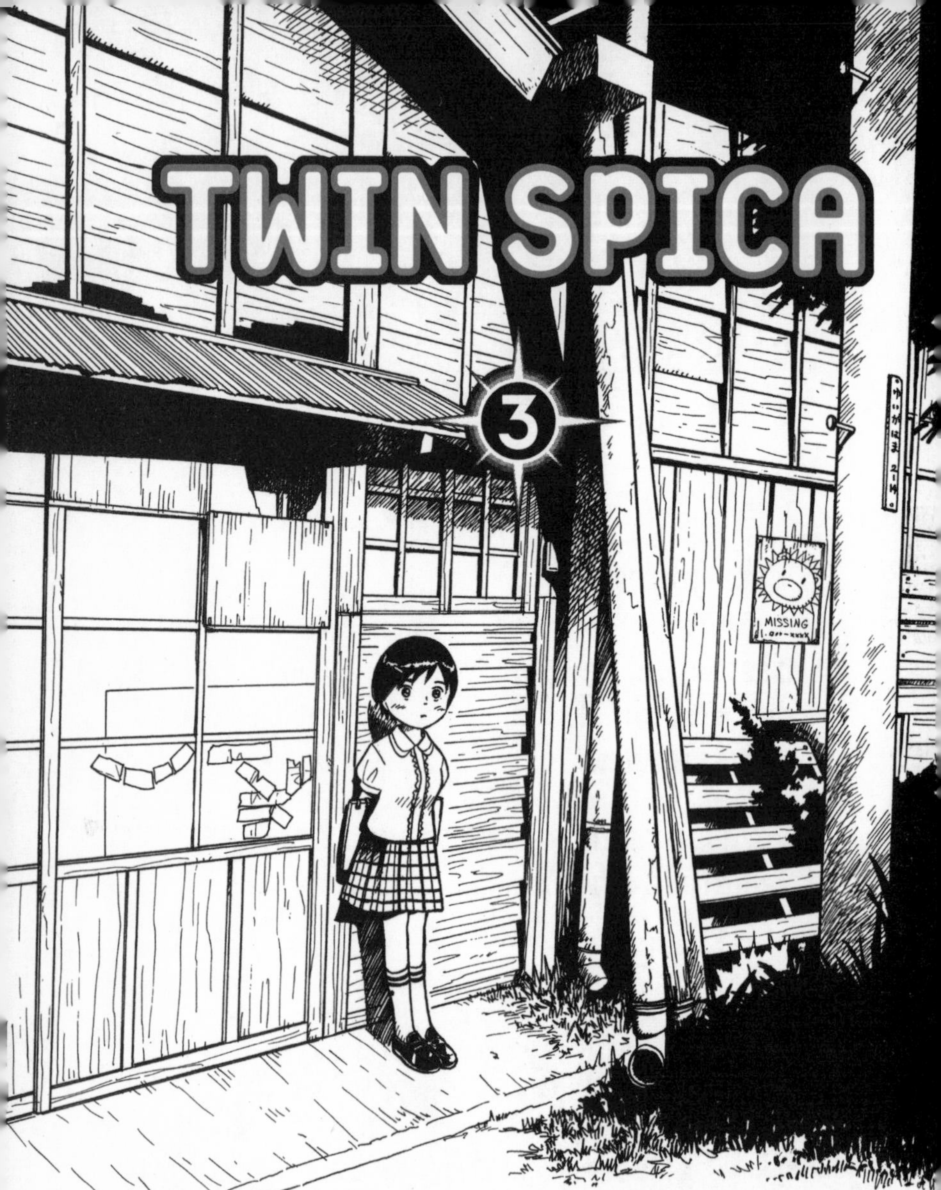
MISSING

Kou Yaginuma

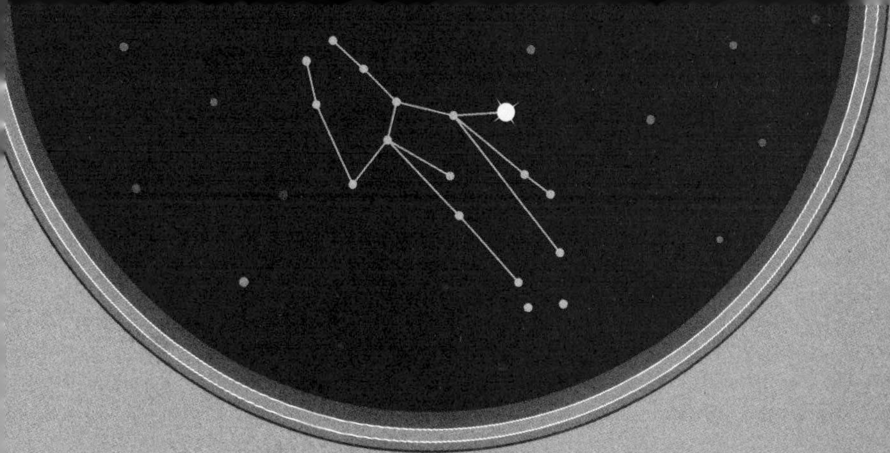

CONTENTS

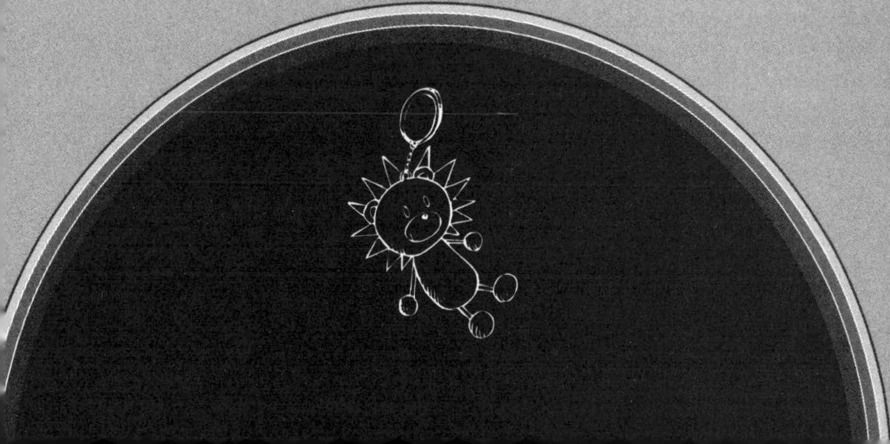

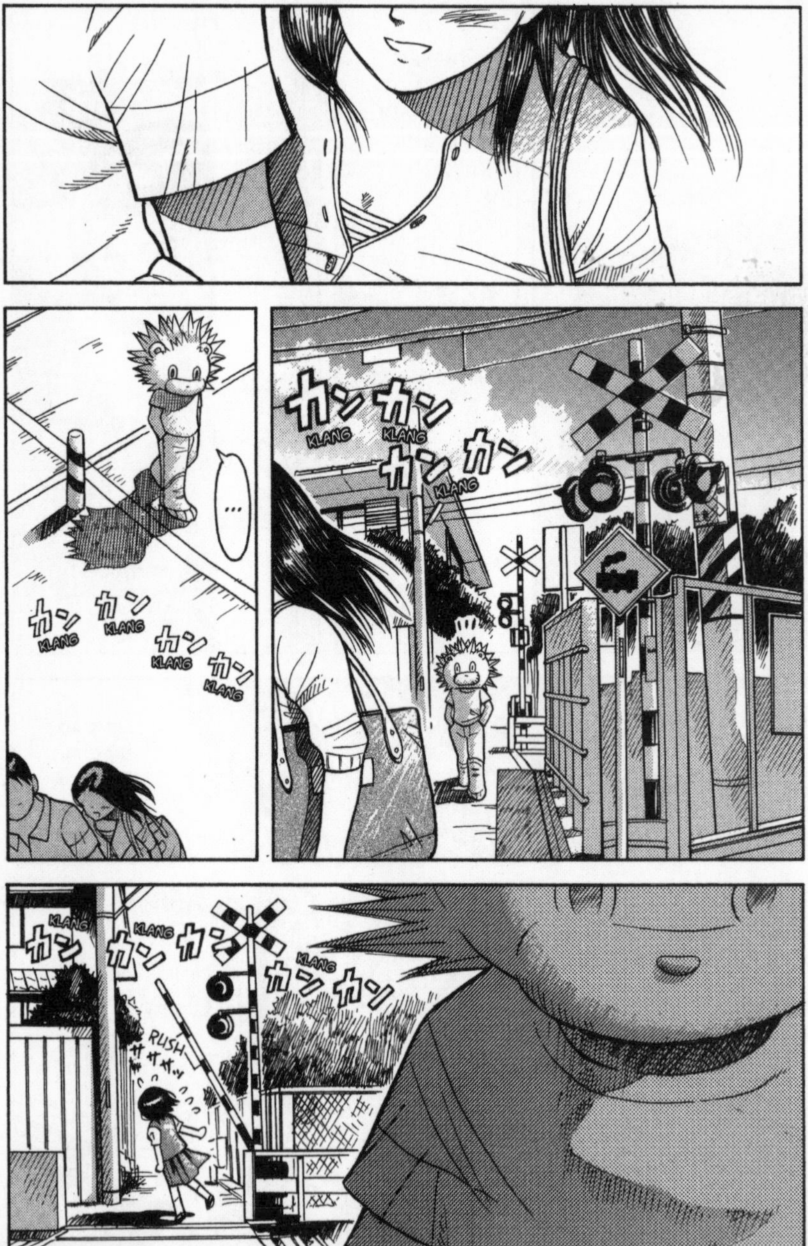
カンカン
KLANG KLANG
カンカン
KLANG
...
カン KLANG
カン KLANG
カン KLANG
カン KLANG
KLANG
カン
KLANG
カン
カン
KLANG
カンカン
RUSH

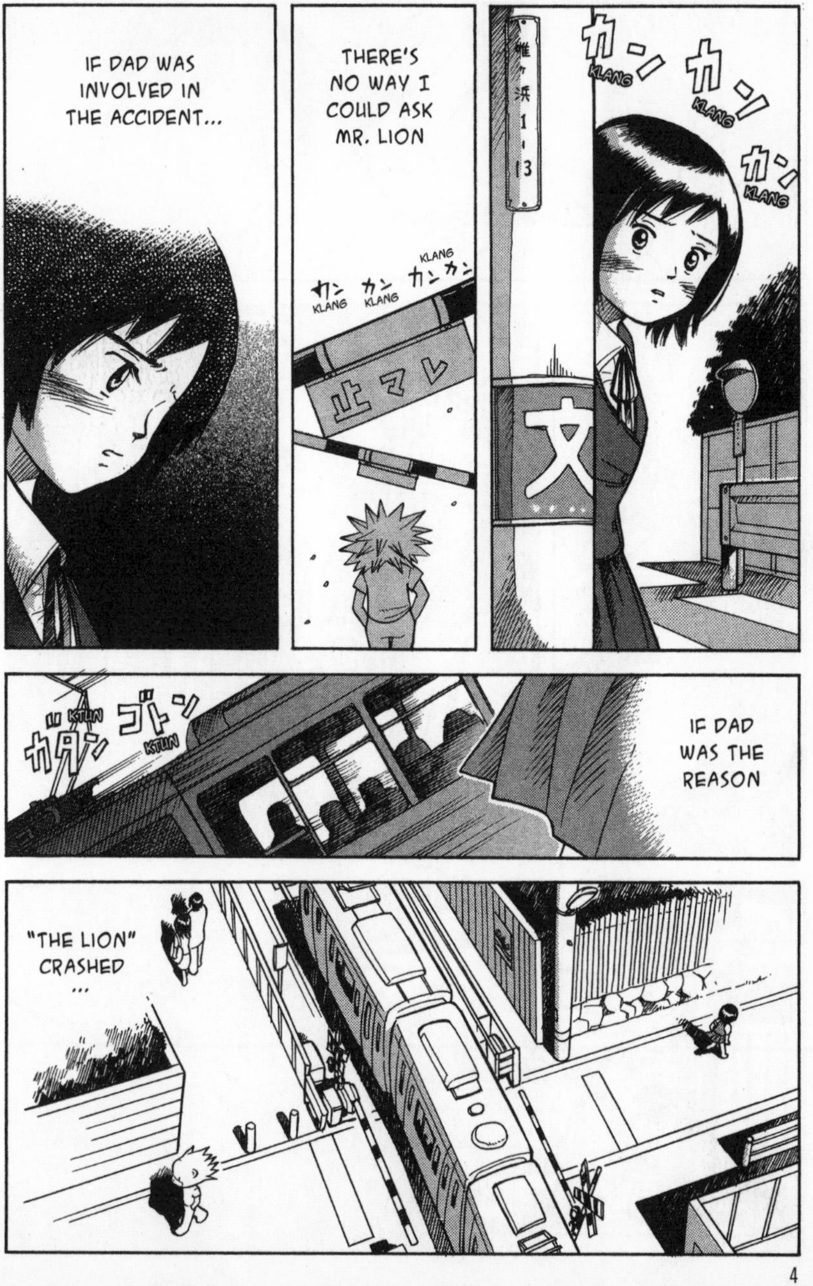

KLANG
KLANG
KLANG
KLANG
KLANG
KLANG
THERE'S NO WAY I COULD ASK MR. LION
止マレ
IF DAD WAS INVOLVED IN THE ACCIDENT...
IF DAD WAS THE REASON
KTUN
KTUN
"THE LION" CRASHED ...

MISSION:09

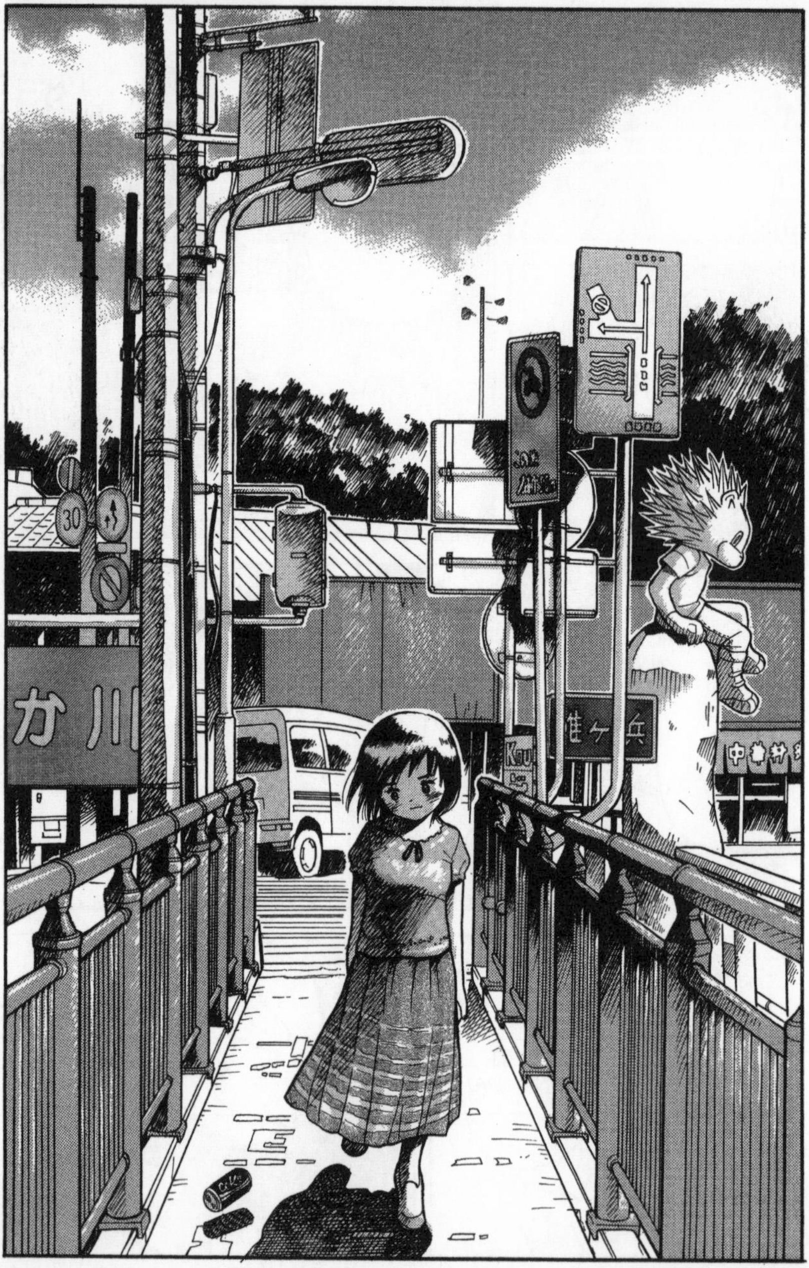
30
カ川

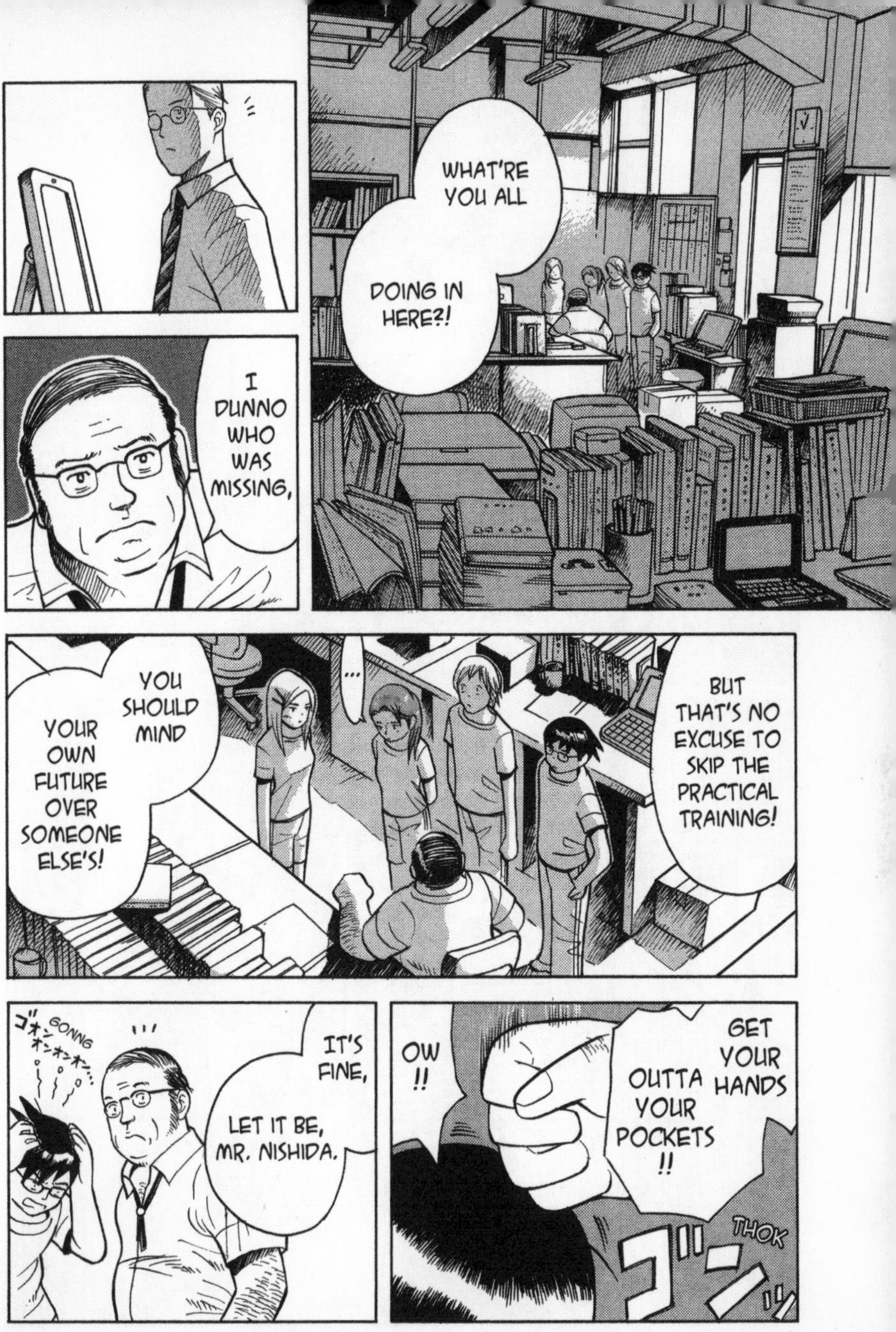
WHAT'RE YOU ALL
DOING IN HERE?!
I DUNNO WHO WAS MISSING,
BUT THAT'S NO EXCUSE TO SKIP THE PRACTICAL TRAINING!
...
YOU SHOULD MIND
YOUR OWN FUTURE OVER SOMEONE ELSE'S!
GET YOUR HANDS
OUTTA YOUR POCKETS !!
THOK
ゴーン
OW !!
IT'S FINE,
LET IT BE, MR. NISHIDA.
ゴオンオンオンオン…
GONNG

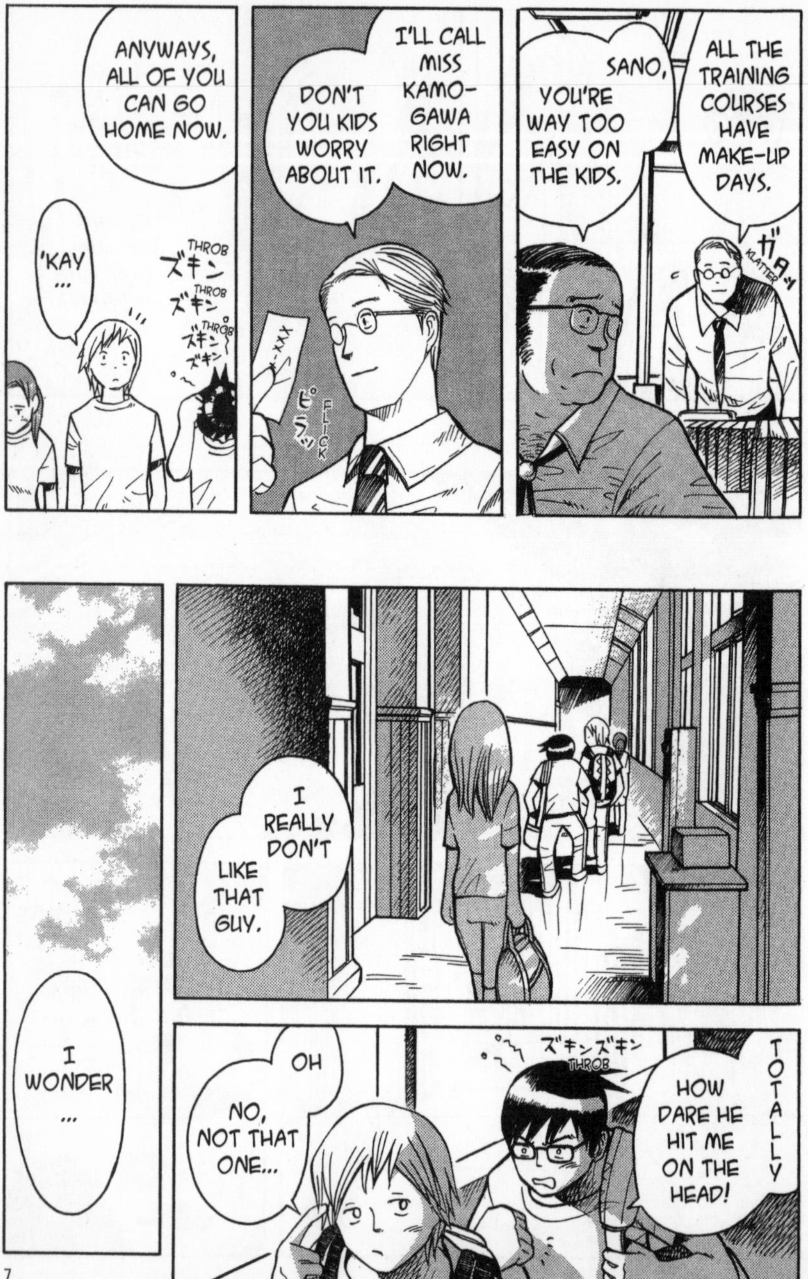
ALL THE TRAINING COURSES HAVE MAKE-UP DAYS.
ガタッ
KLATTER
SANO, YOU'RE WAY TOO EASY ON THE KIDS.
I'LL CALL MISS KAMO-GAWA RIGHT NOW.
DON'T YOU KIDS WORRY ABOUT IT.
ピラッ
FLICK
ANYWAYS, ALL OF YOU CAN GO HOME NOW.
ズキン THROB
ズキン THROB
ズキン THROB
ズキン
'KAY ...
I REALLY DON'T LIKE THAT GUY.
TOTALLY
HOW DARE HE HIT ME ON THE HEAD!
ズキンズキン
THROB
OH
NO, NOT THAT ONE...
I WONDER ...

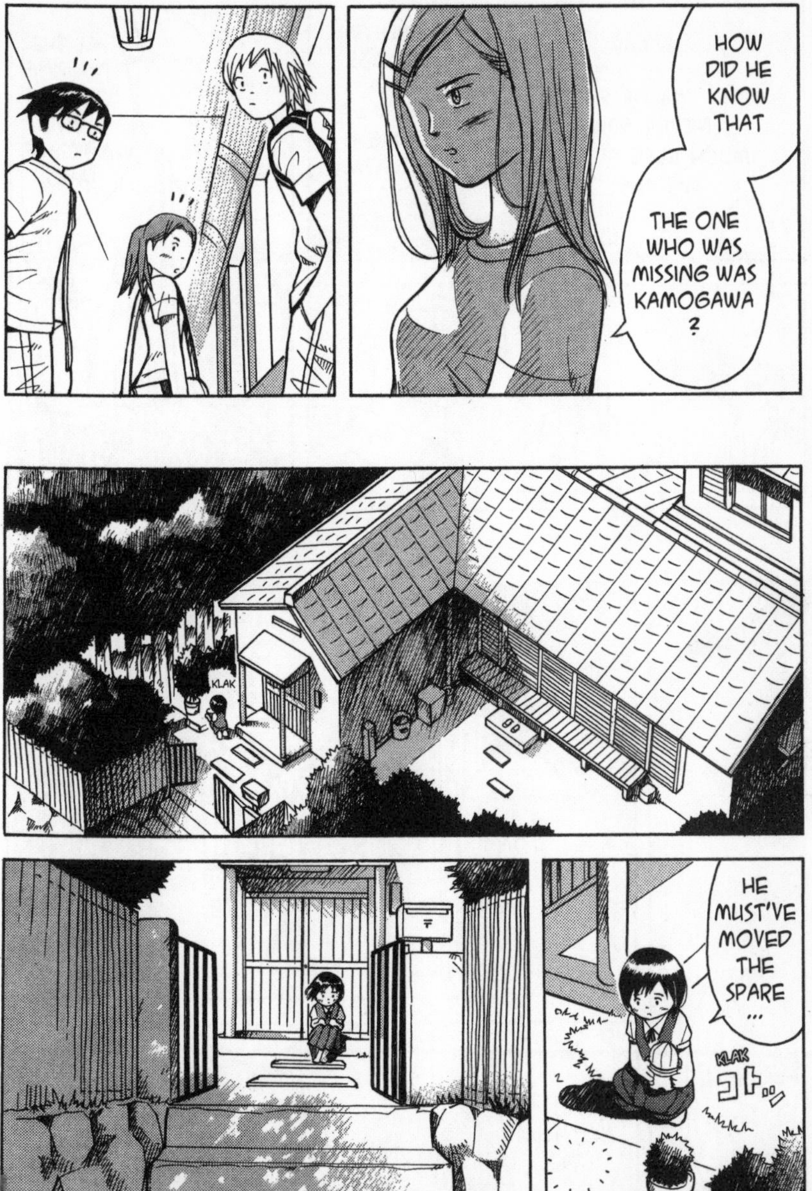
HOW DID HE KNOW THAT
THE ONE WHO WAS MISSING WAS KAMOGAWA ?
KLAK
HE MUST'VE MOVED THE SPARE ...
KLAK
コトッ

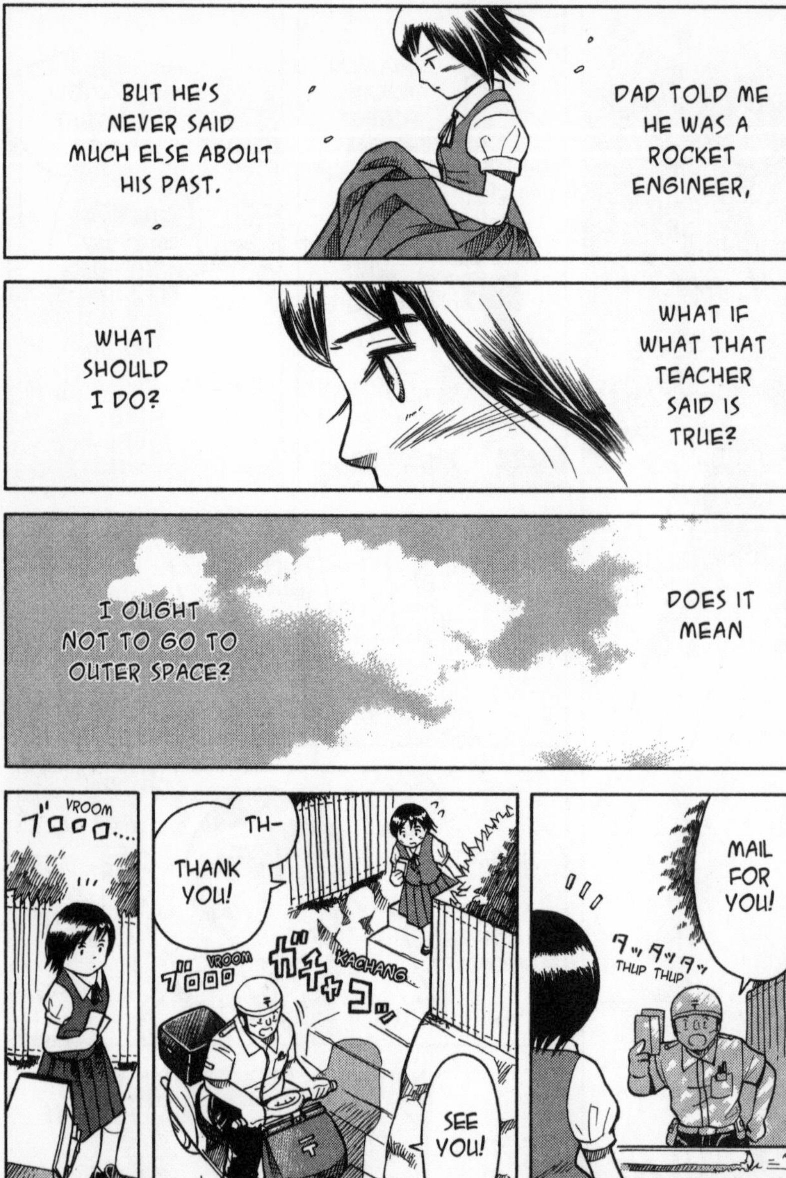
DAD TOLD ME HE WAS A ROCKET ENGINEER,
BUT HE'S NEVER SAID MUCH ELSE ABOUT HIS PAST.
WHAT IF WHAT THAT TEACHER SAID IS TRUE?
WHAT SHOULD I DO?
DOES IT MEAN
I OUGHT NOT TO GO TO OUTER SPACE?
MAIL FOR YOU!
タッタッタッ
THUP THUP
TH- THANK YOU!
ガチャコッ
KACHANG
ブロロロ
VROOM
SEE YOU!
ブロロロ....
VROOM

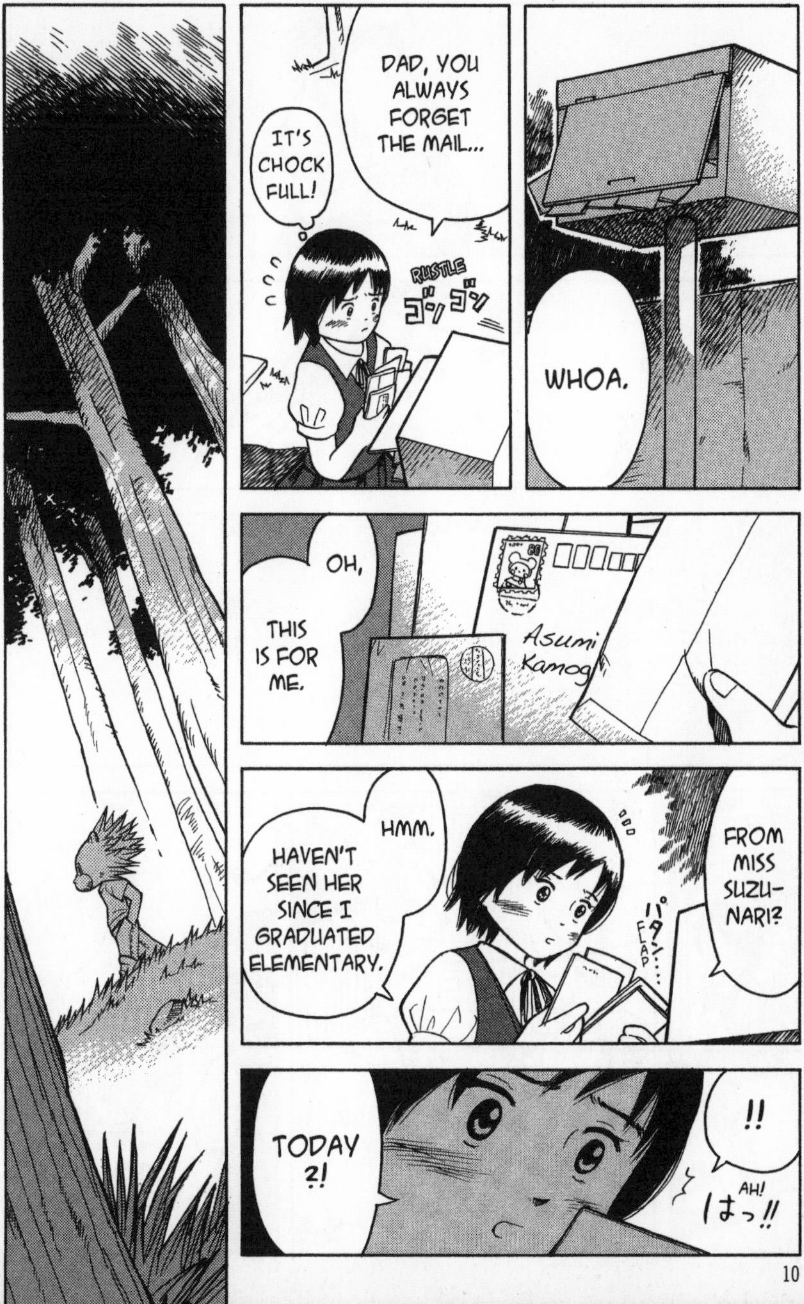
WHOA.
DAD, YOU ALWAYS FORGET THE MAIL...
IT'S CHOCK FULL!
RUSTLE
ゴソゴソ
OH,
THIS IS FOR ME.
Asumi Kamog
FROM MISS SUZU-NARI?
HMM.
HAVEN'T SEEN HER SINCE I GRADUATED ELEMENTARY.
パタン……
FLAP
!!
AH!
はっ!!
TODAY?!

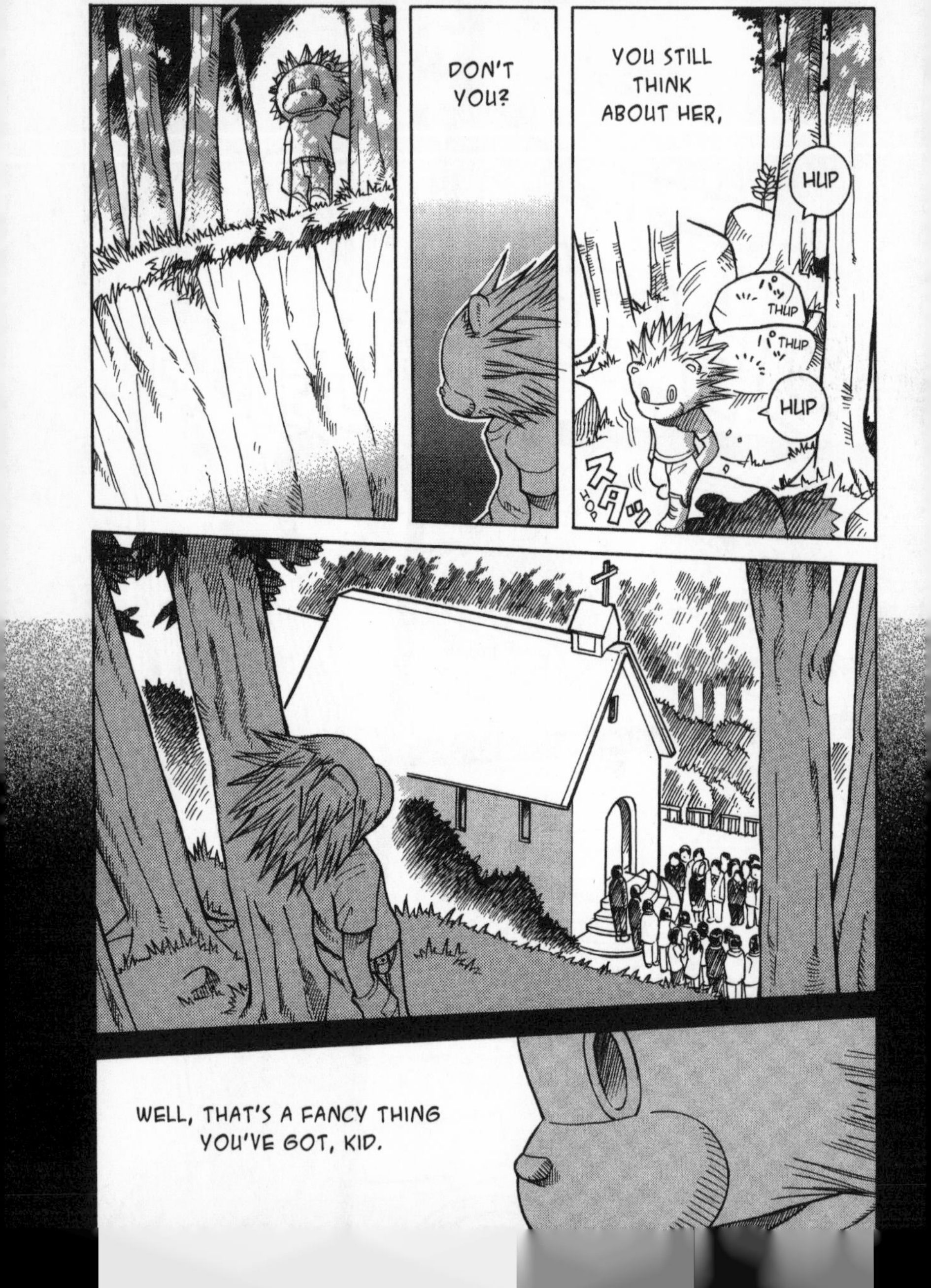
YOU STILL THINK ABOUT HER,
HUP
パッ THUP
パッ THUP
HUP
スタッ HOP
DON'T YOU?
WELL, THAT'S A FANCY THING YOU'VE GOT, KID.

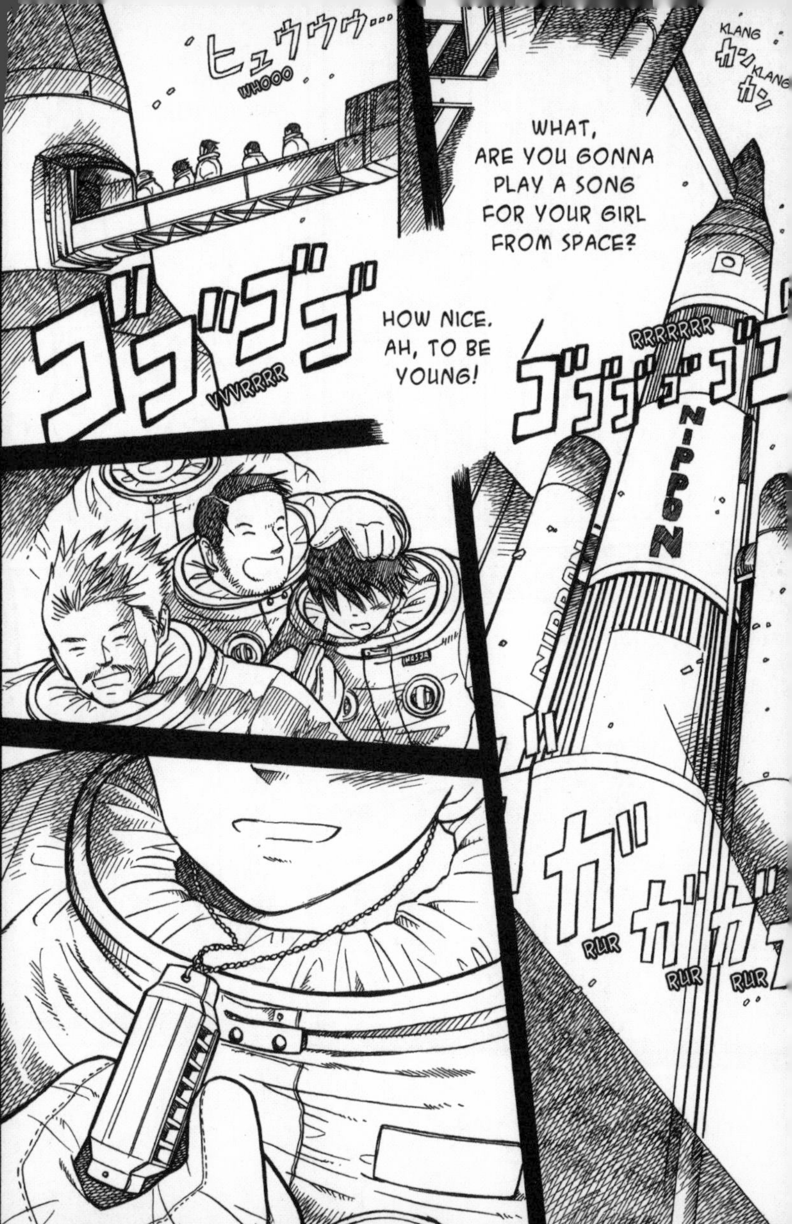
KLANG
カン
KLANG
カン
WHAT, ARE YOU GONNA PLAY A SONG FOR YOUR GIRL FROM SPACE?
RRRRRRR
ゴゴゴゴゴ
NIPPON
ガ
RUR
ガ
RUR
ガ
RUR
ヒュウウウ…
WHOOO
ゴゴゴゴ
VVVRRRR
HOW NICE. AH, TO BE YOUNG!

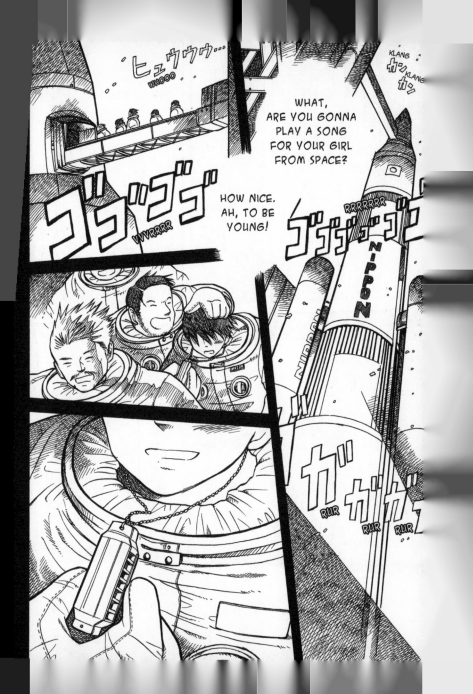

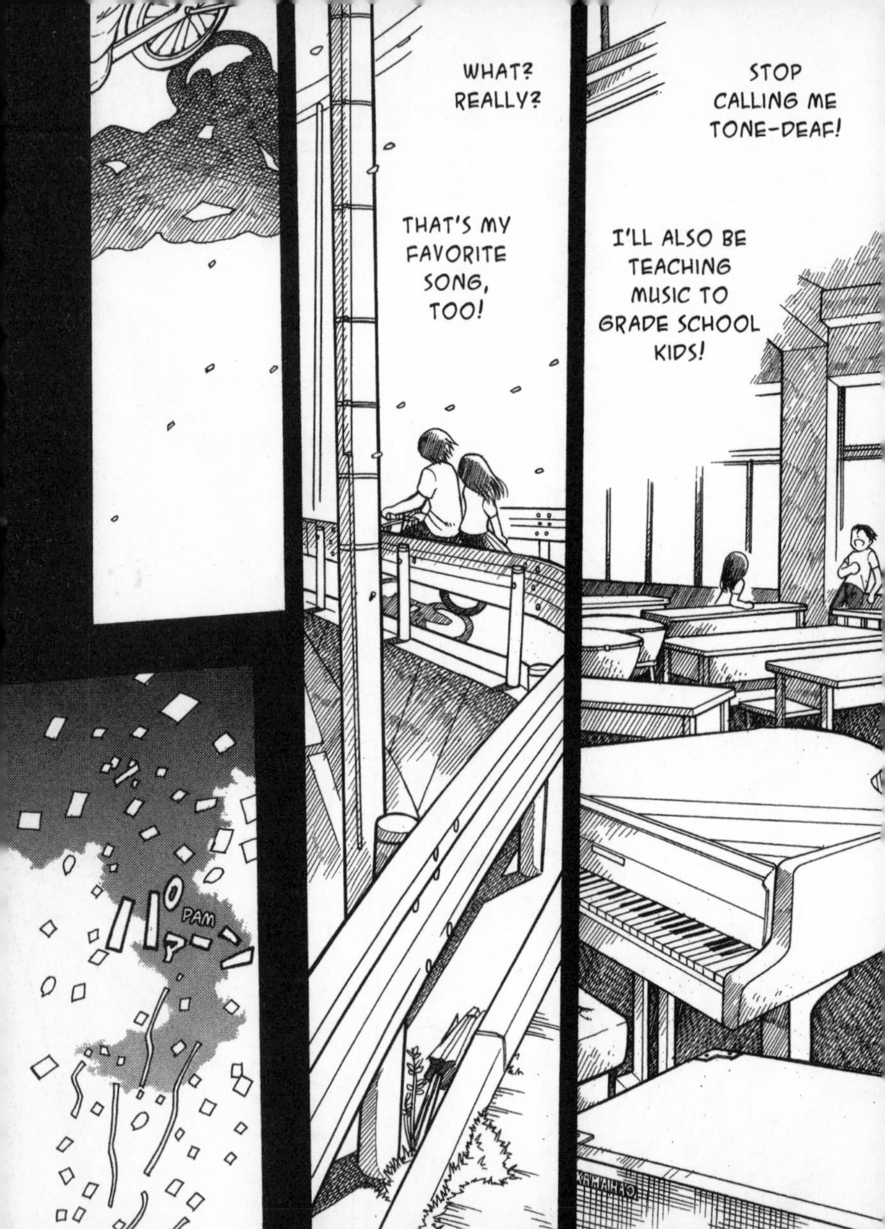
STOP CALLING ME TONE-DEAF!
I'LL ALSO BE TEACHING MUSIC TO GRADE SCHOOL KIDS!
WHAT? REALLY?
THAT'S MY FAVORITE SONG, TOO!
PAM

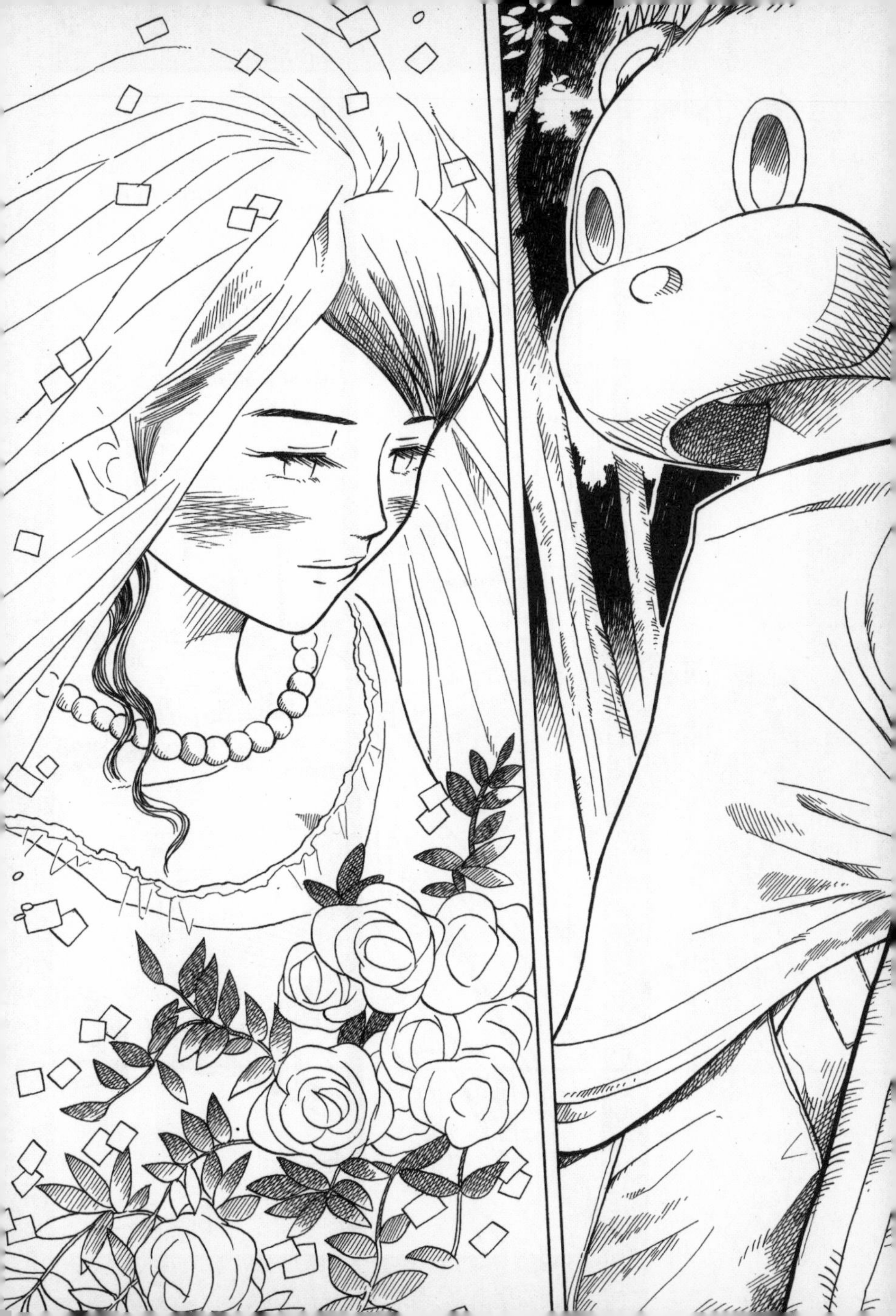

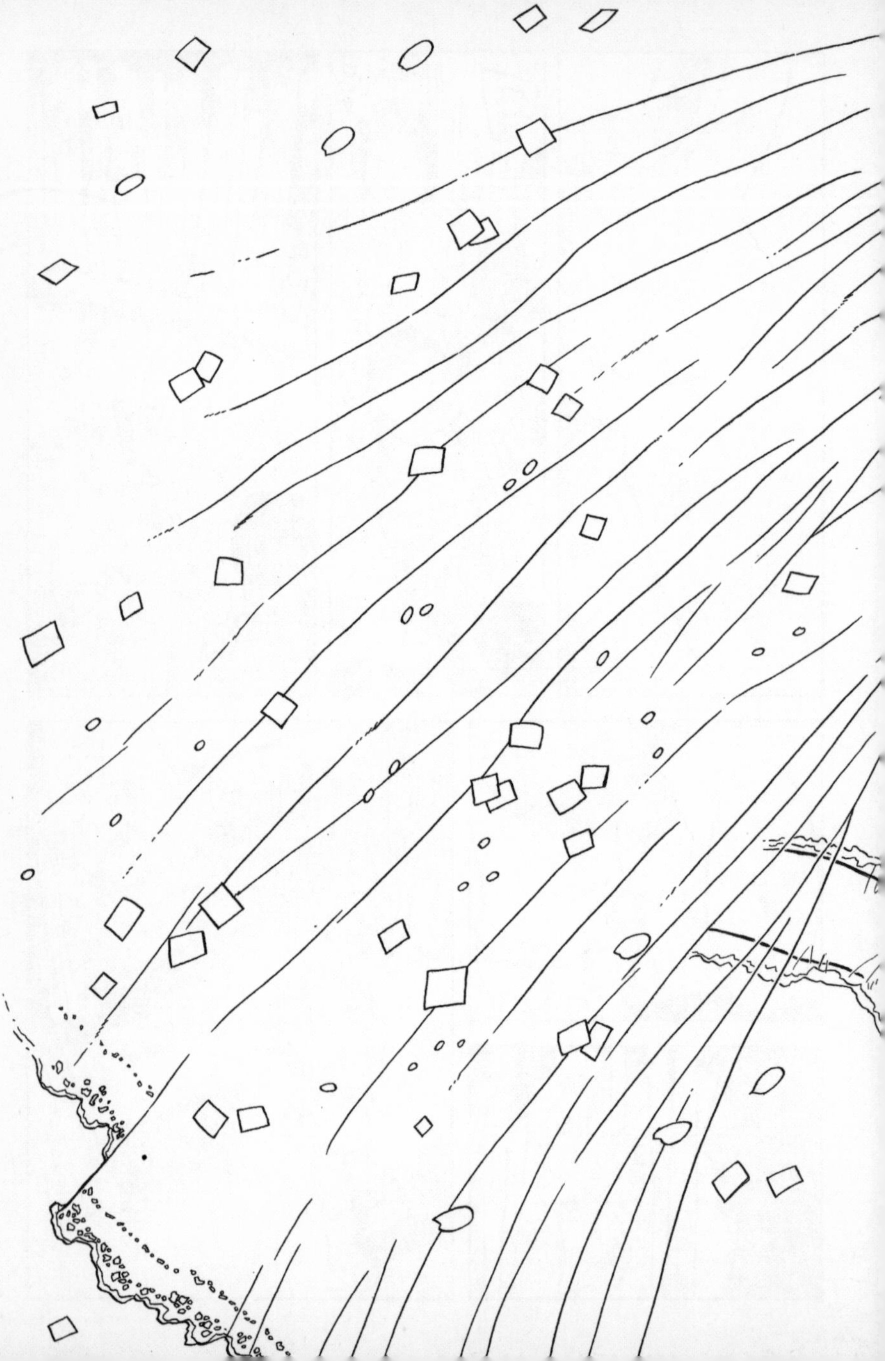

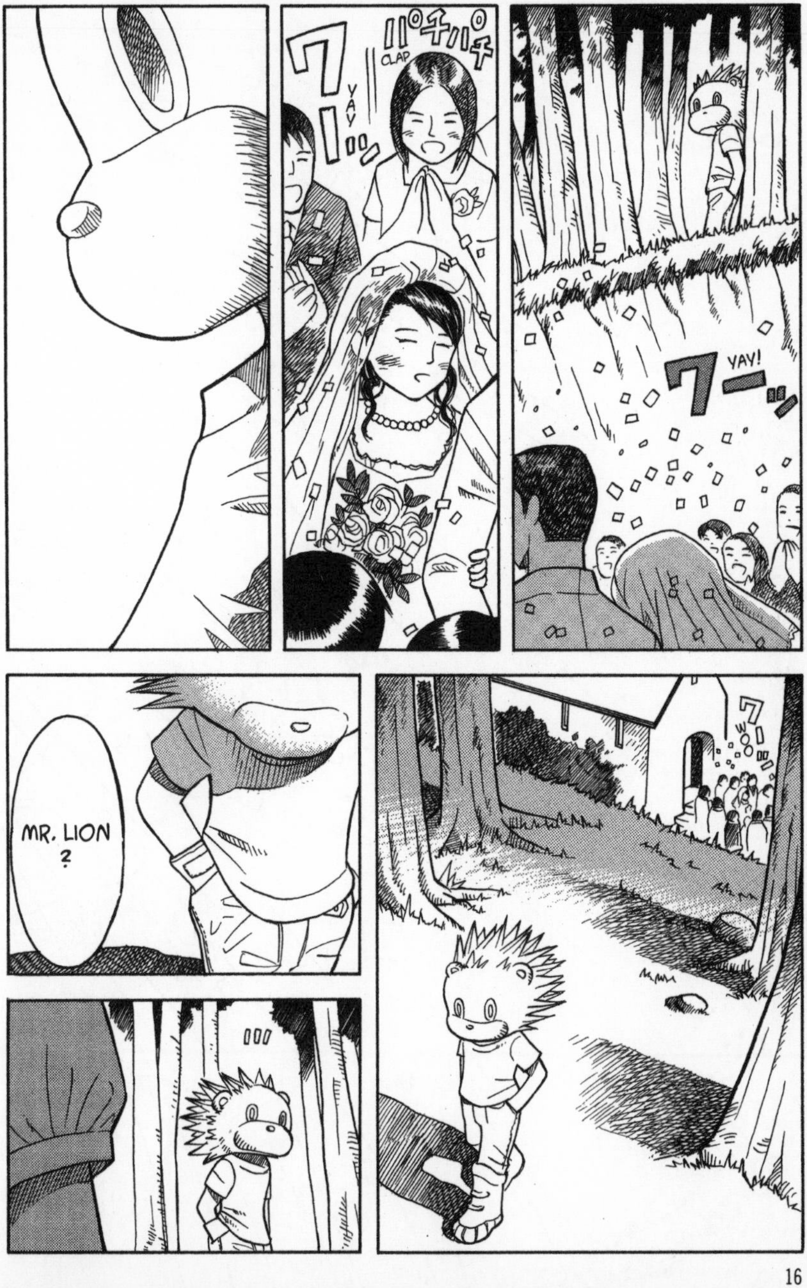
ワーッ
YAY!
パチパチ
CLAP
ワー
YAY!!
ワ
WOO!!
MR. LION ?
!!!

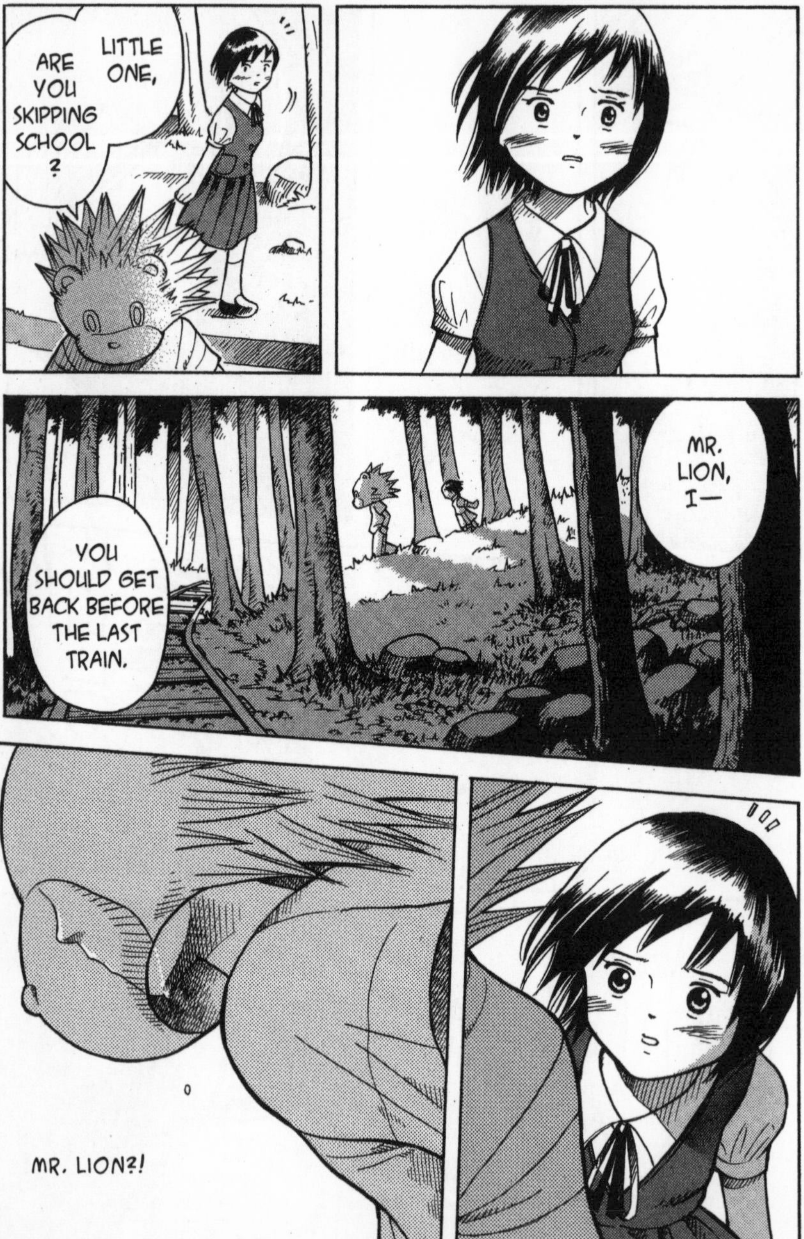
LITTLE ONE, ARE YOU SKIPPING SCHOOL?
MR. LION, I—
YOU SHOULD GET BACK BEFORE THE LAST TRAIN.
MR. LION?!

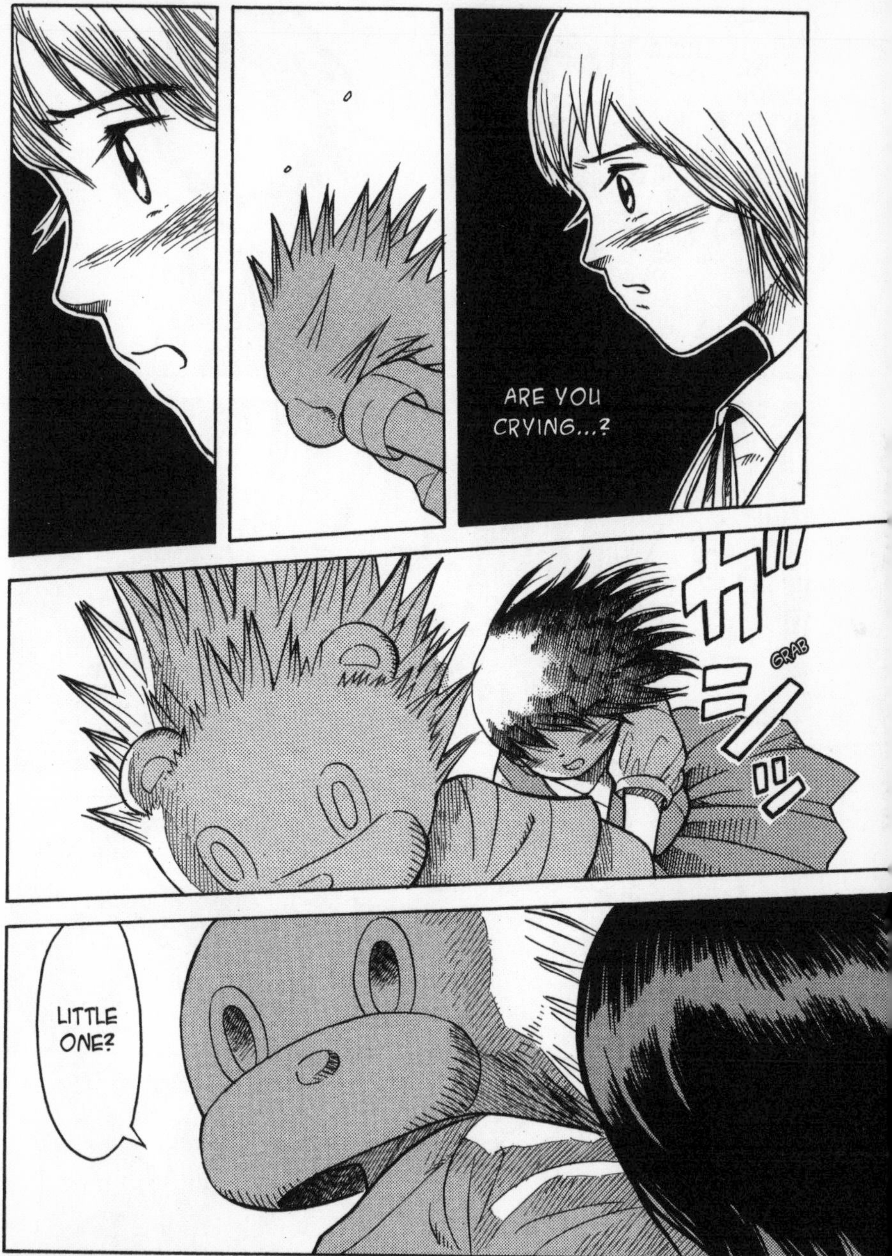
ARE YOU CRYING...?
ガシッ
GRAB
LITTLE ONE?

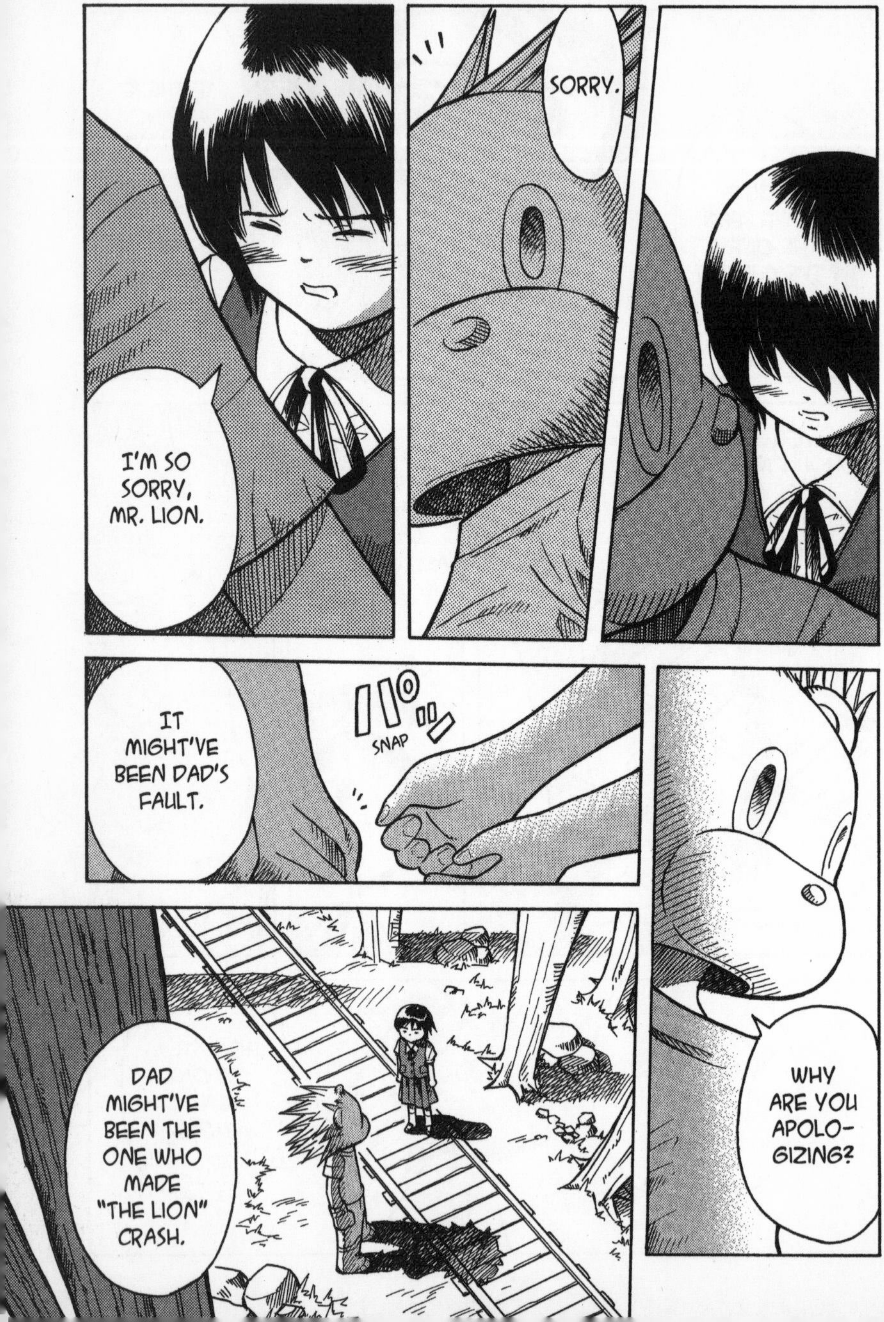
SORRY.
I'M SO SORRY, MR. LION.
WHY ARE YOU APOLO-GIZING?
IT MIGHT'VE BEEN DAD'S FAULT.
SNAP
DAD MIGHT'VE BEEN THE ONE WHO MADE "THE LION" CRASH.

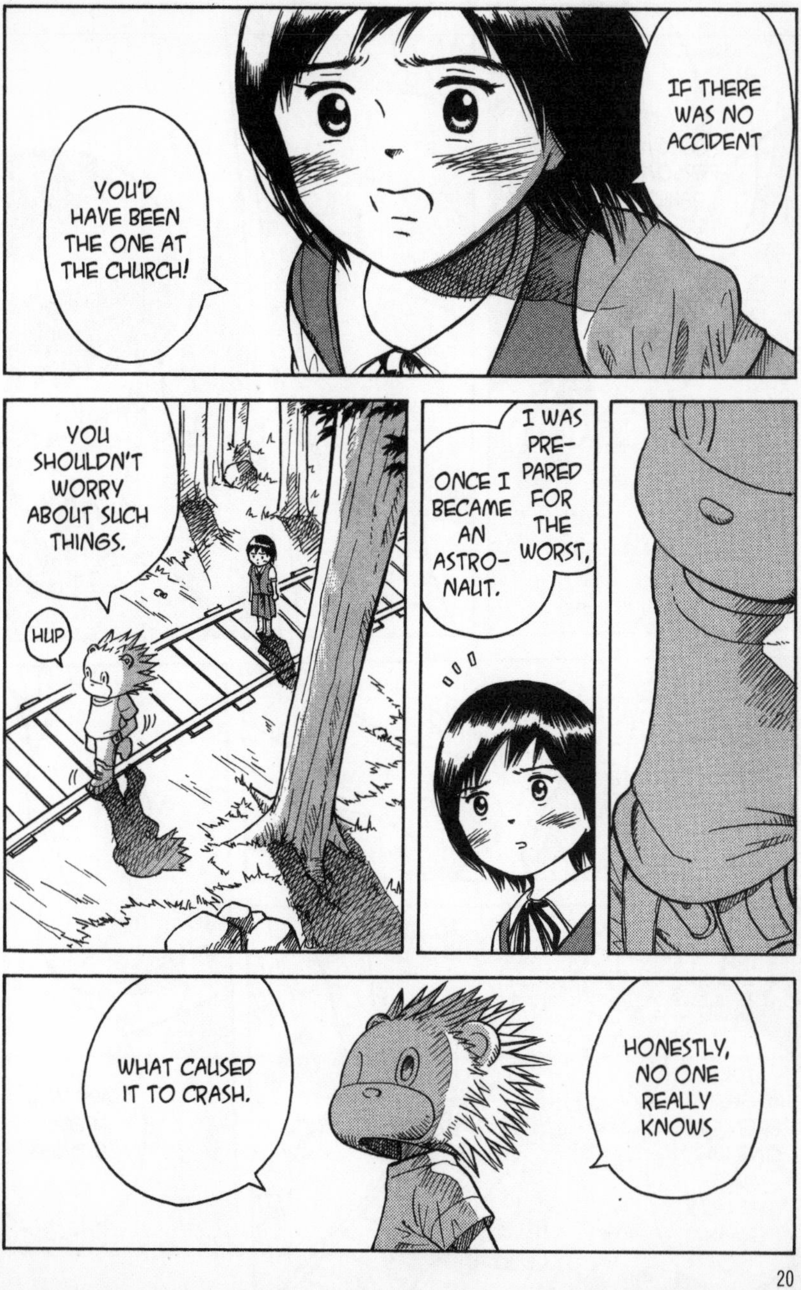
IF THERE WAS NO ACCIDENT
YOU'D HAVE BEEN THE ONE AT THE CHURCH!
I WAS PRE-PARED FOR THE WORST,
ONCE I BECAME AN ASTRO-NAUT.
YOU SHOULDN'T WORRY ABOUT SUCH THINGS.
HUP
HONESTLY, NO ONE REALLY KNOWS
WHAT CAUSED IT TO CRASH.

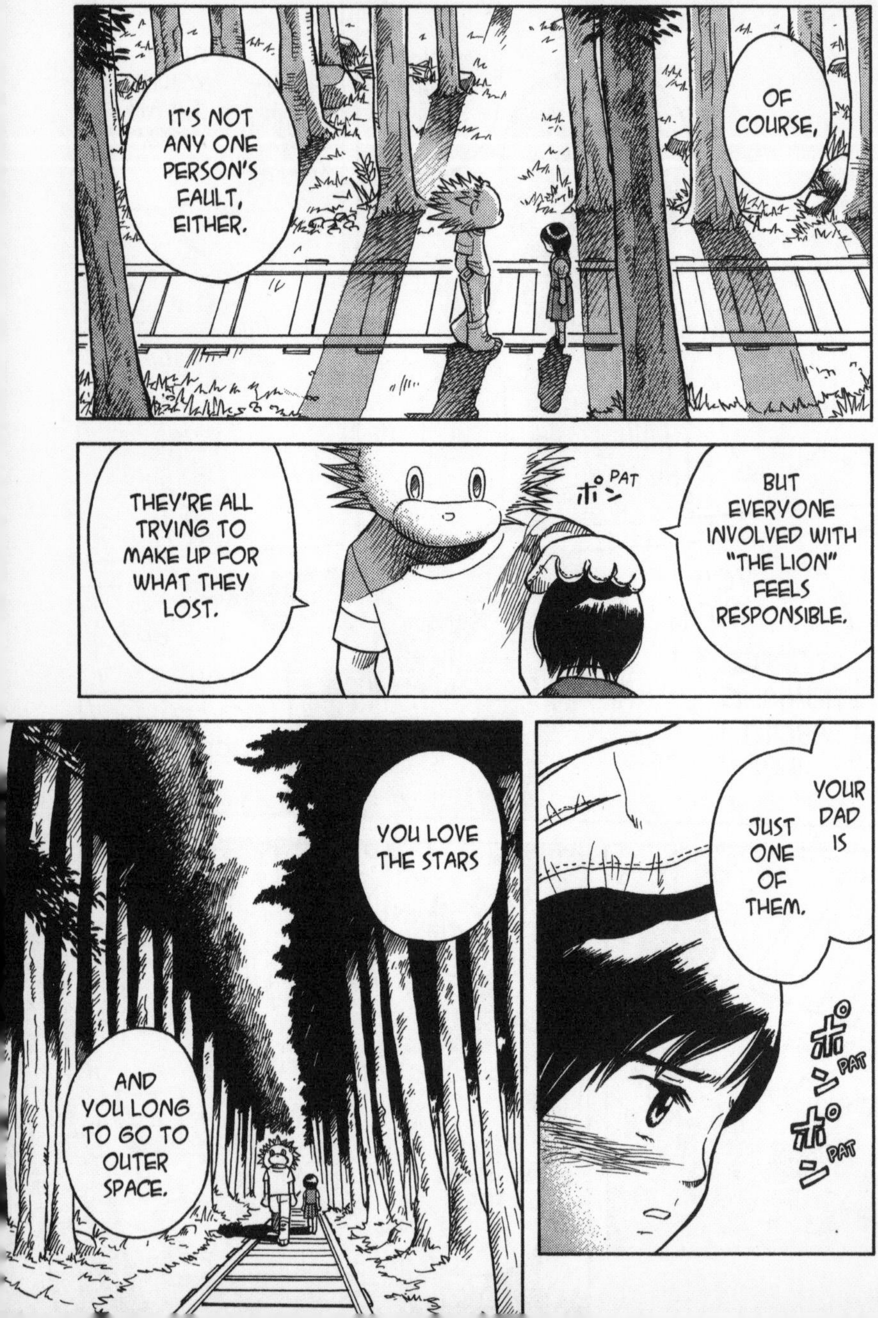
OF COURSE,
IT'S NOT ANY ONE PERSON'S FAULT, EITHER.
BUT EVERYONE INVOLVED WITH "THE LION" FEELS RESPONSIBLE.
ポン PAT
THEY'RE ALL TRYING TO MAKE UP FOR WHAT THEY LOST.
YOUR DAD IS JUST ONE OF THEM.
ポン PAT
ポン PAT
YOU LOVE THE STARS
AND YOU LONG TO GO TO OUTER SPACE.

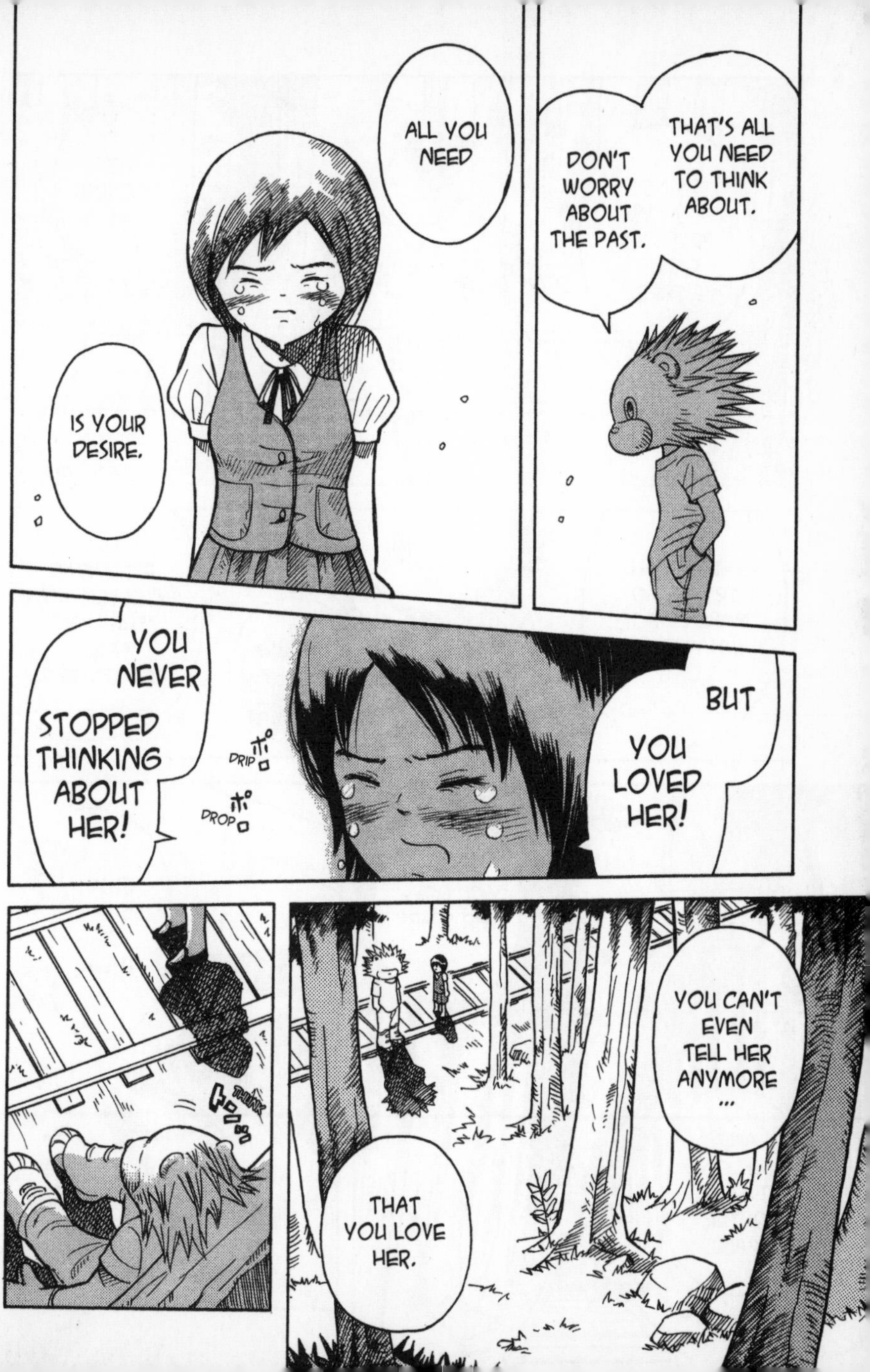
DON'T WORRY ABOUT THE PAST. THAT'S ALL YOU NEED TO THINK ABOUT.
ALL YOU NEED
IS YOUR DESIRE.
BUT YOU LOVED HER!
DRIP
DROP
YOU NEVER STOPPED THINKING ABOUT HER!
YOU CAN'T EVEN TELL HER ANYMORE ...
THAT YOU LOVE HER.
THUNK

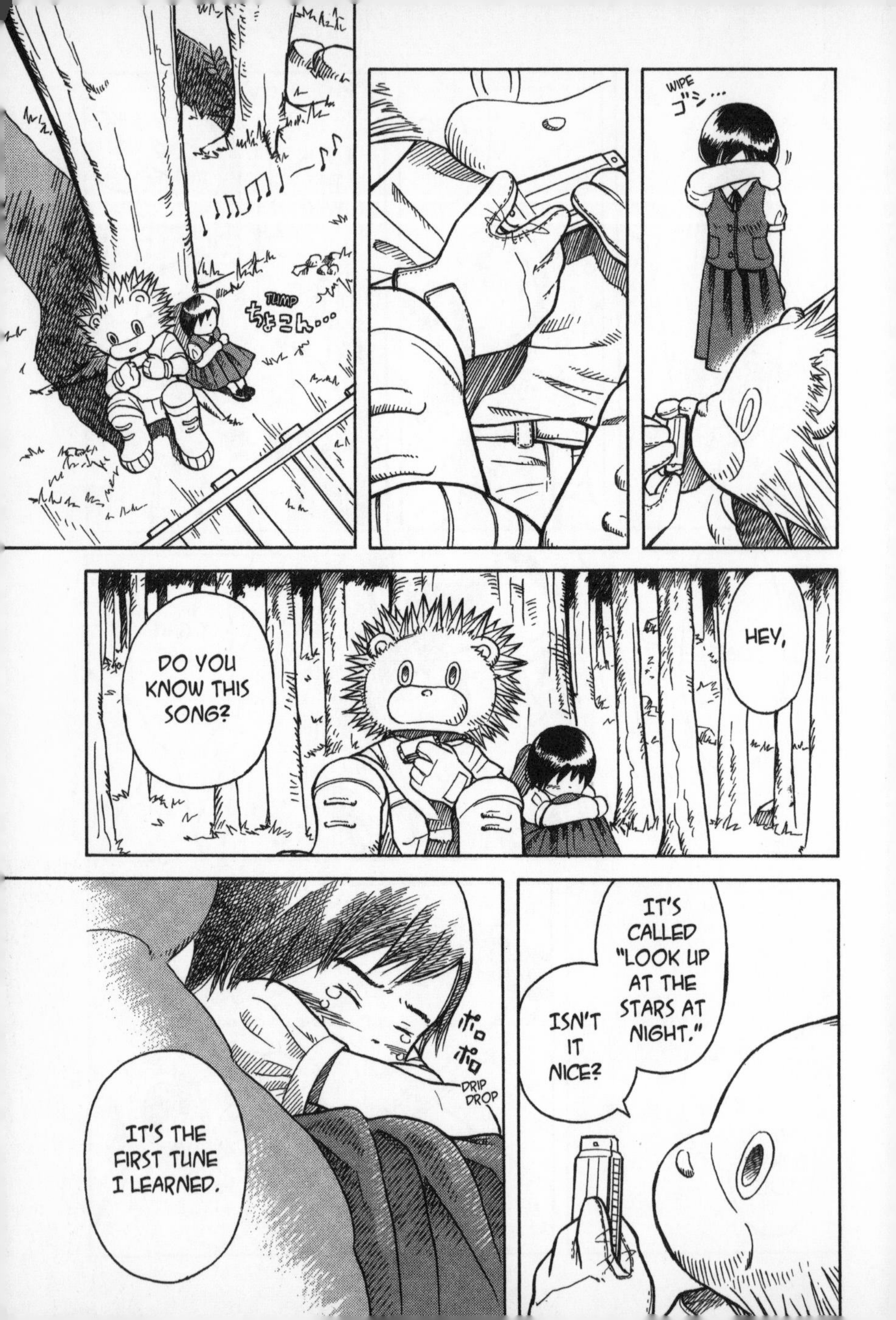
WIPE
ゴシ…
TUMP
ちょこん…
HEY,
DO YOU KNOW THIS SONG?
IT'S CALLED "LOOK UP AT THE STARS AT NIGHT."
ISN'T IT NICE?
ポロ ポロ
DRIP DROP
IT'S THE FIRST TUNE I LEARNED.

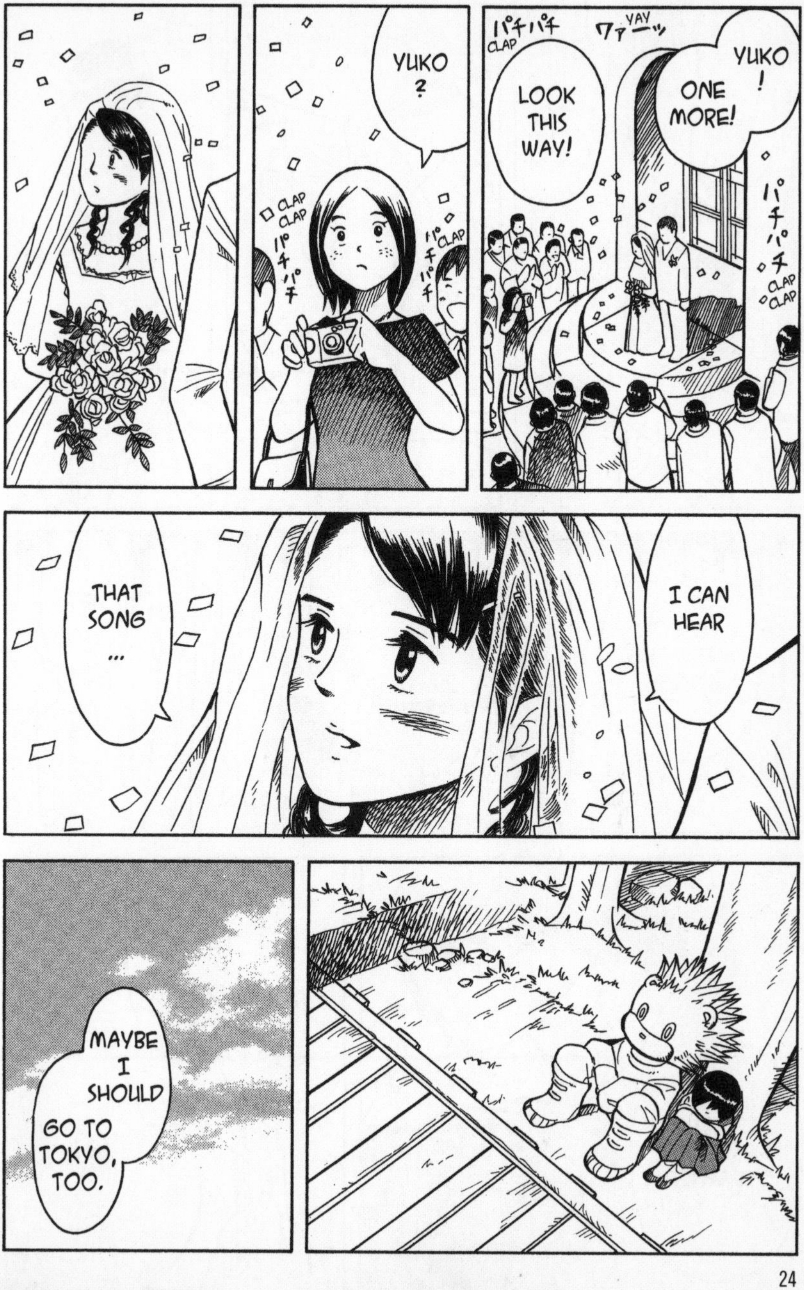
ワァーッ
YAY
YUKO!
ONE MORE!
パチパチ
CLAP CLAP
LOOK THIS WAY!
パチパチ
CLAP
YUKO?
パチパチ
CLAP
パチパチ
CLAP CLAP
I CAN HEAR
THAT SONG ...
MAYBE I SHOULD GO TO TOKYO, TOO.

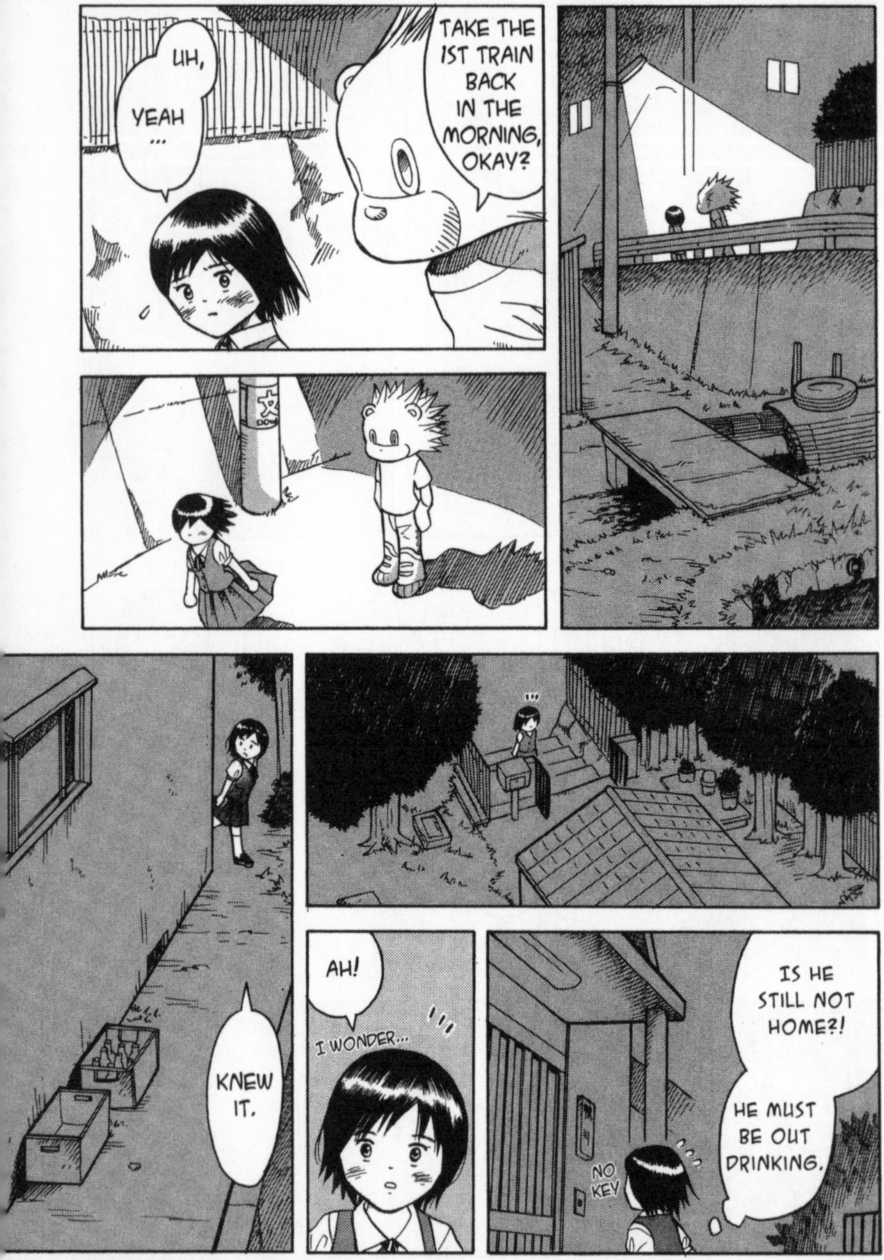
TAKE THE 1ST TRAIN BACK IN THE MORNING, OKAY?
UH, YEAH ...
IS HE STILL NOT HOME?!
HE MUST BE OUT DRINKING.
NO KEY
AH!
I WONDER...
KNEW IT.

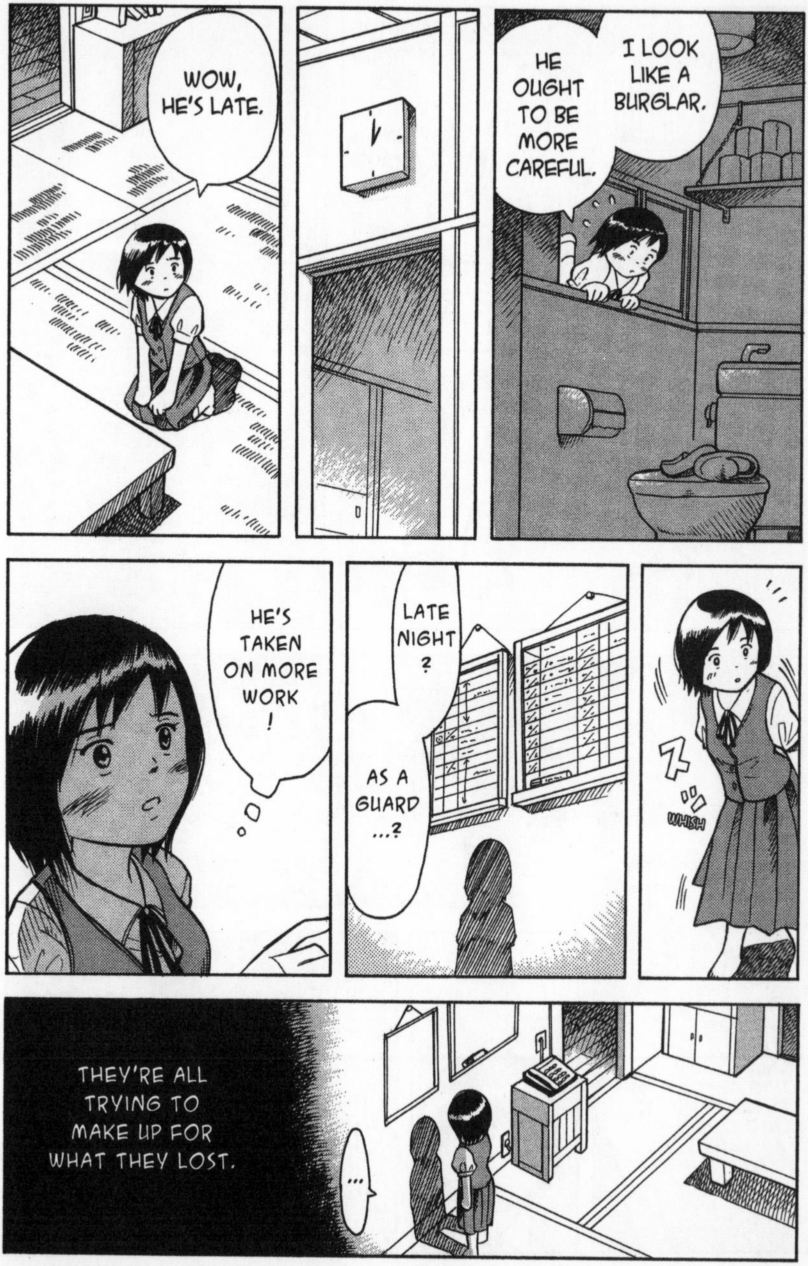
I LOOK LIKE A BURGLAR.
HE OUGHT TO BE MORE CAREFUL.
WOW, HE'S LATE.
WHISH
LATE NIGHT?
AS A GUARD...?
HE'S TAKEN ON MORE WORK!
THEY'RE ALL TRYING TO MAKE UP FOR WHAT THEY LOST.
...

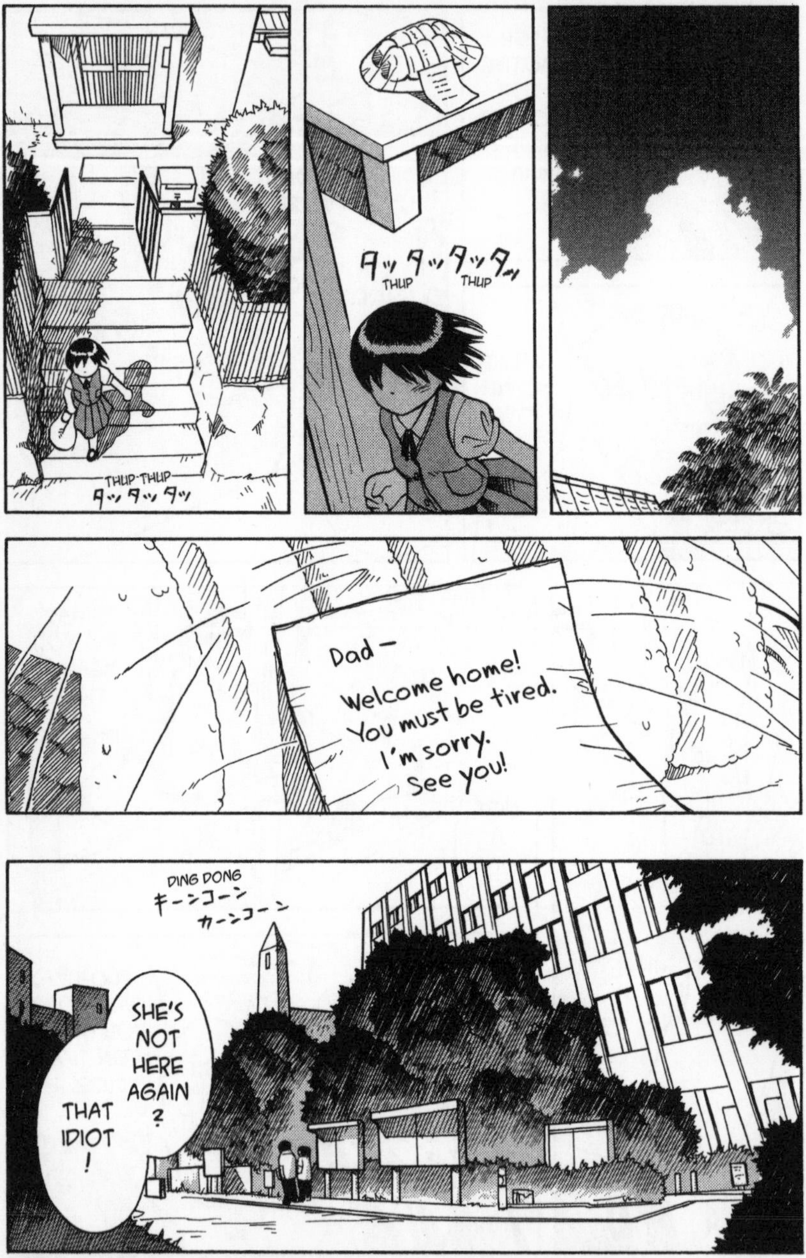
タッタッタッタッ
THUP THUP
THUP-THUP
タッタッタッ
Dad –
Welcome home!
You must be tired.
I'm sorry.
See you!
DING DONG
キーンコーン
カーンコーン
SHE'S NOT HERE AGAIN?
THAT IDIOT!

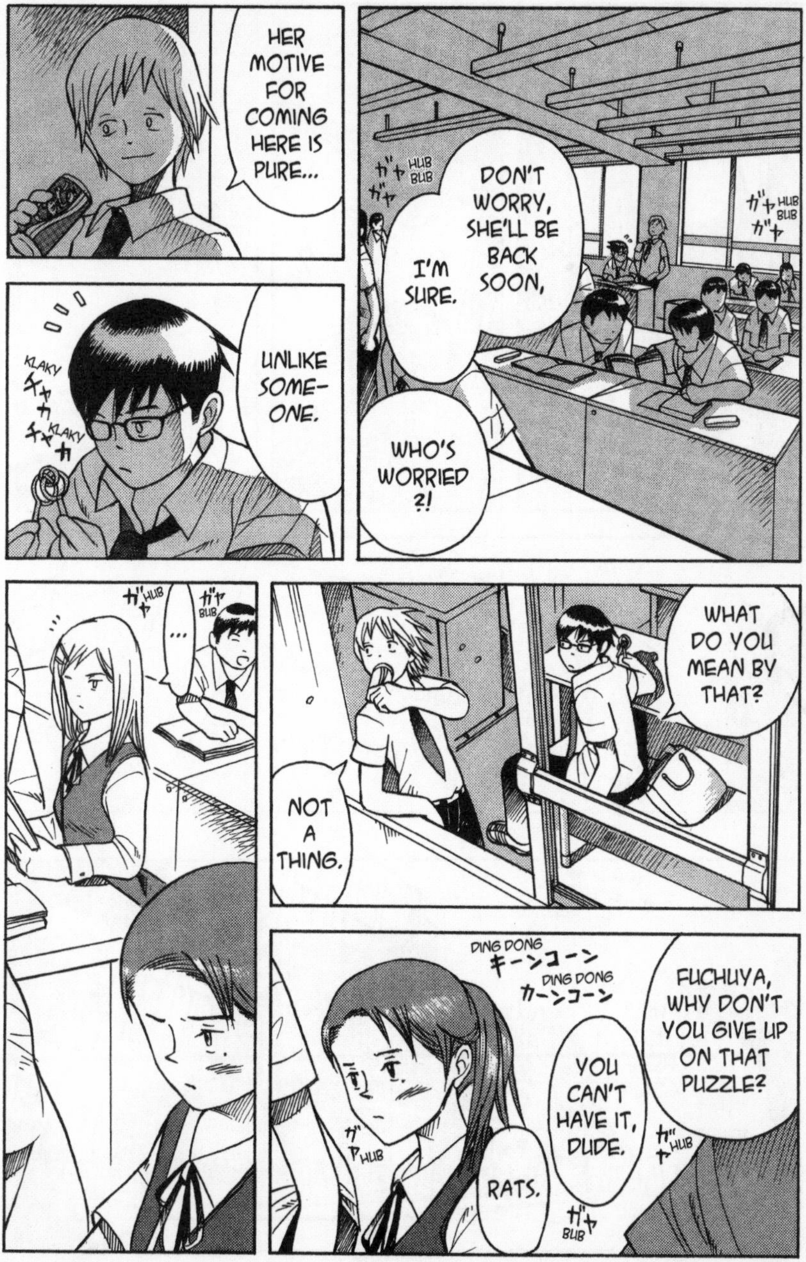
ガヤ HUB BUB
ガヤ
DON'T WORRY, SHE'LL BE BACK SOON,
I'M SURE.
ガヤ HUB BUB
ガヤ
WHO'S WORRIED?!
HER MOTIVE FOR COMING HERE IS PURE...
UNLIKE SOME-ONE.
KLAKY カチャ
カ
KLAKY カチャ
カ
WHAT DO YOU MEAN BY THAT?
NOT A THING.
DING DONG キーンコーン
DING DONG カーンコーン
FUCHUYA, WHY DON'T YOU GIVE UP ON THAT PUZZLE?
ガヤ HUB
YOU CAN'T HAVE IT, DUDE.
ガヤ HUB
RATS.
ガヤ BUB
ガヤ HUB
ガヤ BUB
...

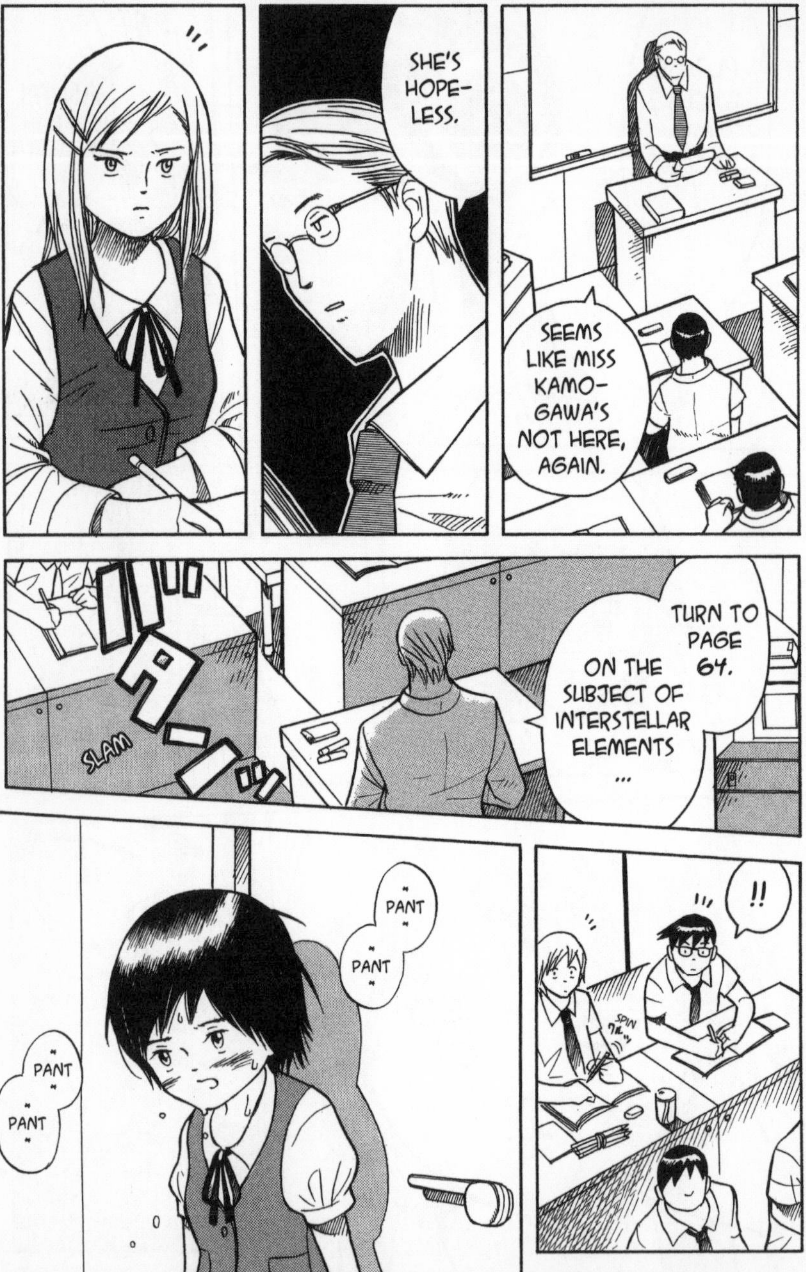
SEEMS LIKE MISS KAMO-GAWA'S NOT HERE, AGAIN.
SHE'S HOPE-LESS.
TURN TO PAGE 64.
ON THE SUBJECT OF INTERSTELLAR ELEMENTS ...
SLAM
!!
SPIN
PANT
PANT
PANT
PANT

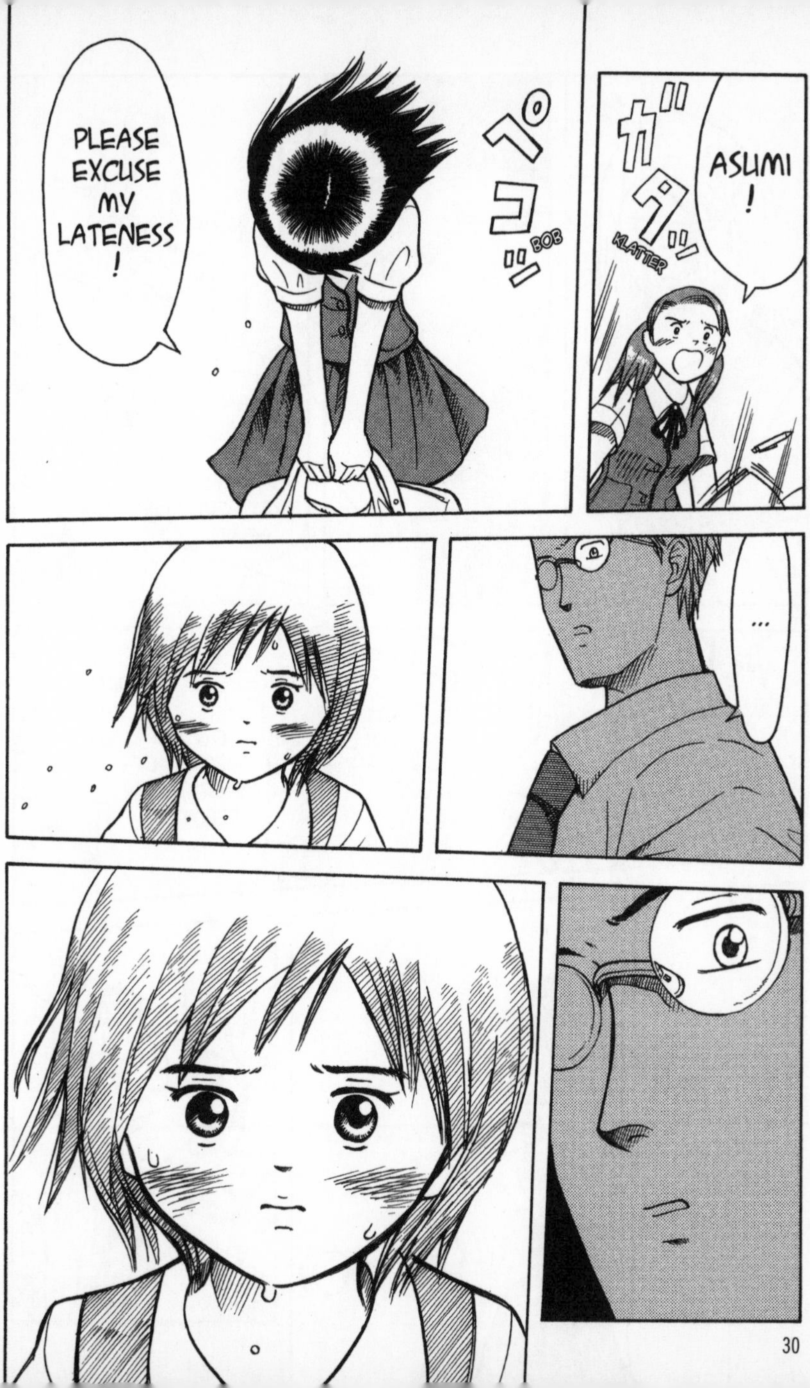
ASUMI!
KLATTER
PLEASE EXCUSE MY LATENESS!
BOB
...

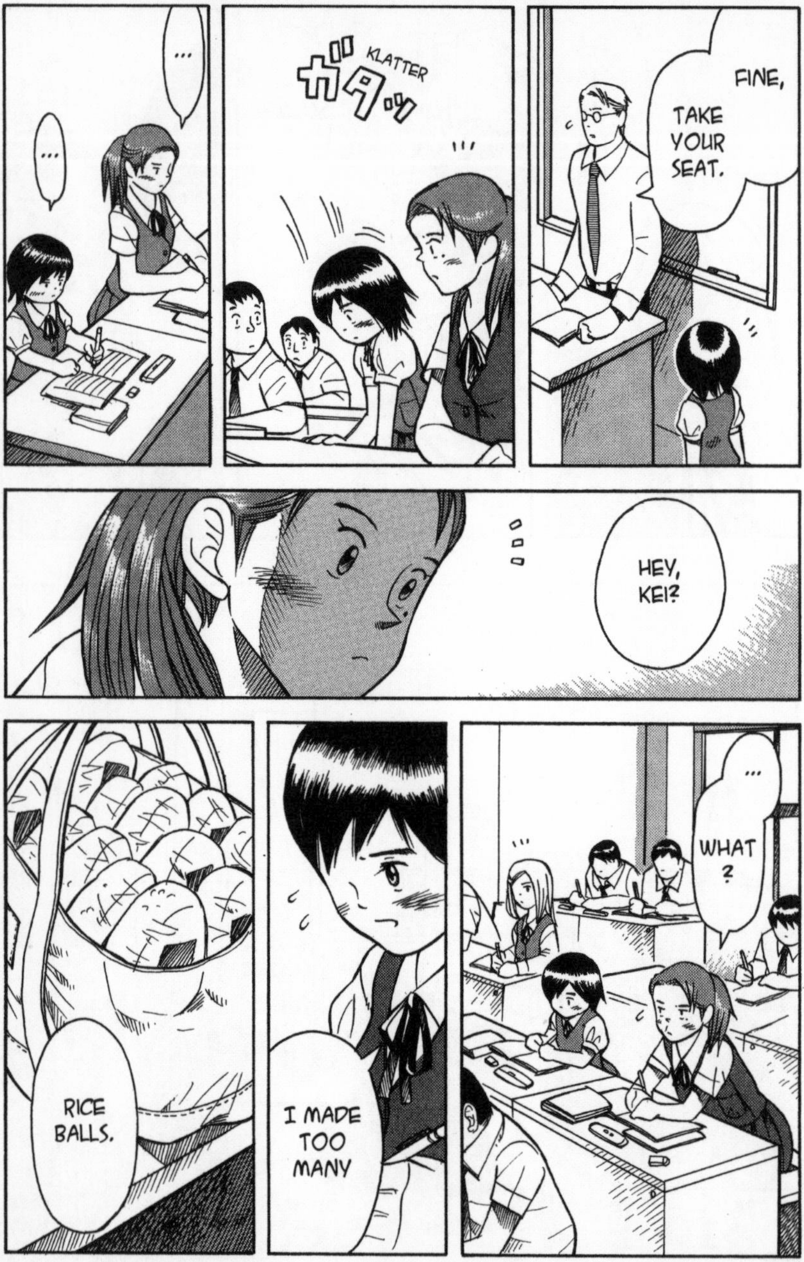
FINE,
TAKE YOUR SEAT.
ガタッ
KLATTER
...
...
HEY, KEI?
...
WHAT ?
I MADE TOO MANY
RICE BALLS.

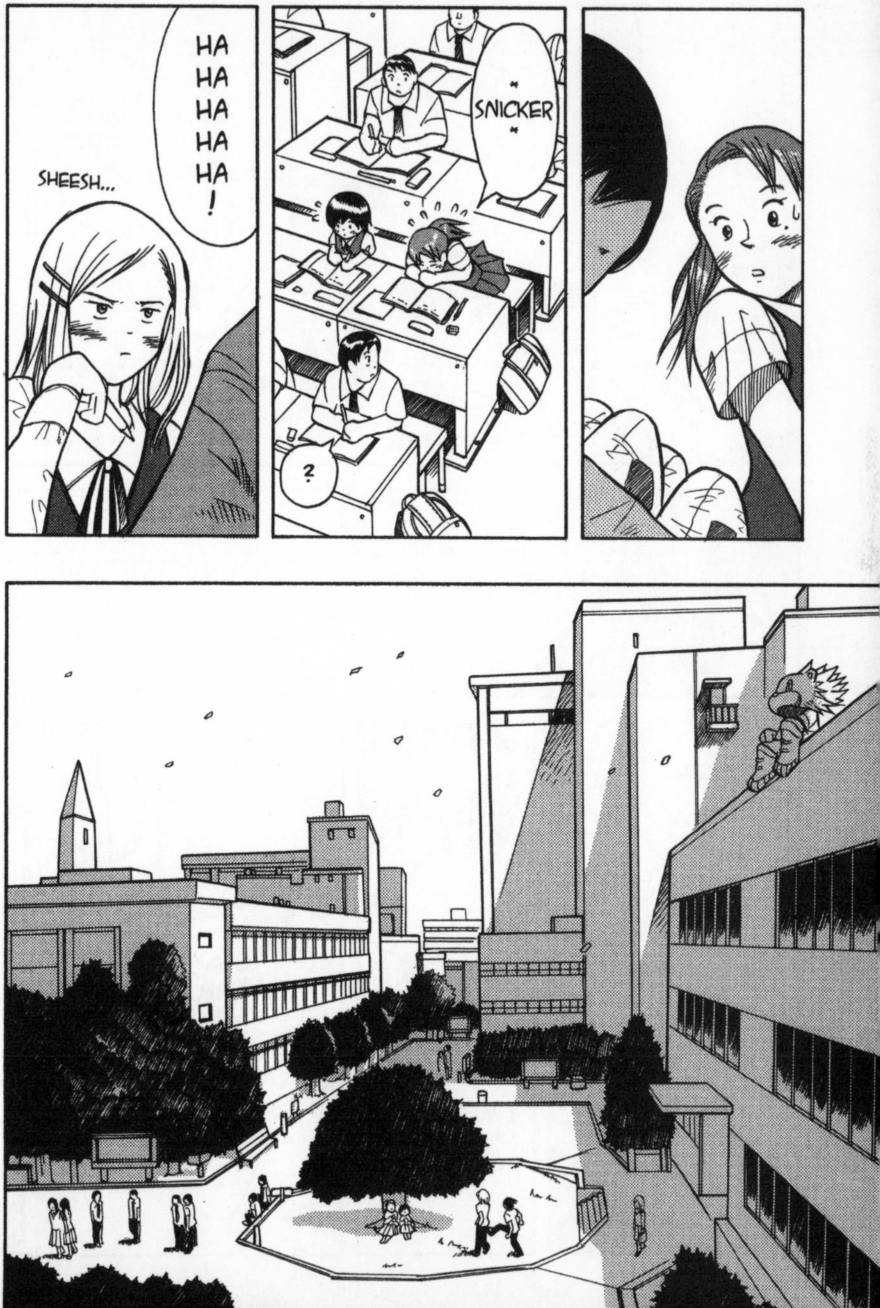
SNICKER
?
HA HA HA HA HA!
SHEESH...

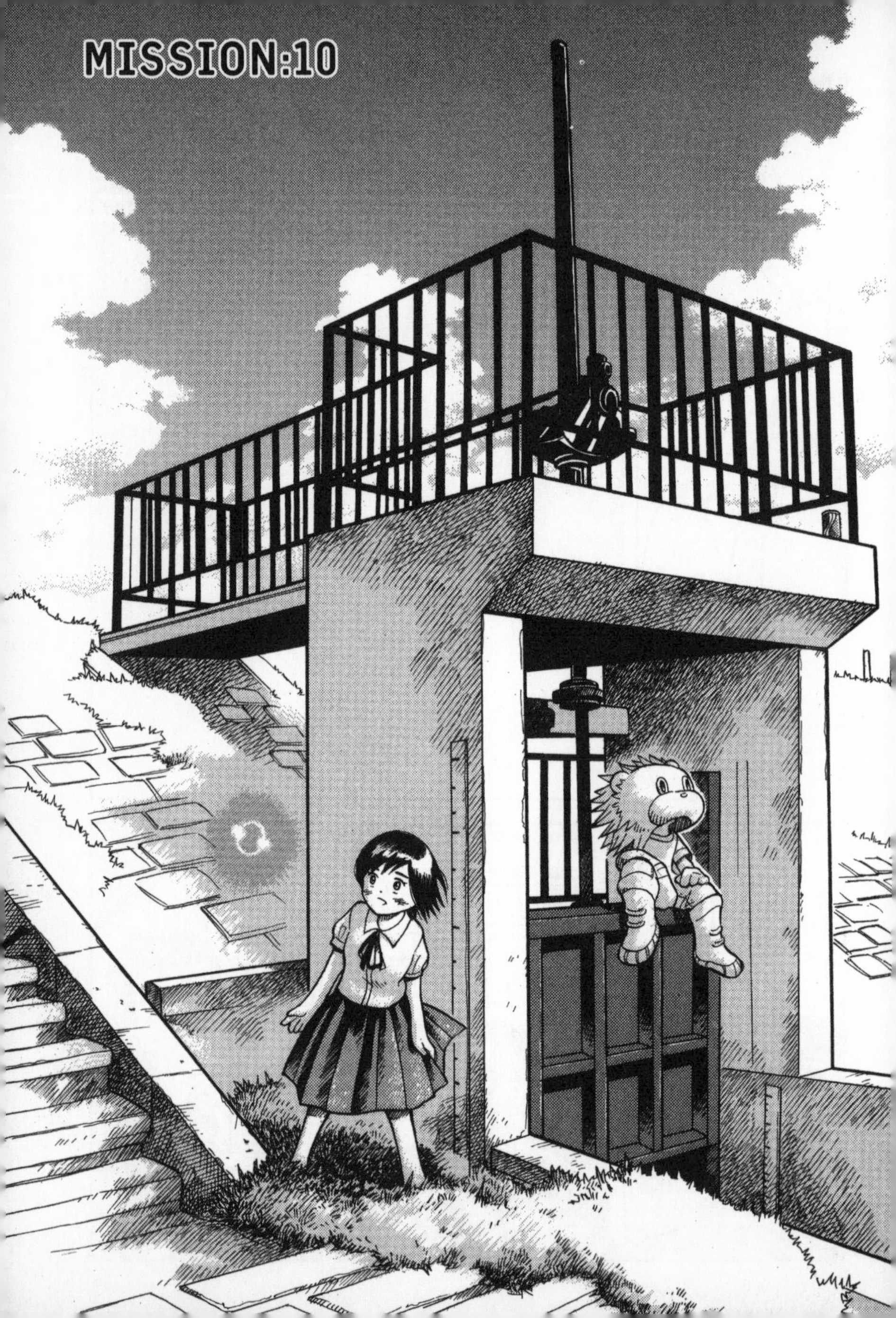
MISSION:10

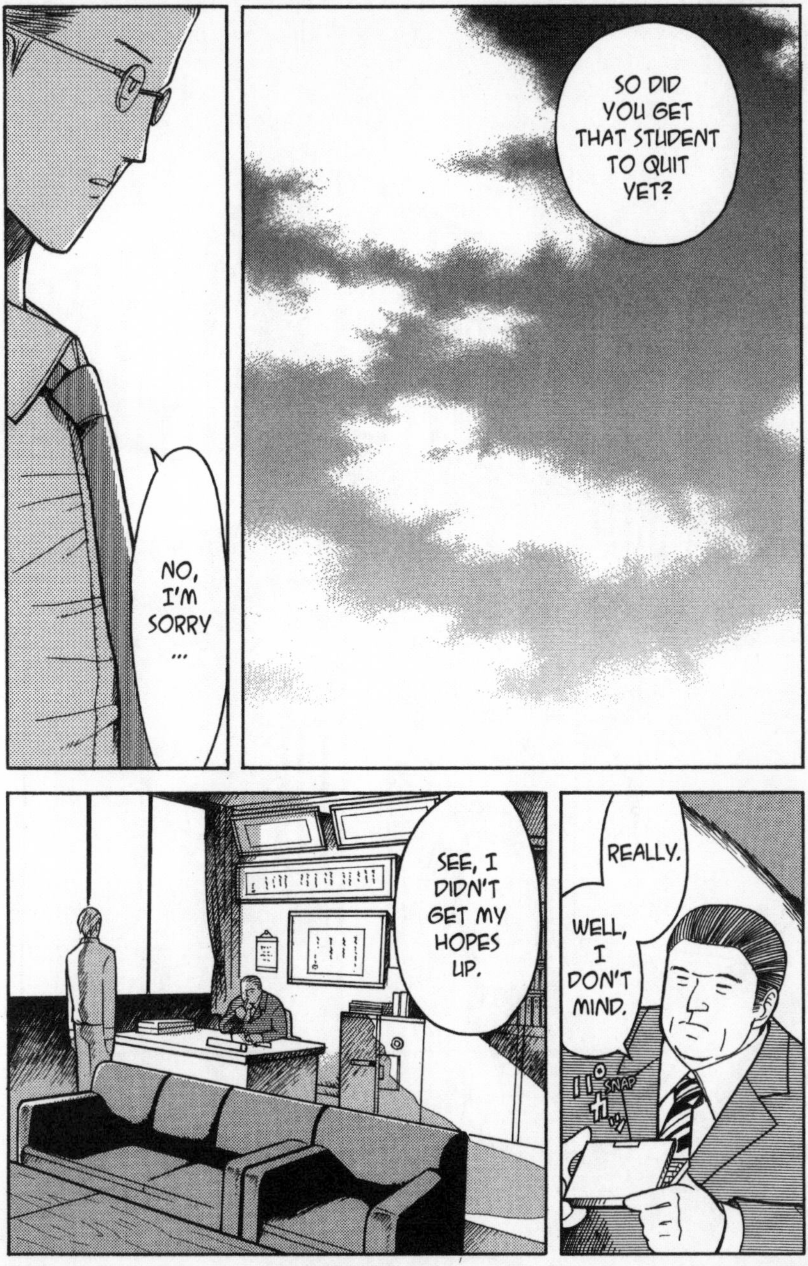
SO DID YOU GET THAT STUDENT TO QUIT YET?
NO, I'M SORRY ...
REALLY.
WELL, I DON'T MIND.
SNAP
SEE, I DIDN'T GET MY HOPES UP.

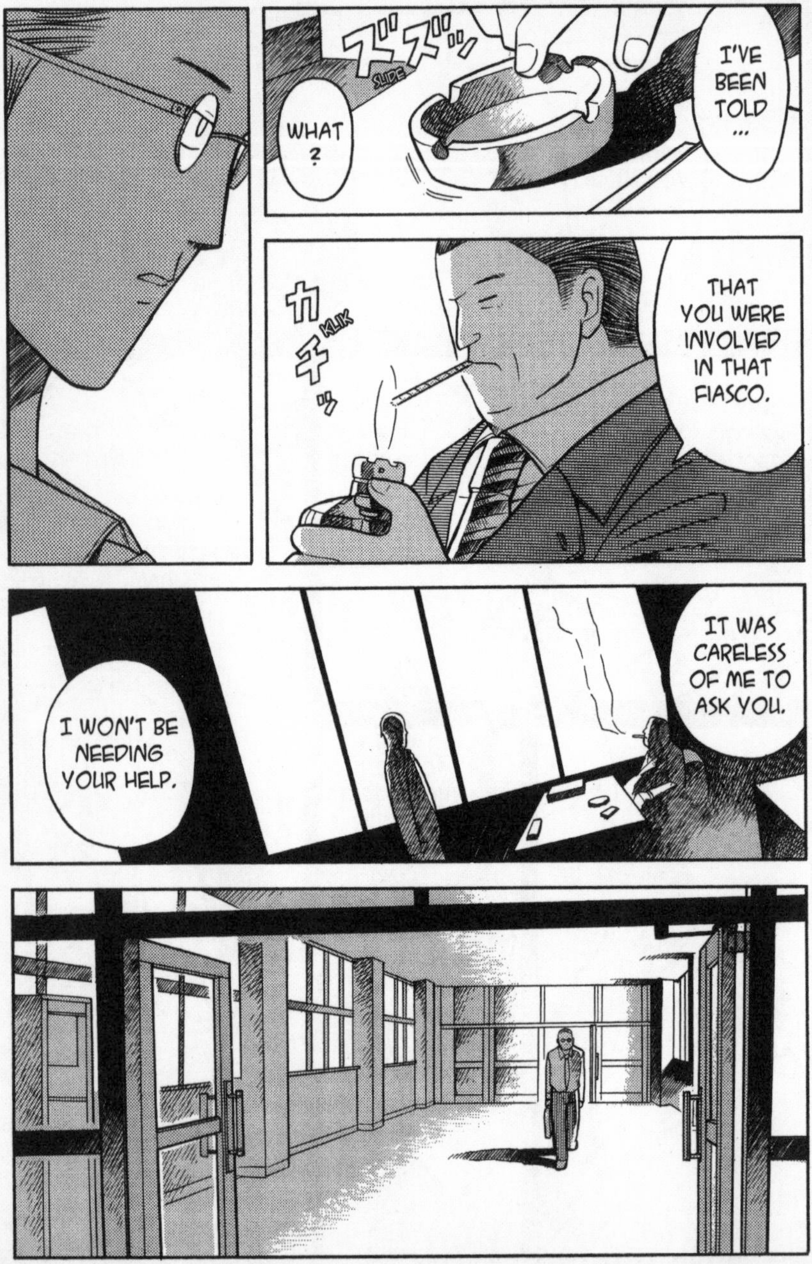
I'VE BEEN TOLD ...
ズズッ
SLIDE
WHAT?
THAT YOU WERE INVOLVED IN THAT FIASCO.
カチッ
KLIK
IT WAS CARELESS OF ME TO ASK YOU.
I WON'T BE NEEDING YOUR HELP.

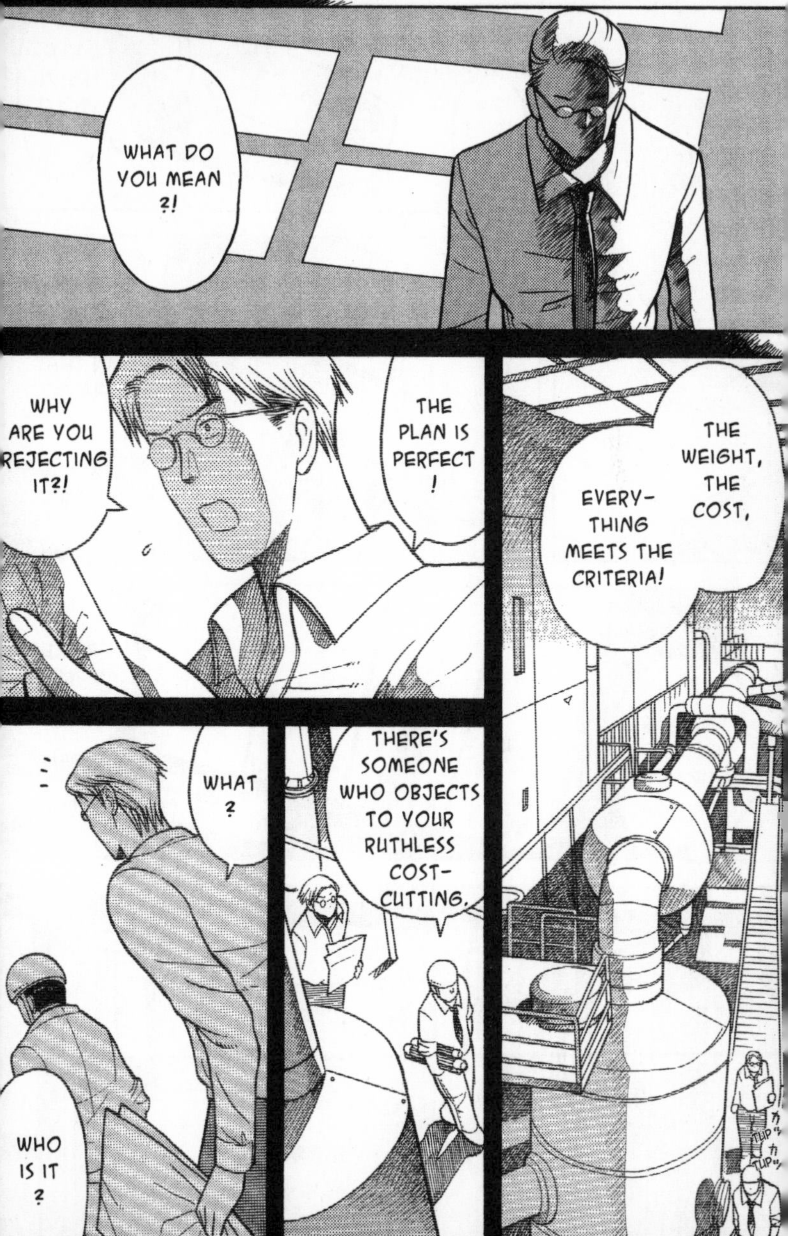
WHAT DO YOU MEAN ?!
THE WEIGHT, THE COST,
EVERY-THING MEETS THE CRITERIA!
TUP
TUP
THE PLAN IS PERFECT !
WHY ARE YOU REJECTING IT?!
THERE'S SOMEONE WHO OBJECTS TO YOUR RUTHLESS COST-CUTTING.
WHAT ?
...
WHO IS IT ?

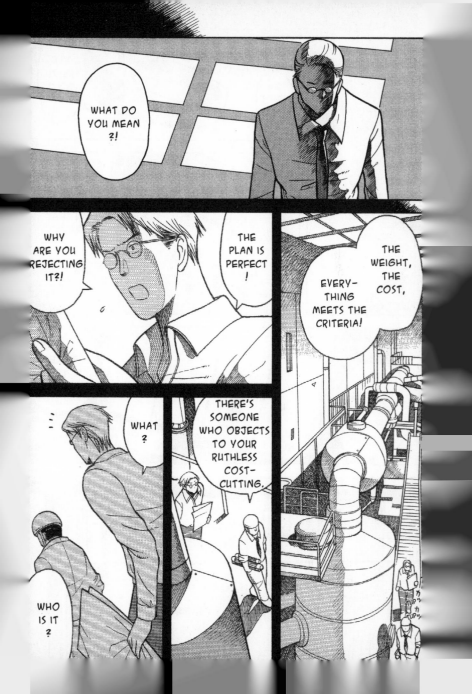

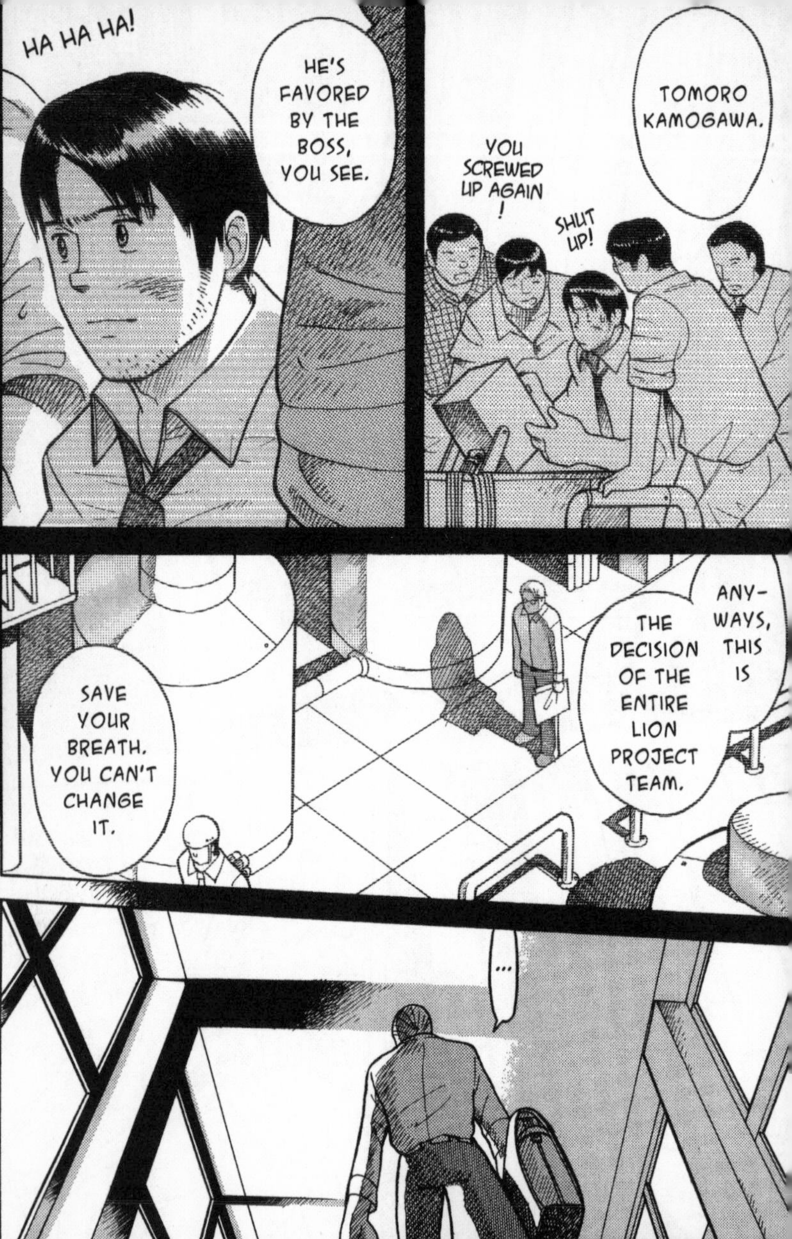
TOMORO KAMOGAWA.
YOU SCREWED UP AGAIN!
SHUT UP!
HE'S FAVORED BY THE BOSS, YOU SEE.
HA HA HA!
ANYWAYS, THIS IS THE DECISION OF THE ENTIRE LION PROJECT TEAM.
SAVE YOUR BREATH. YOU CAN'T CHANGE IT.
...

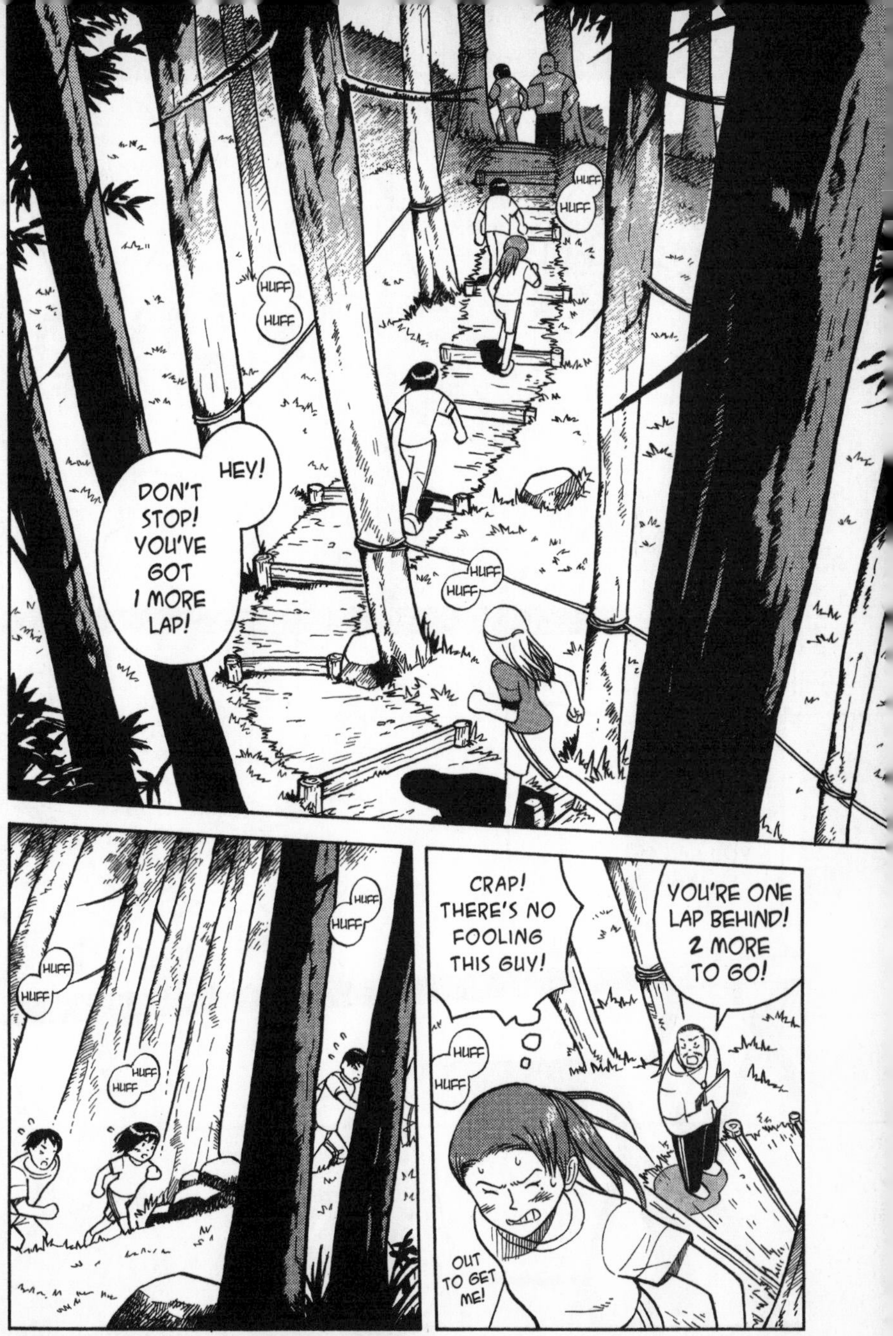
HUFF HUFF
HUFF HUFF
HEY! DON'T STOP! YOU'VE GOT 1 MORE LAP!
HUFF HUFF
YOU'RE ONE LAP BEHIND! 2 MORE TO GO!
CRAP! THERE'S NO FOOLING THIS GUY!
HUFF HUFF
OUT TO GET ME!
HUFF HUFF
HUFF HUFF
HUFF HUFF

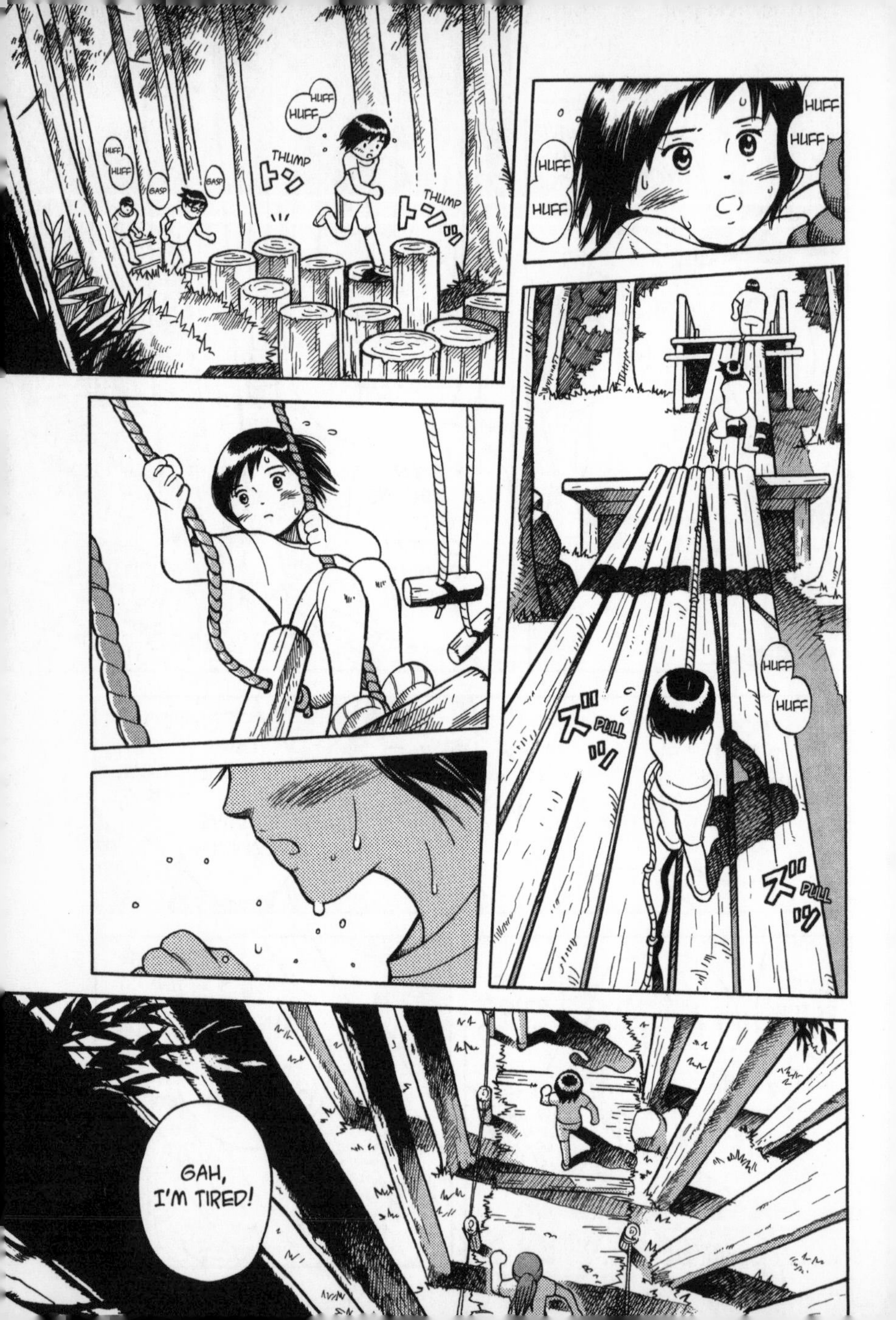
HUFF
HUFF
HUFF
HUFF
HUFF
HUFF
HUFF
HUFF
GASP
GASP
THUMP
THUMP
HUFF
HUFF
PULL
PULL
GAH, I'M TIRED!

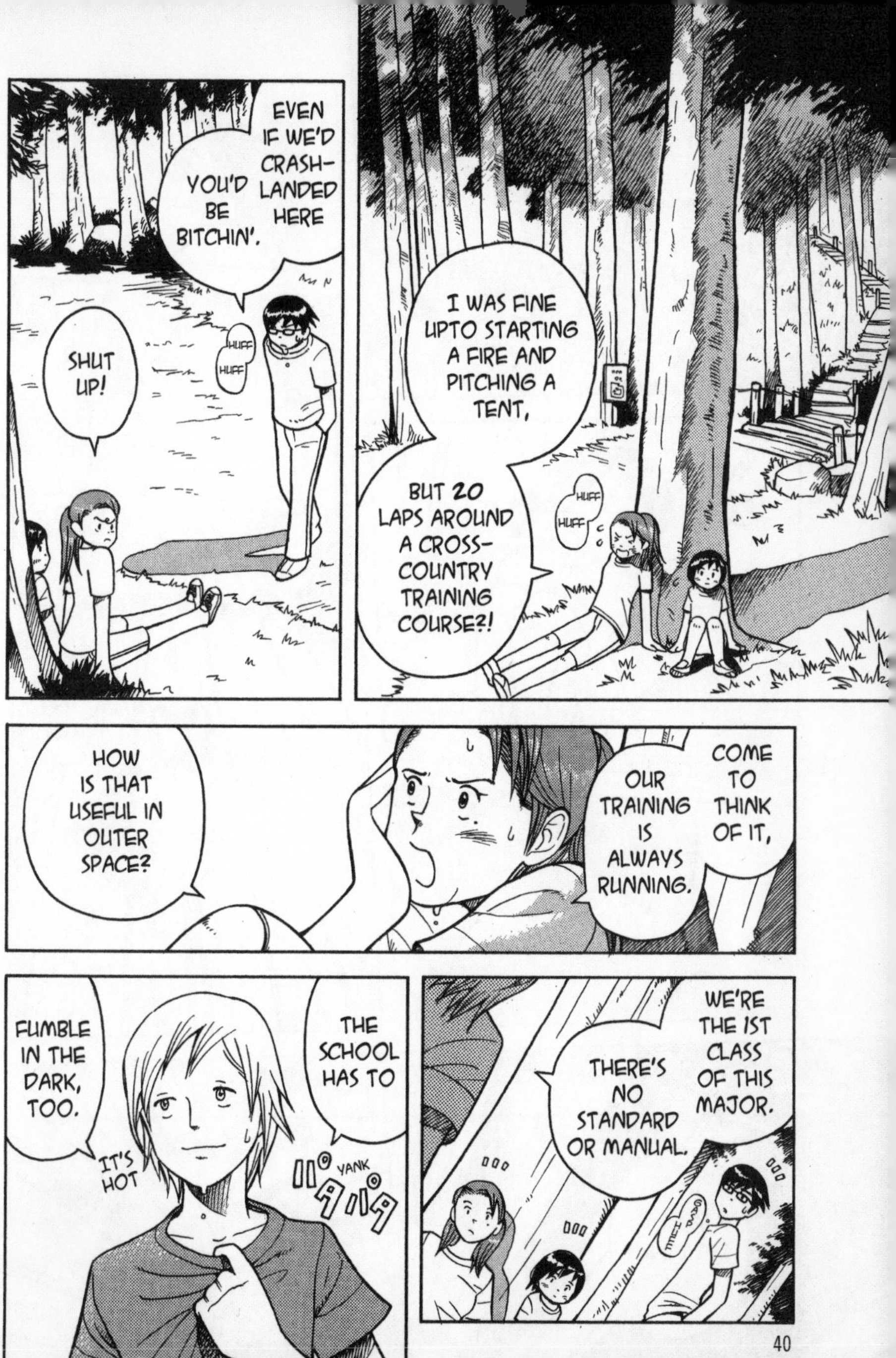
I WAS FINE UPTO STARTING A FIRE AND PITCHING A TENT,
BUT 20 LAPS AROUND A CROSS-COUNTRY TRAINING COURSE?!
HUFF
HUFF
EVEN IF WE'D CRASH-LANDED HERE YOU'D BE BITCHIN'.
HUFF
HUFF
SHUT UP!
COME TO THINK OF IT, OUR TRAINING IS ALWAYS RUNNING.
HOW IS THAT USEFUL IN OUTER SPACE?
WE'RE THE 1ST CLASS OF THIS MAJOR.
THERE'S NO STANDARD OR MANUAL.
THE SCHOOL HAS TO
FUMBLE IN THE DARK, TOO.
YANK
IT'S HOT

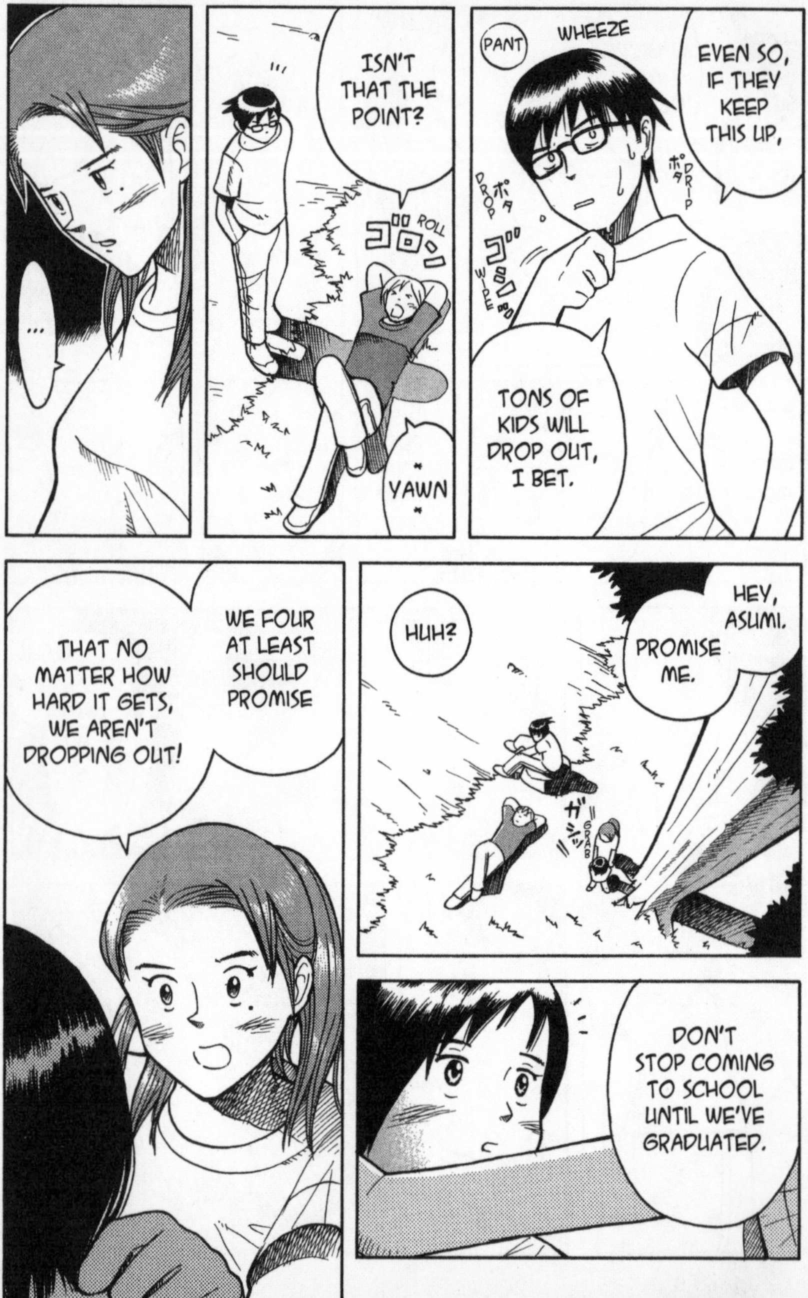
PANT
WHEEZE
EVEN SO, IF THEY KEEP THIS UP,
DRIP
DROP
WIPE
TONS OF KIDS WILL DROP OUT, I BET.
ISN'T THAT THE POINT?
ROLL
YAWN
...
HEY, ASUMI.
PROMISE ME.
HUH?
GRAB
DON'T STOP COMING TO SCHOOL UNTIL WE'VE GRADUATED.
WE FOUR AT LEAST SHOULD PROMISE
THAT NO MATTER HOW HARD IT GETS, WE AREN'T DROPPING OUT!

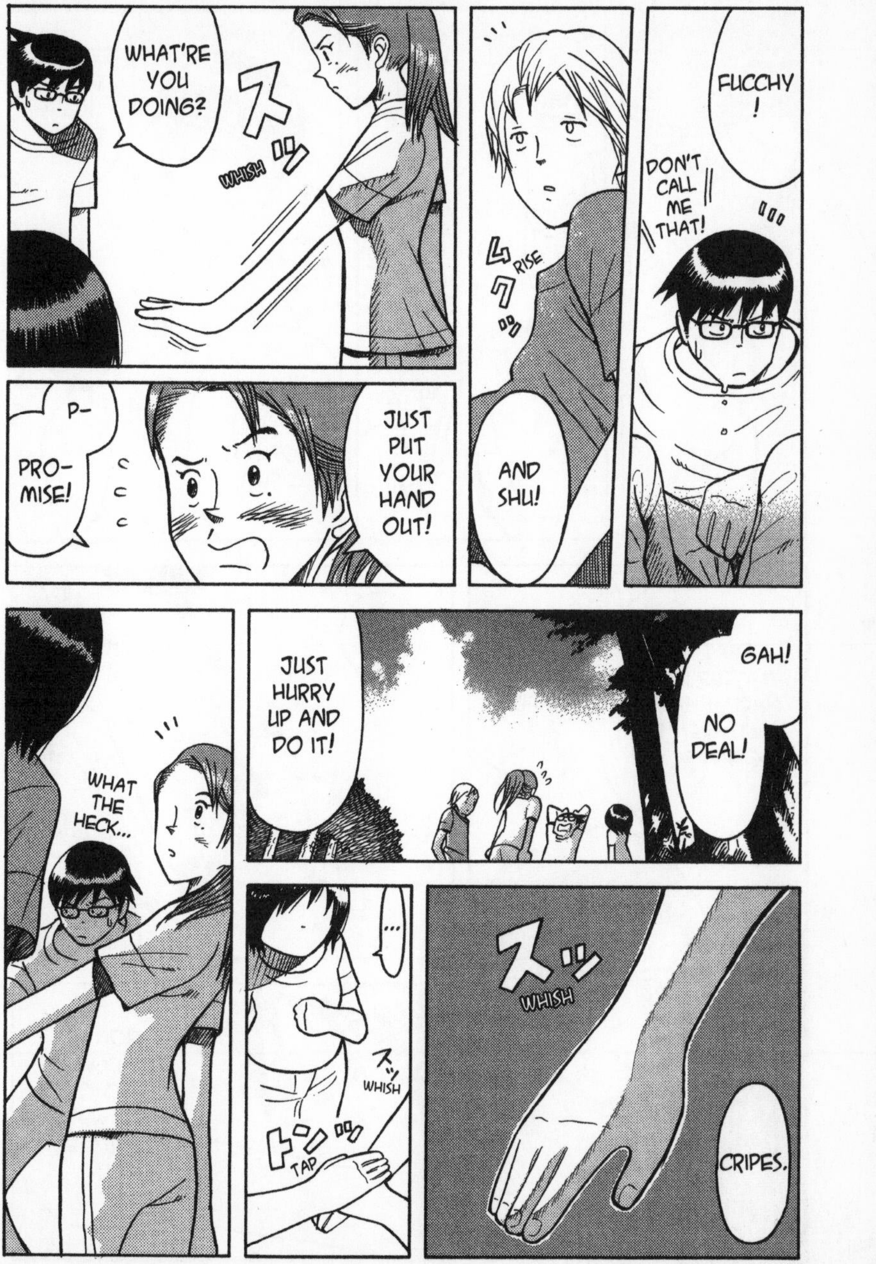
FUCCHY !
DON'T CALL ME THAT!
RISE
AND SHU!
WHAT'RE YOU DOING?
WHISH
JUST PUT YOUR HAND OUT!
P-
PRO-MISE!
GAH!
NO DEAL!
JUST HURRY UP AND DO IT!
WHISH
CRIPES.
...
WHISH
TAP
WHAT THE HECK...

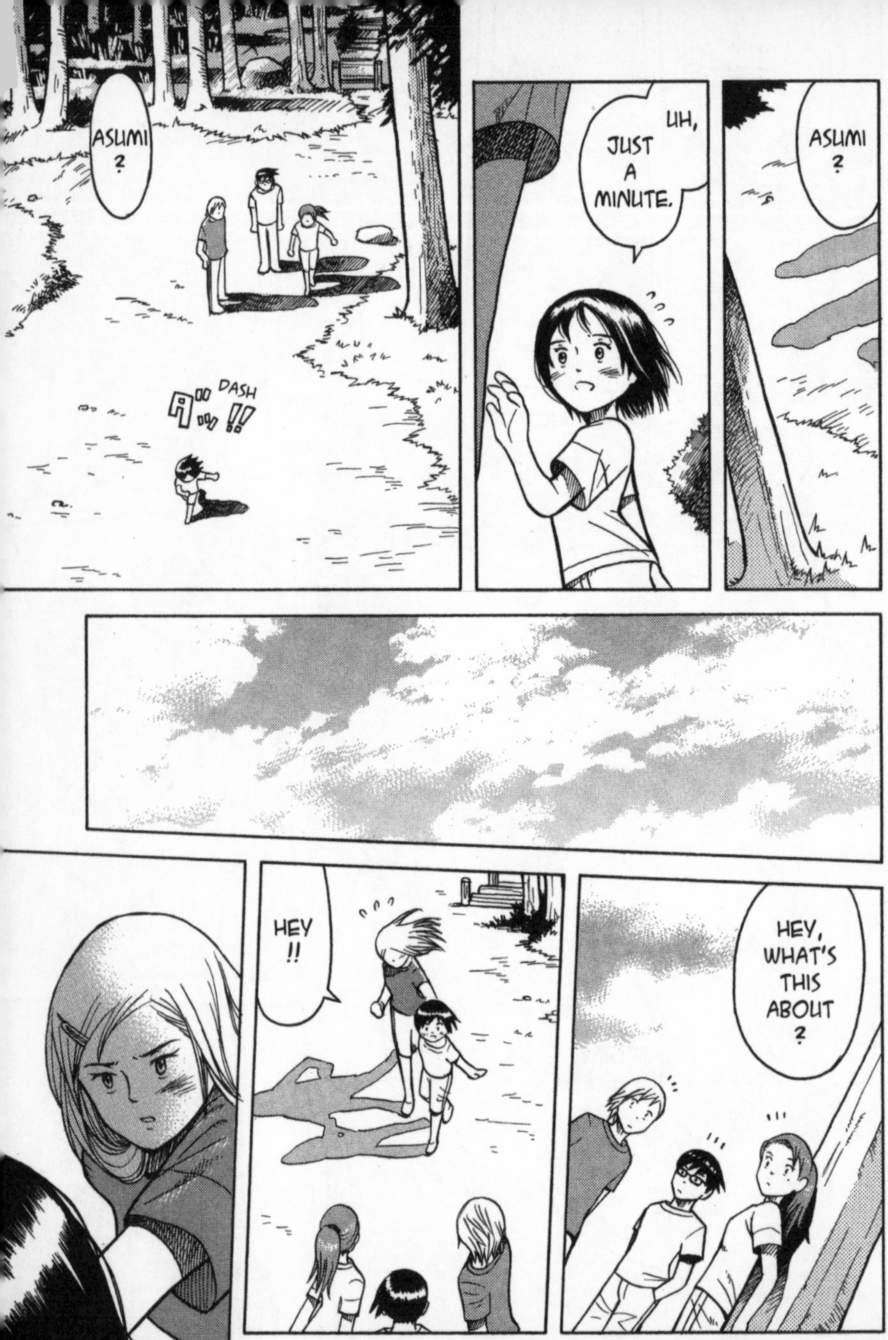
ASUMI?
UH, JUST A MINUTE.
ASUMI?
ダッ!!
DASH
HEY, WHAT'S THIS ABOUT?
HEY!!

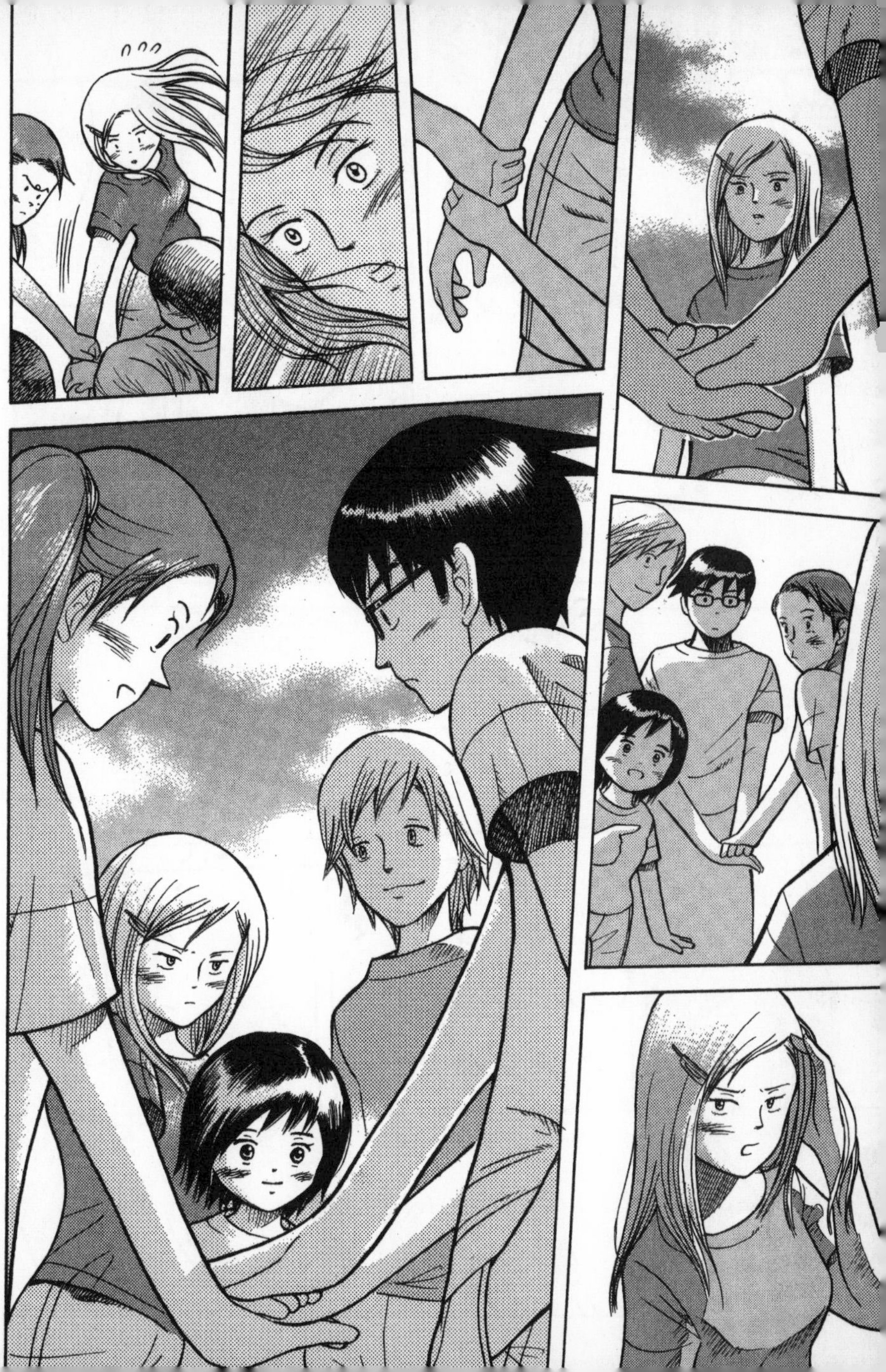

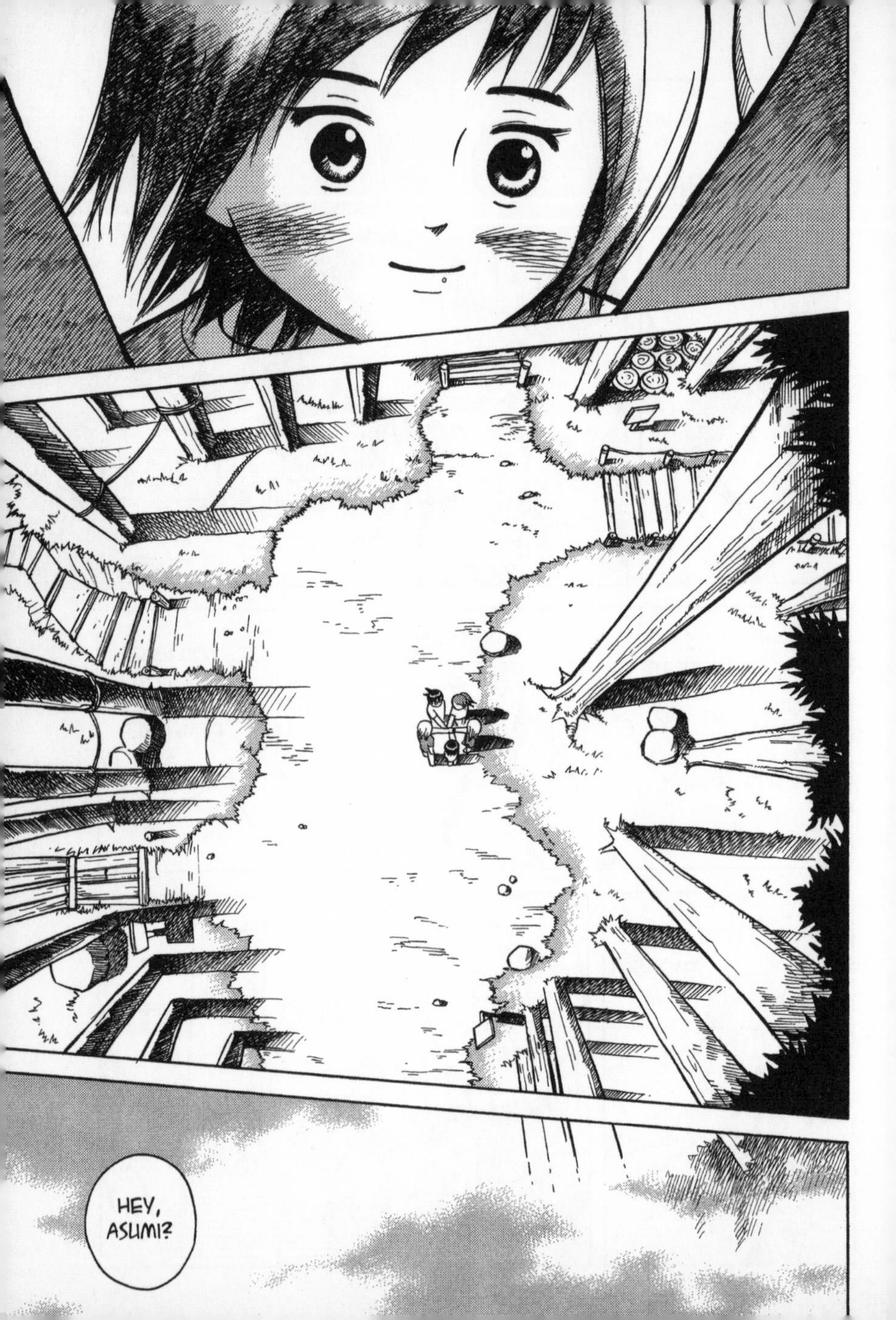
HEY, ASUMI?

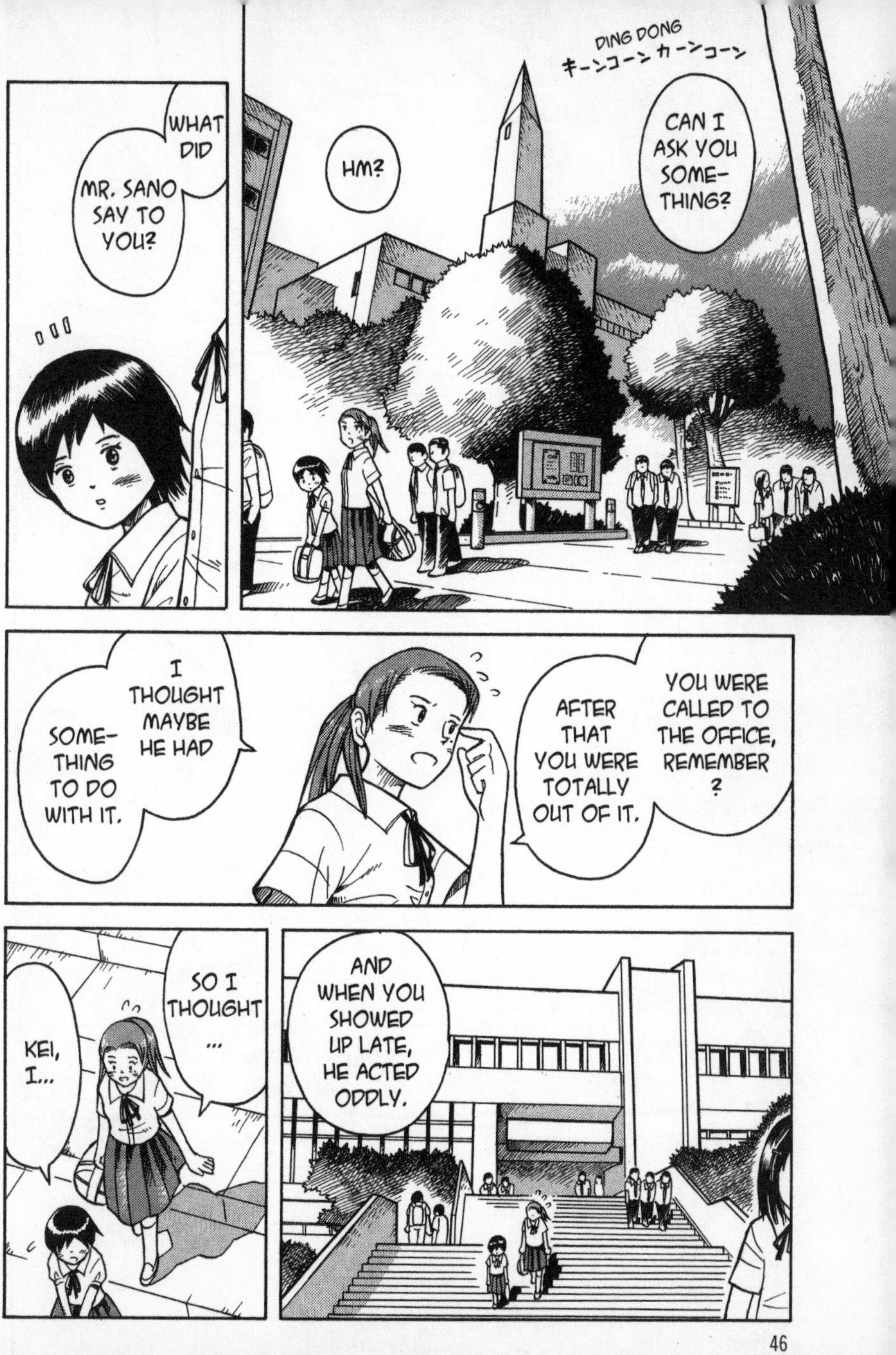
DING DONG
キーンコーン カーンコーン
CAN I ASK YOU SOME-THING?
HM?
WHAT DID MR. SANO SAY TO YOU?
YOU WERE CALLED TO THE OFFICE, REMEMBER?
AFTER THAT YOU WERE TOTALLY OUT OF IT.
I THOUGHT MAYBE HE HAD SOME-THING TO DO WITH IT.
AND WHEN YOU SHOWED UP LATE, HE ACTED ODDLY.
SO I THOUGHT ...
KEI, I...

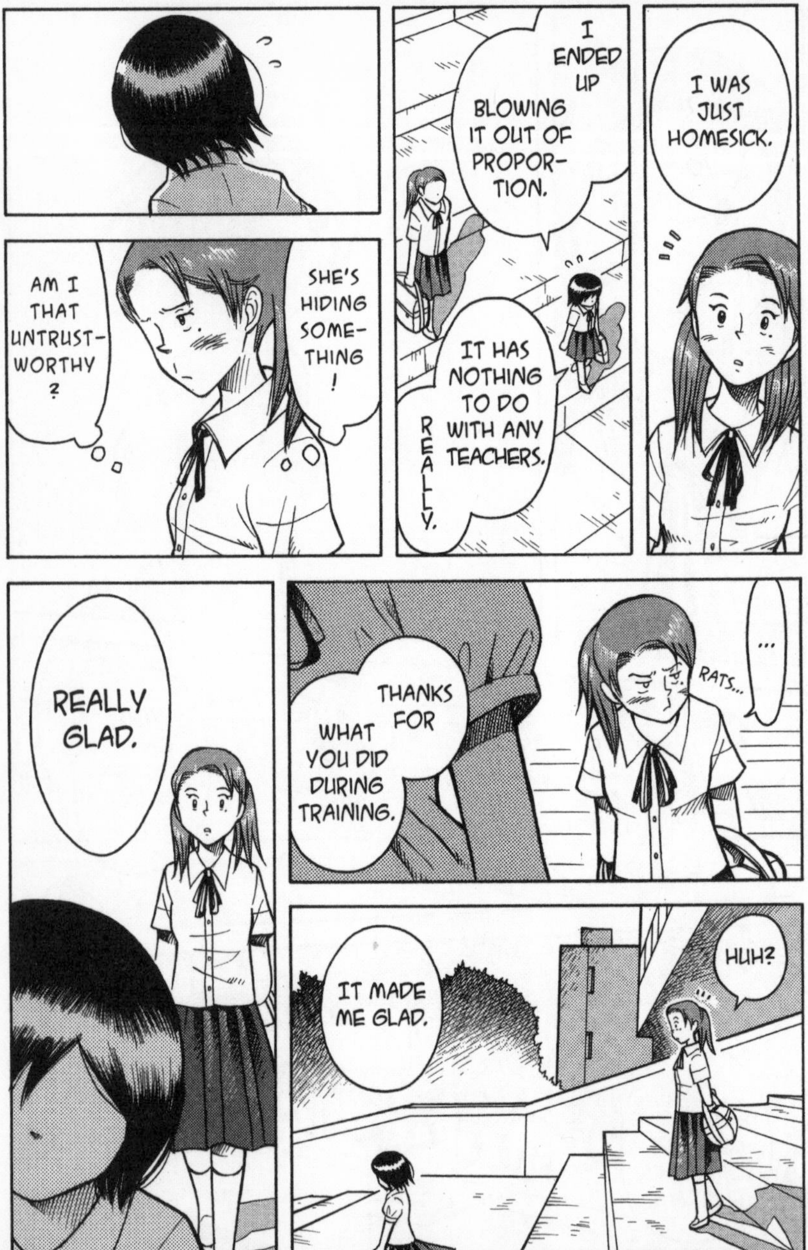
I WAS JUST HOMESICK.
I ENDED UP BLOWING IT OUT OF PROPORTION.
IT HAS NOTHING TO DO WITH ANY TEACHERS.
REALLY.
SHE'S HIDING SOMETHING!
AM I THAT UNTRUSTWORTHY?
...
RATS...
THANKS FOR WHAT YOU DID DURING TRAINING.
HUH?
IT MADE ME GLAD.
REALLY GLAD.

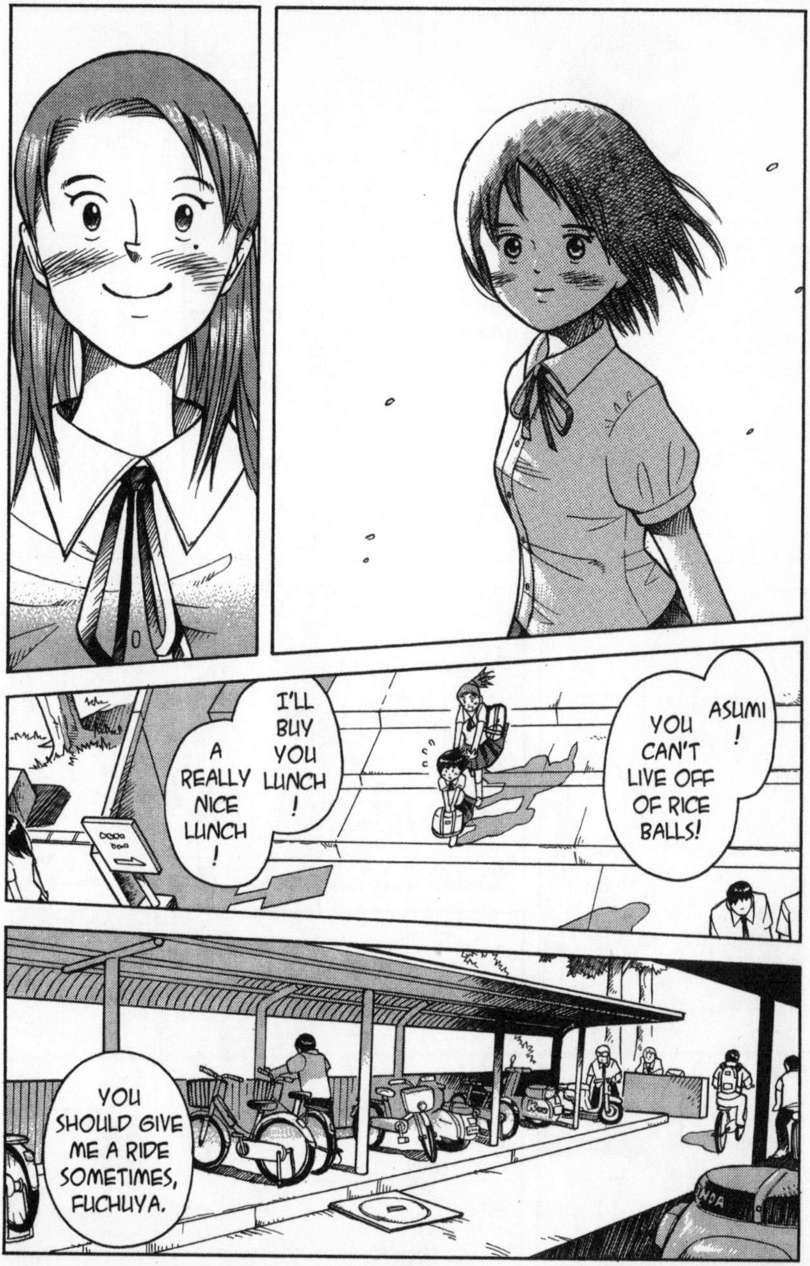
ASUMI! YOU CAN'T LIVE OFF OF RICE BALLS!
I'LL BUY YOU LUNCH!
A REALLY NICE LUNCH!
YOU SHOULD GIVE ME A RIDE SOMETIMES, FUCHUYA.

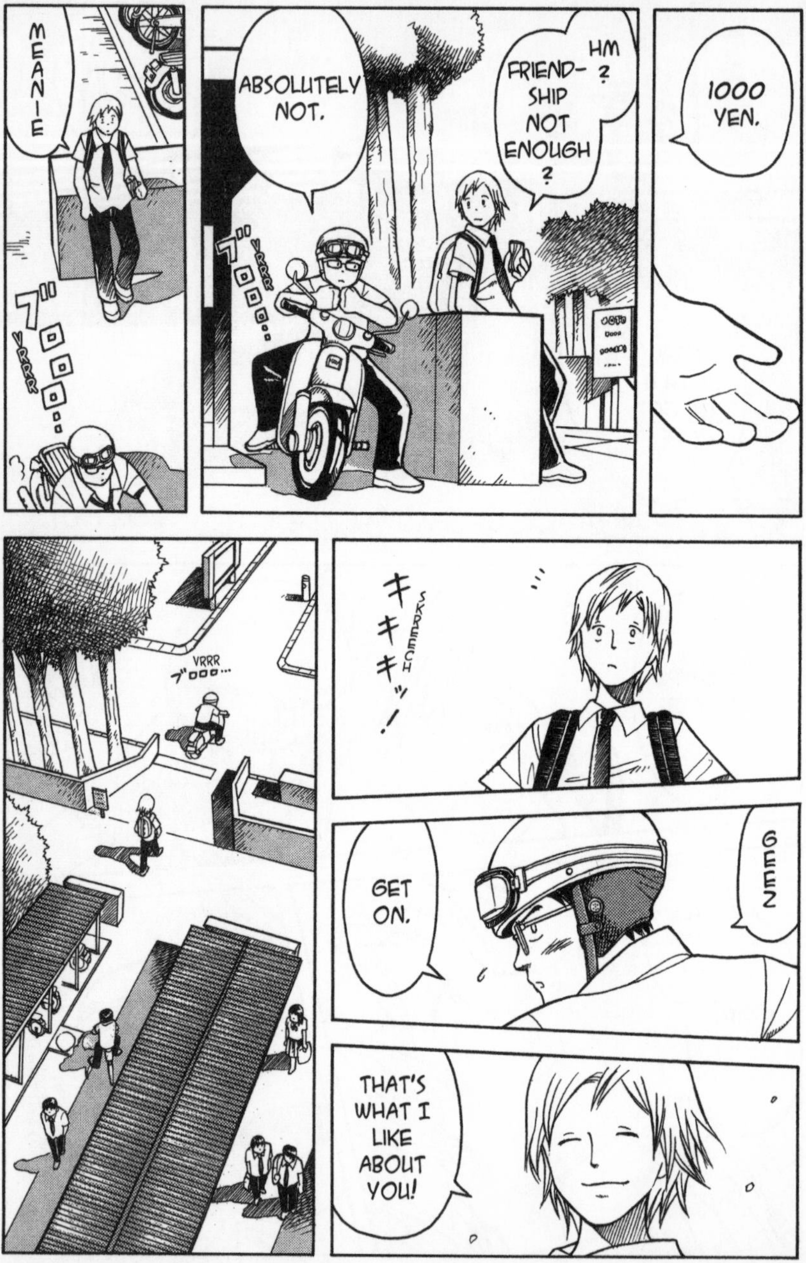
1000 YEN.
HM? FRIEND-SHIP NOT ENOUGH?
ABSOLUTELY NOT.
VRRR
MEANIE
VRRR
キキキッ!
SKREECH
GEEZ
GET ON.
THAT'S WHAT I LIKE ABOUT YOU!
VRRR...

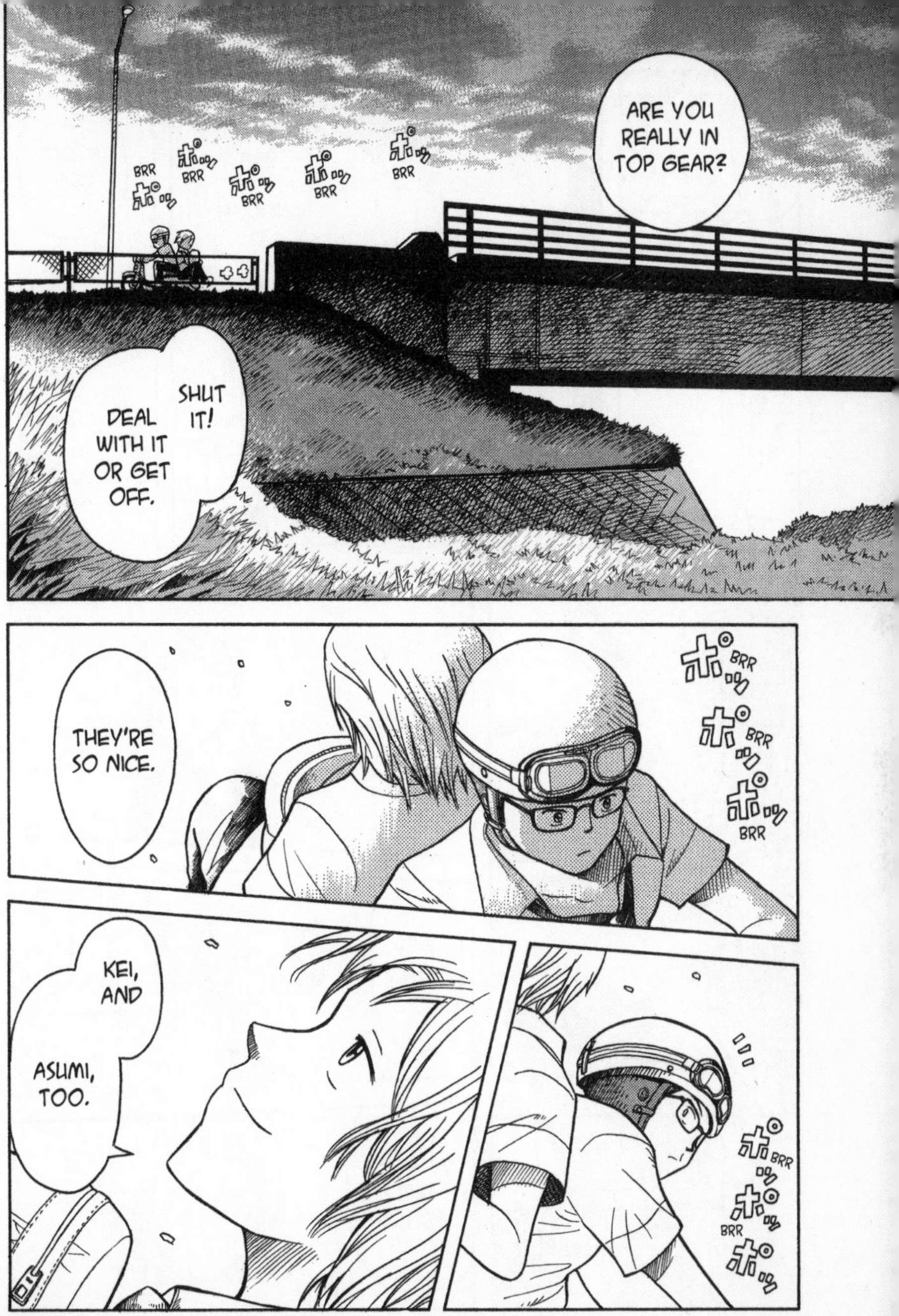
ARE YOU REALLY IN TOP GEAR?
BRR
BRR
BRR
BRR
BRR
SHUT IT!
DEAL WITH IT OR GET OFF.
BRR
BRR
BRR
THEY'RE SO NICE.
BRR
BRR
KEI, AND
ASUMI, TOO.

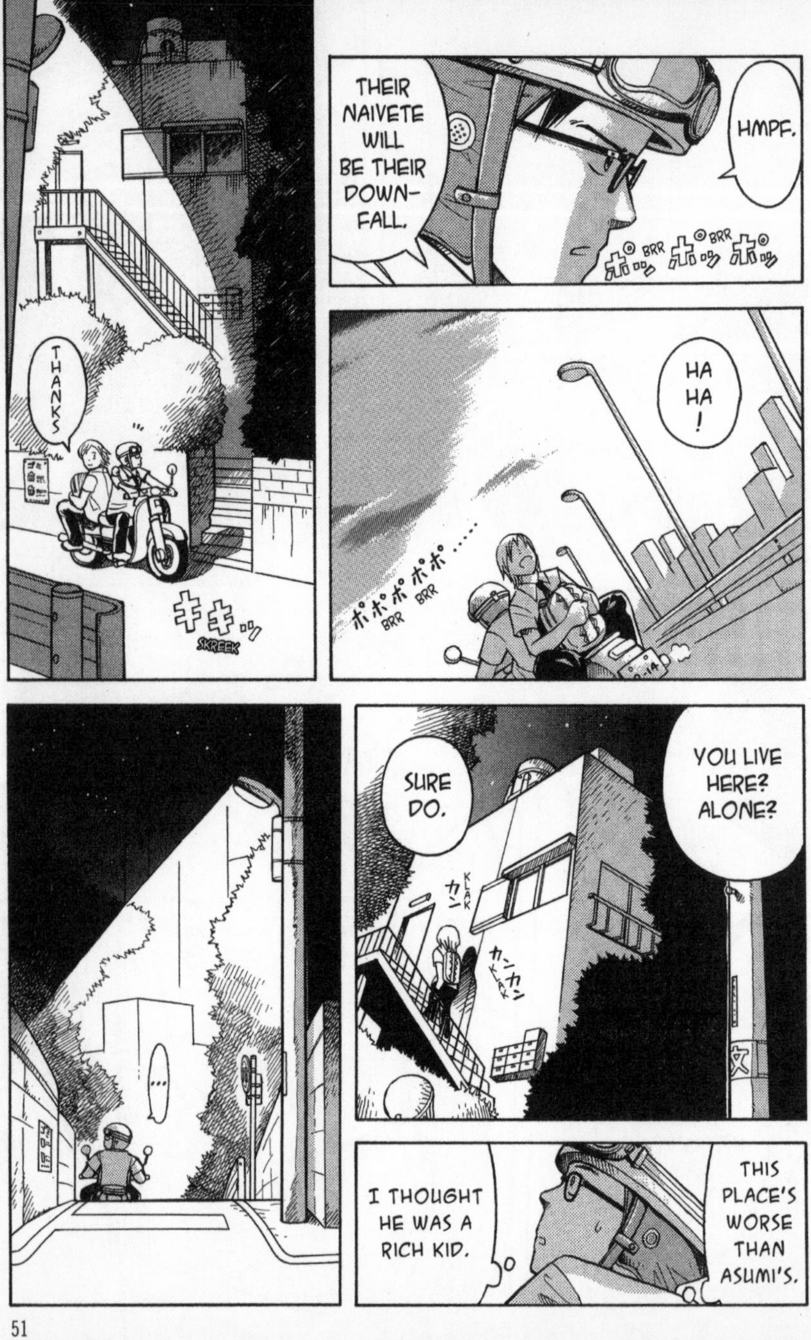
HMPF.
THEIR NAIVETE WILL BE THEIR DOWNFALL.
ポッ BRR ポッ BRR ポッ
HA HA!
ポポポポ BRR BRR
THANKS
キキッ SKREEK
YOU LIVE HERE? ALONE?
SURE DO.
カン KLAK
カンカン KLAK
THIS PLACE'S WORSE THAN ASUMI'S.
I THOUGHT HE WAS A RICH KID.
...

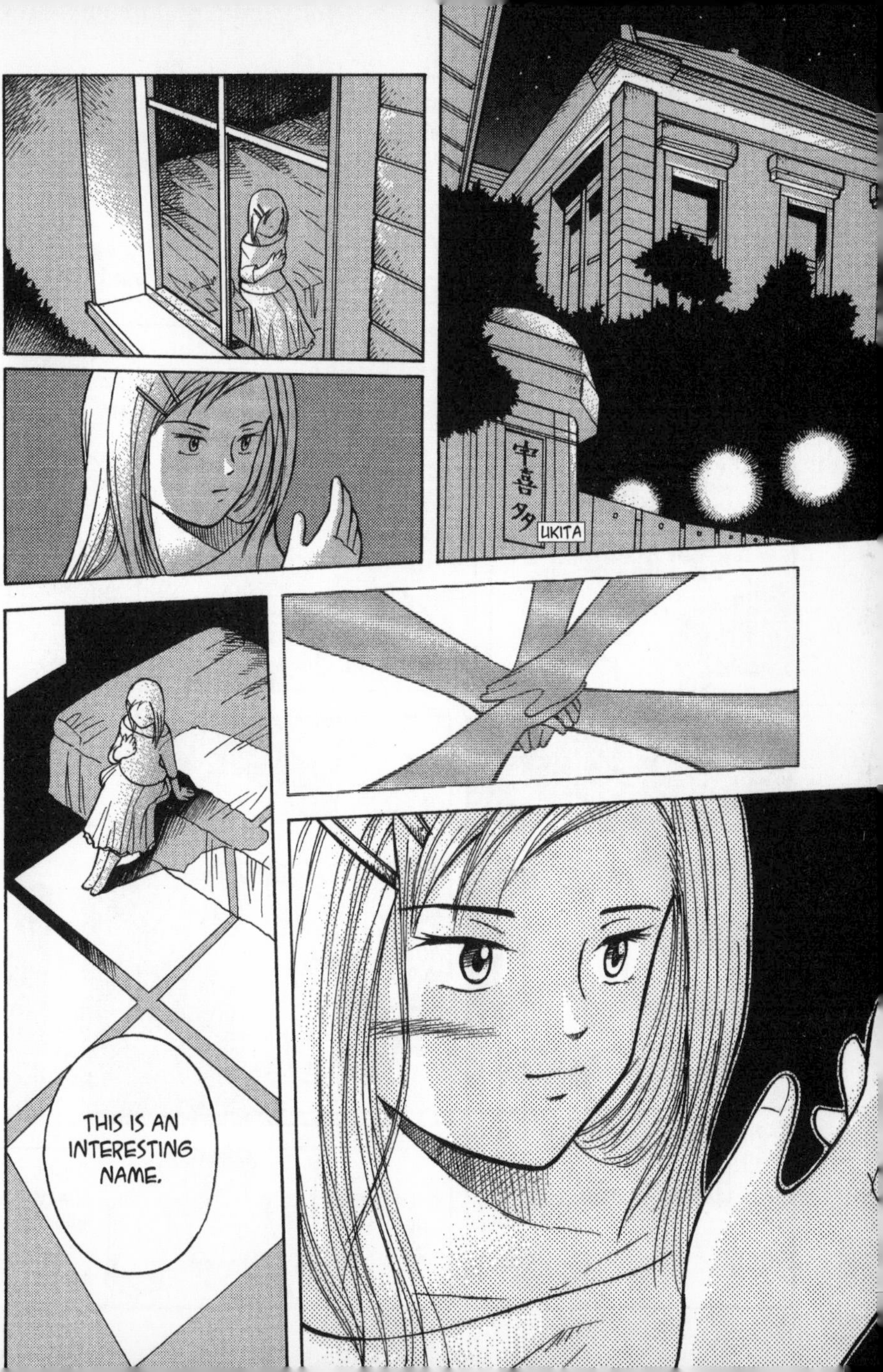

宇喜多
UKITA
THIS IS AN INTERESTING NAME.

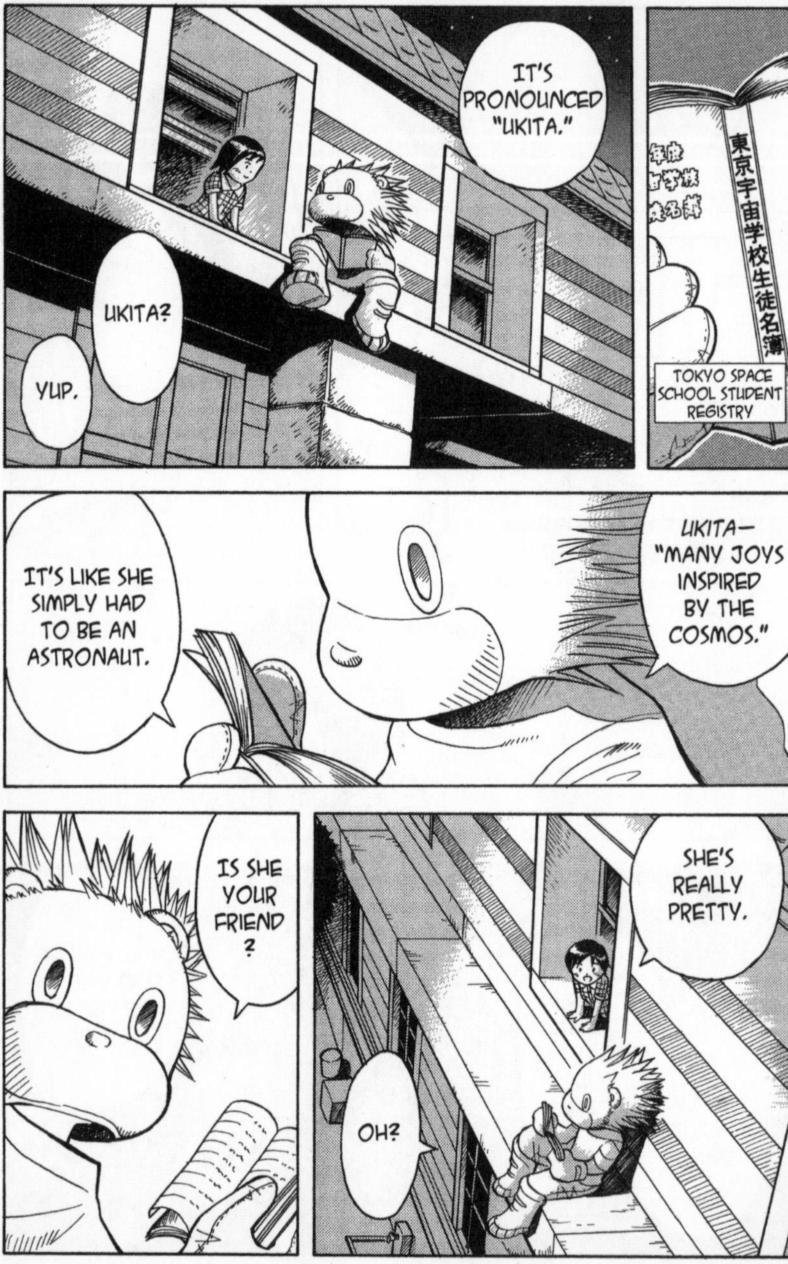
東京宇宙学校生徒名簿
TOKYO SPACE SCHOOL STUDENT REGISTRY
IT'S PRONOUNCED "UKITA."
UKITA?
YUP.
UKITA— "MANY JOYS INSPIRED BY THE COSMOS."
IT'S LIKE SHE SIMPLY HAD TO BE AN ASTRONAUT.
SHE'S REALLY PRETTY.
OH?
IS SHE YOUR FRIEND?

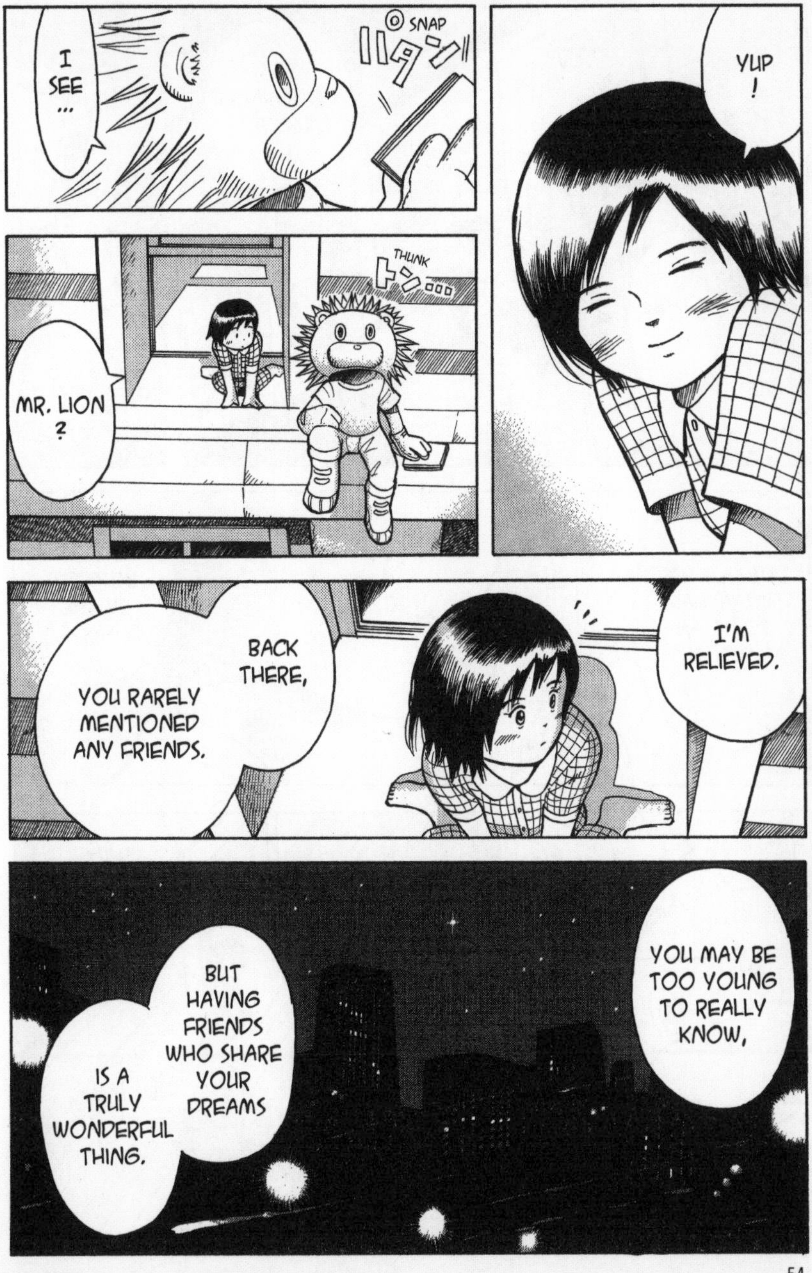
YUP!
SNAP
I SEE...
THUNK
MR. LION?
I'M RELIEVED.
BACK THERE,
YOU RARELY MENTIONED ANY FRIENDS.
YOU MAY BE TOO YOUNG TO REALLY KNOW,
BUT HAVING FRIENDS WHO SHARE YOUR DREAMS
IS A TRULY WONDERFUL THING.

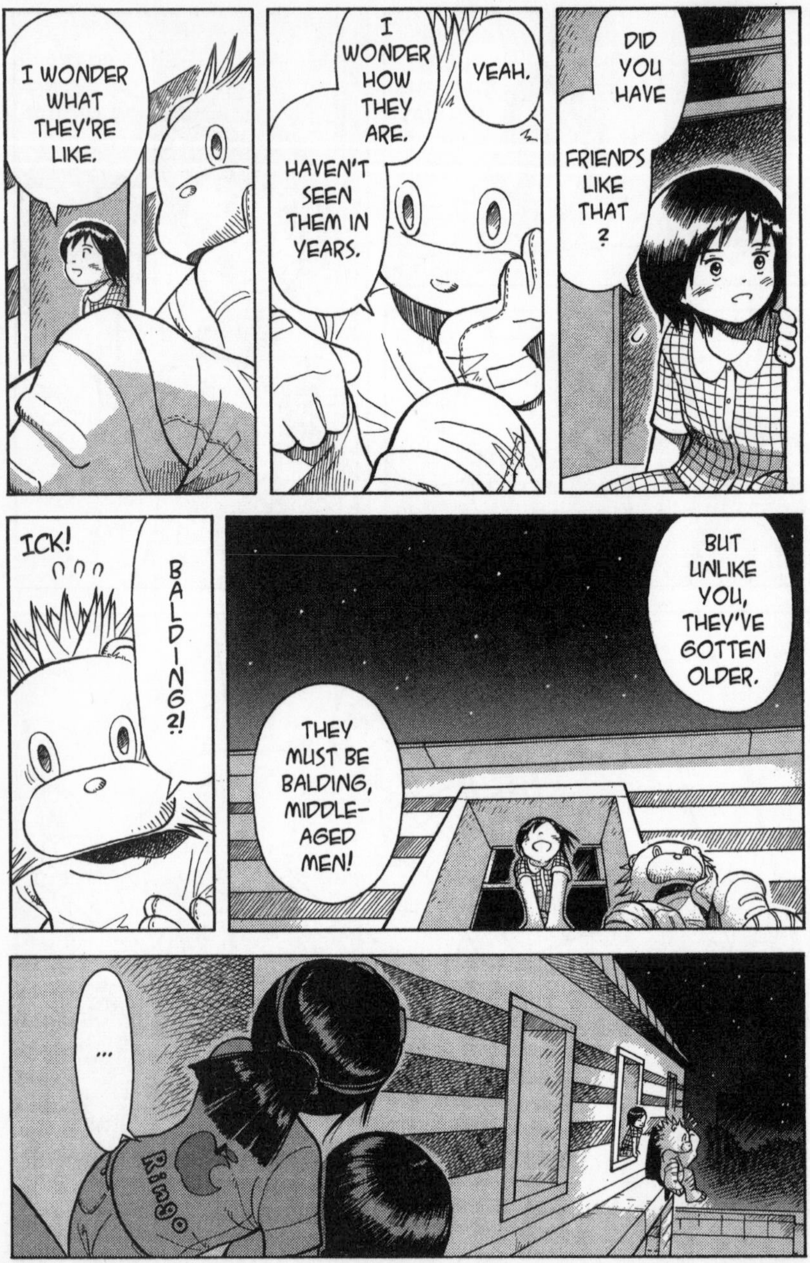
DID YOU HAVE FRIENDS LIKE THAT?
YEAH.
I WONDER HOW THEY ARE.
HAVEN'T SEEN THEM IN YEARS.
I WONDER WHAT THEY'RE LIKE.
BUT UNLIKE YOU, THEY'VE GOTTEN OLDER.
THEY MUST BE BALDING, MIDDLE-AGED MEN!
BALDING?!
ICK!
...
Ring

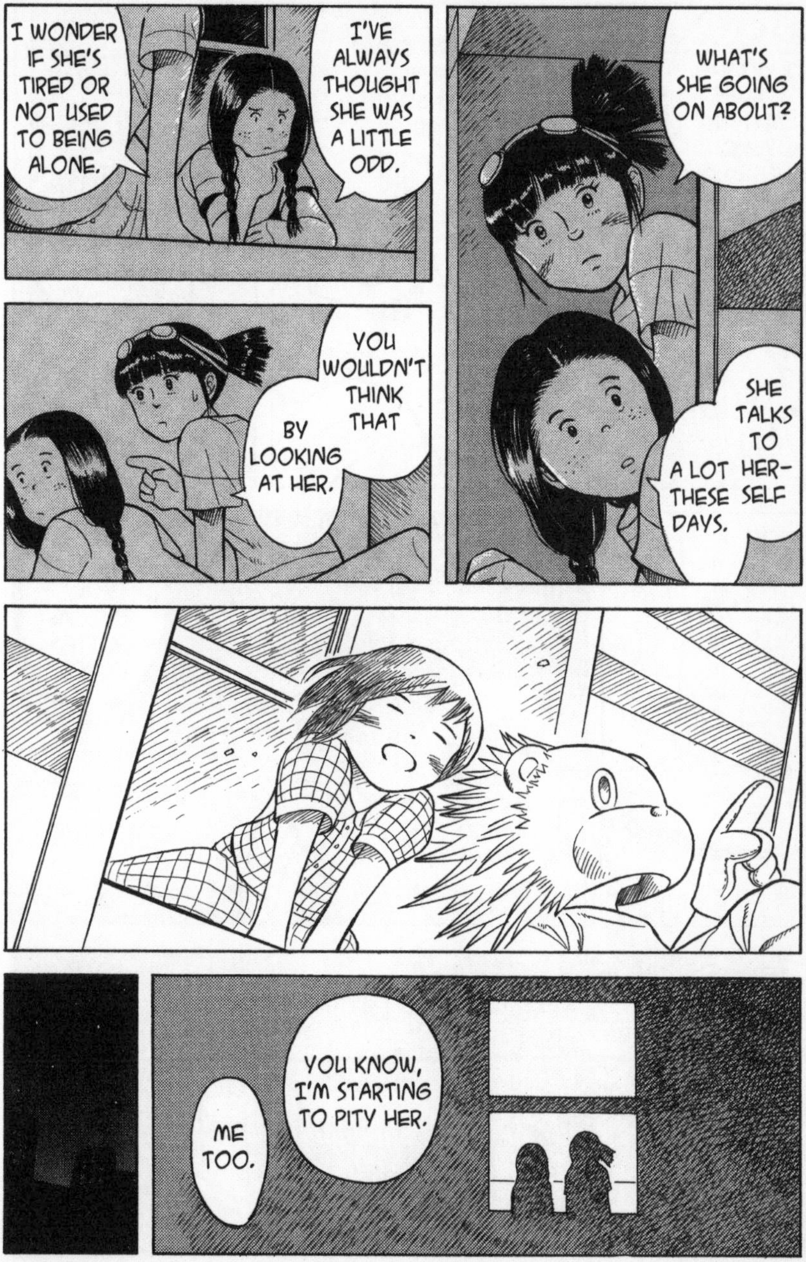
WHAT'S SHE GOING ON ABOUT?
SHE TALKS TO HERSELF A LOT THESE DAYS.
I'VE ALWAYS THOUGHT SHE WAS A LITTLE ODD.
I WONDER IF SHE'S TIRED OR NOT USED TO BEING ALONE.
YOU WOULDN'T THINK THAT BY LOOKING AT HER.
YOU KNOW, I'M STARTING TO PITY HER.
ME TOO.

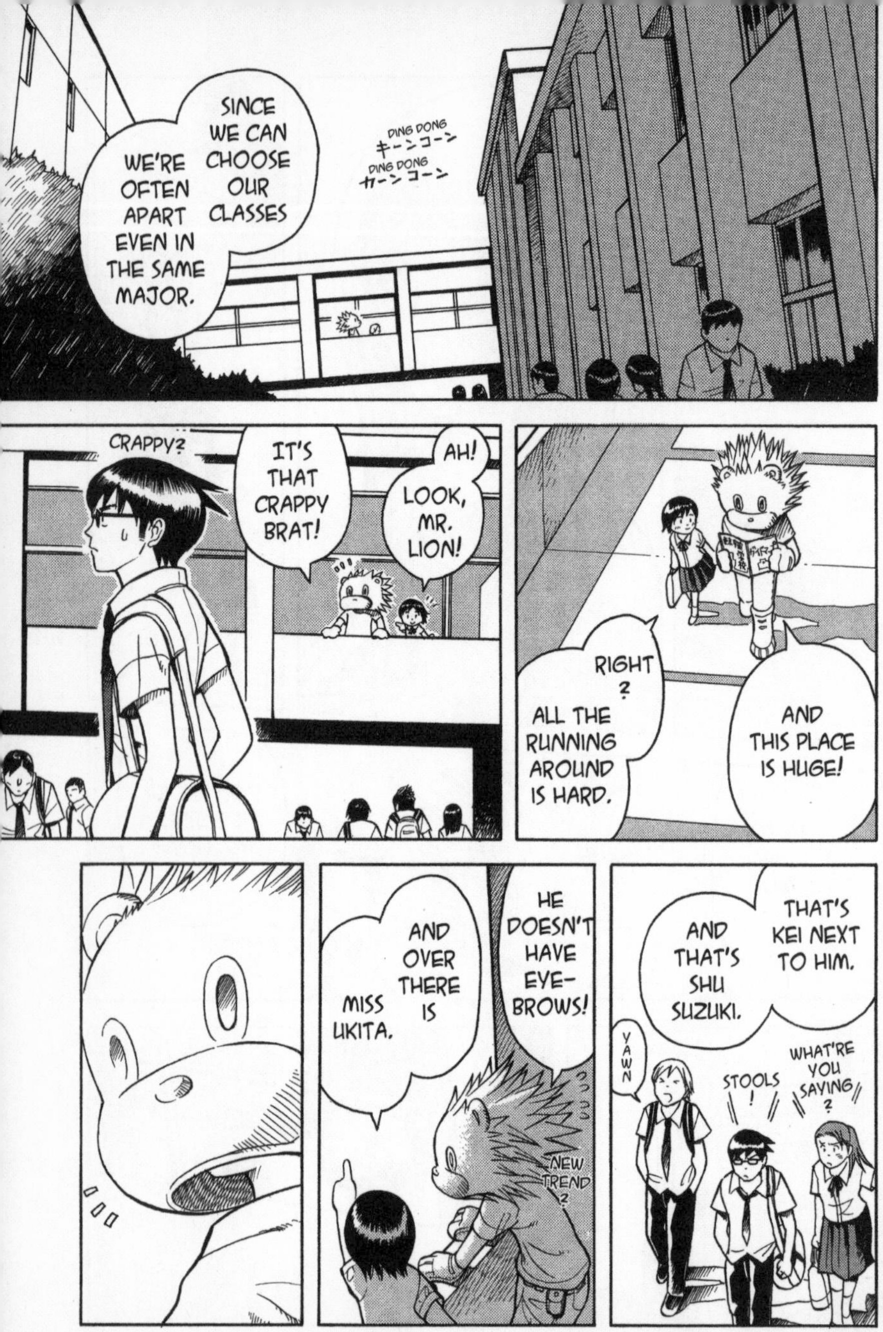
DING DONG
キーンコーン
DING DONG
カーンコーン
SINCE WE CAN CHOOSE OUR CLASSES
WE'RE OFTEN APART EVEN IN THE SAME MAJOR.
AND THIS PLACE IS HUGE!
ALL THE RUNNING AROUND IS HARD. RIGHT?
AH! LOOK, MR. LION!
IT'S THAT CRAPPY BRAT!
CRAPPY?
THAT'S KEI NEXT TO HIM.
AND THAT'S SHU SUZUKI.
YAWN
WHAT'RE YOU SAYING?
STOOLS!
HE DOESN'T HAVE EYE-BROWS!
AND OVER THERE IS MISS UKITA.
NEW TREND?

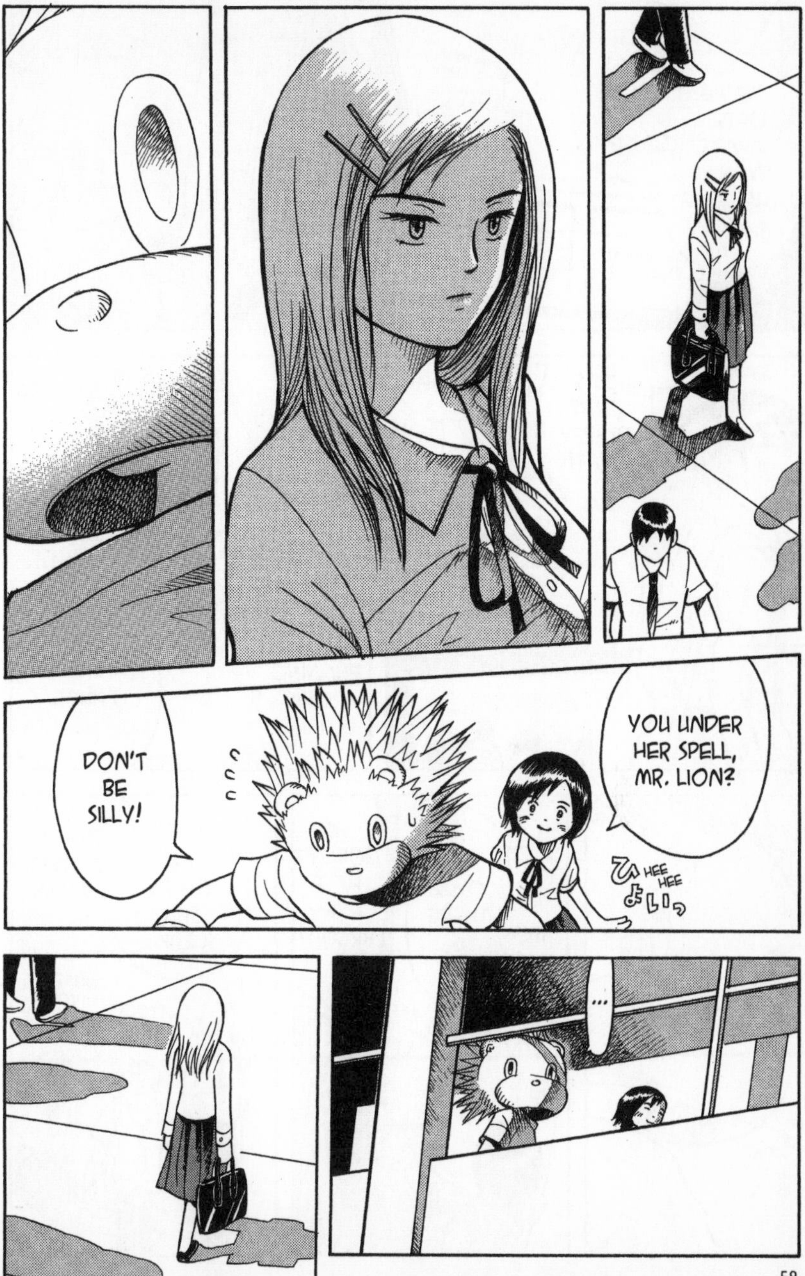
YOU UNDER HER SPELL, MR. LION?
HEE HEE
ひよいっ
DON'T BE SILLY!
...

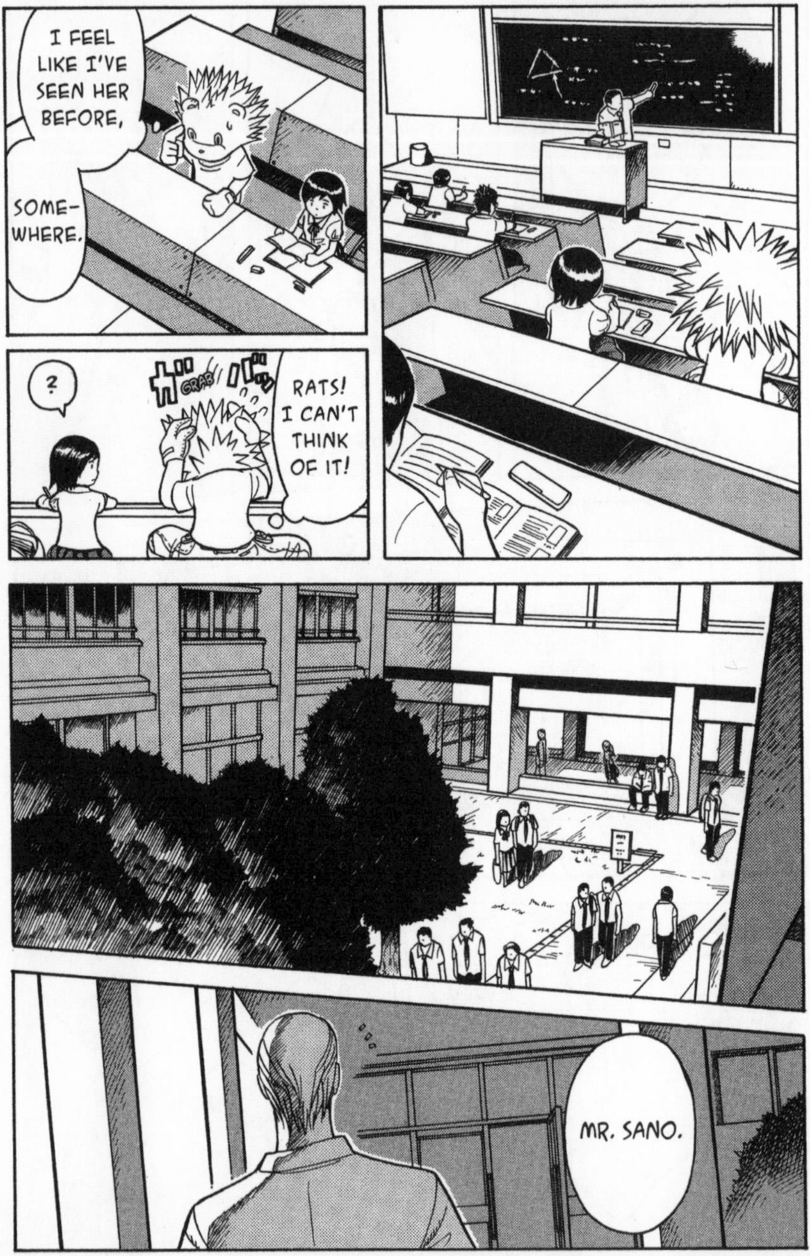
I FEEL LIKE I'VE SEEN HER BEFORE,
SOME-WHERE.
?
GRAB
RATS! I CAN'T THINK OF IT!
MR. SANO.

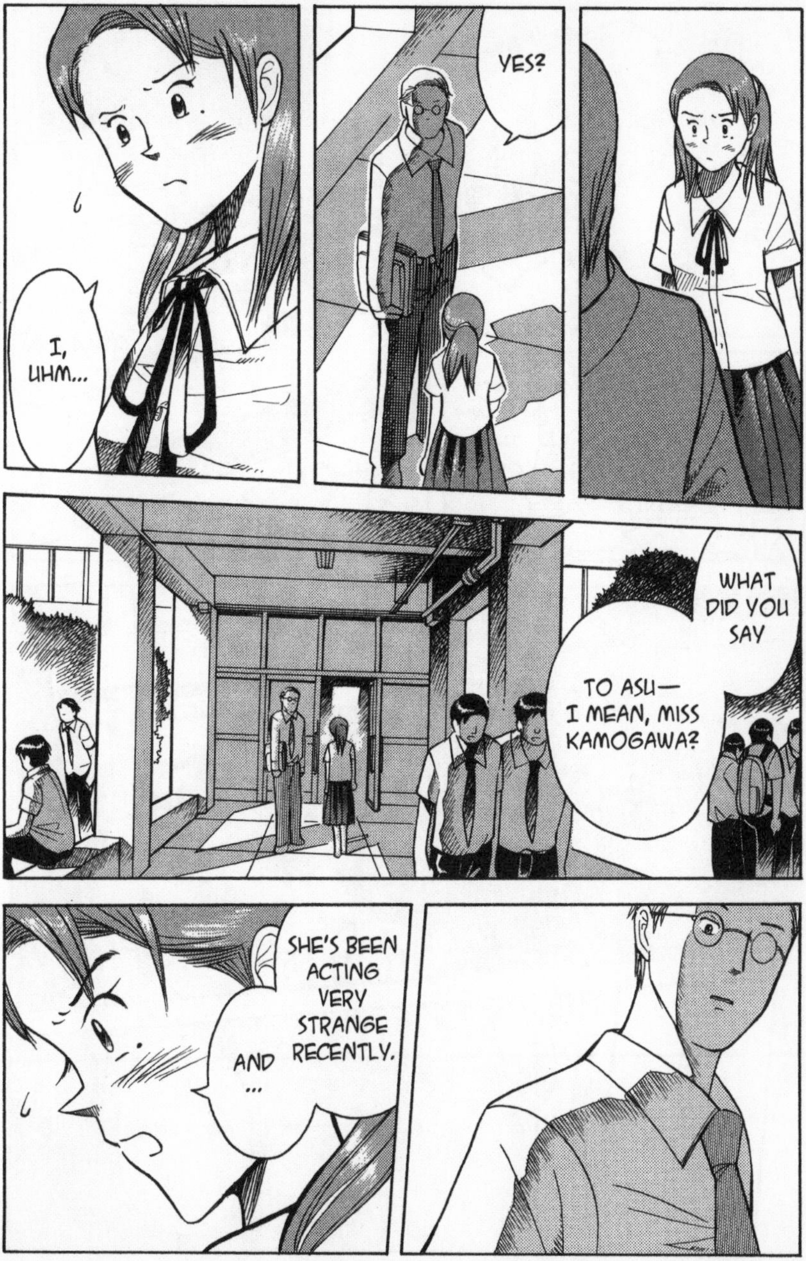
YES?
I, UHM...
WHAT DID YOU SAY
TO ASU— I MEAN, MISS KAMOGAWA?
SHE'S BEEN ACTING VERY STRANGE RECENTLY.
AND ...

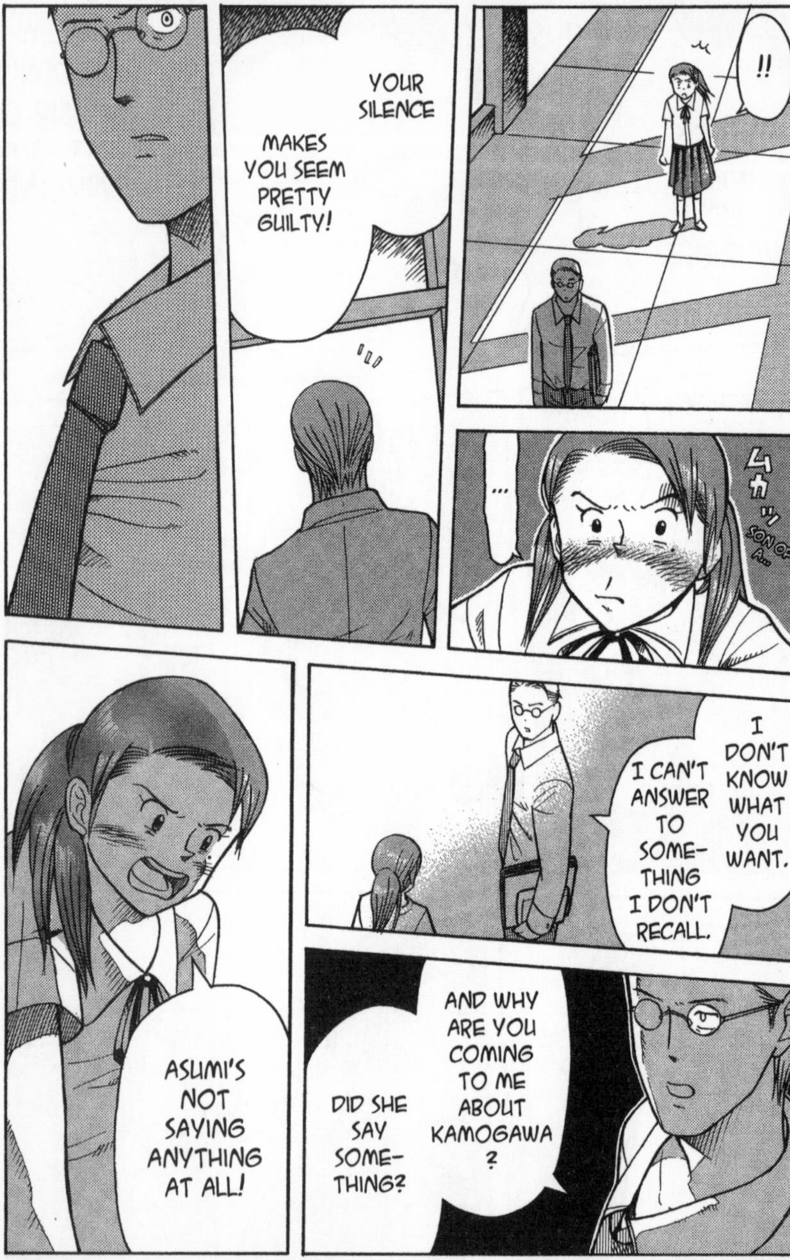
ム
!!
...
ムカッ
SON OF A...
YOUR SILENCE
MAKES YOU SEEM PRETTY GUILTY!
I DON'T KNOW WHAT YOU WANT.
I CAN'T ANSWER TO SOME-THING I DON'T RECALL.
AND WHY ARE YOU COMING TO ME ABOUT KAMOGAWA?
DID SHE SAY SOME-THING?
ASUMI'S NOT SAYING ANYTHING AT ALL!

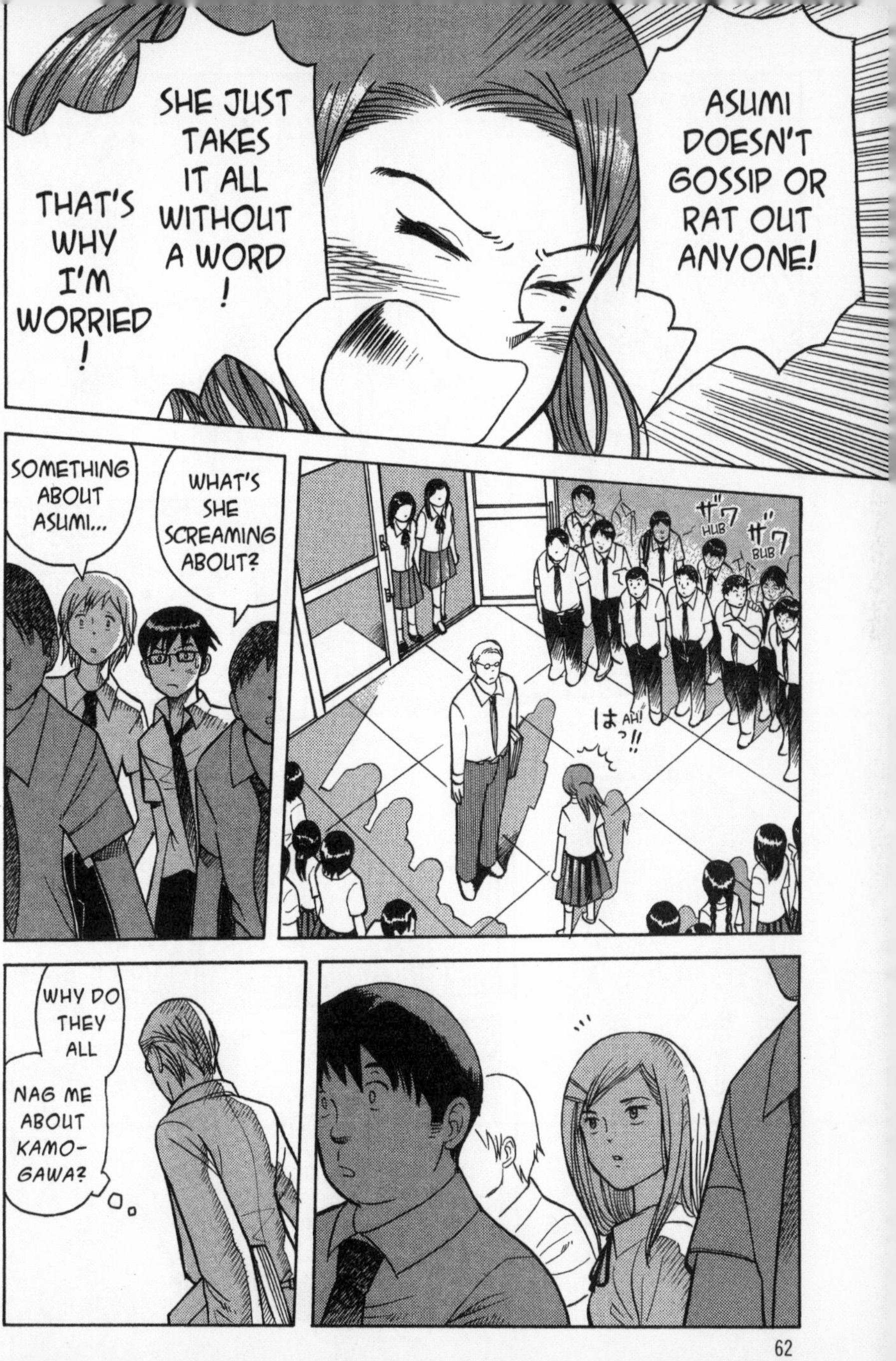
ASUMI DOESN'T GOSSIP OR RAT OUT ANYONE!
SHE JUST TAKES IT ALL WITHOUT A WORD!
THAT'S WHY I'M WORRIED!
ザワ HUB
ザワ BUB
は AH!?!!
WHAT'S SHE SCREAMING ABOUT?
SOMETHING ABOUT ASUMI...
WHY DO THEY ALL NAG ME ABOUT KAMO-GAWA?

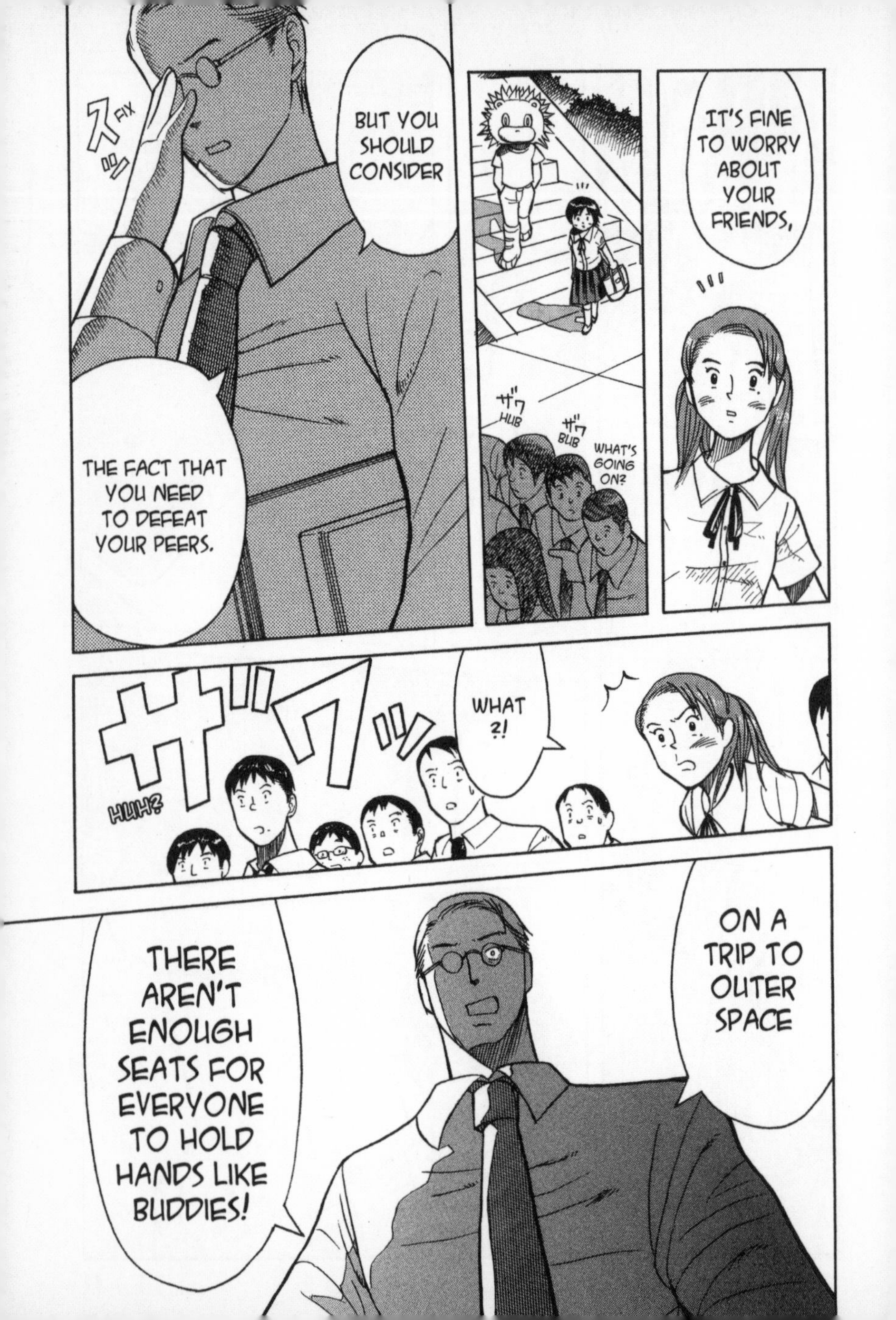
IT'S FINE TO WORRY ABOUT YOUR FRIENDS,
HUB
BUB
WHAT'S GOING ON?
BUT YOU SHOULD CONSIDER
FIX
THE FACT THAT YOU NEED TO DEFEAT YOUR PEERS.
WHAT ?!
HUH?
ON A TRIP TO OUTER SPACE
THERE AREN'T ENOUGH SEATS FOR EVERYONE TO HOLD HANDS LIKE BUDDIES!

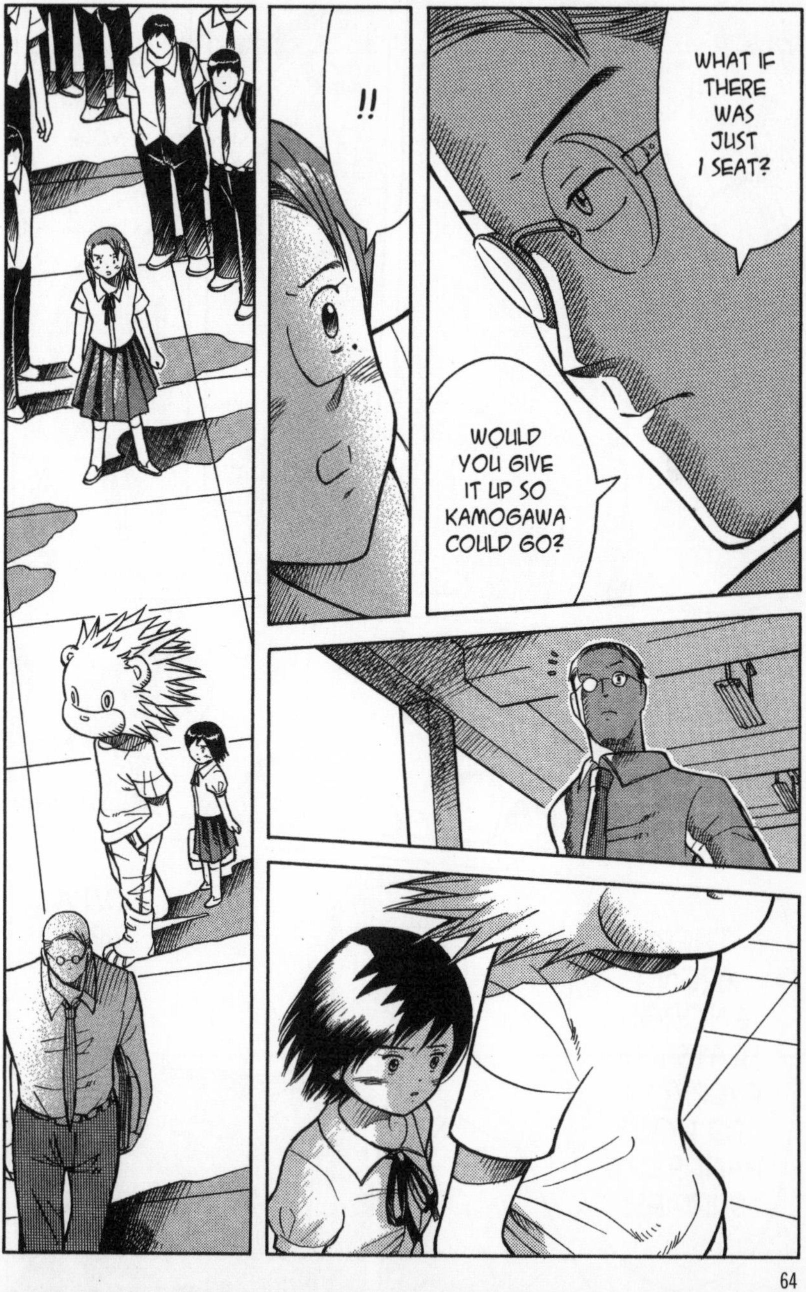
WHAT IF THERE WAS JUST 1 SEAT?
WOULD YOU GIVE IT UP SO KAMOGAWA COULD GO?
!!

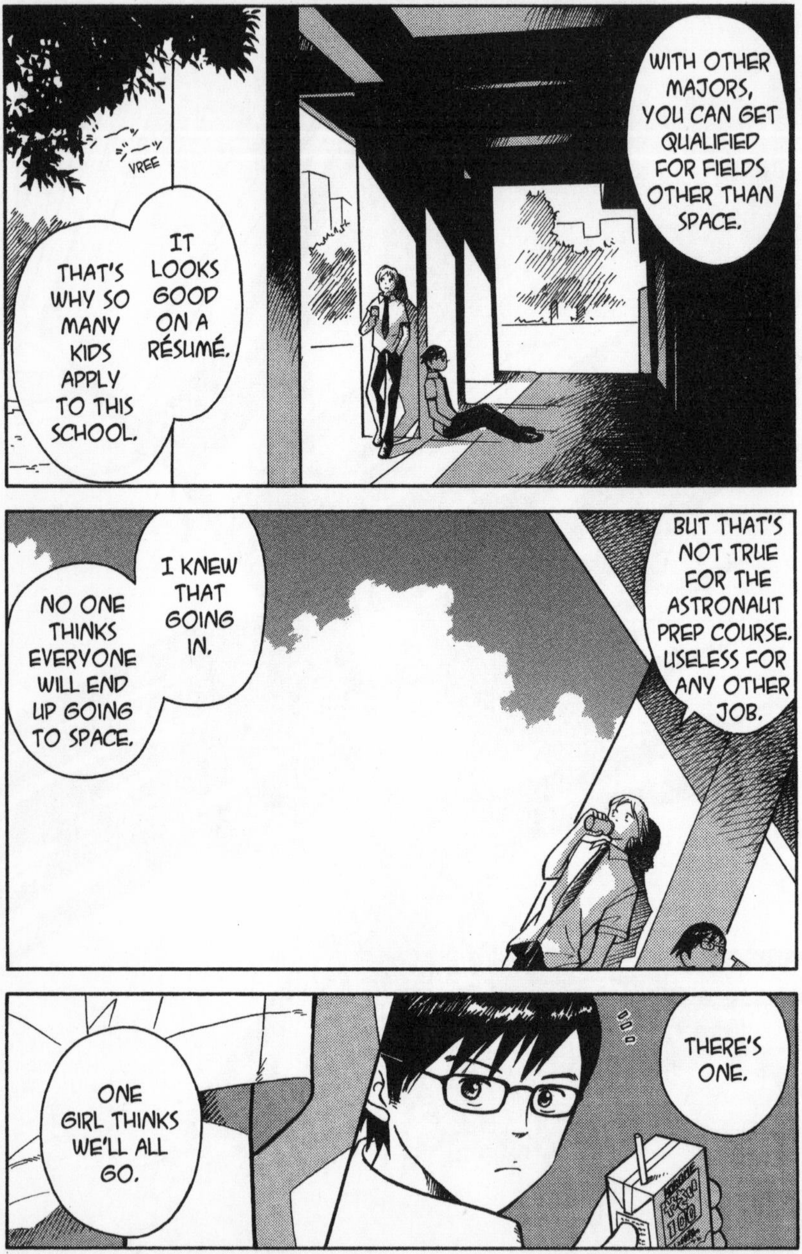
WITH OTHER MAJORS, YOU CAN GET QUALIFIED FOR FIELDS OTHER THAN SPACE.
IT LOOKS GOOD ON A RÉSUMÉ.
THAT'S WHY SO MANY KIDS APPLY TO THIS SCHOOL.
VREE
BUT THAT'S NOT TRUE FOR THE ASTRONAUT PREP COURSE. USELESS FOR ANY OTHER JOB.
I KNEW THAT GOING IN.
NO ONE THINKS EVERYONE WILL END UP GOING TO SPACE.
THERE'S ONE.
ONE GIRL THINKS WE'LL ALL GO.

MISSION:11

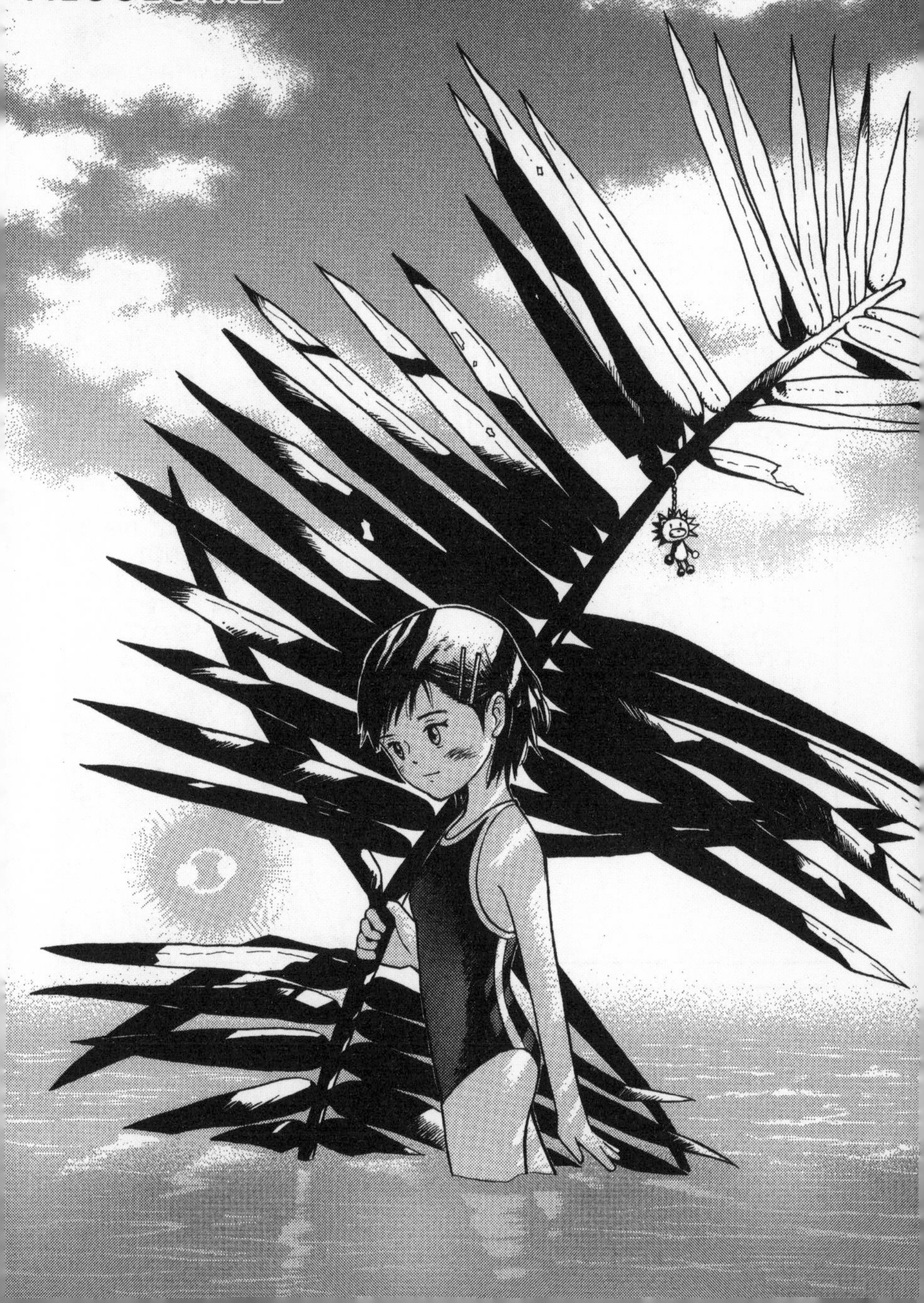

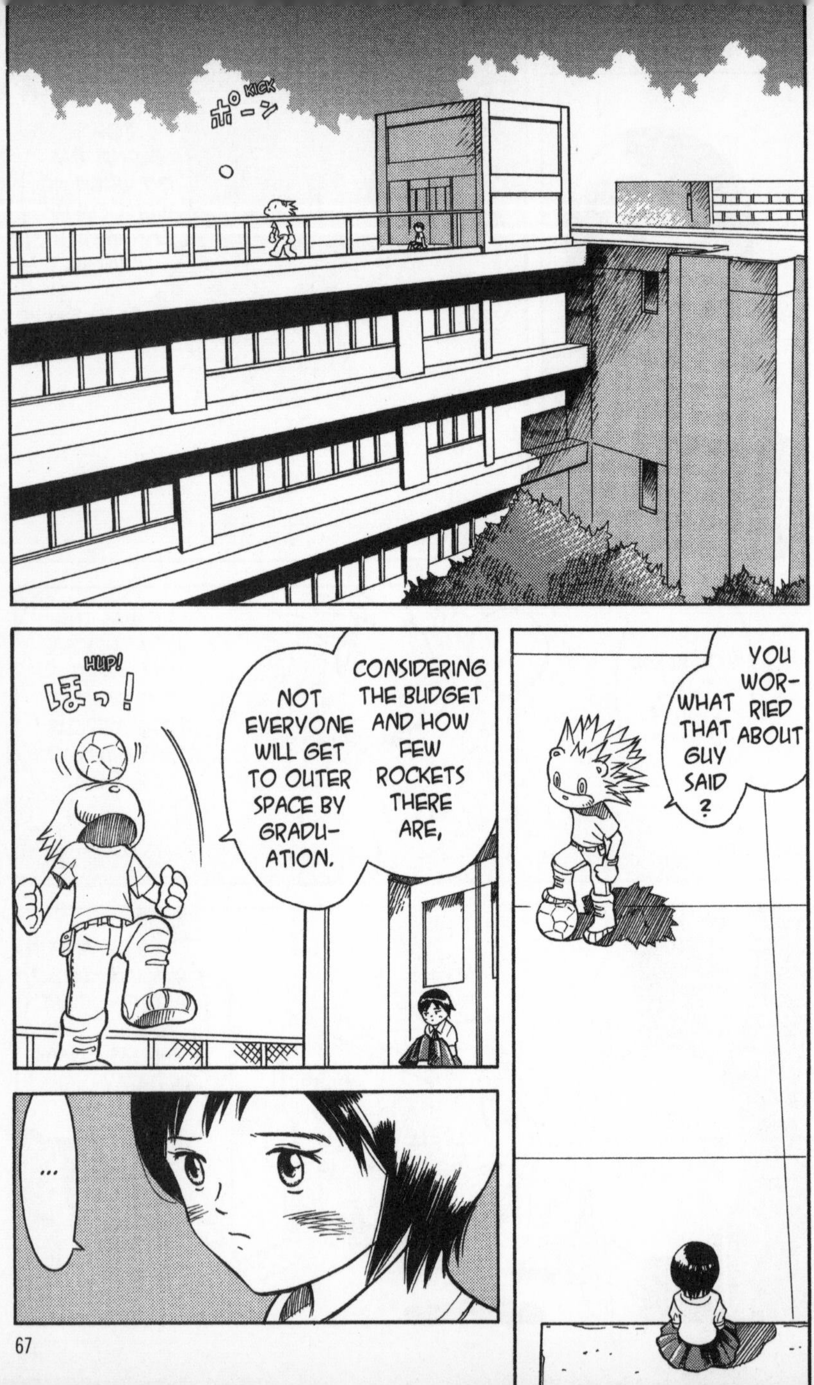
ポーン KICK
YOU WORRIED ABOUT WHAT THAT GUY SAID?
CONSIDERING THE BUDGET AND HOW FEW ROCKETS THERE ARE,
NOT EVERYONE WILL GET TO OUTER SPACE BY GRADUATION.
ほっ! HUP!
...

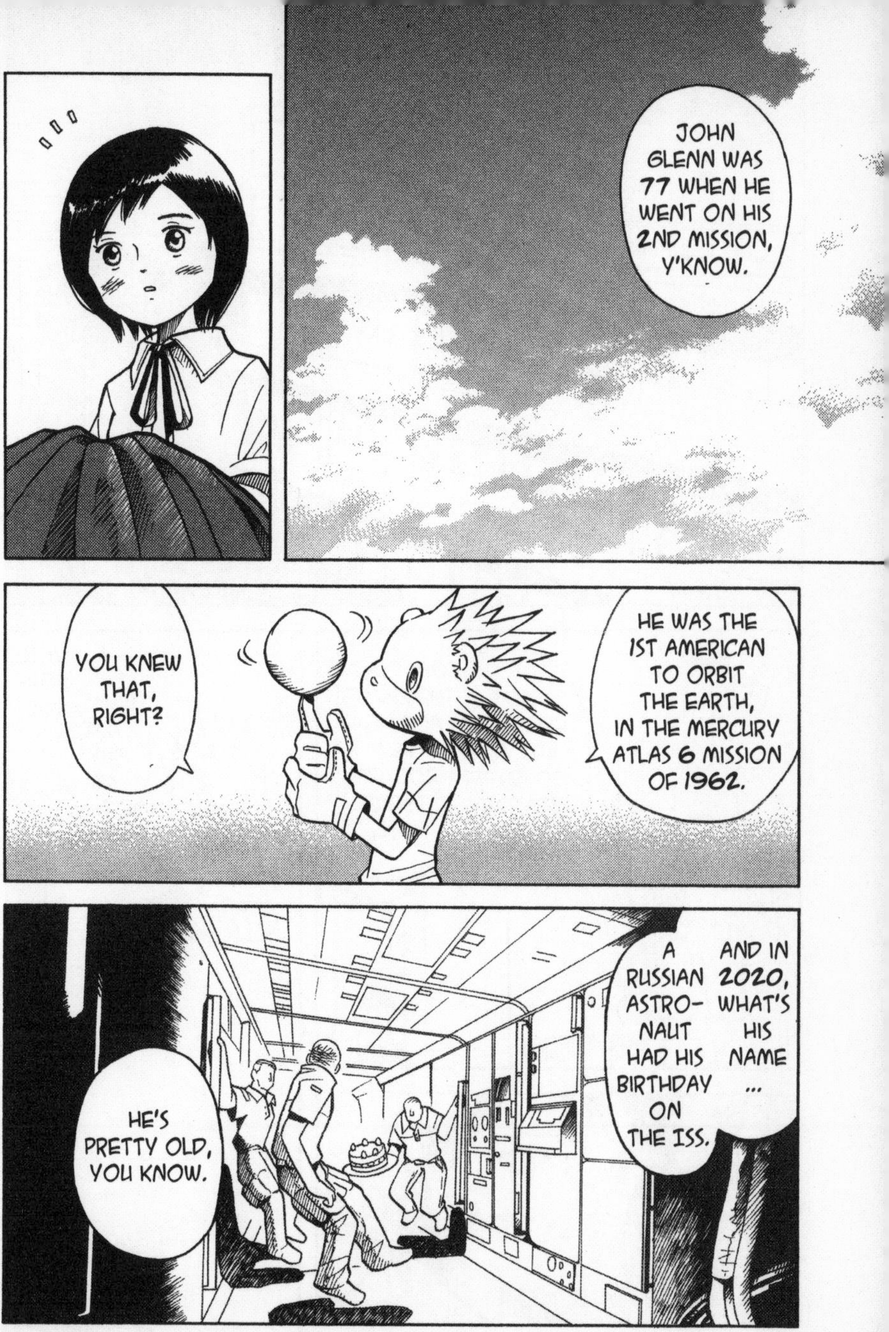
JOHN GLENN WAS 77 WHEN HE WENT ON HIS 2ND MISSION, Y'KNOW.
HE WAS THE 1ST AMERICAN TO ORBIT THE EARTH, IN THE MERCURY ATLAS 6 MISSION OF 1962.
YOU KNEW THAT, RIGHT?
AND IN 2020, WHAT'S HIS NAME ...
A RUSSIAN ASTRO-NAUT HAD HIS BIRTHDAY ON THE ISS.
HE'S PRETTY OLD, YOU KNOW.

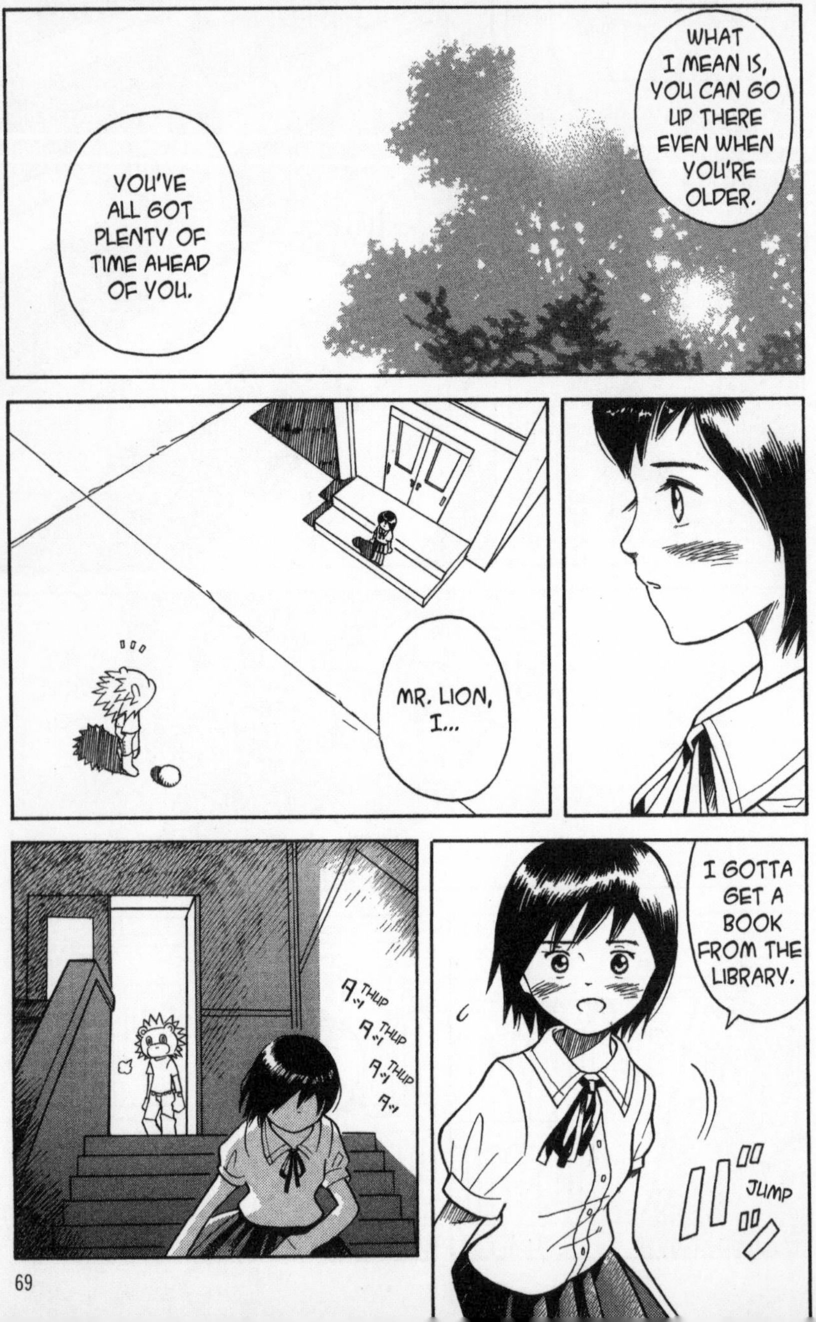
WHAT I MEAN IS, YOU CAN GO UP THERE EVEN WHEN YOU'RE OLDER.
YOU'VE ALL GOT PLENTY OF TIME AHEAD OF YOU.
MR. LION, I...
I GOTTA GET A BOOK FROM THE LIBRARY.
JUMP
THUP
THUP
THUP

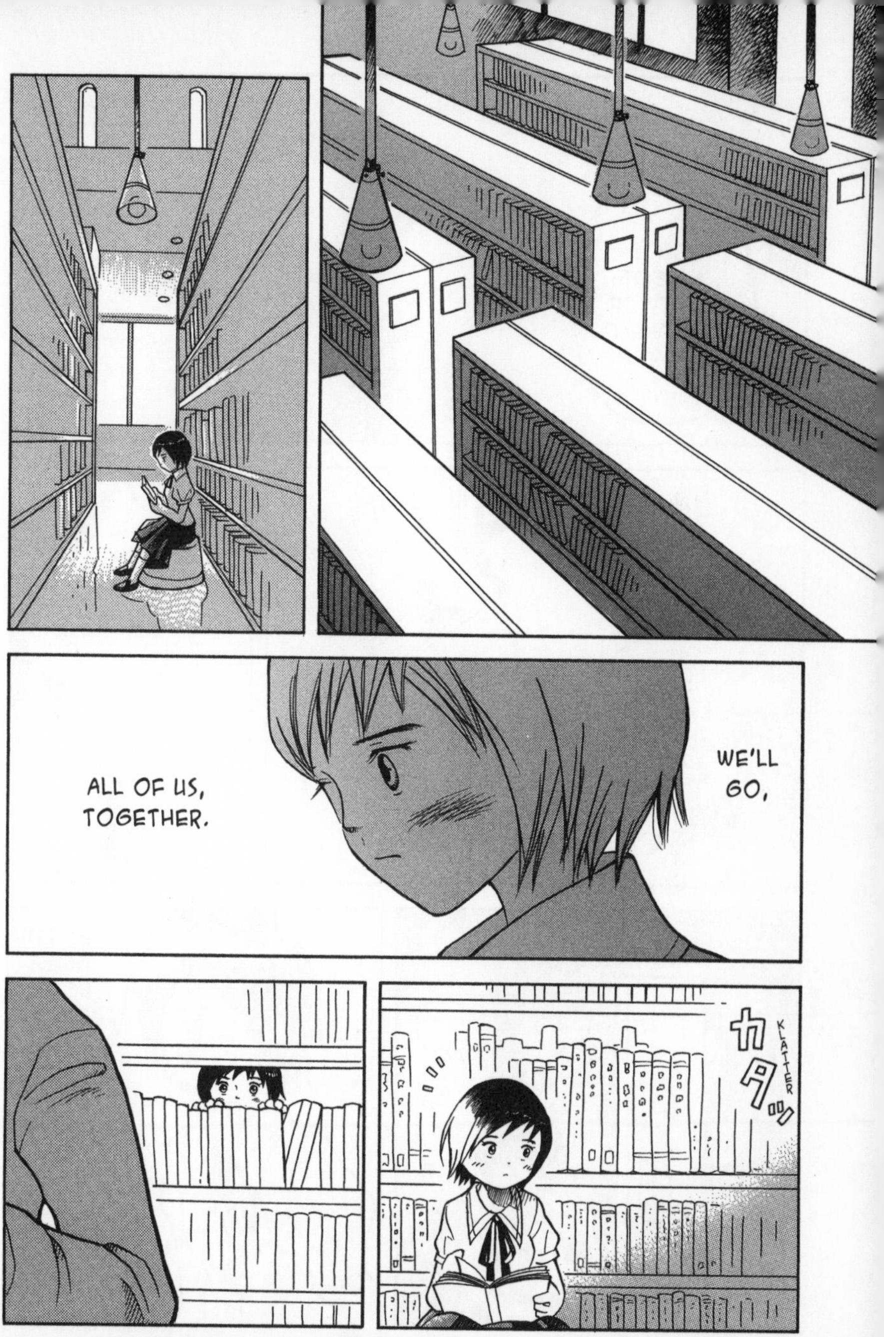
WE'LL GO,
ALL OF US, TOGETHER.
カタッ
KLATTER

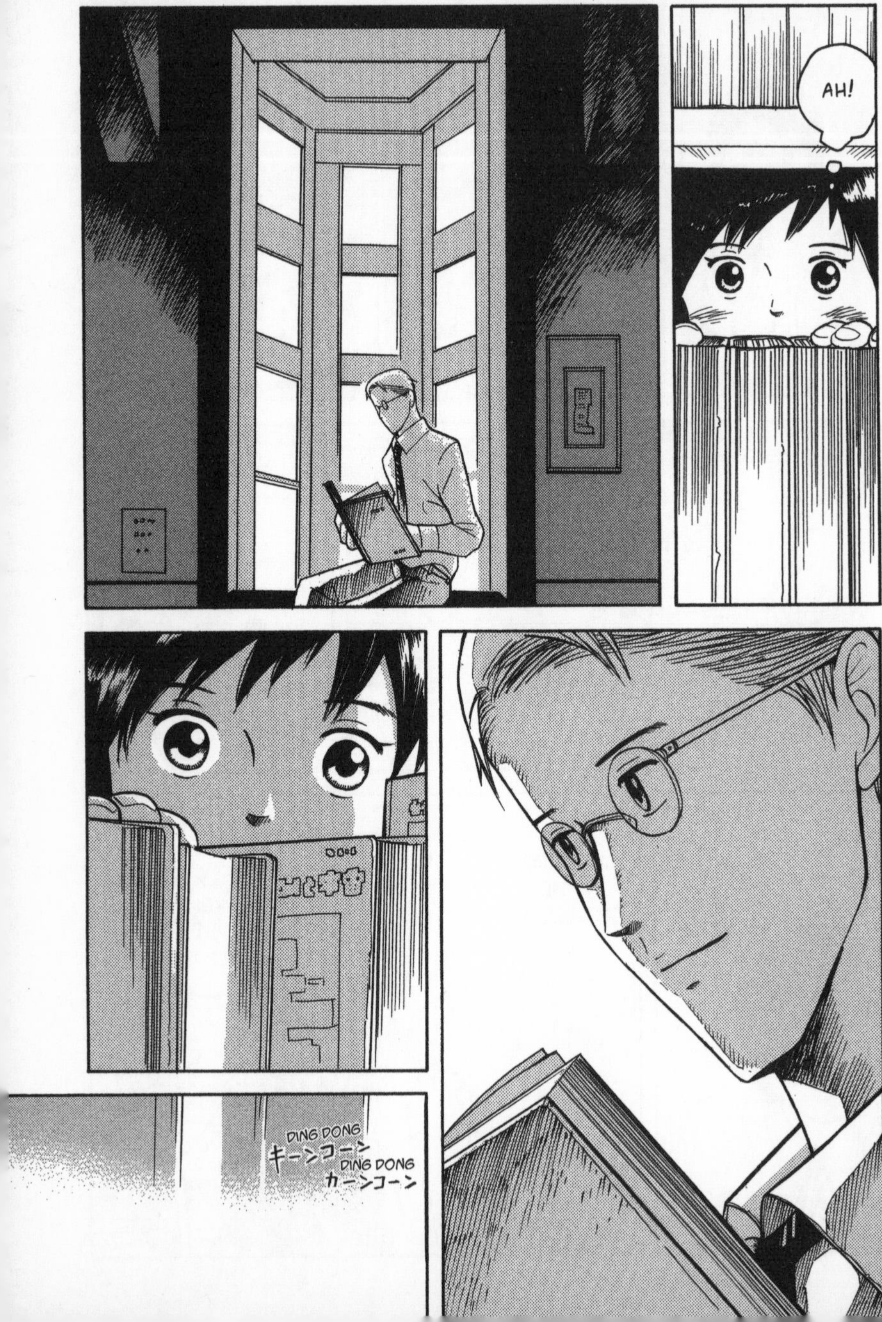
AH!
DING DONG
キーンコーン
DING DONG
カーンコーン

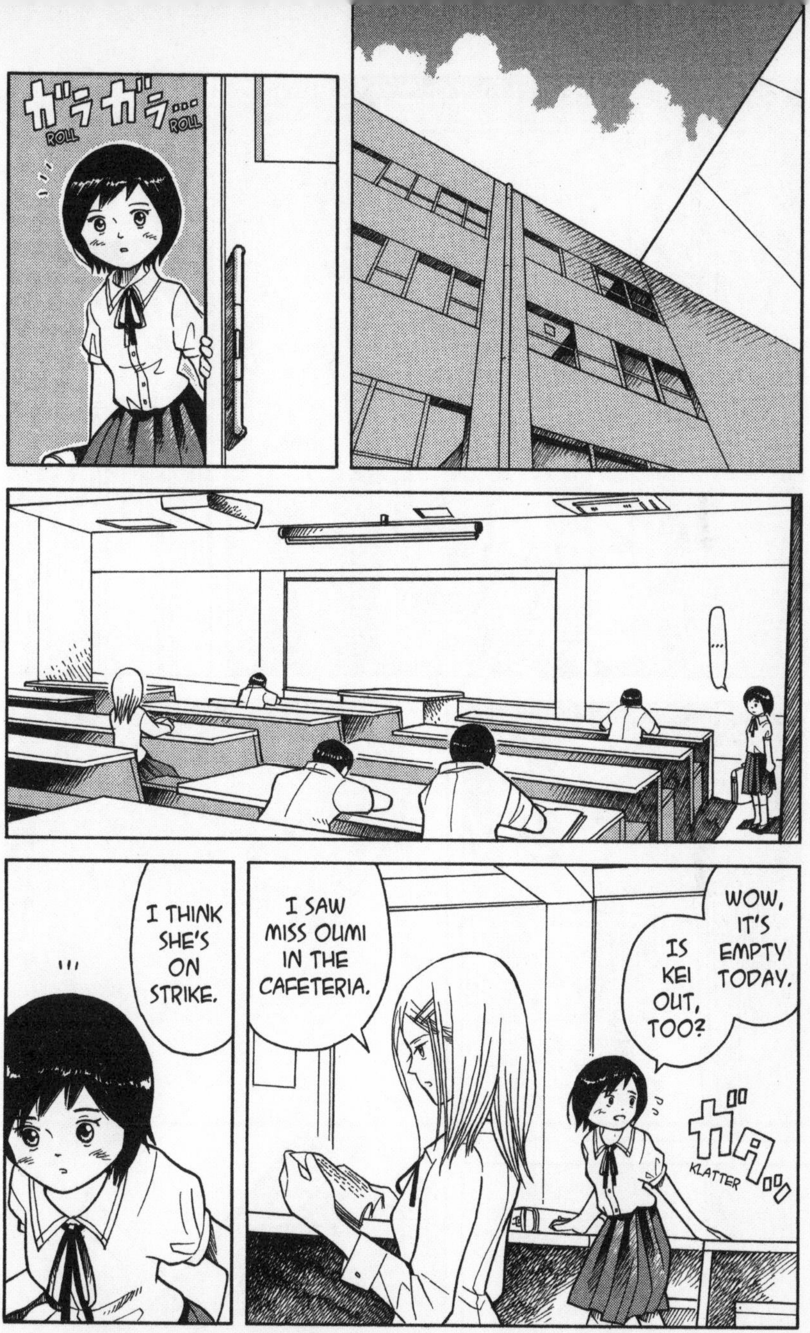
ガラガラ...
ROLL ROLL
...
WOW, IT'S EMPTY TODAY.
IS KEI OUT, TOO?
I SAW MISS OUMI IN THE CAFETERIA.
ガタッ
KLATTER
I THINK SHE'S ON STRIKE.
...

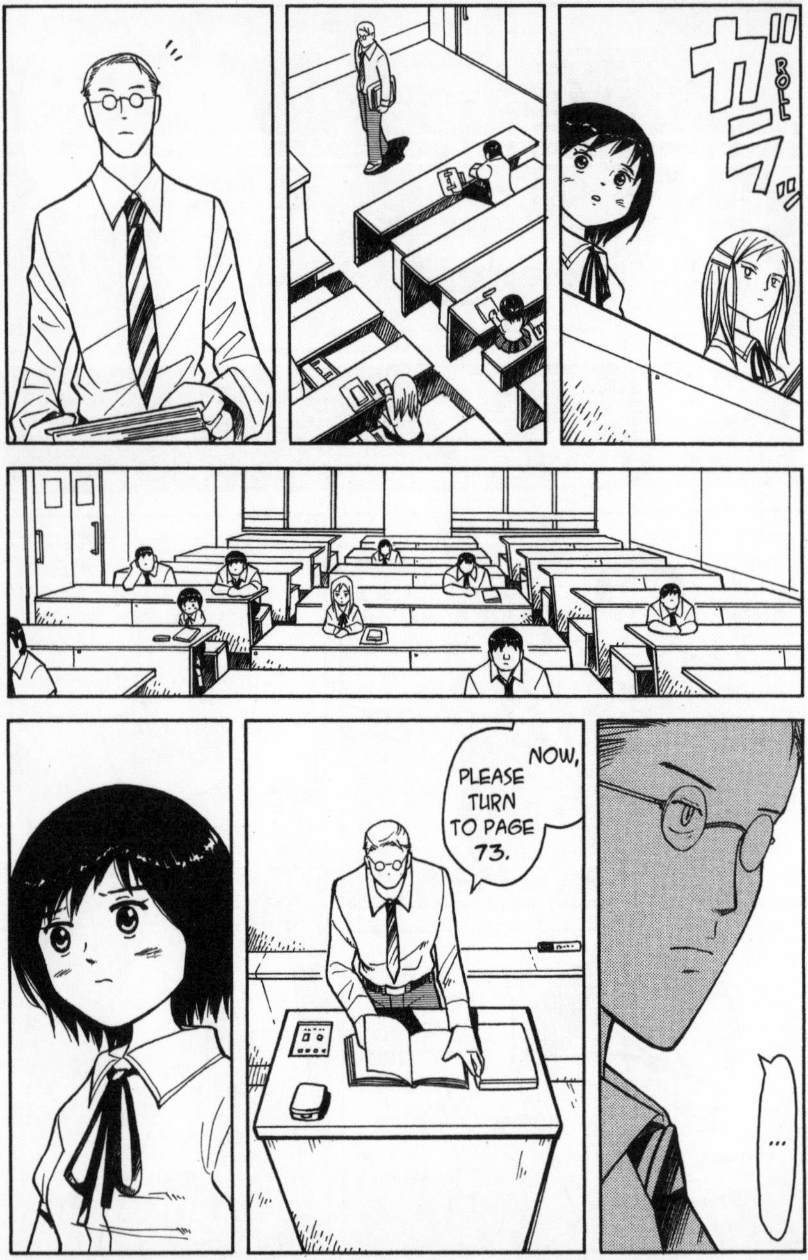
ガラ
ROLL
...
NOW, PLEASE TURN TO PAGE 73.

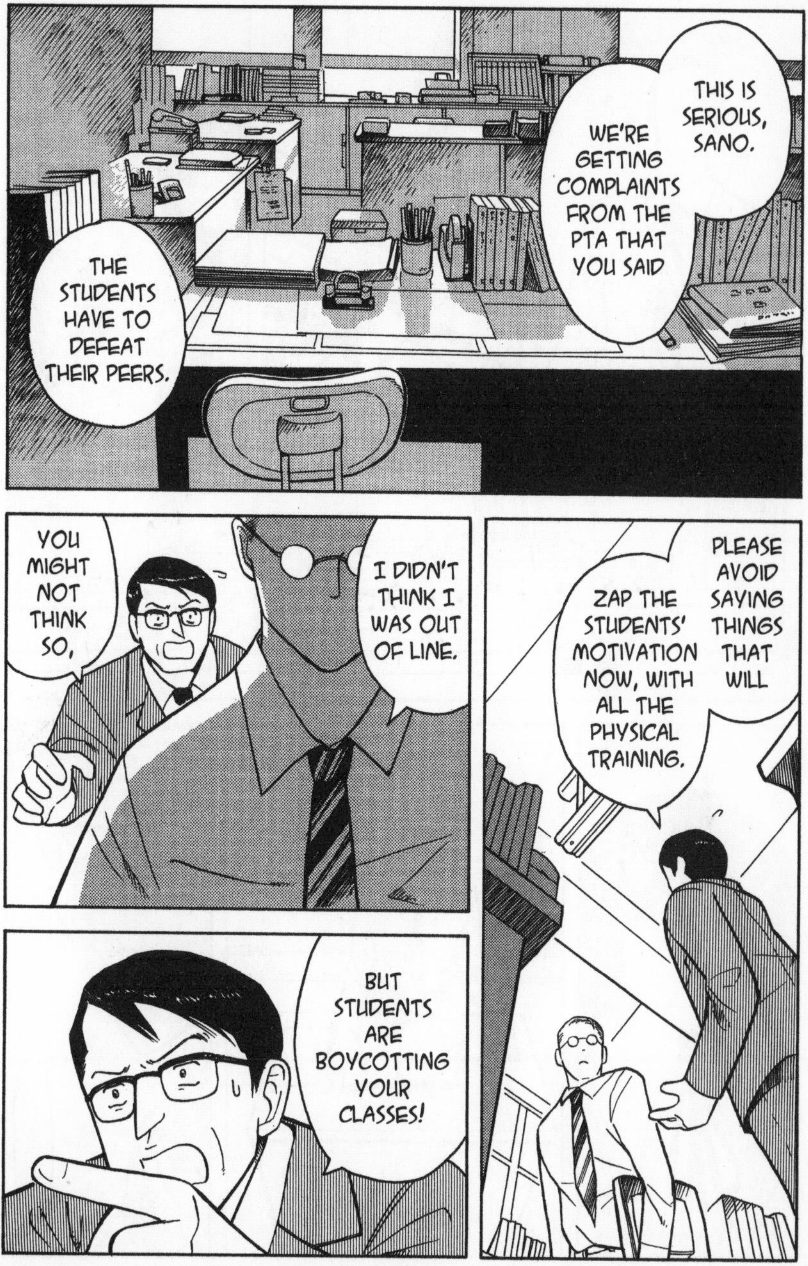
THIS IS SERIOUS, SANO.
WE'RE GETTING COMPLAINTS FROM THE PTA THAT YOU SAID
THE STUDENTS HAVE TO DEFEAT THEIR PEERS.
PLEASE AVOID SAYING THINGS THAT WILL
ZAP THE STUDENTS' MOTIVATION NOW, WITH ALL THE PHYSICAL TRAINING.
I DIDN'T THINK I WAS OUT OF LINE.
YOU MIGHT NOT THINK SO,
BUT STUDENTS ARE BOYCOTTING YOUR CLASSES!

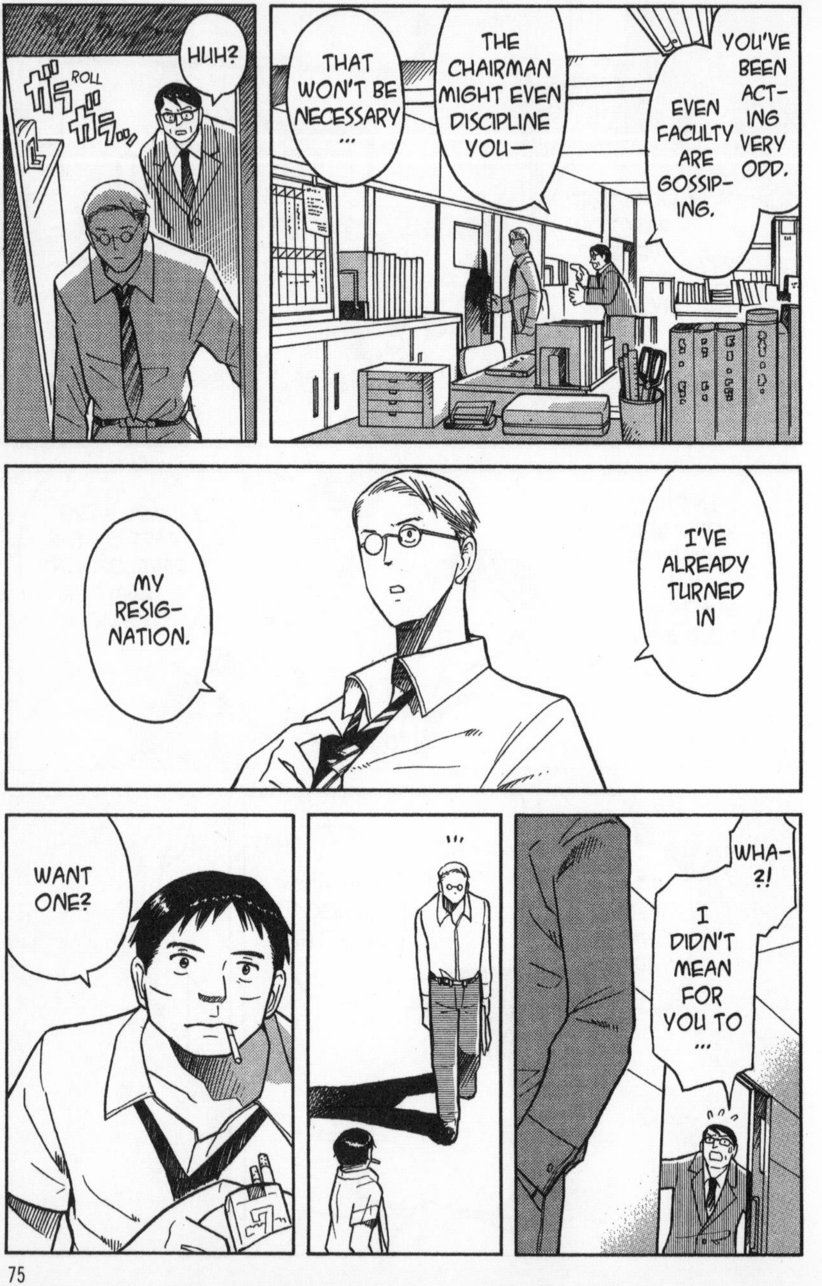
YOU'VE BEEN ACT- ING VERY ODD.
EVEN FACULTY ARE GOSSIP- ING.
THE CHAIRMAN MIGHT EVEN DISCIPLINE YOU—
THAT WON'T BE NECESSARY ...
HUH?
ROLL
I'VE ALREADY TURNED IN
MY RESIG- NATION.
WHA- ?!
I DIDN'T MEAN FOR YOU TO ...
WANT ONE?

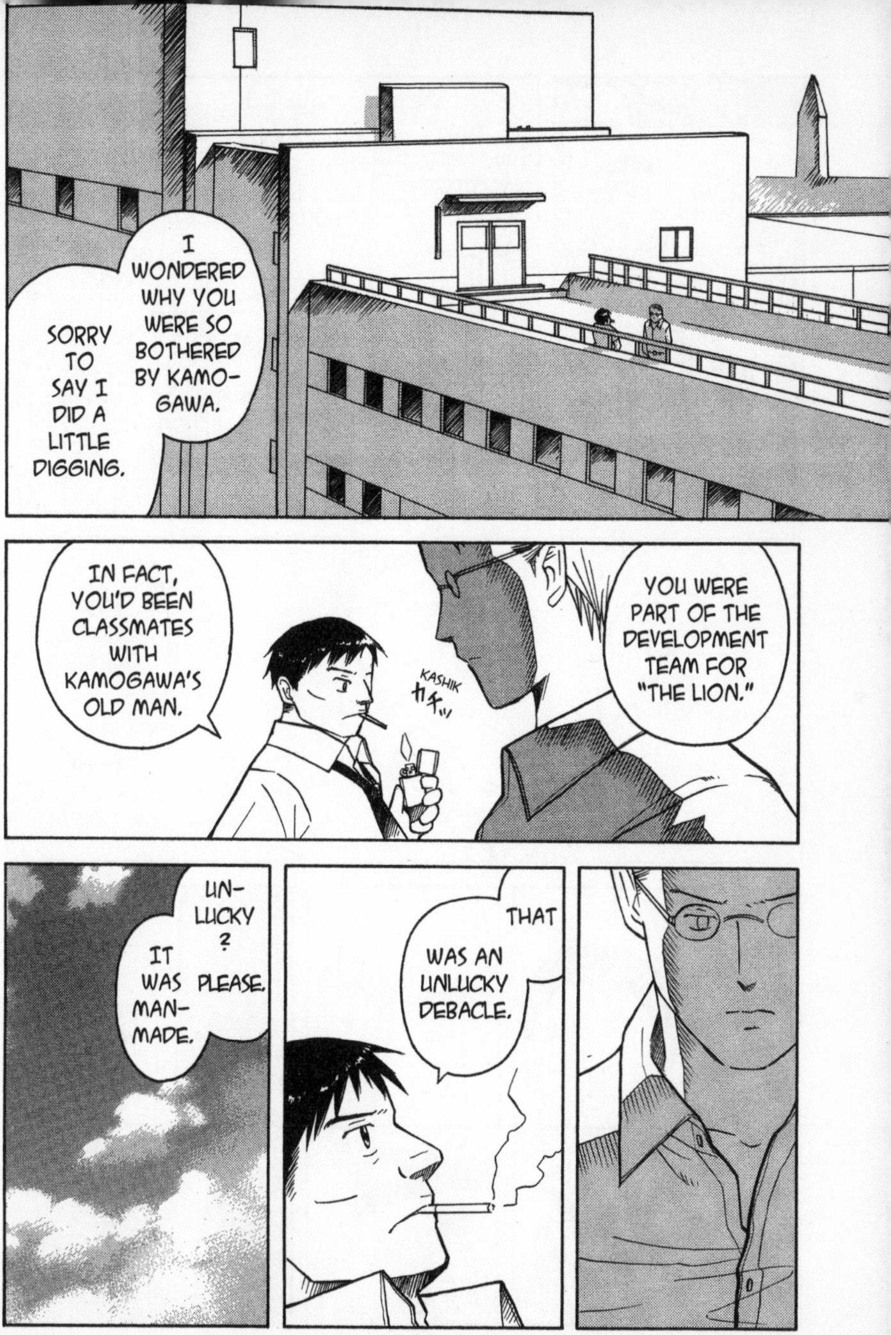
I WONDERED WHY YOU WERE SO BOTHERED BY KAMO-GAWA.
SORRY TO SAY I DID A LITTLE DIGGING.
YOU WERE PART OF THE DEVELOPMENT TEAM FOR "THE LION."
KASHIK
IN FACT, YOU'D BEEN CLASSMATES WITH KAMOGAWA'S OLD MAN.
THAT
WAS AN UNLUCKY DEBACLE.
UN-LUCKY? PLEASE.
IT WAS MAN-MADE.

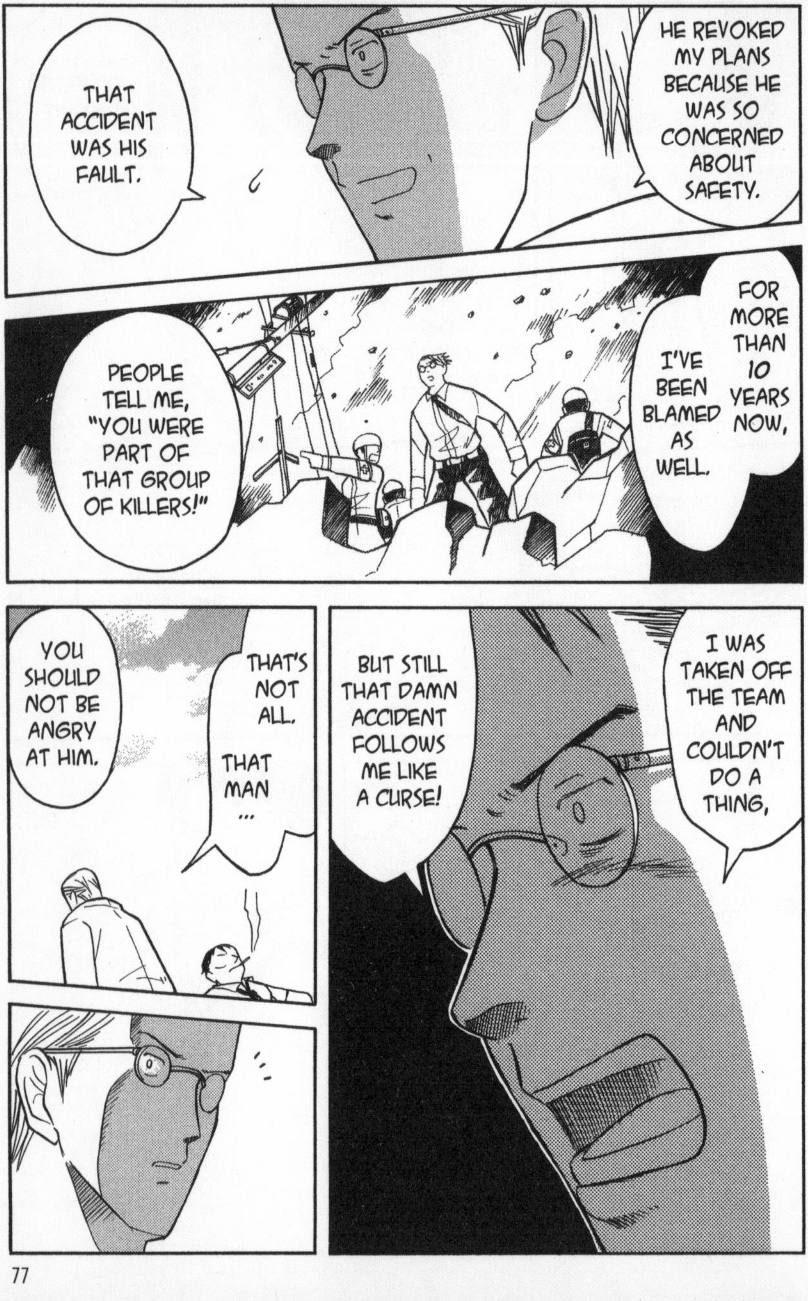
HE REVOKED MY PLANS BECAUSE HE WAS SO CONCERNED ABOUT SAFETY.
THAT ACCIDENT WAS HIS FAULT.
FOR MORE THAN 10 YEARS NOW,
I'VE BEEN BLAMED AS WELL.
PEOPLE TELL ME, "YOU WERE PART OF THAT GROUP OF KILLERS!"
I WAS TAKEN OFF THE TEAM AND COULDN'T DO A THING,
BUT STILL THAT DAMN ACCIDENT FOLLOWS ME LIKE A CURSE!
THAT'S NOT ALL.
THAT MAN ...
YOU SHOULD NOT BE ANGRY AT HIM.

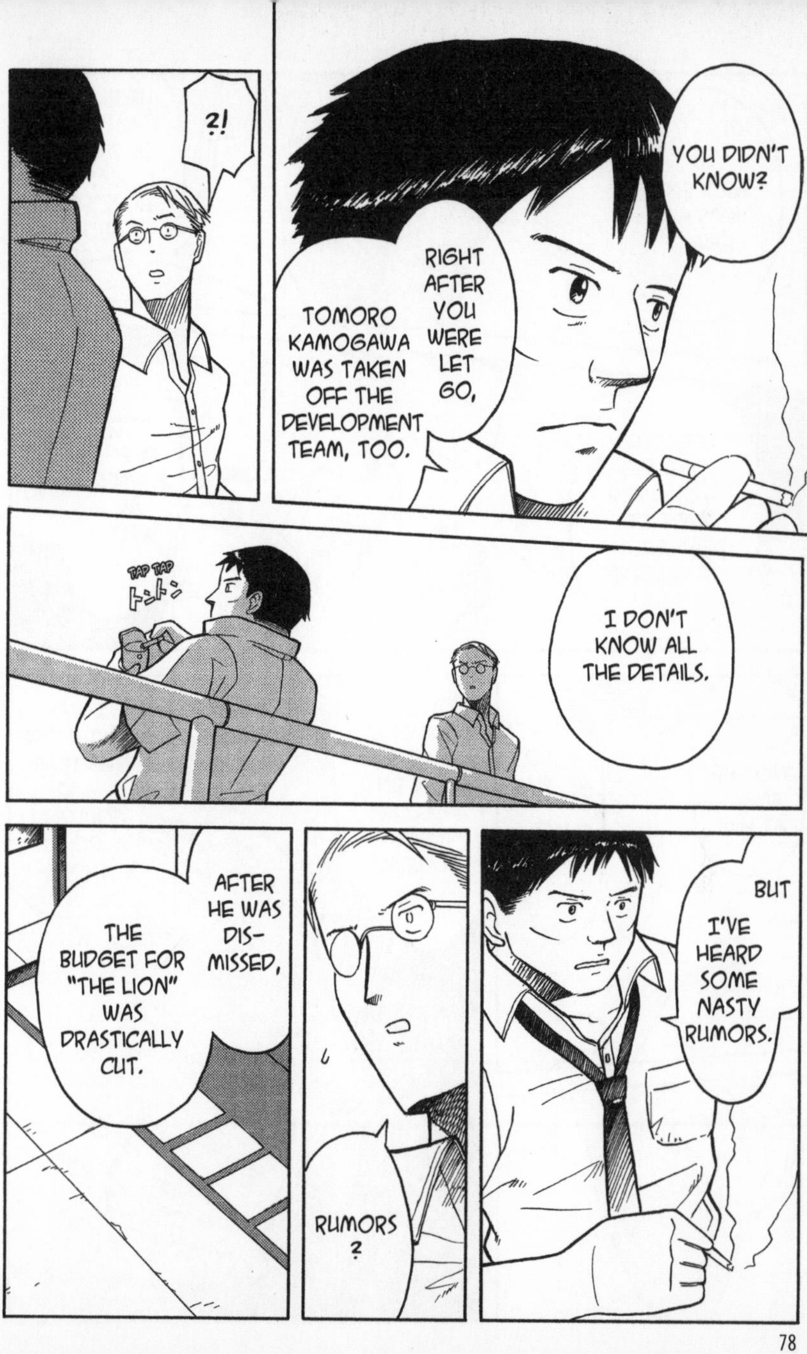
YOU DIDN'T KNOW?
RIGHT AFTER YOU WERE LET GO,
TOMORO KAMOGAWA WAS TAKEN OFF THE DEVELOPMENT TEAM, TOO.
?!
I DON'T KNOW ALL THE DETAILS.
TAP TAP
トントン
BUT I'VE HEARD SOME NASTY RUMORS.
RUMORS?
AFTER HE WAS DIS-MISSED,
THE BUDGET FOR "THE LION" WAS DRASTICALLY CUT.

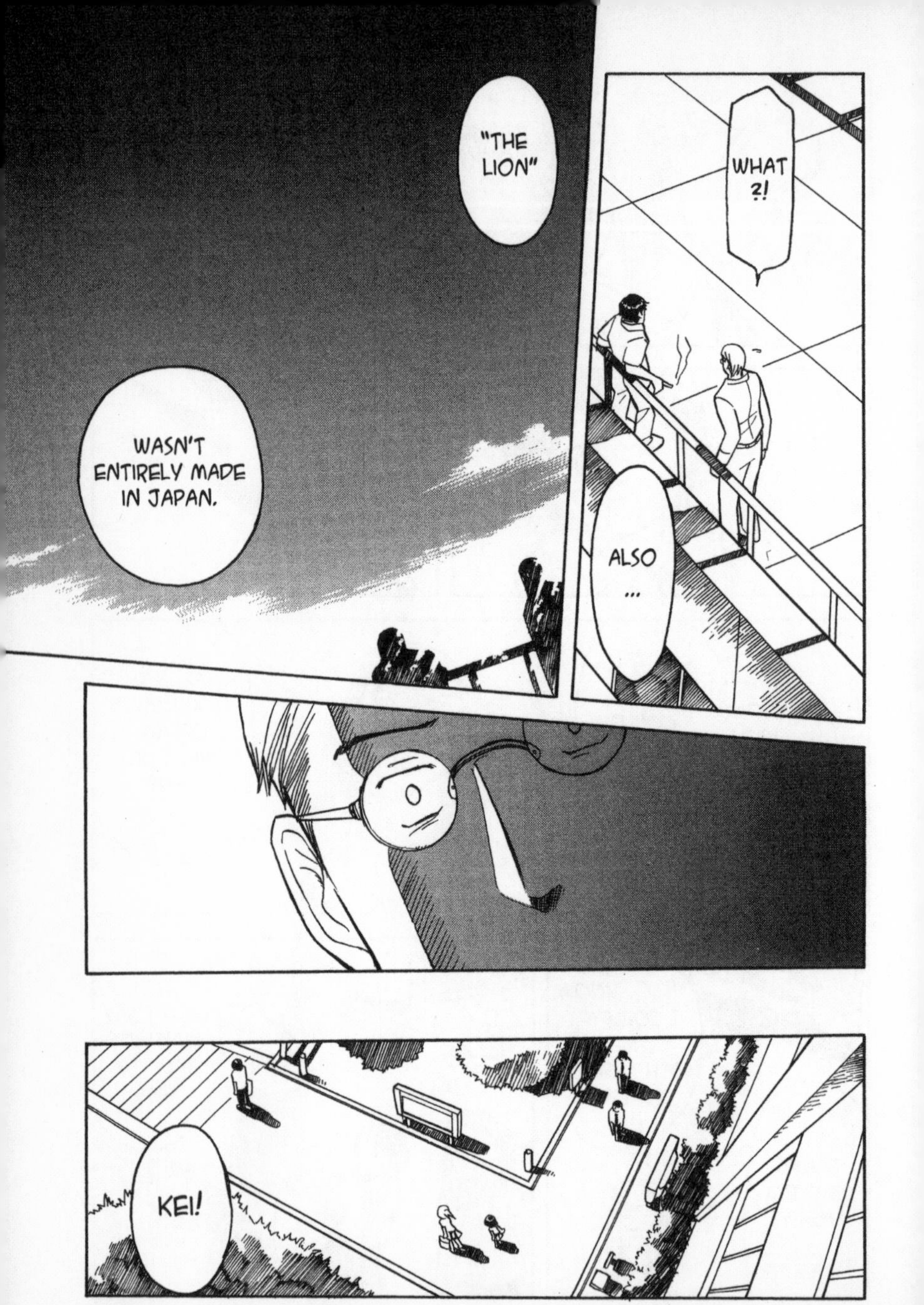
WHAT ?!
ALSO ...
"THE LION"
WASN'T ENTIRELY MADE IN JAPAN.
KEI!

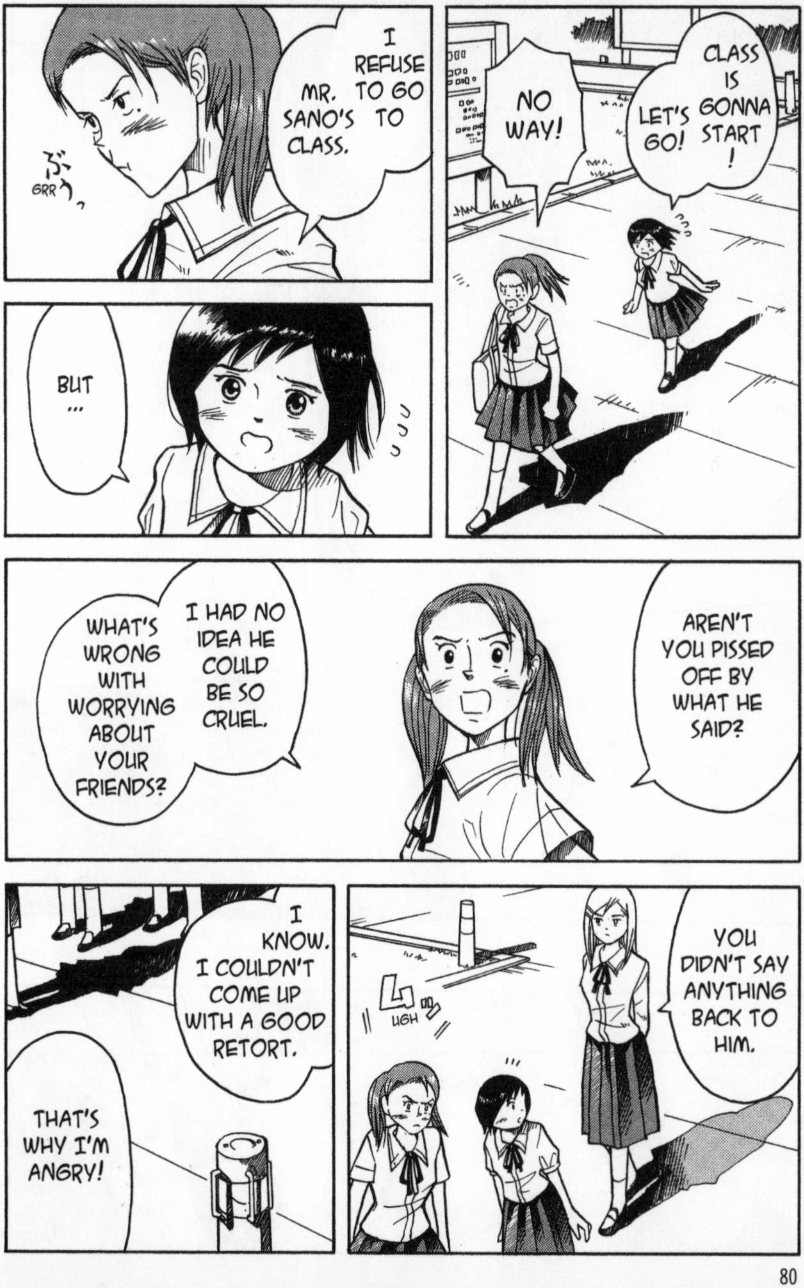
CLASS IS GONNA START!
LET'S GO!
NO WAY!
I REFUSE TO GO TO MR. SANO'S CLASS.
ぶぅっ GRR
BUT...
AREN'T YOU PISSED OFF BY WHAT HE SAID?
I HAD NO IDEA HE COULD BE SO CRUEL.
WHAT'S WRONG WITH WORRYING ABOUT YOUR FRIENDS?
YOU DIDN'T SAY ANYTHING BACK TO HIM.
ムッ UGH
I KNOW. I COULDN'T COME UP WITH A GOOD RETORT.
THAT'S WHY I'M ANGRY!

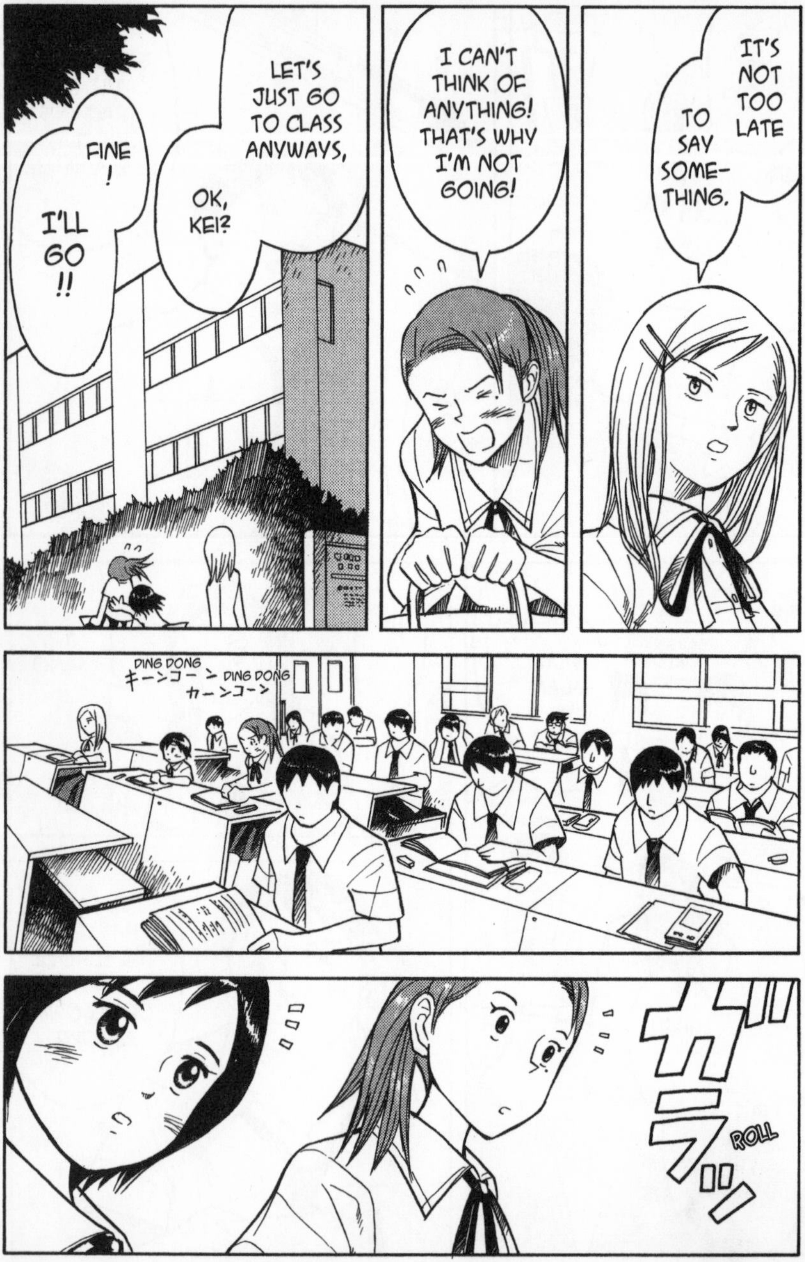
IT'S NOT TOO LATE TO SAY SOME-THING.
I CAN'T THINK OF ANYTHING! THAT'S WHY I'M NOT GOING!
LET'S JUST GO TO CLASS ANYWAYS, OK, KEI?
FINE! I'LL GO!!
キーンコーン DING DONG
カーンコーン DING DONG
ガラッ ROLL

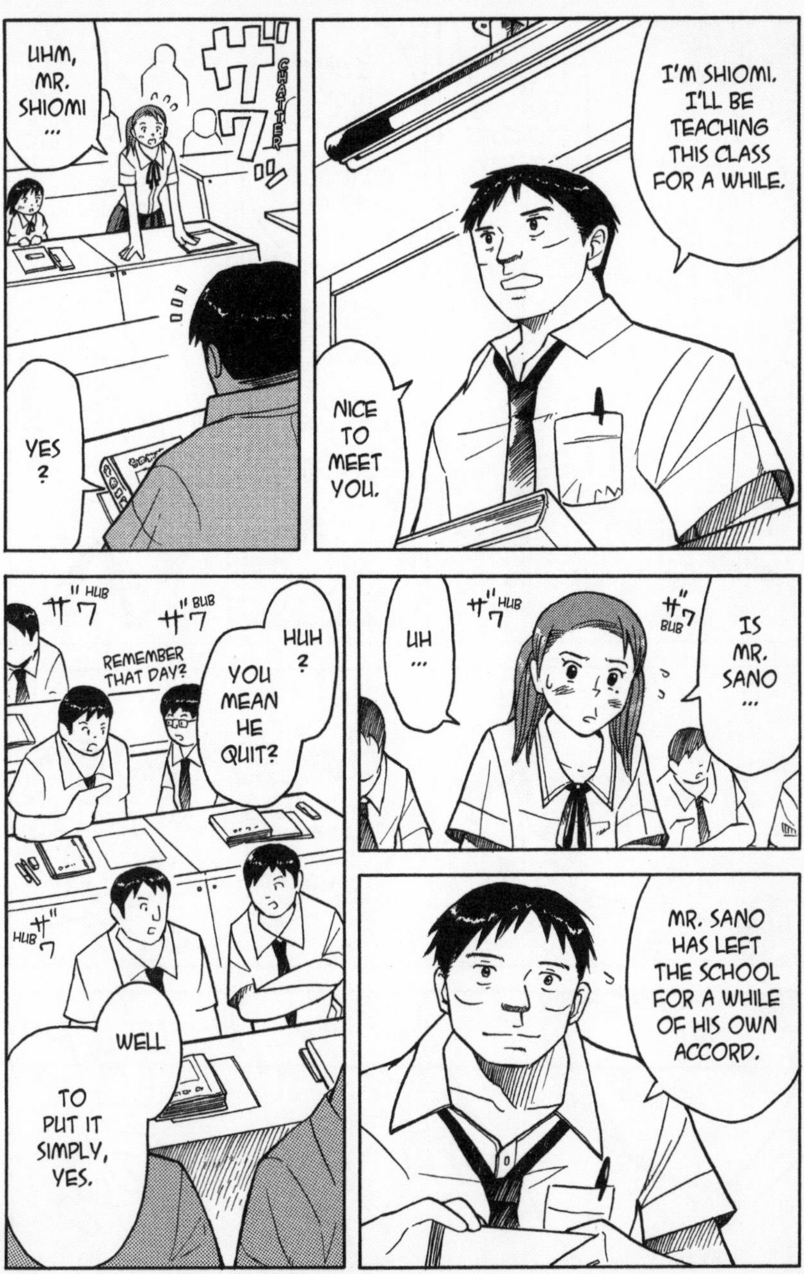
I'M SHIOMI. I'LL BE TEACHING THIS CLASS FOR A WHILE.
NICE TO MEET YOU.
ザワ
CHATTER
UHM, MR. SHIOMI ...
YES ?
ザワ BUB
IS MR. SANO ...
ザワ HUB
UH ...
MR. SANO HAS LEFT THE SCHOOL FOR A WHILE OF HIS OWN ACCORD.
ザワ BUB
ザワ HUB
HUH ?
YOU MEAN HE QUIT?
REMEMBER THAT DAY?
ザワ HUB
WELL
TO PUT IT SIMPLY, YES.

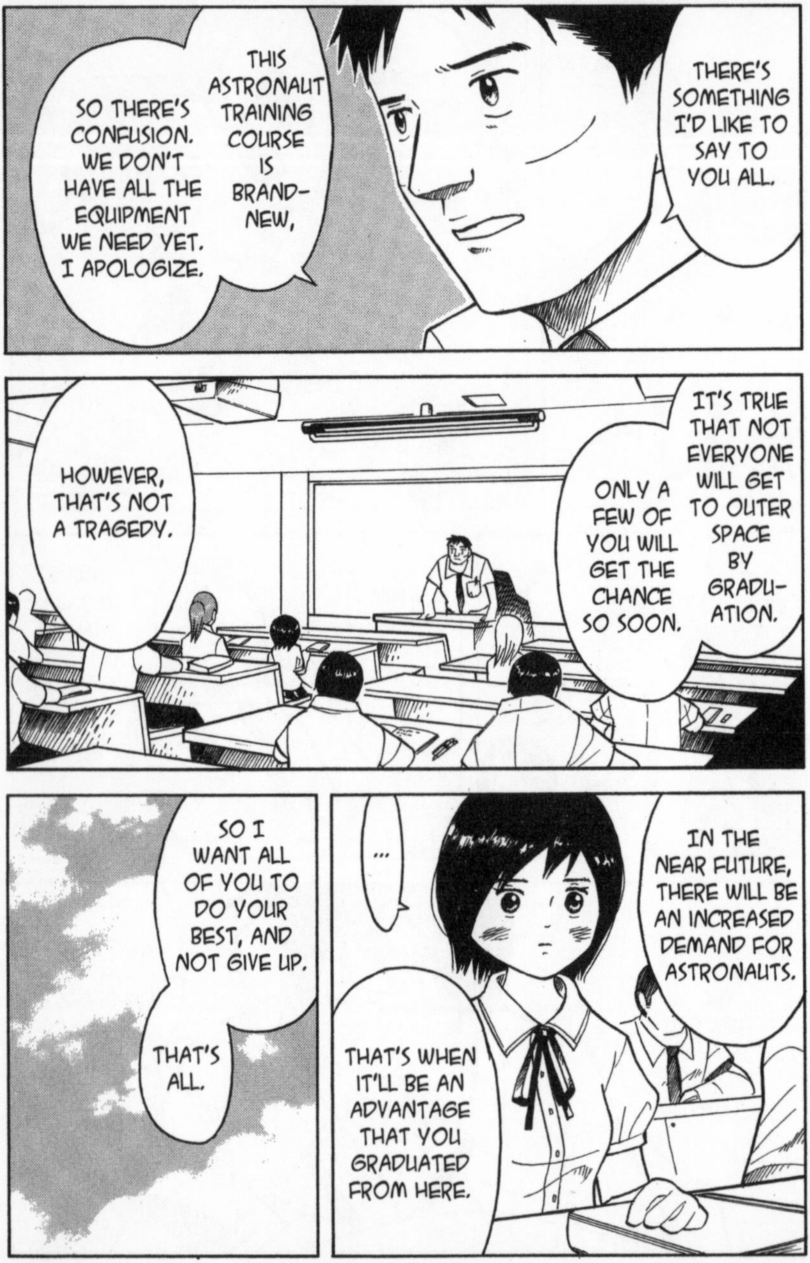
THERE'S SOMETHING I'D LIKE TO SAY TO YOU ALL.
THIS ASTRONAUT TRAINING COURSE IS BRAND-NEW,
SO THERE'S CONFUSION. WE DON'T HAVE ALL THE EQUIPMENT WE NEED YET. I APOLOGIZE.
IT'S TRUE THAT NOT EVERYONE WILL GET TO OUTER SPACE BY GRADUATION.
ONLY A FEW OF YOU WILL GET THE CHANCE SO SOON.
HOWEVER, THAT'S NOT A TRAGEDY.
IN THE NEAR FUTURE, THERE WILL BE AN INCREASED DEMAND FOR ASTRONAUTS.
...
THAT'S WHEN IT'LL BE AN ADVANTAGE THAT YOU GRADUATED FROM HERE.
SO I WANT ALL OF YOU TO DO YOUR BEST, AND NOT GIVE UP.
THAT'S ALL.

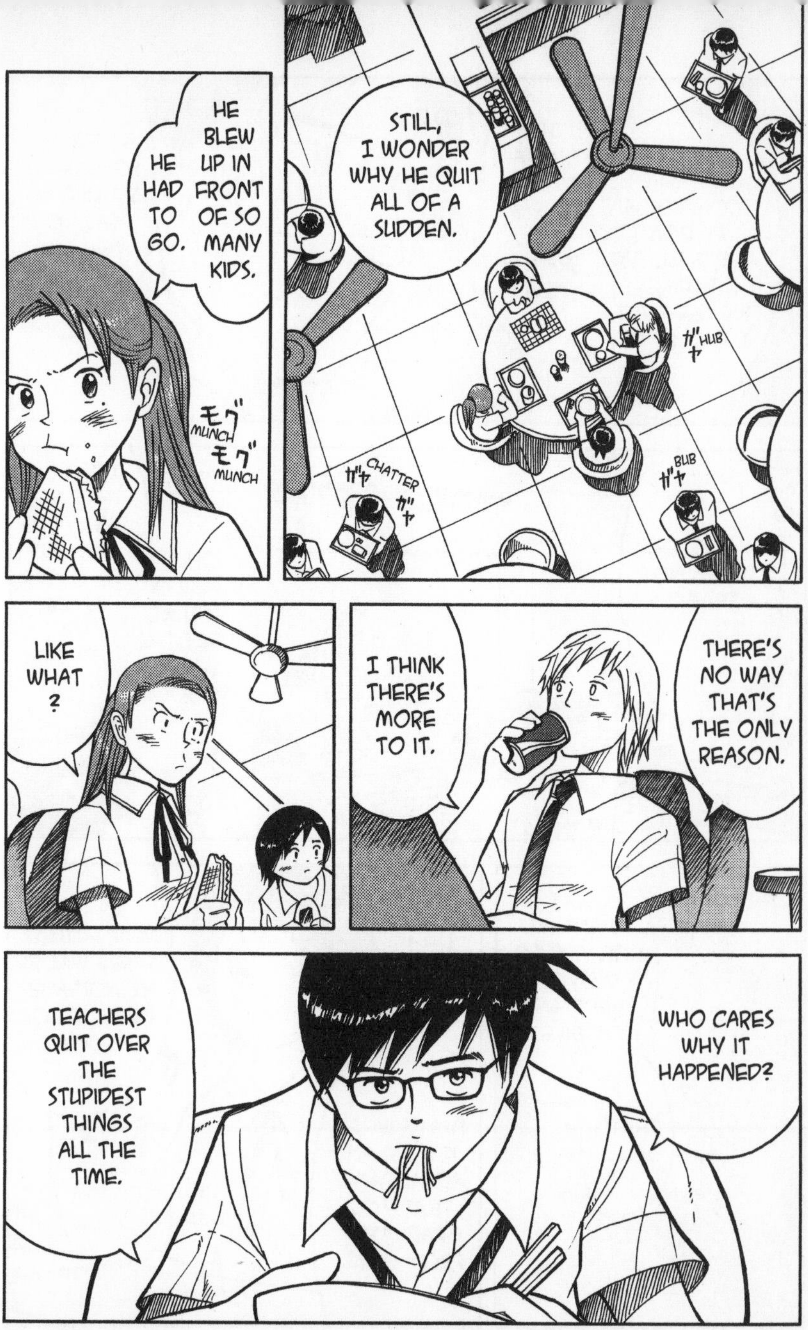
STILL, I WONDER WHY HE QUIT ALL OF A SUDDEN.
ガヤ HUB
ガヤ BUB
ガヤ CHATTER ガヤ
HE BLEW UP IN FRONT OF SO MANY KIDS.
HE HAD TO GO.
モグ MUNCH モグ MUNCH
THERE'S NO WAY THAT'S THE ONLY REASON.
I THINK THERE'S MORE TO IT.
LIKE WHAT?
WHO CARES WHY IT HAPPENED?
TEACHERS QUIT OVER THE STUPIDEST THINGS ALL THE TIME.

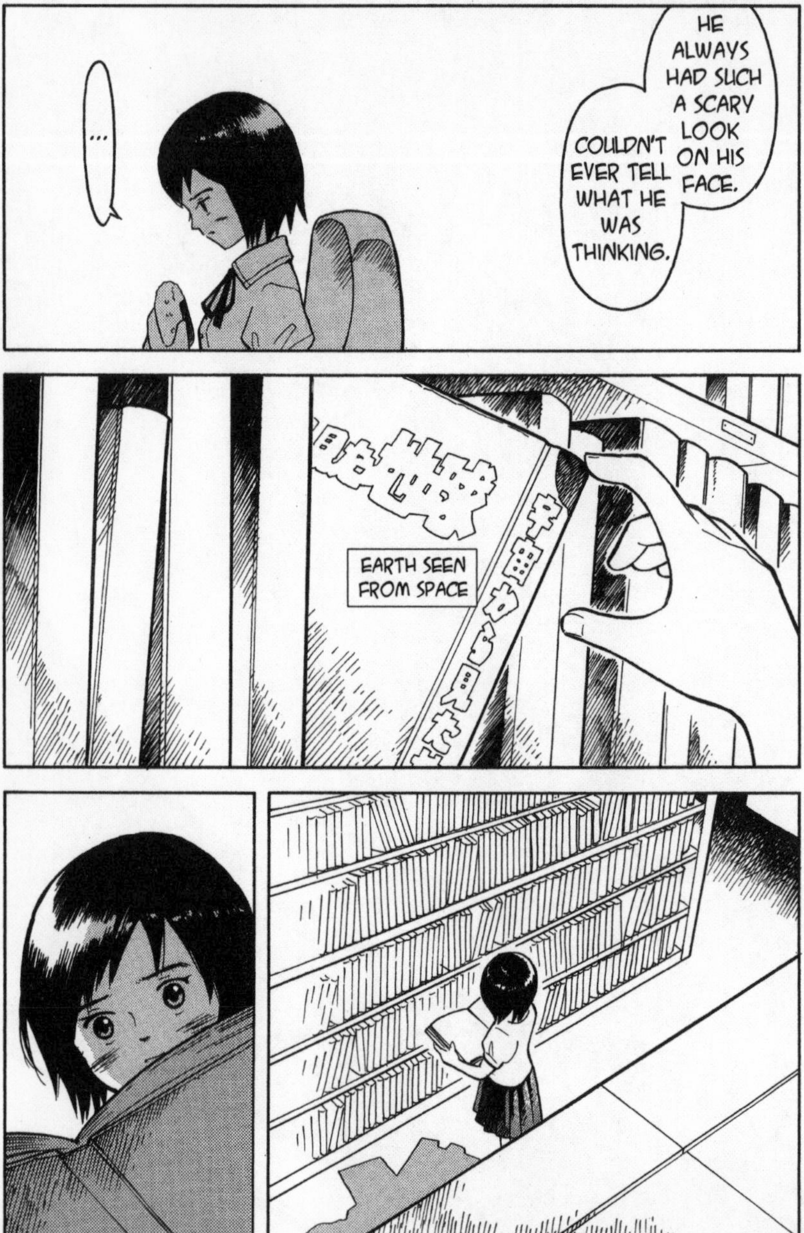
HE ALWAYS HAD SUCH A SCARY LOOK ON HIS FACE.
COULDN'T EVER TELL WHAT HE WAS THINKING.
...
宇宙から見た
EARTH SEEN FROM SPACE

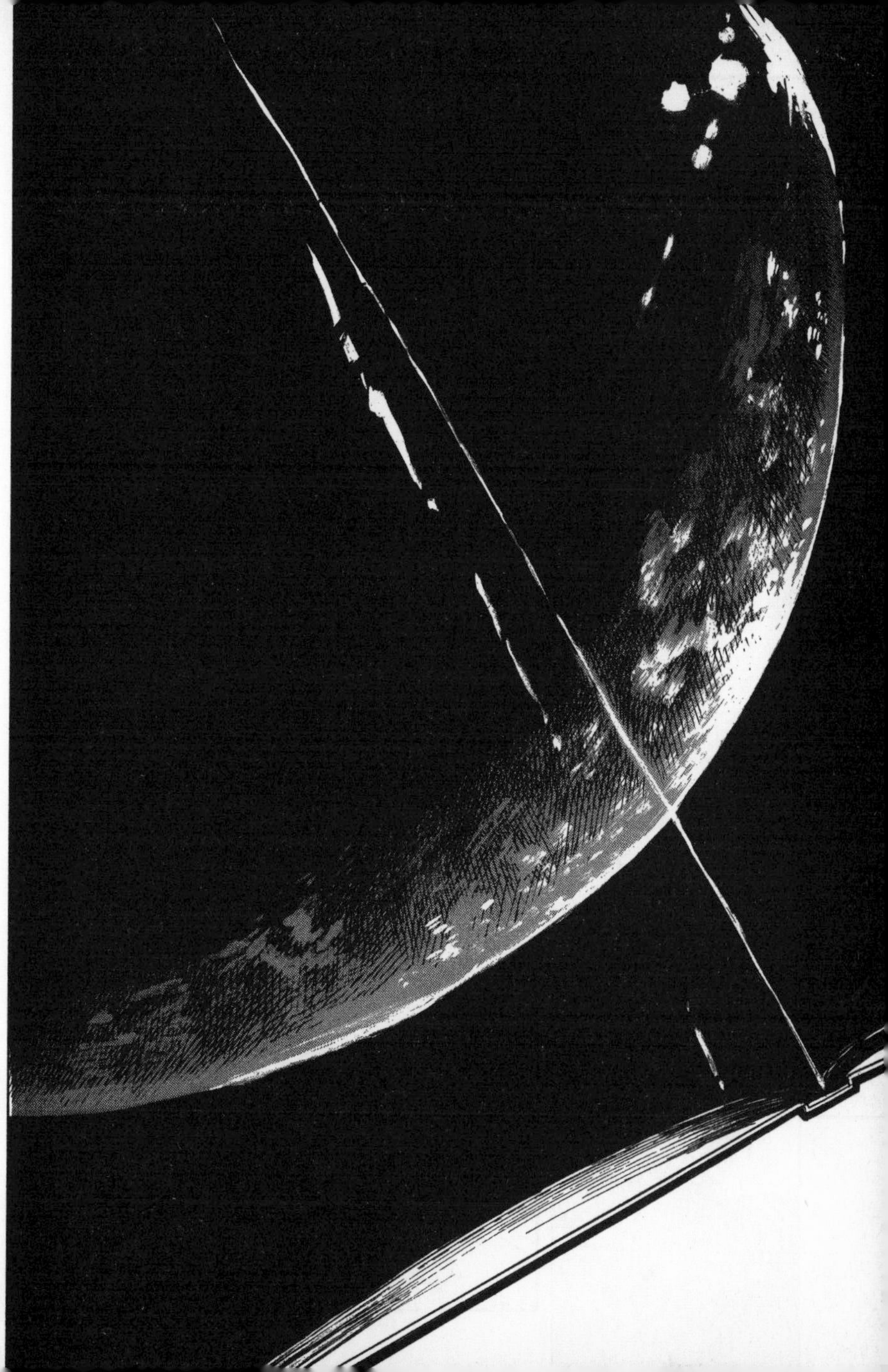

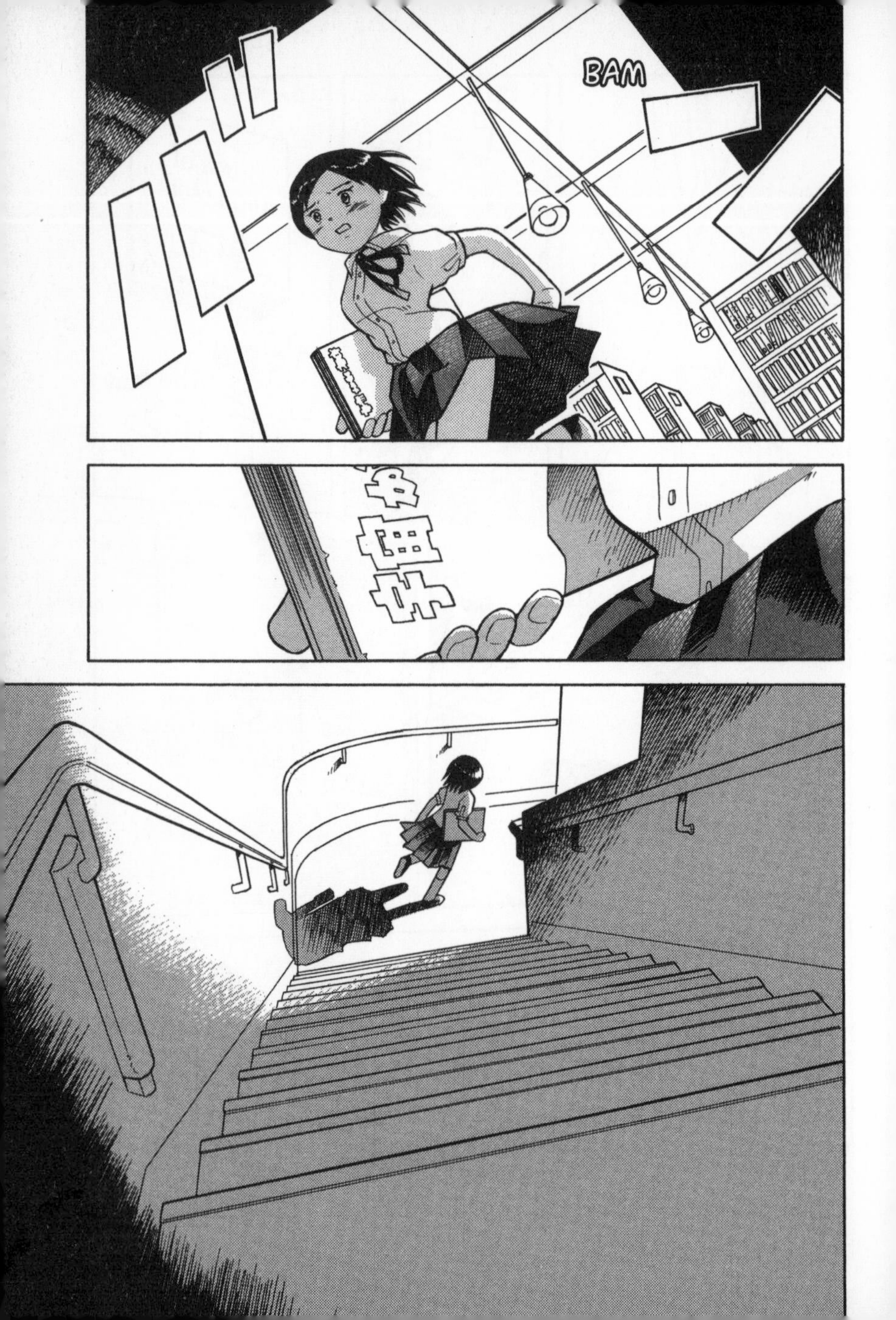
BAM

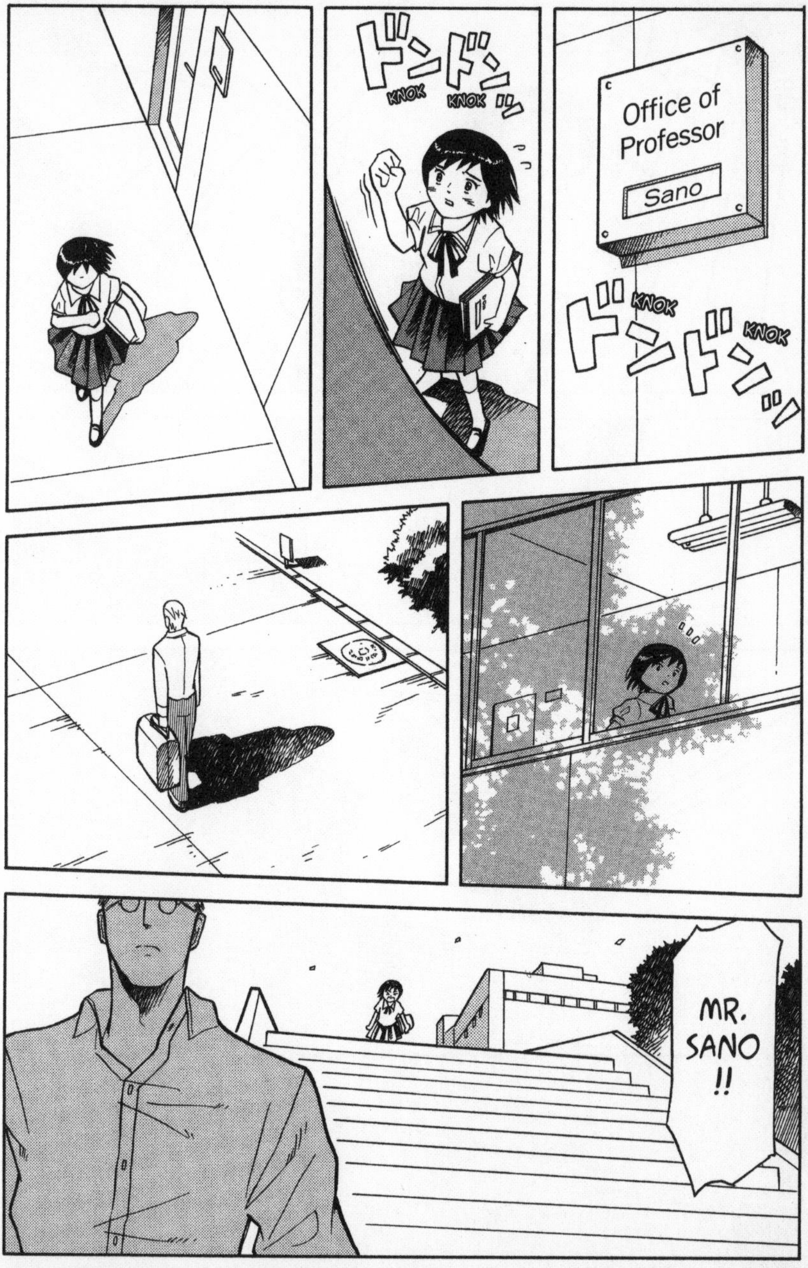
Office of Professor
Sano
ドンドン
KNOK KNOK
ドンドン
KNOK KNOK
MR. SANO !!

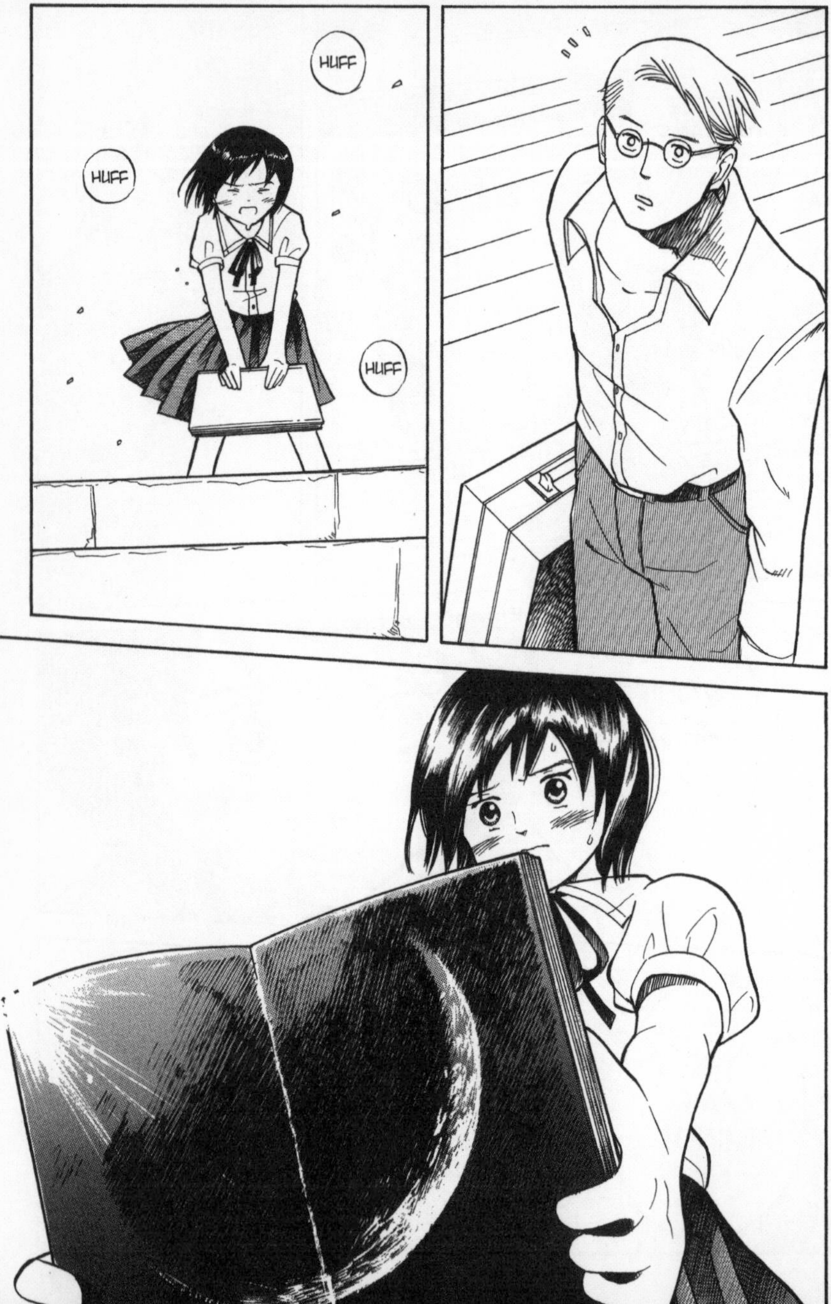
HUFF
HUFF
HUFF

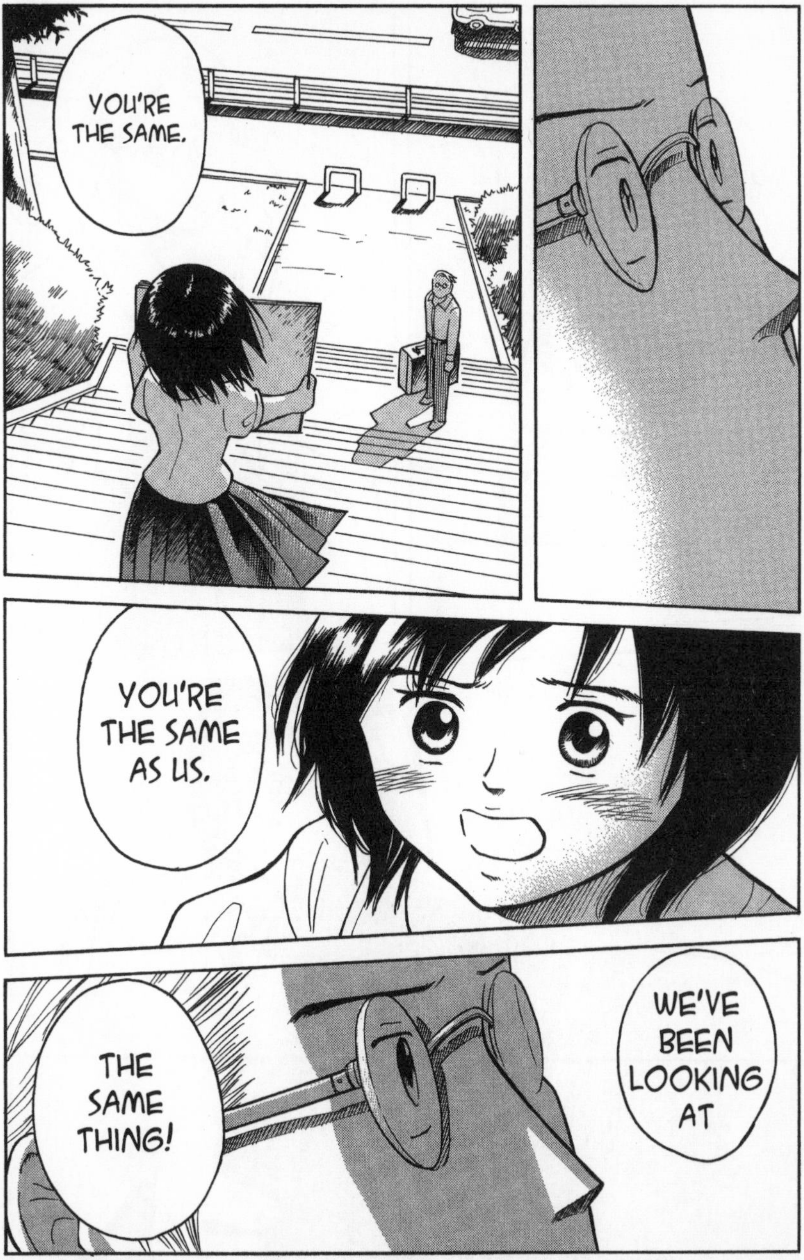
YOU'RE THE SAME.
YOU'RE THE SAME AS US.
WE'VE BEEN LOOKING AT
THE SAME THING!

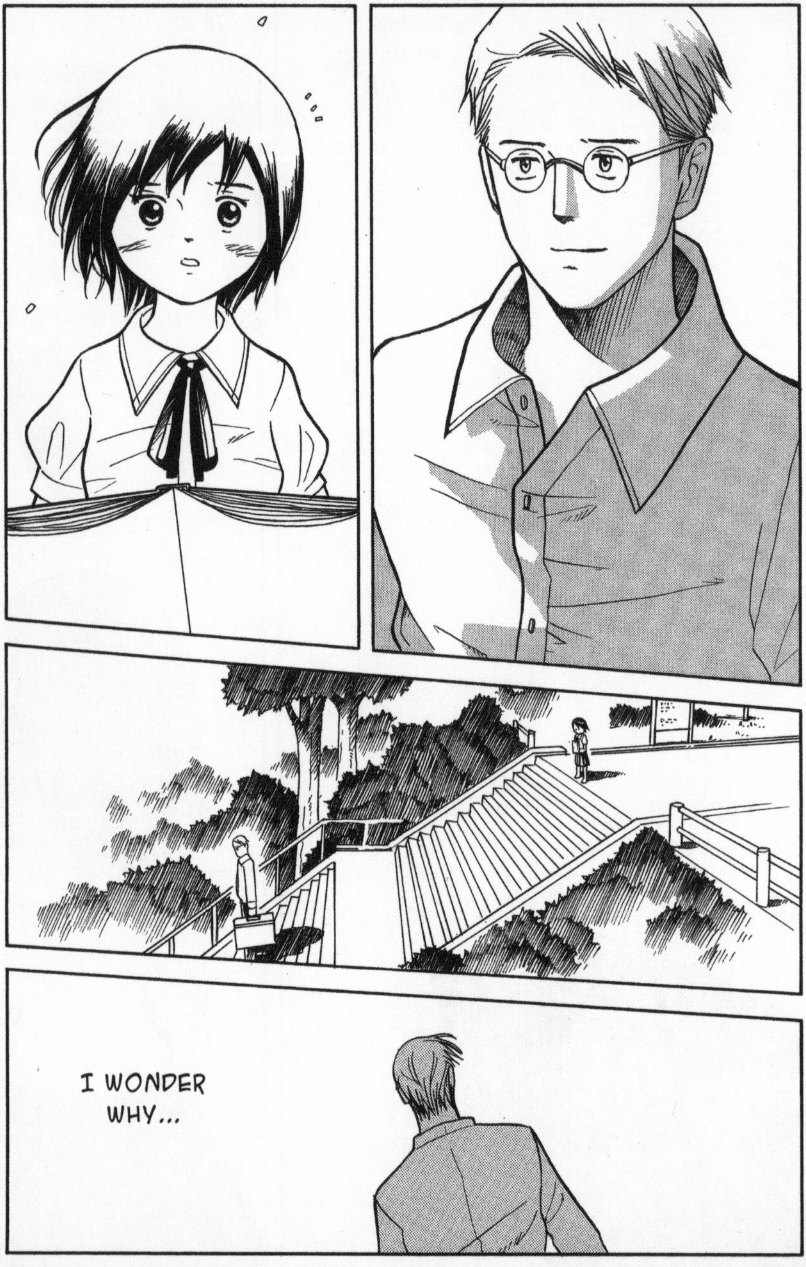
I WONDER WHY...

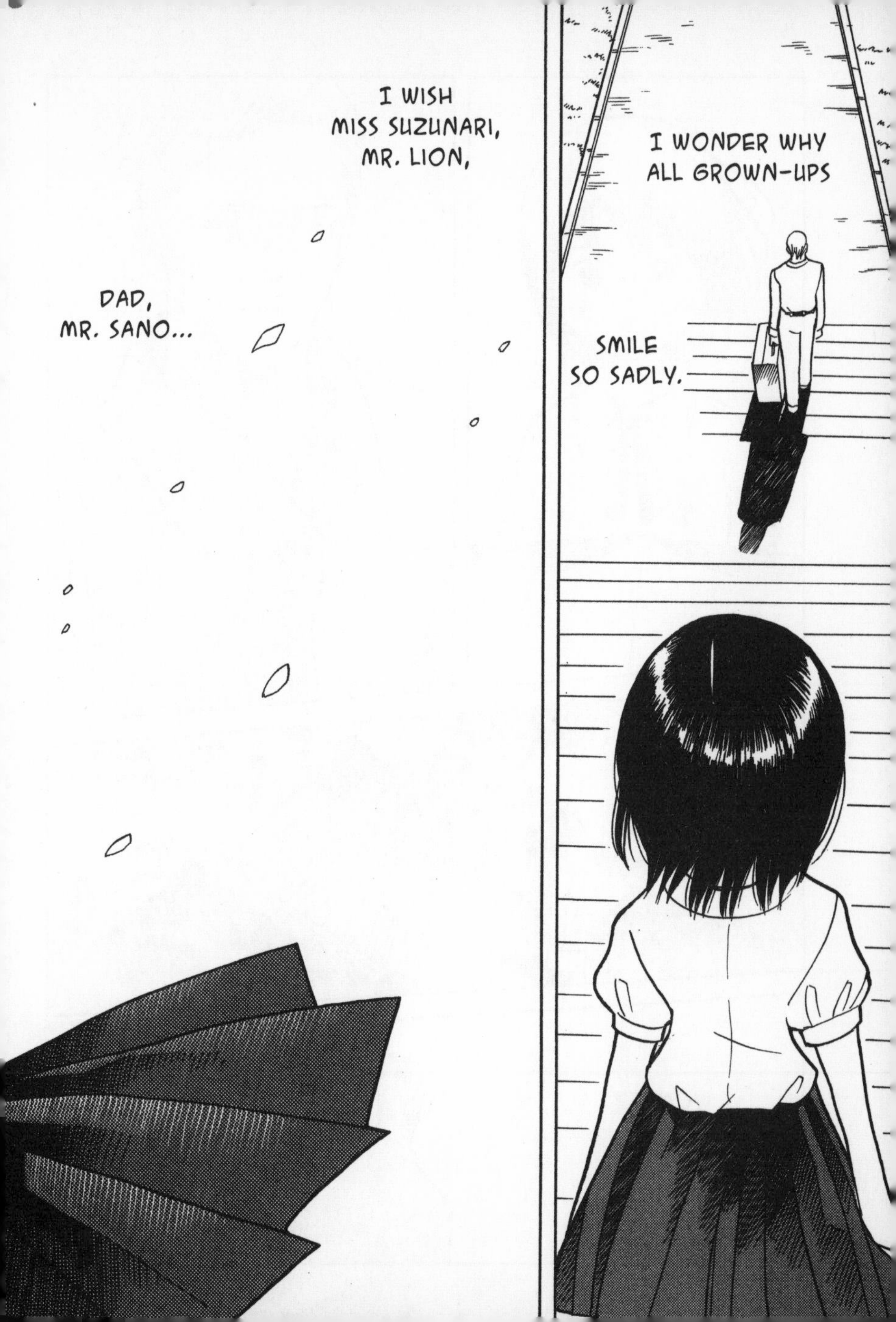
I WONDER WHY ALL GROWN-UPS
SMILE SO SADLY.
I WISH MISS SUZUNARI, MR. LION,
DAD, MR. SANO...

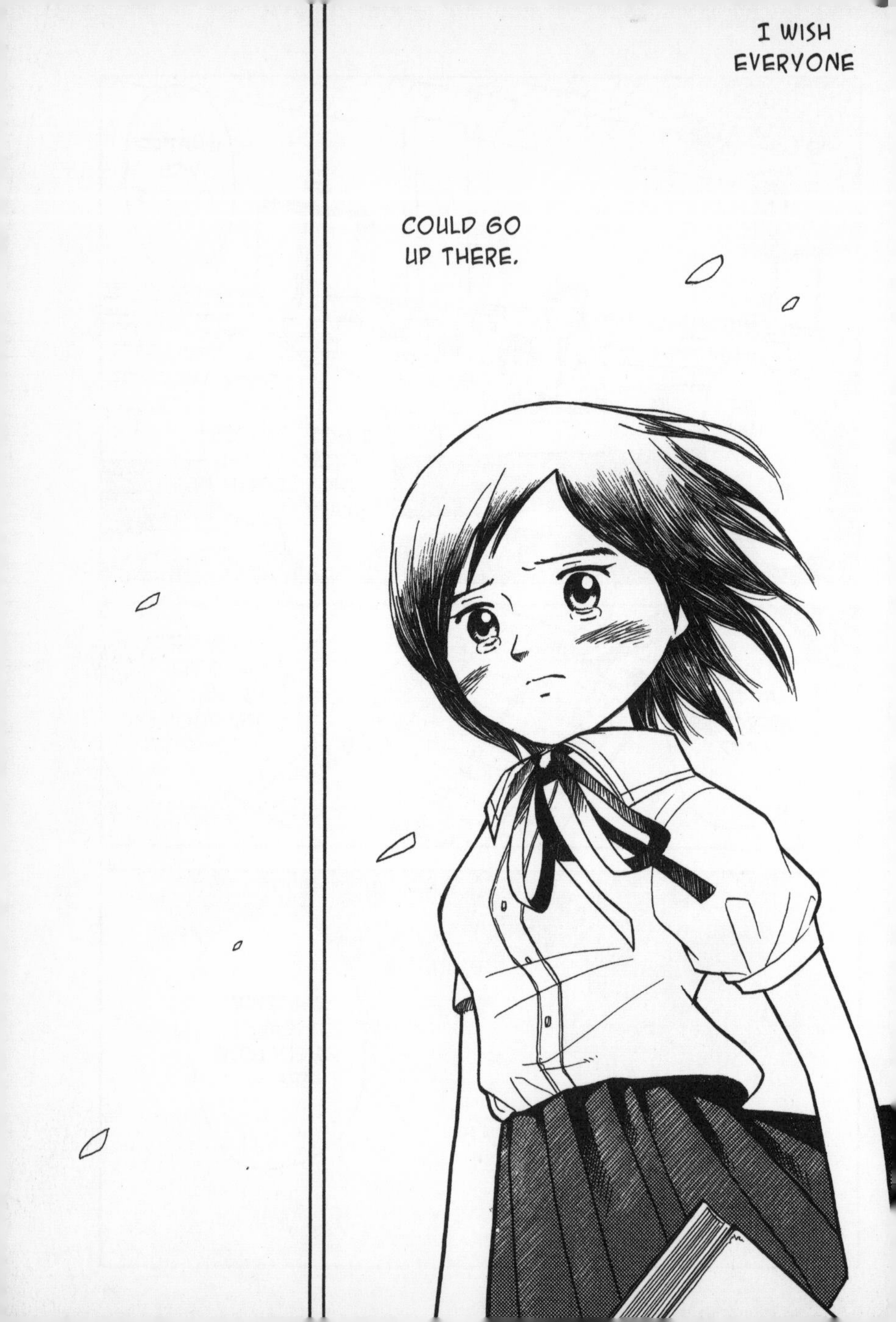
I WISH EVERYONE
COULD GO UP THERE.

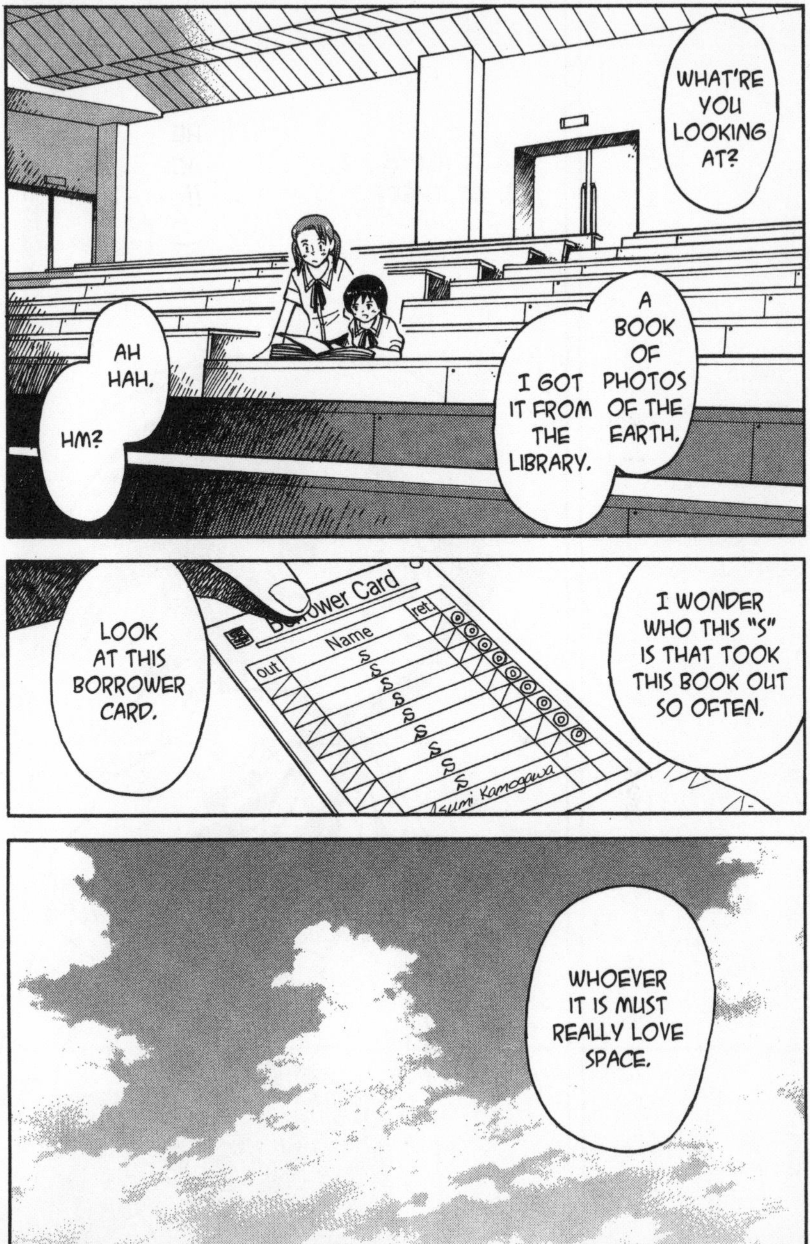
WHAT'RE YOU LOOKING AT?
A BOOK OF PHOTOS OF THE EARTH.
I GOT IT FROM THE LIBRARY.
AH HAH.
HM?
I WONDER WHO THIS "S" IS THAT TOOK THIS BOOK OUT SO OFTEN.
LOOK AT THIS BORROWER CARD.
Borrower Card
Name
out
ret.
Asumi Kamogawa
WHOEVER IT IS MUST REALLY LOVE SPACE.

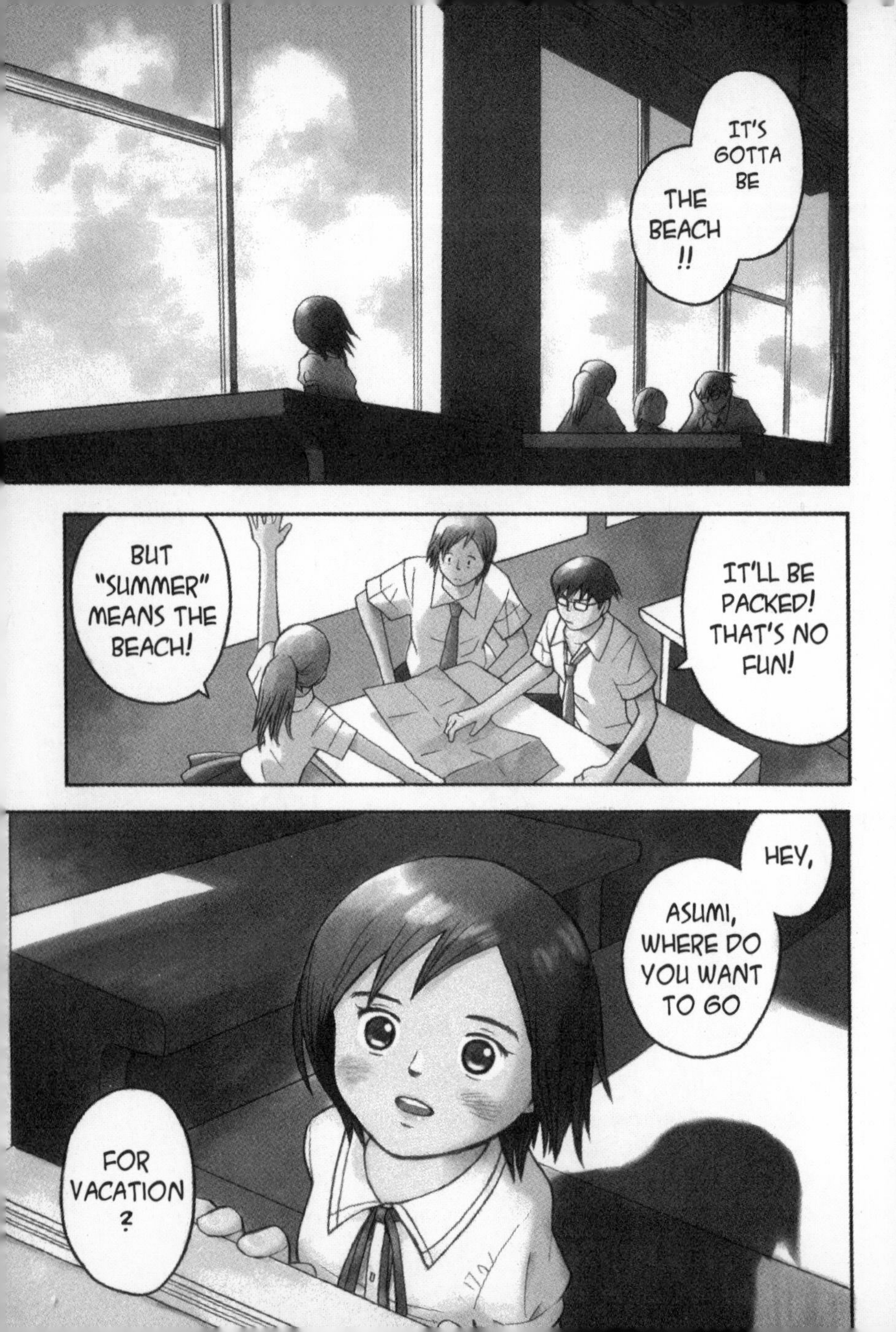
IT'S GOTTA BE THE BEACH !!
IT'LL BE PACKED! THAT'S NO FUN!
BUT "SUMMER" MEANS THE BEACH!
HEY, ASUMI, WHERE DO YOU WANT TO GO
FOR VACATION ?

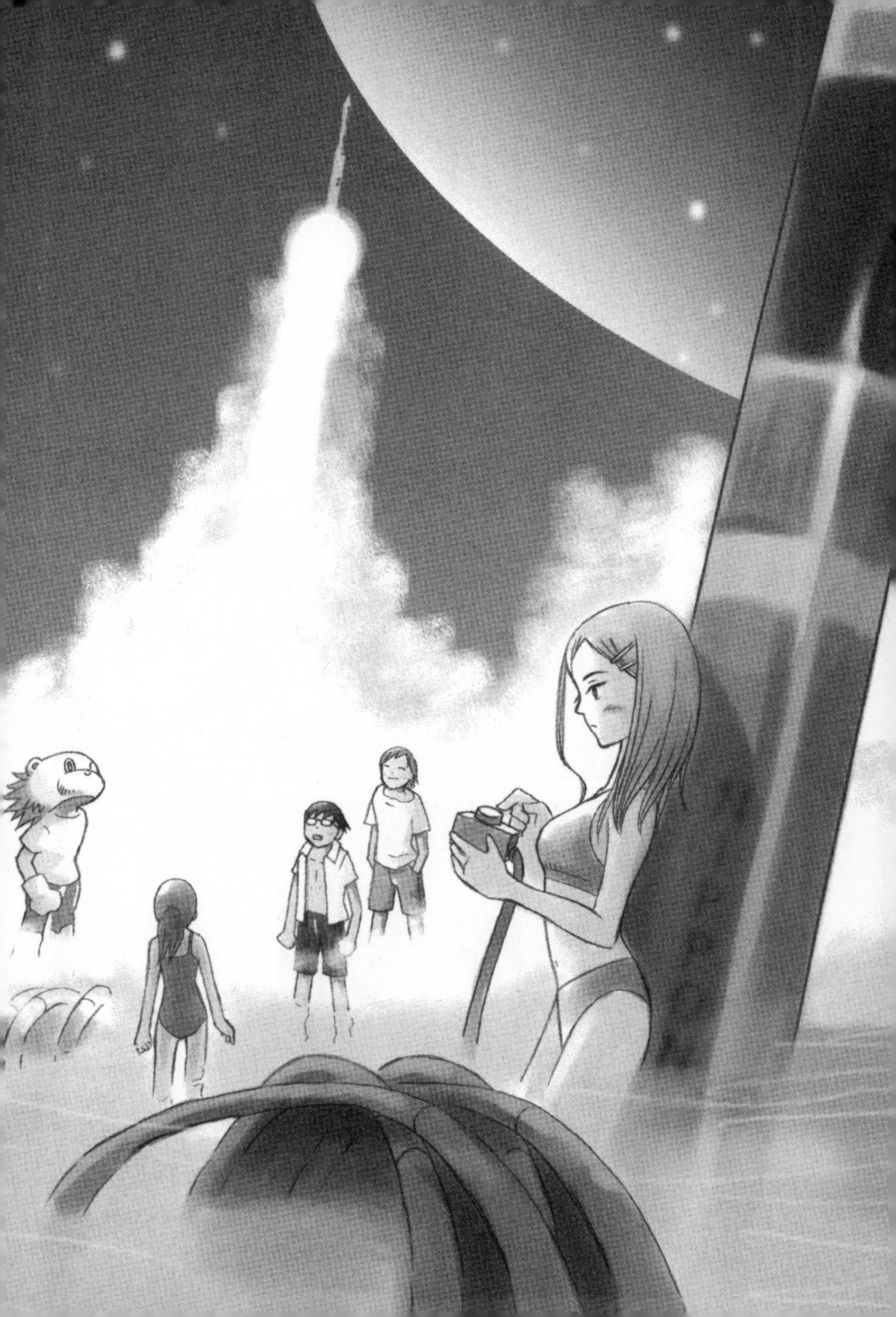

MISSION:12

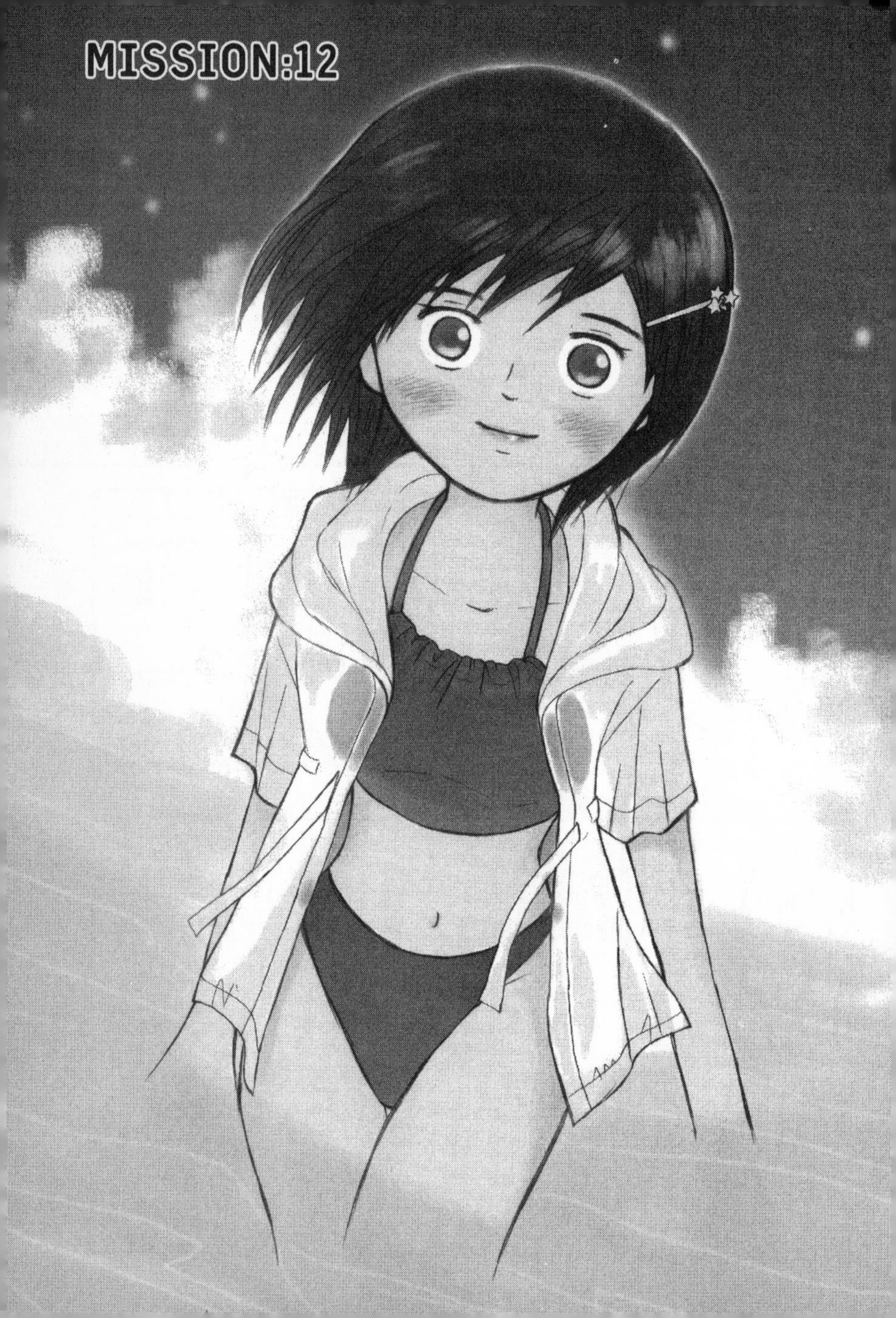

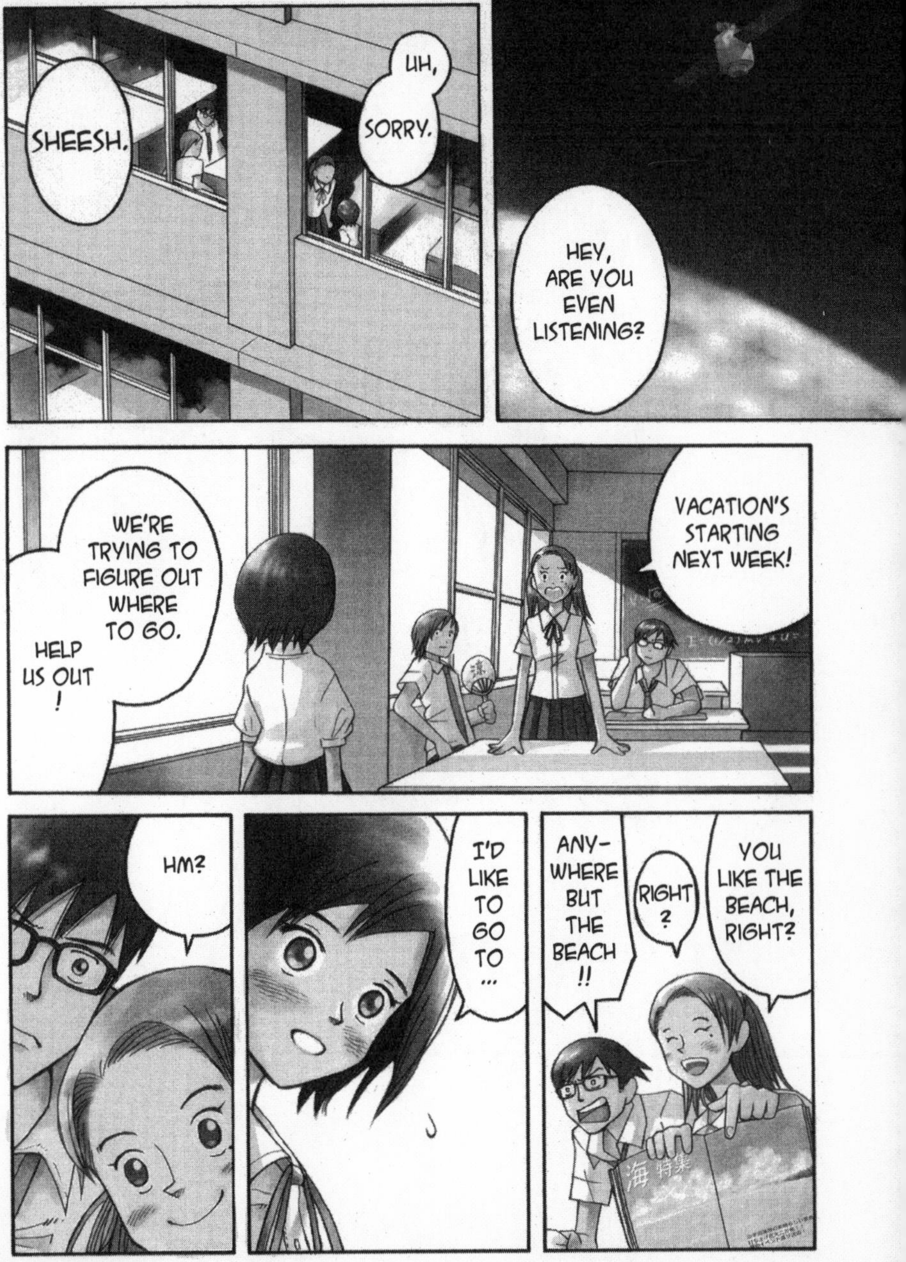
HEY, ARE YOU EVEN LISTENING?
UH, SORRY.
SHEESH.
VACATION'S STARTING NEXT WEEK!
WE'RE TRYING TO FIGURE OUT WHERE TO GO.
HELP US OUT!
YOU LIKE THE BEACH, RIGHT?
RIGHT?
ANY-WHERE BUT THE BEACH!!
I'D LIKE TO GO TO...
HM?

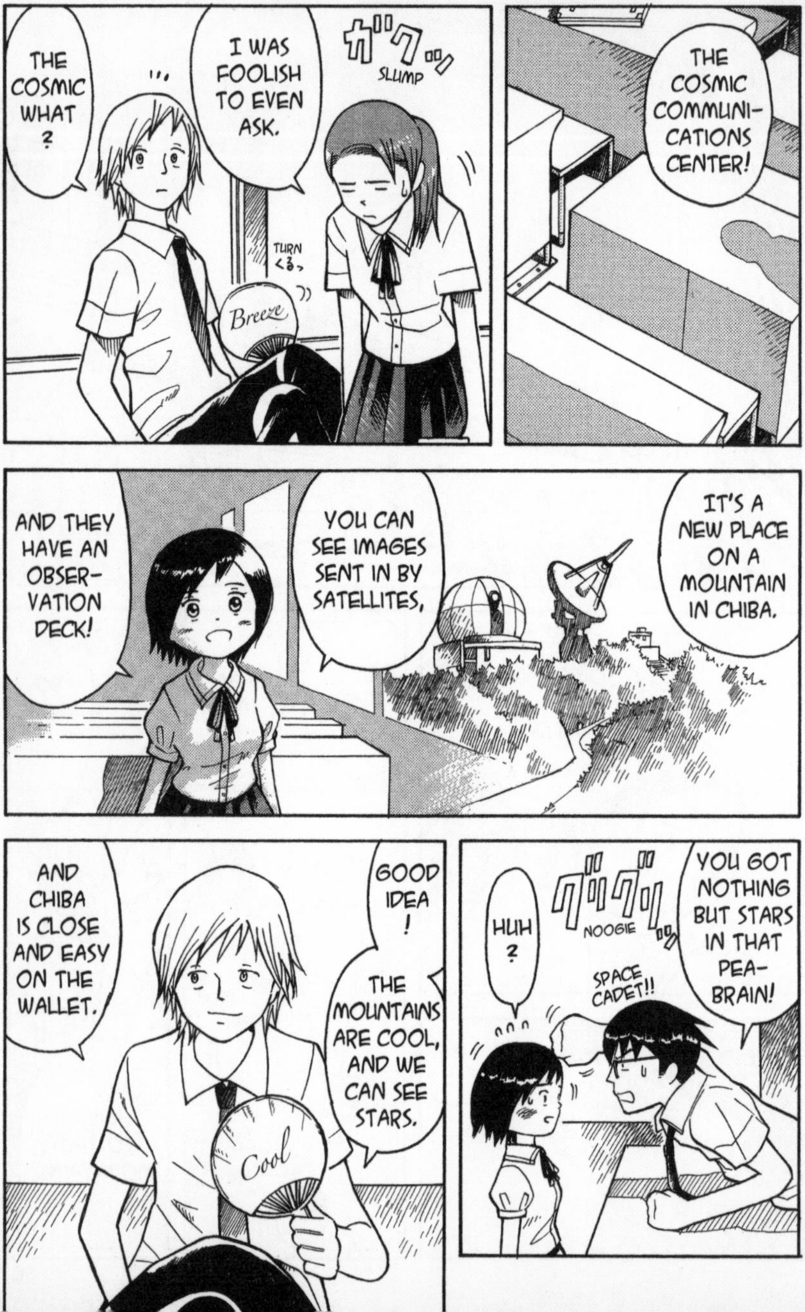
THE COSMIC COMMUNI-CATIONS CENTER!
ガクッ
SLUMP
I WAS FOOLISH TO EVEN ASK.
THE COSMIC WHAT?
TURN
くるっ
Breeze
IT'S A NEW PLACE ON A MOUNTAIN IN CHIBA.
YOU CAN SEE IMAGES SENT IN BY SATELLITES,
AND THEY HAVE AN OBSER-VATION DECK!
YOU GOT NOTHING BUT STARS IN THAT PEA-BRAIN!
グリグリ
NOOGIE
HUH?
SPACE CADET!!
GOOD IDEA!
THE MOUNTAINS ARE COOL, AND WE CAN SEE STARS.
AND CHIBA IS CLOSE AND EASY ON THE WALLET.
Cool

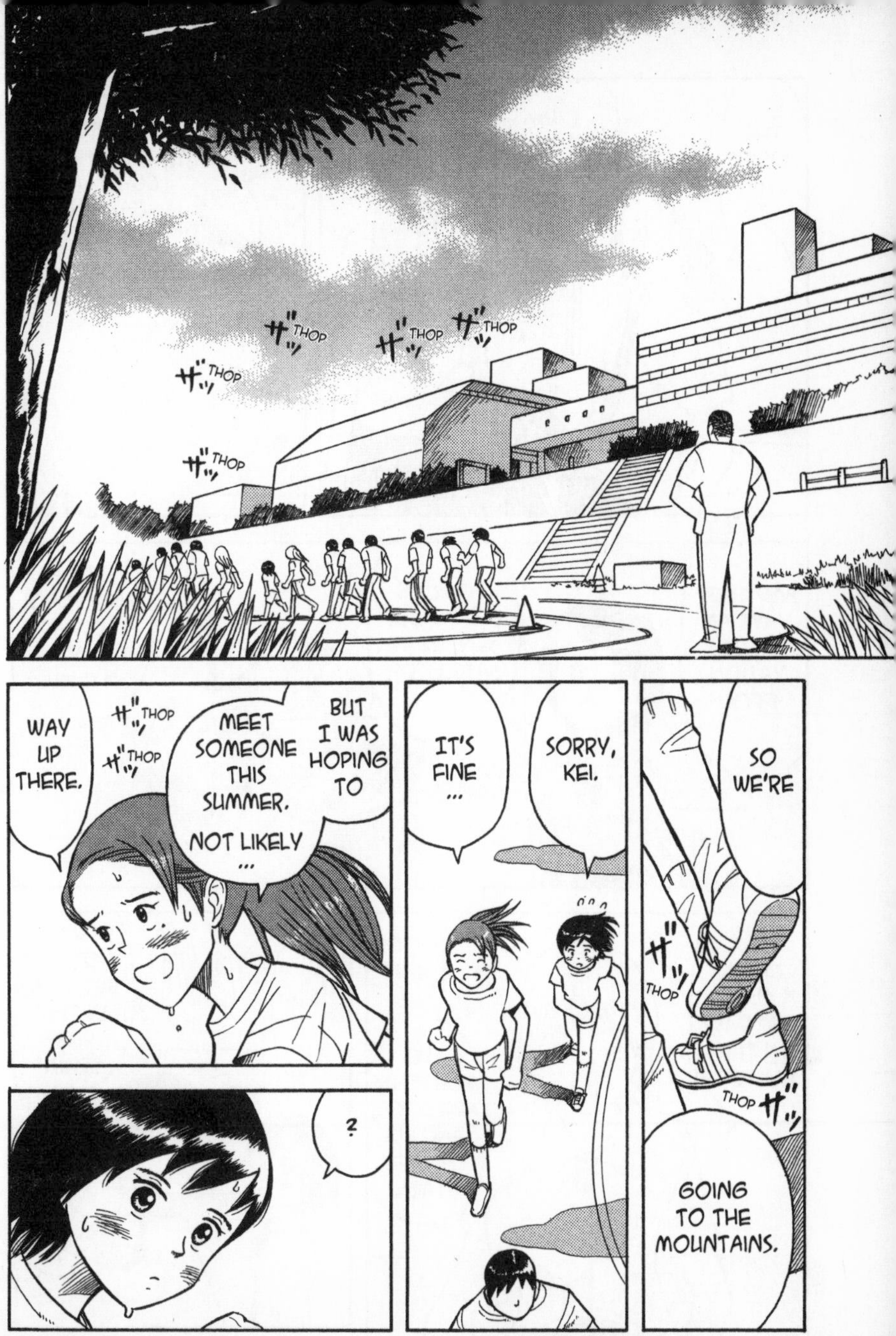
ザッ THOP
ザッ THOP
ザッ THOP
ザッ THOP
ザッ THOP
SO WE'RE
ザッ THOP
THOP ザッ
GOING TO THE MOUNTAINS.
SORRY, KEI.
IT'S FINE ...
BUT I WAS HOPING TO
MEET SOMEONE THIS SUMMER.
NOT LIKELY ...
ザッ THOP
ザッ THOP
WAY UP THERE.
?

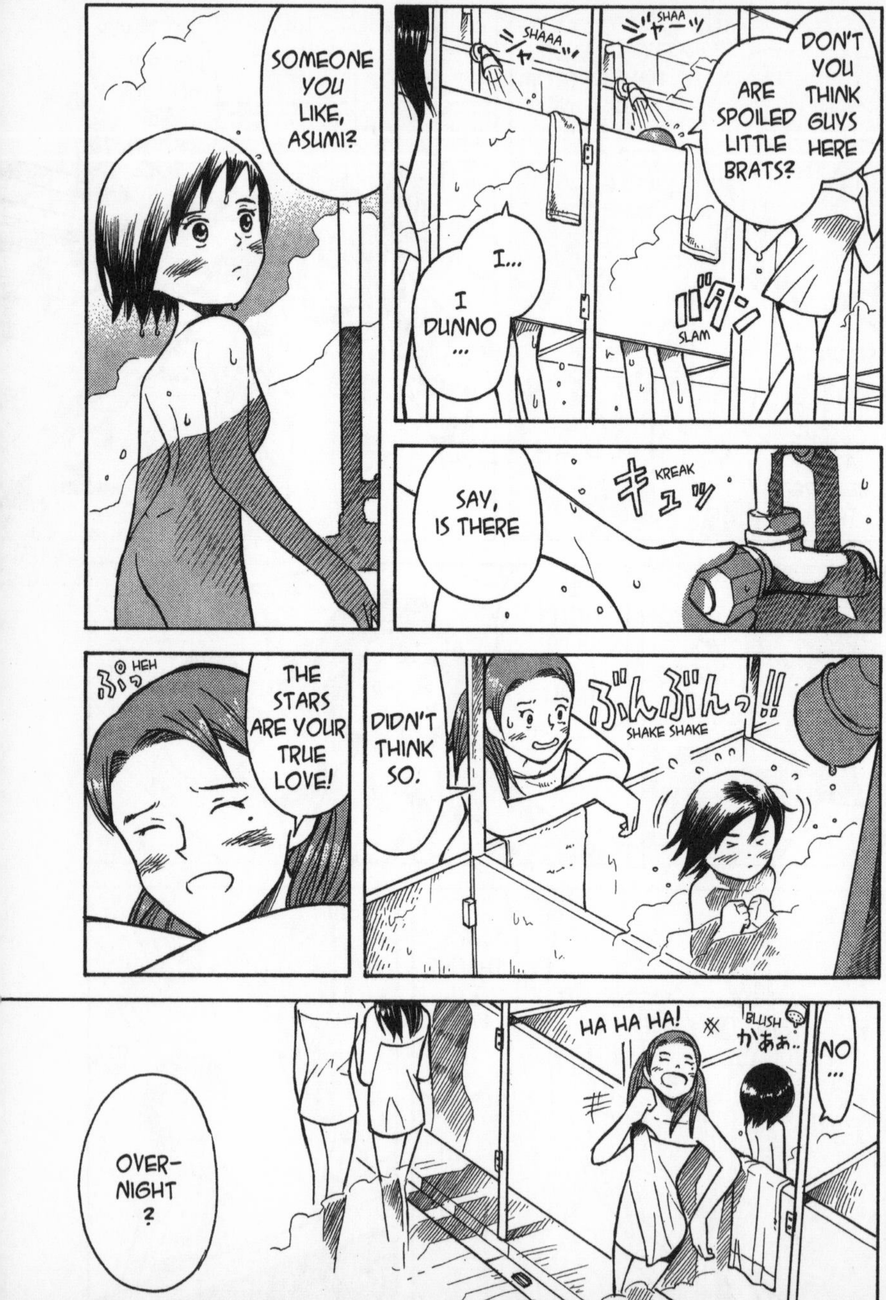

ジャーッ SHAA
DON'T YOU THINK GUYS HERE ARE SPOILED LITTLE BRATS?
ジャーッ SHAAA
I... I DUNNO ...
バタン SLAM
キュッ KREAK
SAY, IS THERE
SOMEONE YOU LIKE, ASUMI?
ぶんぶんっ!! SHAKE SHAKE
DIDN'T THINK SO.
THE STARS ARE YOUR TRUE LOVE!
ぷっ HEH
NO ...
かあぁ.. BLUSH
HA HA HA!
OVER-NIGHT?

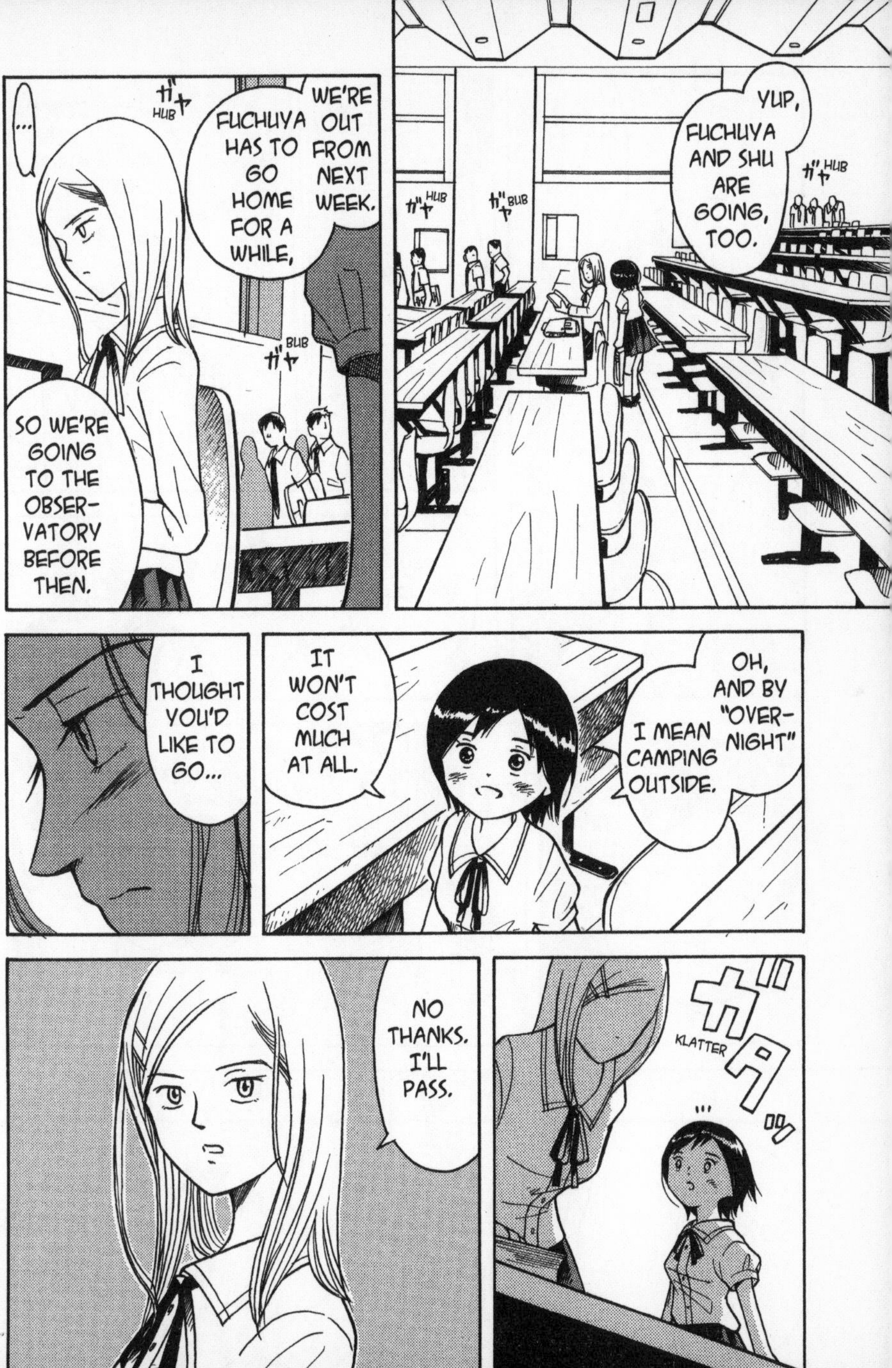
YUP, FUCHUYA AND SHU ARE GOING, TOO.
ガヤ HUB
ガヤ BUB
ガヤ HUB
WE'RE OUT FROM NEXT WEEK.
FUCHUYA HAS TO GO HOME FOR A WHILE,
ガヤ HUB
...
ガヤ BUB
SO WE'RE GOING TO THE OBSER-VATORY BEFORE THEN.
OH, AND BY "OVER-NIGHT" I MEAN CAMPING OUTSIDE.
IT WON'T COST MUCH AT ALL.
I THOUGHT YOU'D LIKE TO GO...
ガタッ KLATTER
NO THANKS. I'LL PASS.

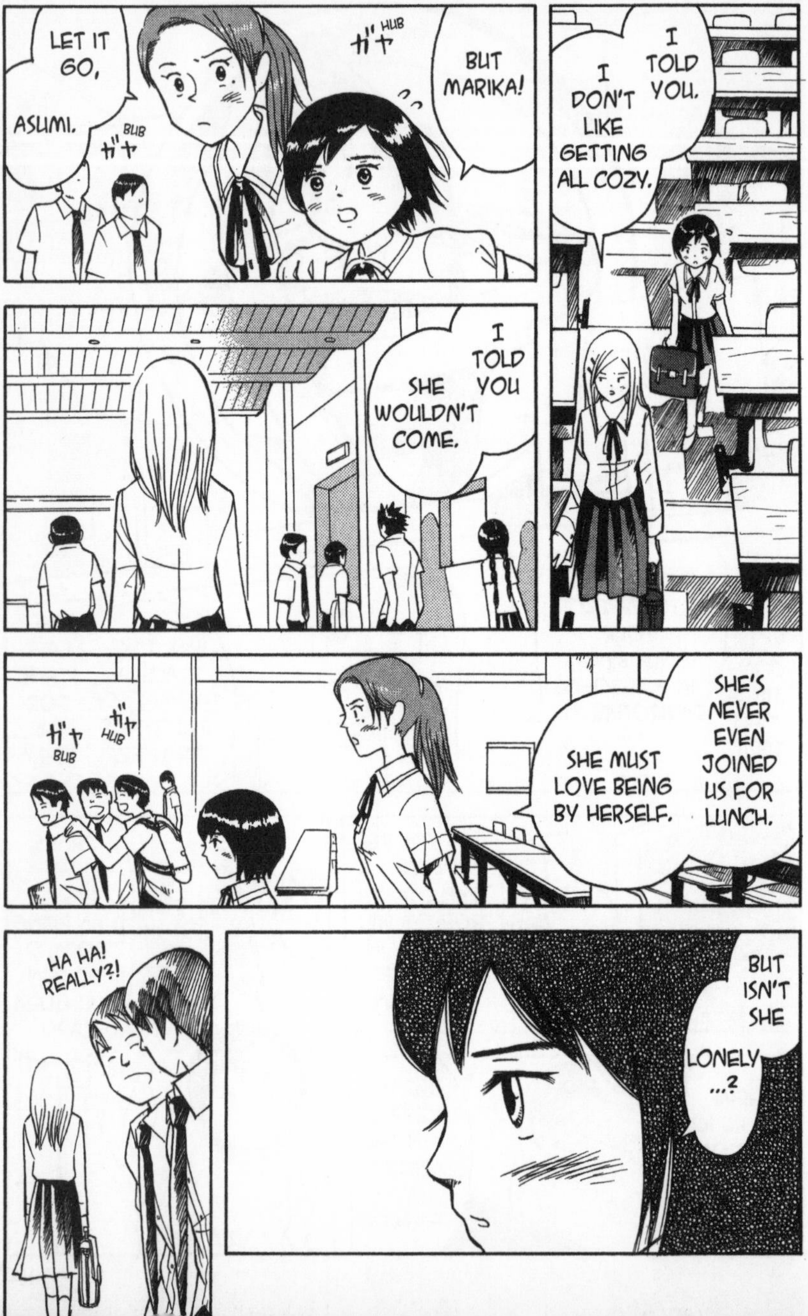
I TOLD YOU. I DON'T LIKE GETTING ALL COZY.
BUT MARIKA!
ガヤ HUB
LET IT GO, ASUMI.
ガヤ BUB
I TOLD YOU SHE WOULDN'T COME.
SHE'S NEVER EVEN JOINED US FOR LUNCH. SHE MUST LOVE BEING BY HERSELF.
ガヤ HUB
ガヤ BUB
BUT ISN'T SHE LONELY ...?
HA HA! REALLY?!

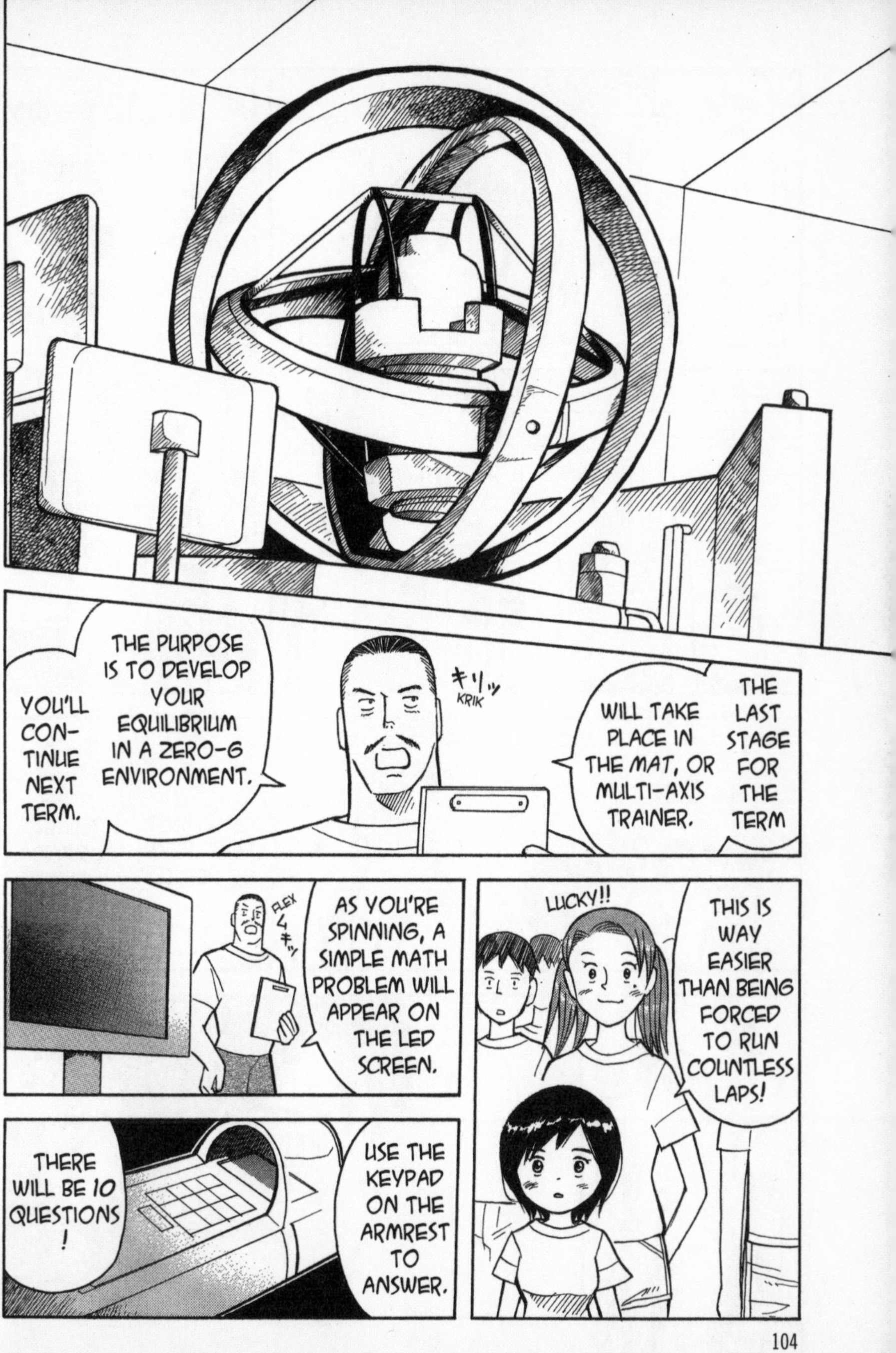
THE LAST STAGE FOR THE TERM
WILL TAKE PLACE IN THE MAT, OR MULTI-AXIS TRAINER.
キリッ KRIK
THE PURPOSE IS TO DEVELOP YOUR EQUILIBRIUM IN A ZERO-G ENVIRONMENT.
YOU'LL CONTINUE NEXT TERM.
THIS IS WAY EASIER THAN BEING FORCED TO RUN COUNTLESS LAPS!
LUCKY!!
AS YOU'RE SPINNING, A SIMPLE MATH PROBLEM WILL APPEAR ON THE LED SCREEN.
ムキッ FLEX
USE THE KEYPAD ON THE ARMREST TO ANSWER.
THERE WILL BE 10 QUESTIONS!

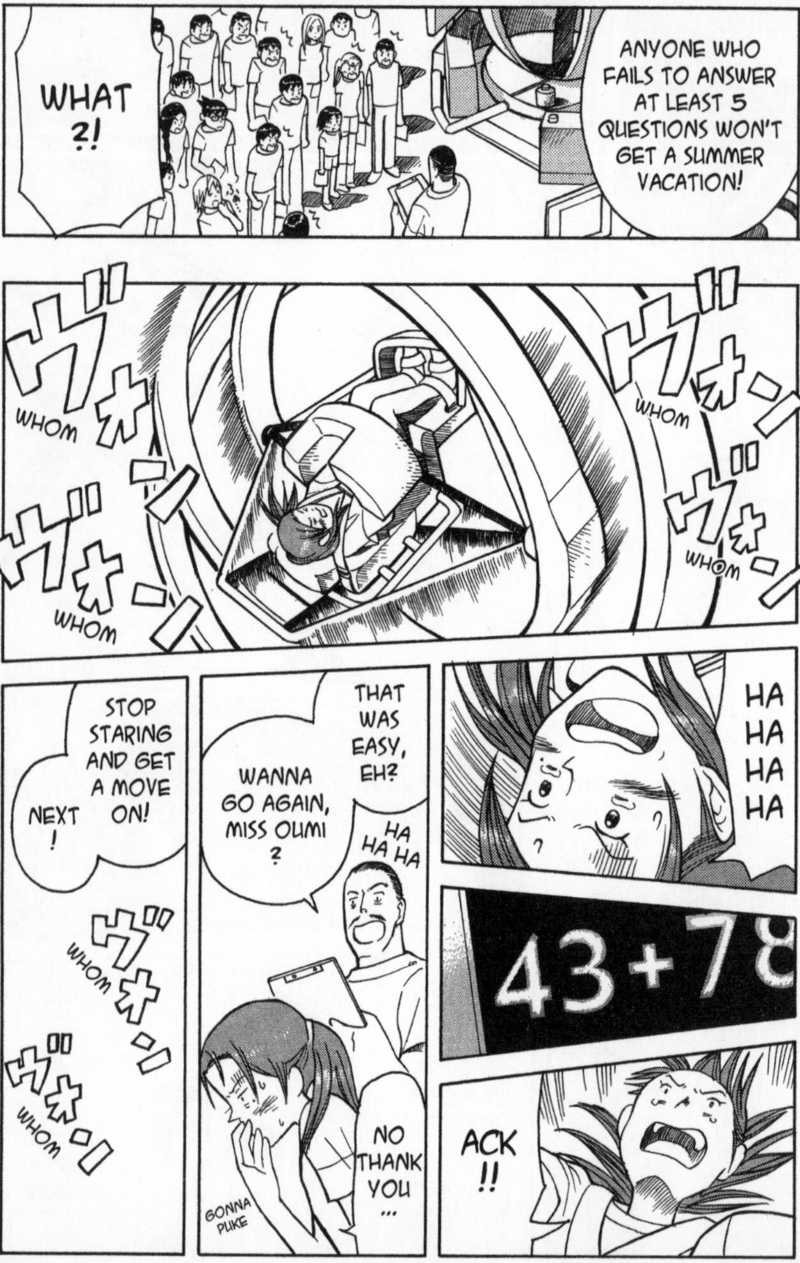
ANYONE WHO FAILS TO ANSWER AT LEAST 5 QUESTIONS WON'T GET A SUMMER VACATION!
WHAT ?!
ヴォーン
WHOM
ヴォーン
WHOM
ヴォーン
WHOM
ヴォーン
WHOM
HA HA HA HA
43+78
ACK !!
THAT WAS EASY, EH?
WANNA GO AGAIN, MISS OUMI ?
HA HA HA
NO THANK YOU ...
GONNA PUKE
STOP STARING AND GET A MOVE ON!
NEXT !
ヴォーン
WHOM
ヴォーン
WHOM

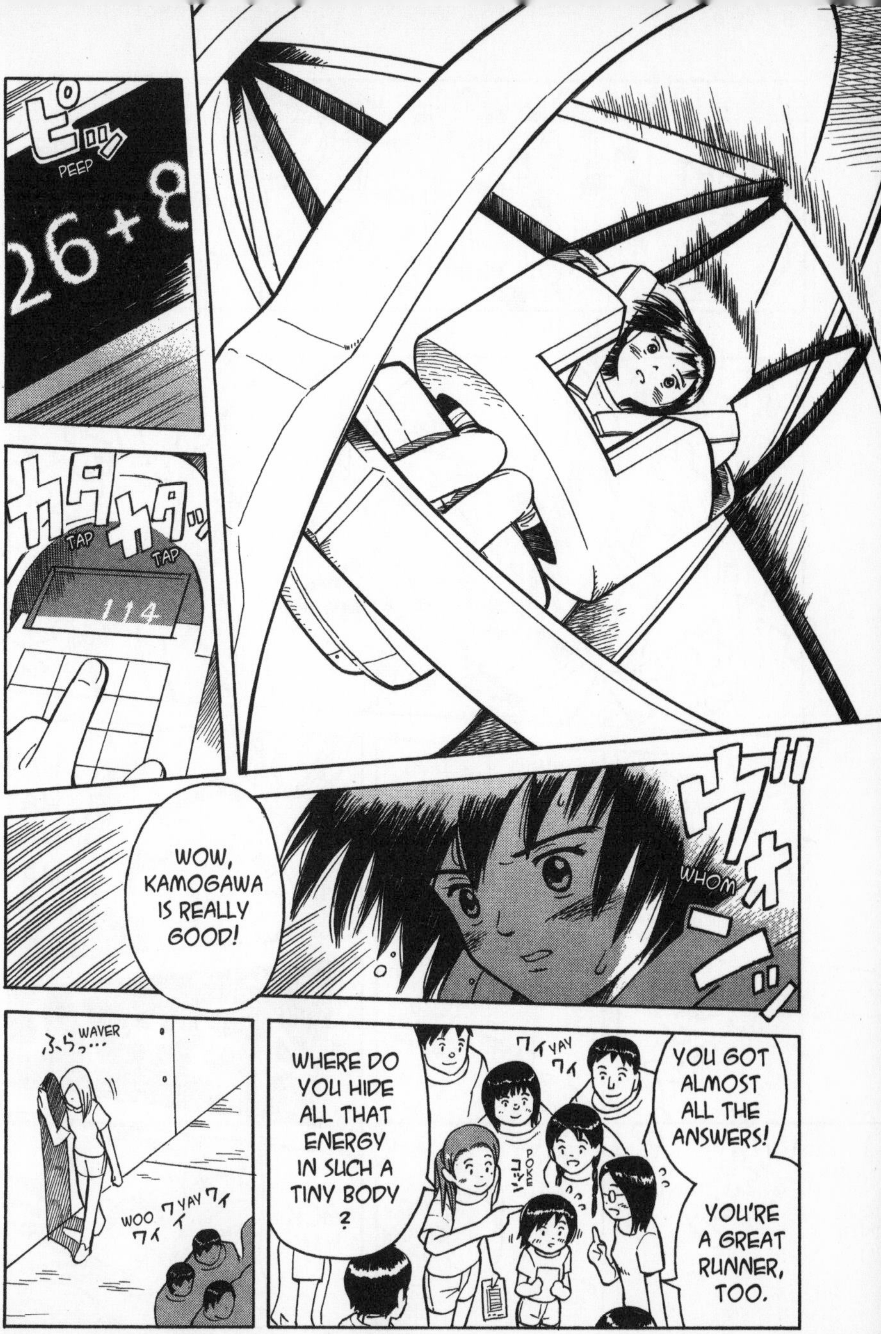

PEEP
26+8
TAP TAP
114
WHOM
WOW, KAMOGAWA IS REALLY GOOD!
YOU GOT ALMOST ALL THE ANSWERS!
YAY
WHERE DO YOU HIDE ALL THAT ENERGY IN SUCH A TINY BODY?
POKE
YOU'RE A GREAT RUNNER, TOO.
WAVER
WOO YAY

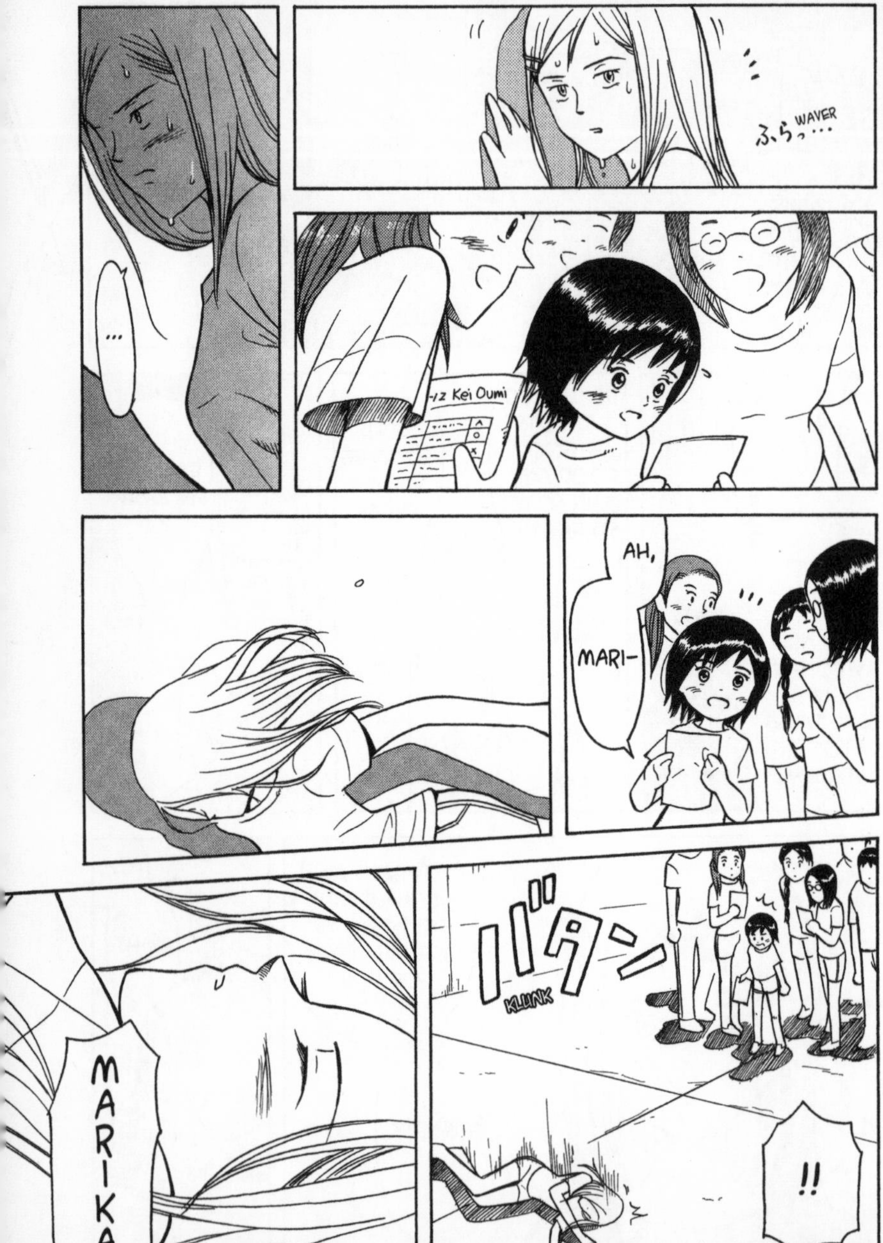
ふらっ…
WAVER
Kei Oumi
…
AH,
MARI-
バタン
KLUNK
!!
MARIKA!

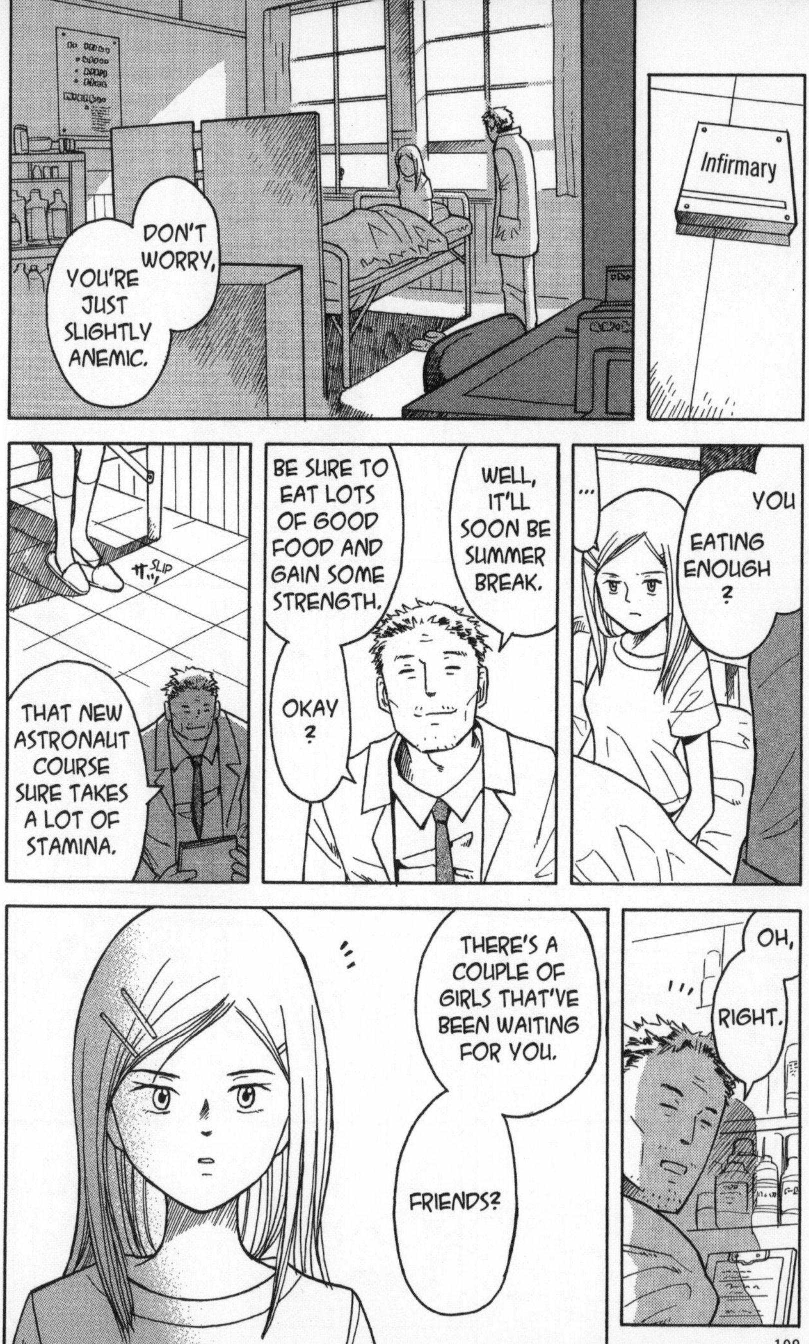
Infirmary
DON'T WORRY, YOU'RE JUST SLIGHTLY ANEMIC.
YOU
EATING ENOUGH?
...
WELL, IT'LL SOON BE SUMMER BREAK.
BE SURE TO EAT LOTS OF GOOD FOOD AND GAIN SOME STRENGTH.
OKAY?
SLIP
THAT NEW ASTRONAUT COURSE SURE TAKES A LOT OF STAMINA.
OH, RIGHT.
THERE'S A COUPLE OF GIRLS THAT'VE BEEN WAITING FOR YOU.
FRIENDS?

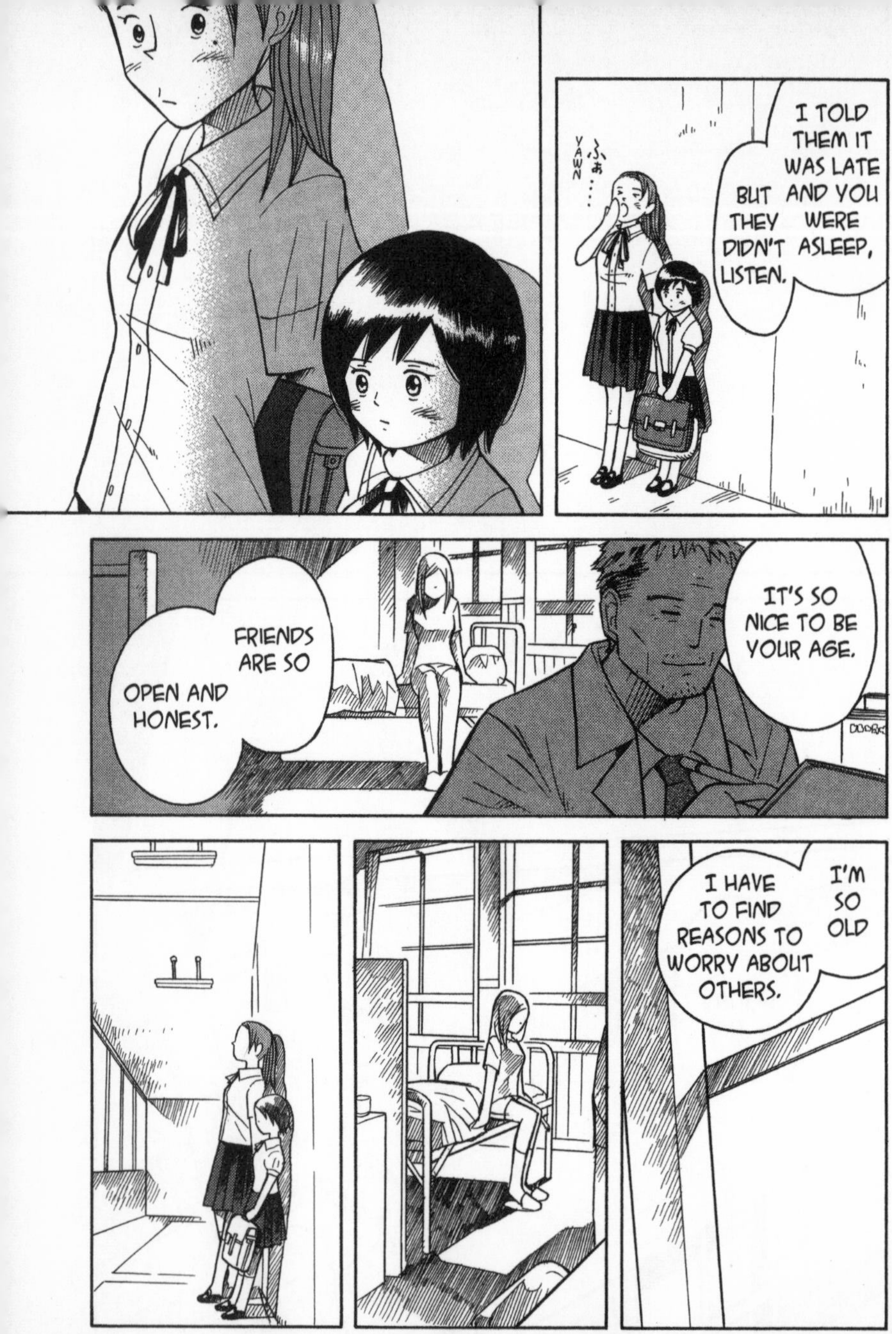
I TOLD THEM IT WAS LATE AND YOU WERE ASLEEP,
BUT THEY DIDN'T LISTEN.
ふぁ……
YAWN
IT'S SO NICE TO BE YOUR AGE.
FRIENDS ARE SO OPEN AND HONEST.
I'M SO OLD
I HAVE TO FIND REASONS TO WORRY ABOUT OTHERS.

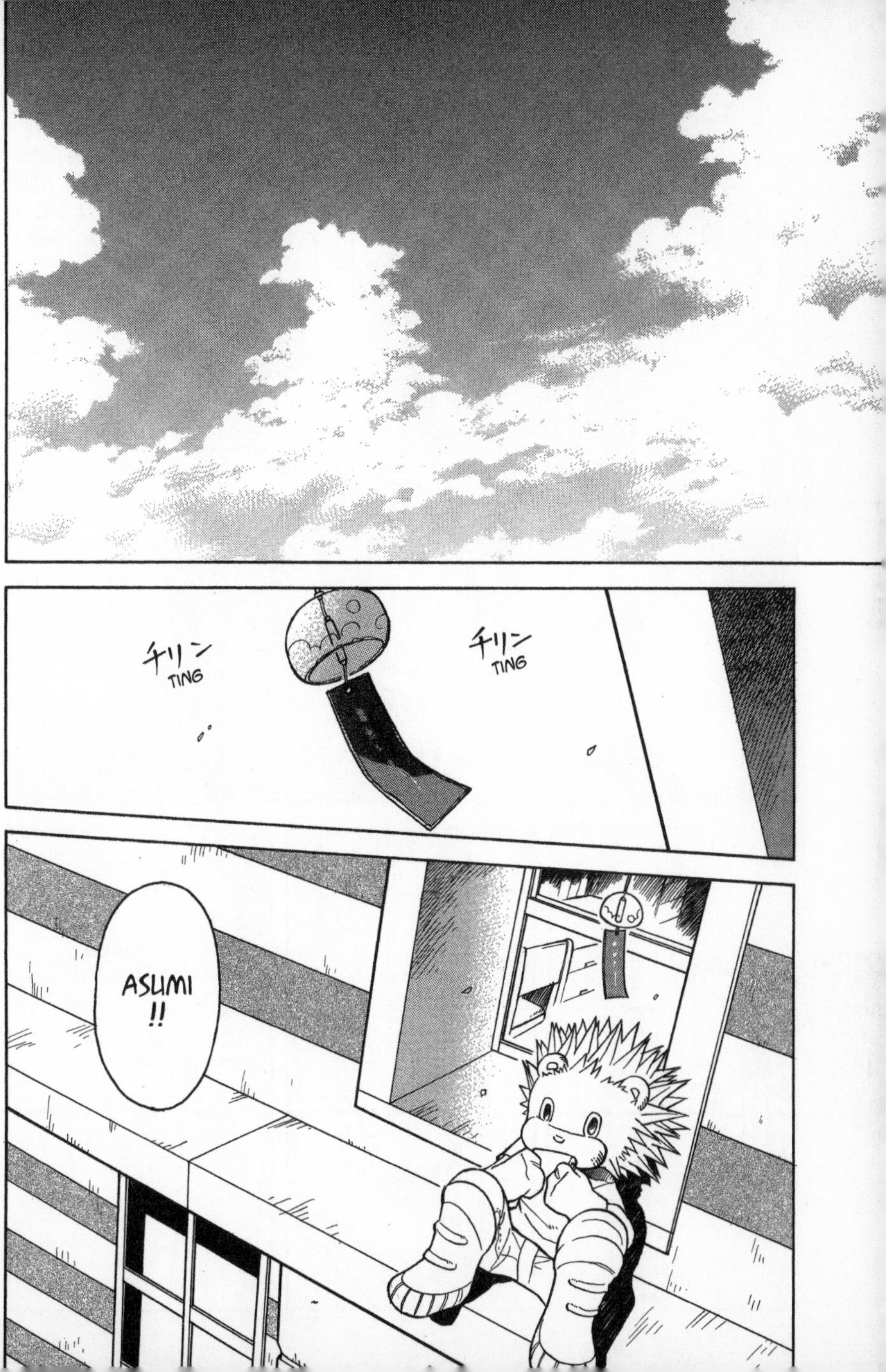
チリン
TING
チリン
TING
ASUMI !!

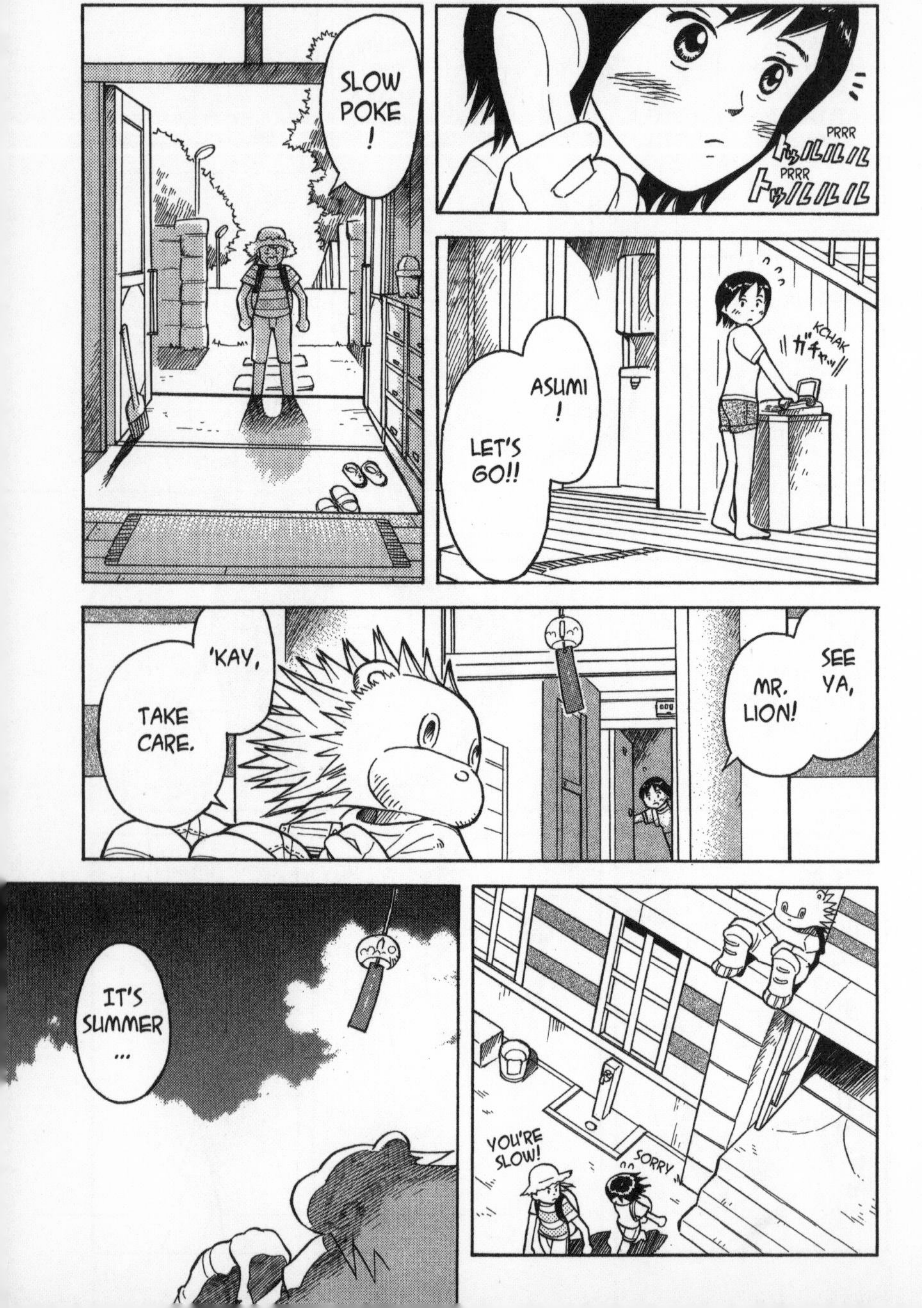
PRRR
トゥルルルル
PRRR
トゥルルルル
ASUMI!
LET'S GO!!
KCHAK
ガチャッ
SLOW POKE!
SEE YA, MR. LION!
'KAY, TAKE CARE.
YOU'RE SLOW!
SORRY
IT'S SUMMER...

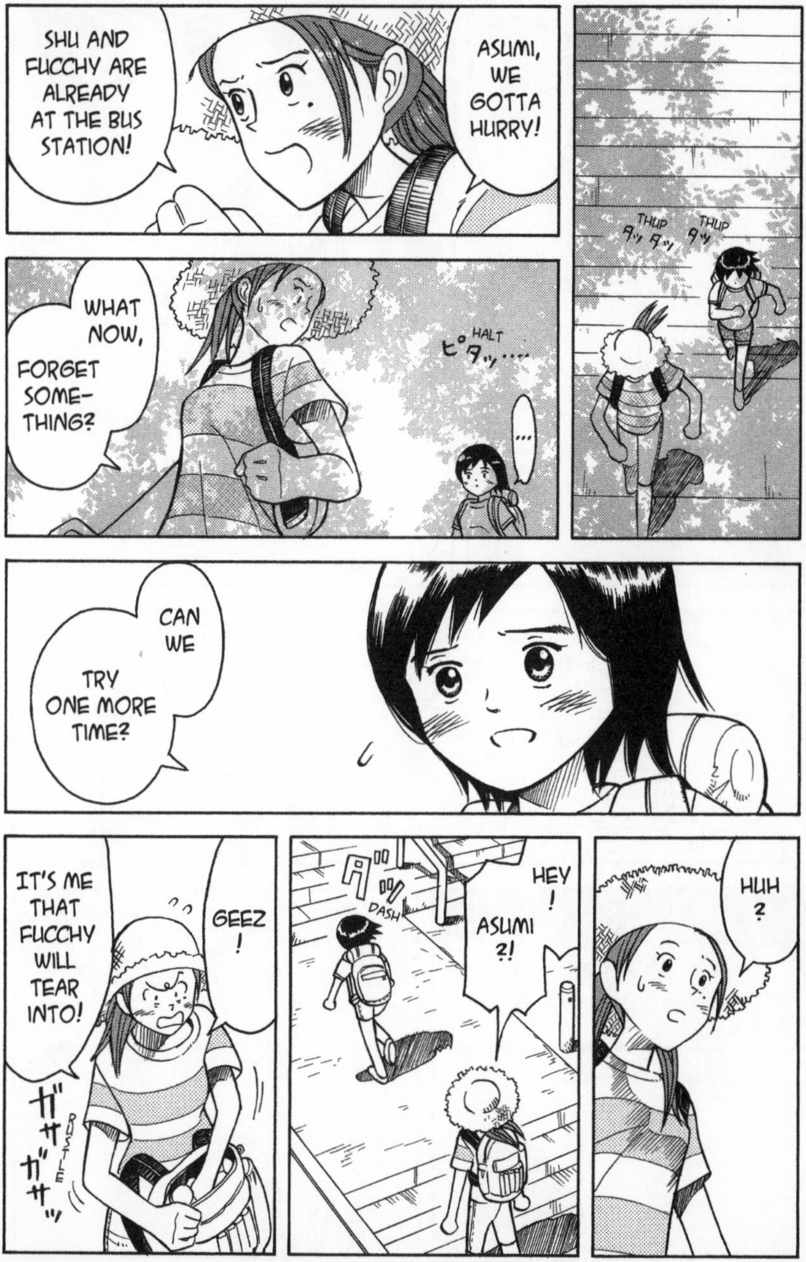

THUP THUP
タッ タッ タッ
ASUMI, WE GOTTA HURRY!
SHU AND FUCCHY ARE ALREADY AT THE BUS STATION!
HALT
ピタッ…
...
WHAT NOW, FORGET SOME-THING?
CAN WE TRY ONE MORE TIME?
HUH?
HEY! ASUMI?!
ダッ
DASH
GEEZ!
IT'S ME THAT FUCCHY WILL TEAR INTO!
ガサガサッ
RUSTLE

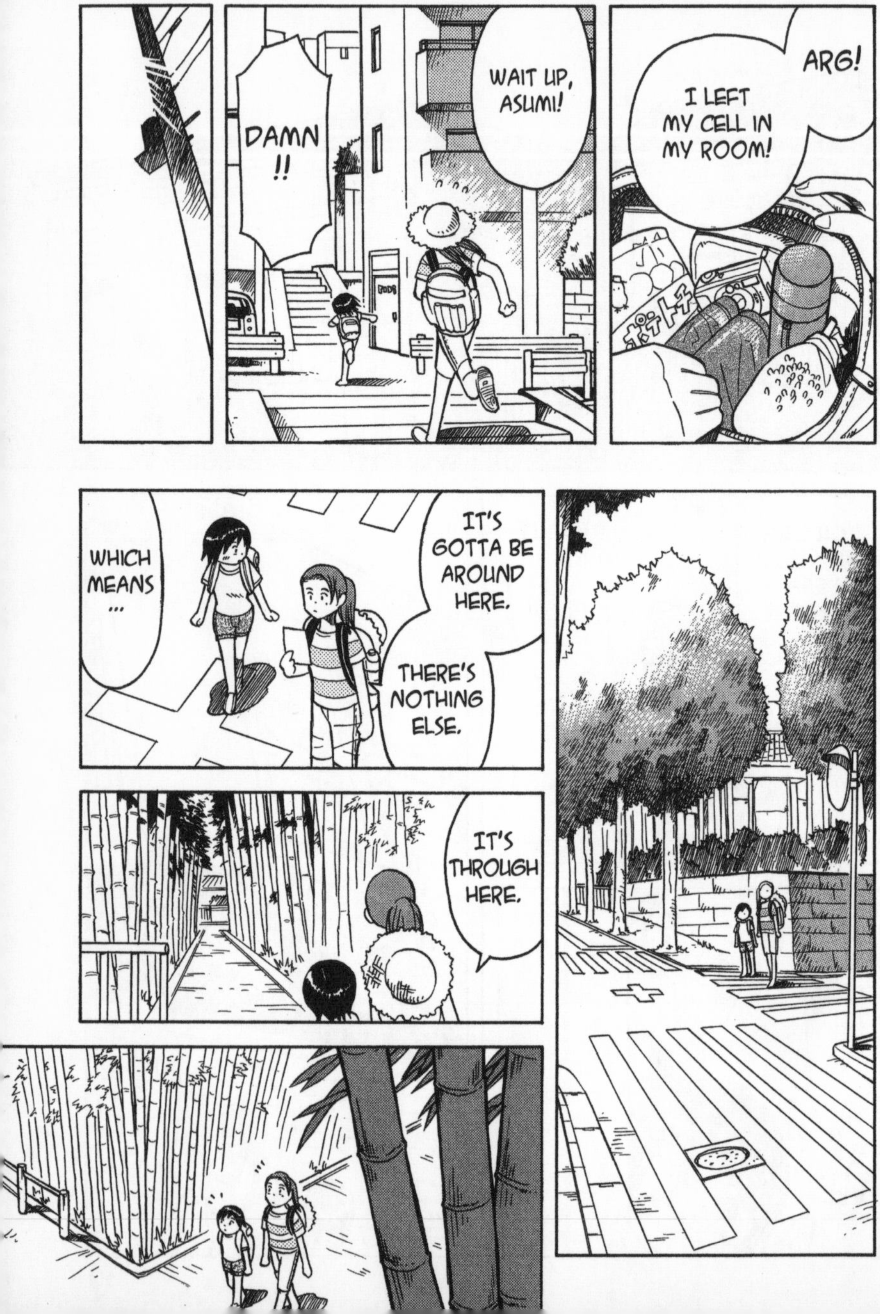
ARG!
I LEFT MY CELL IN MY ROOM!
WAIT UP, ASUMI!
DAMN !!
IT'S GOTTA BE AROUND HERE.
THERE'S NOTHING ELSE.
WHICH MEANS ...
IT'S THROUGH HERE.

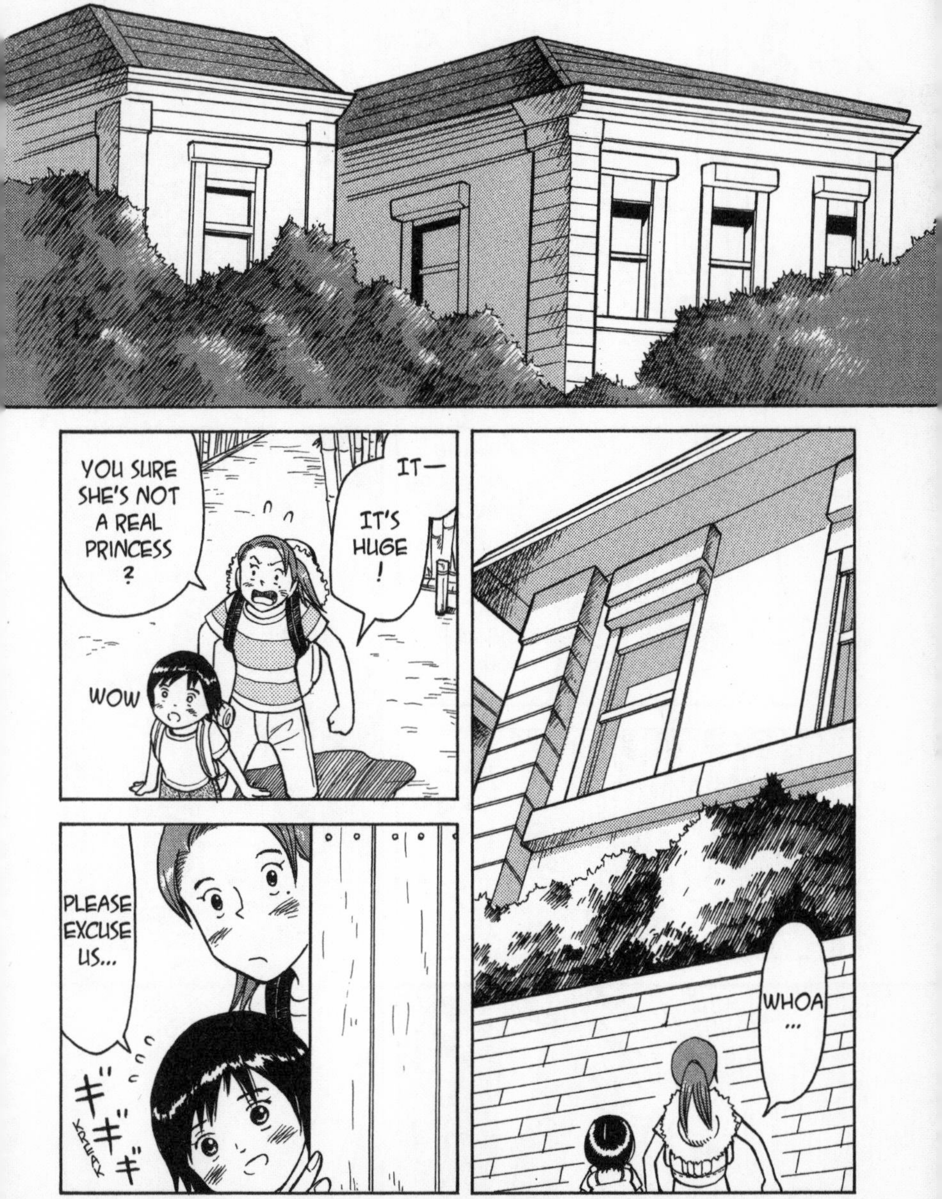
WHOA ...
IT—
IT'S HUGE!
YOU SURE SHE'S NOT A REAL PRINCESS?
WOW
PLEASE EXCUSE US...
ギギギ
KREEK

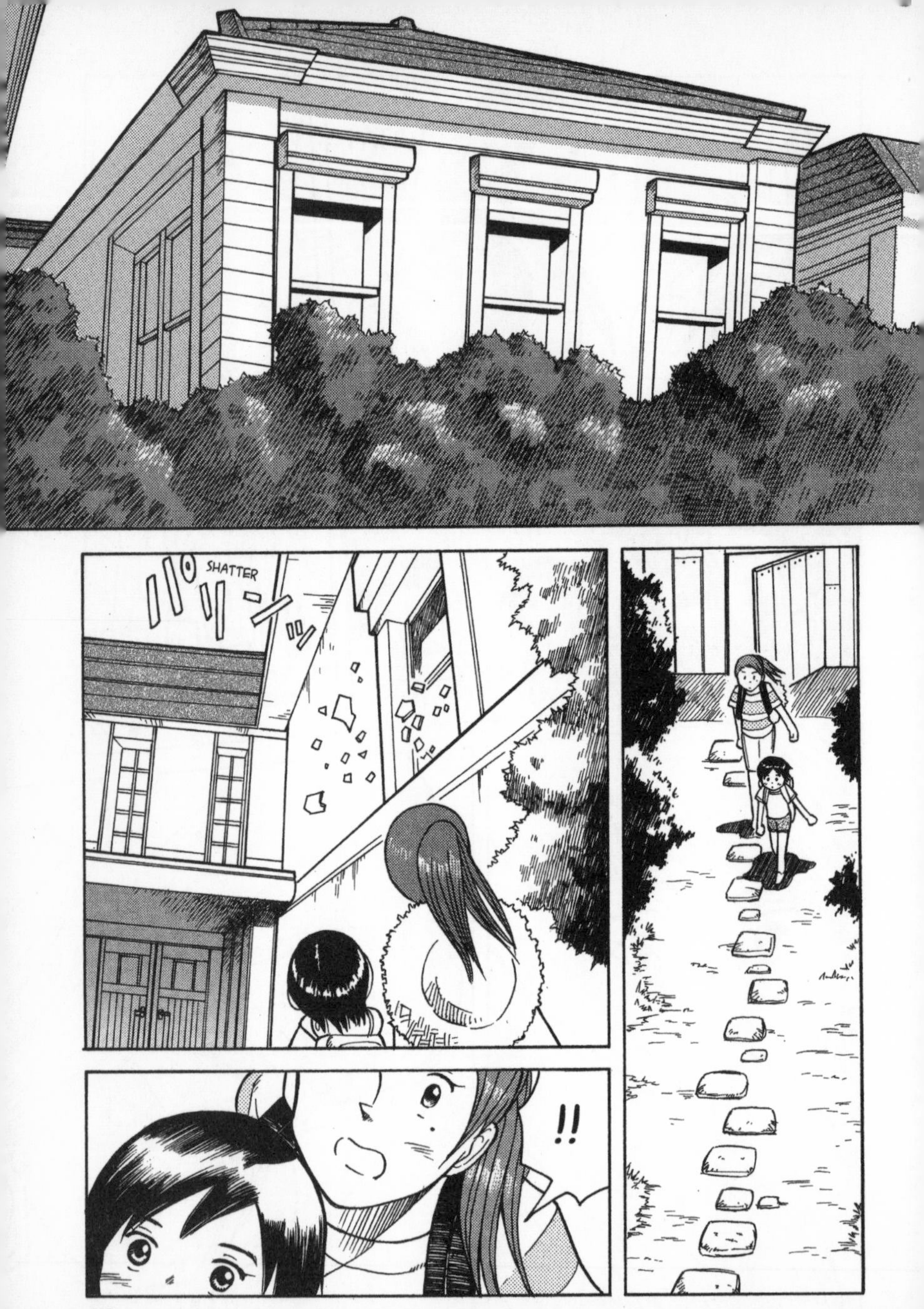
パリ
SHATTER
!!

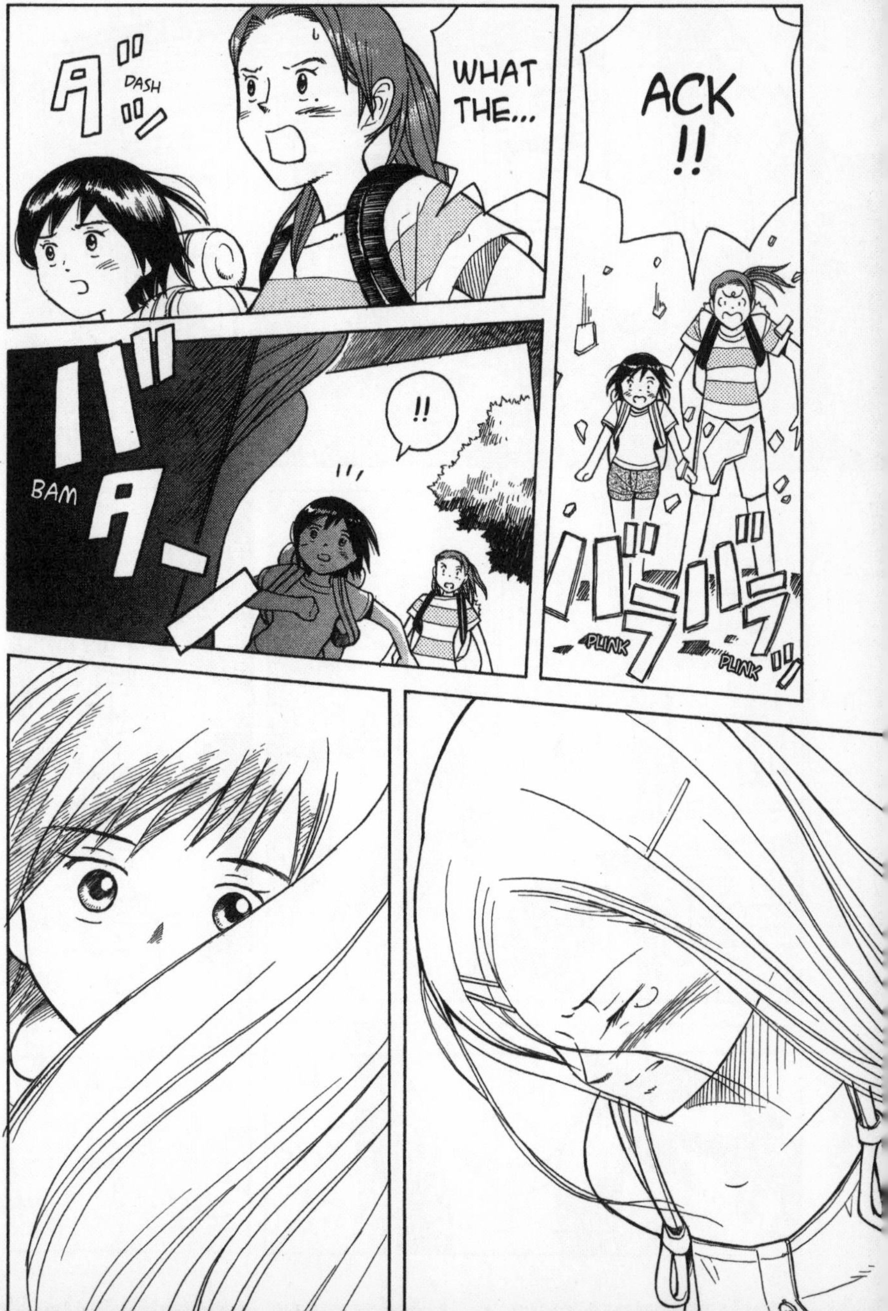
ACK !!
PLINK
PLINK
WHAT THE...
DASH
!!
BAM

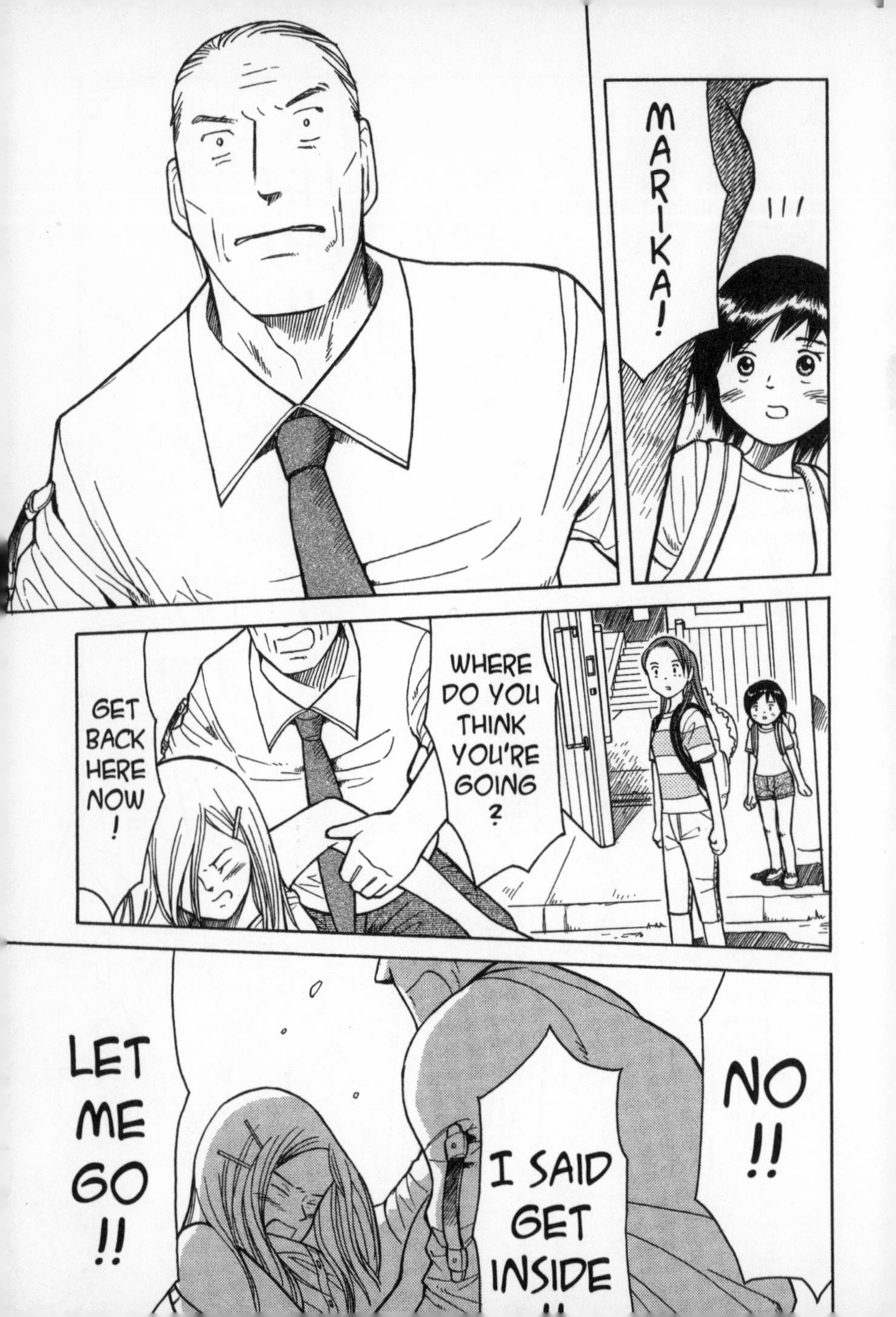
MARIKA!
WHERE DO YOU THINK YOU'RE GOING?
GET BACK HERE NOW!
NO!!
I SAID GET INSIDE !!
LET ME GO!!

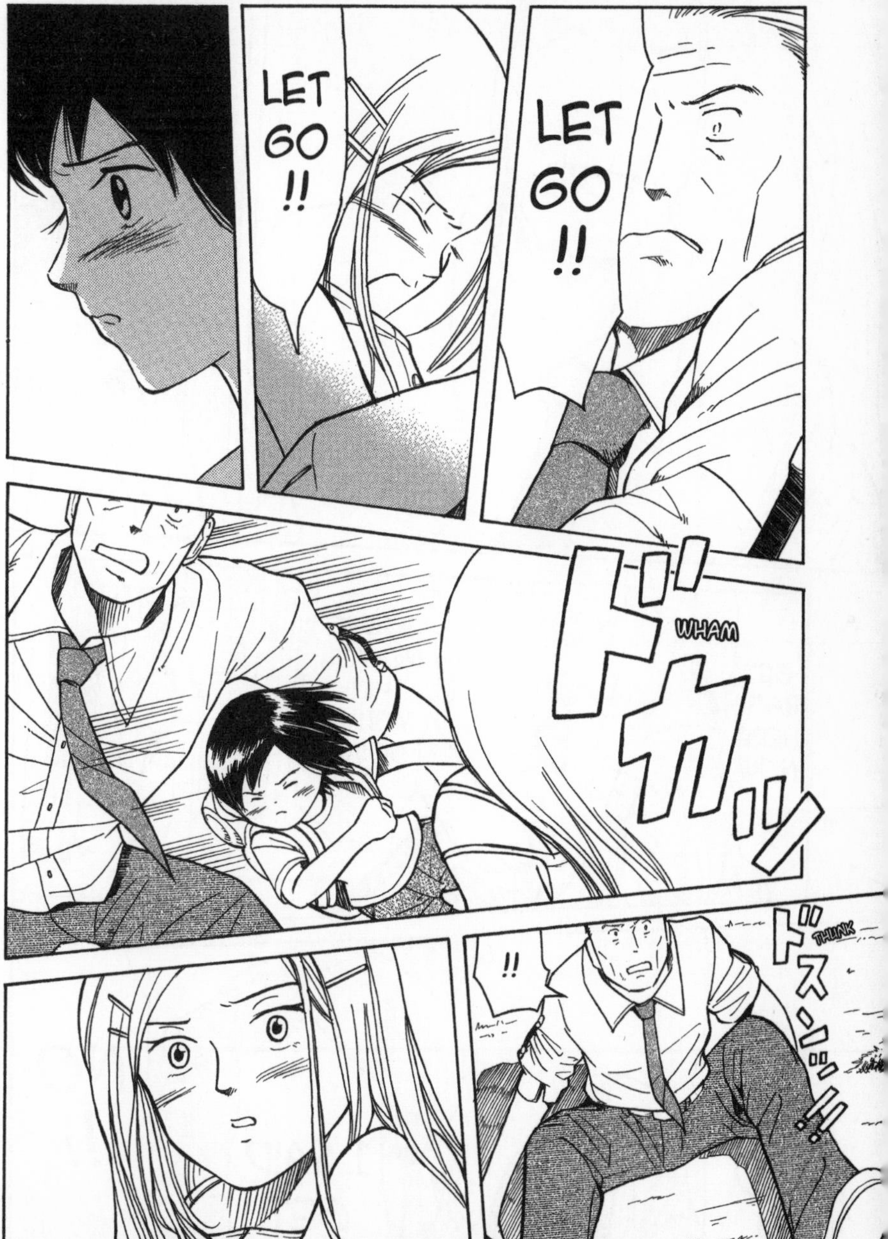
LET GO !!
LET GO !!
ドガッ
WHAM
!!
ドスン!!
THUNK

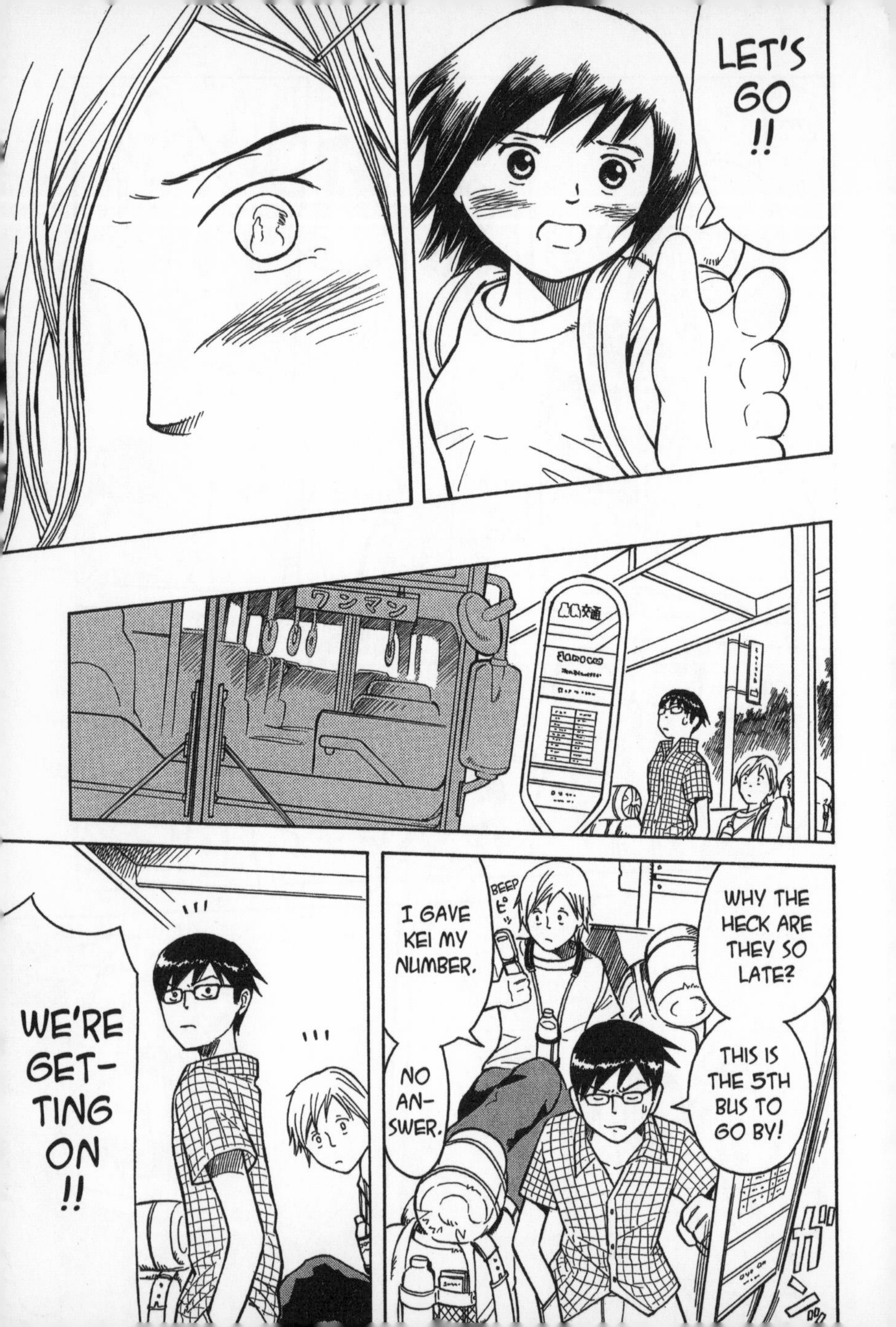
LET'S GO !!
ワンマン
WHY THE HECK ARE THEY SO LATE?
BEEP ピッ
I GAVE KEI MY NUMBER.
THIS IS THE 5TH BUS TO GO BY!
NO AN-SWER.
WE'RE GET-TING ON !!

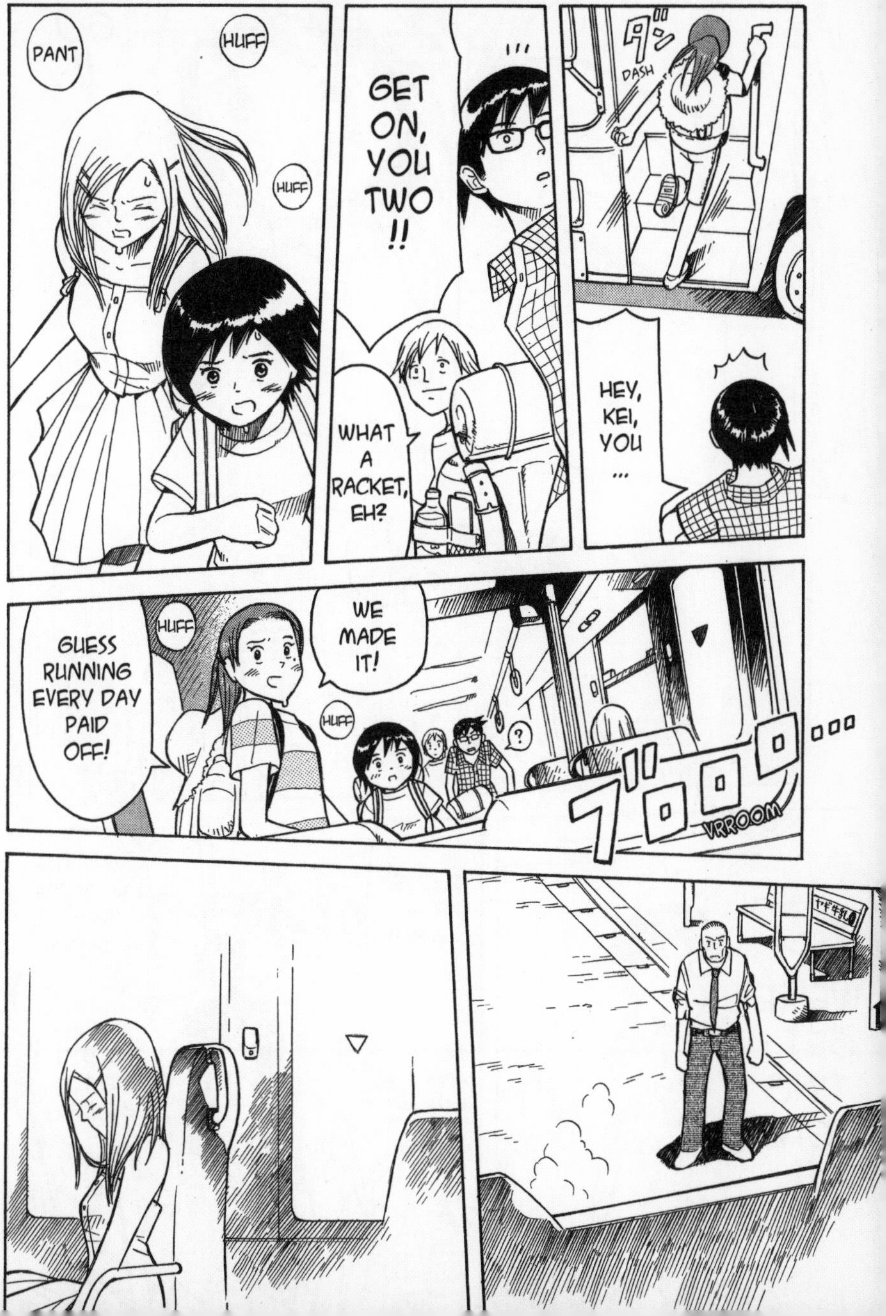
DASH
HEY, KEI, YOU ...
GET ON, YOU TWO !!
WHAT A RACKET, EH?
HUFF
PANT
HUFF
VRROOM
WE MADE IT!
HUFF
GUESS RUNNING EVERY DAY PAID OFF!
HUFF
?

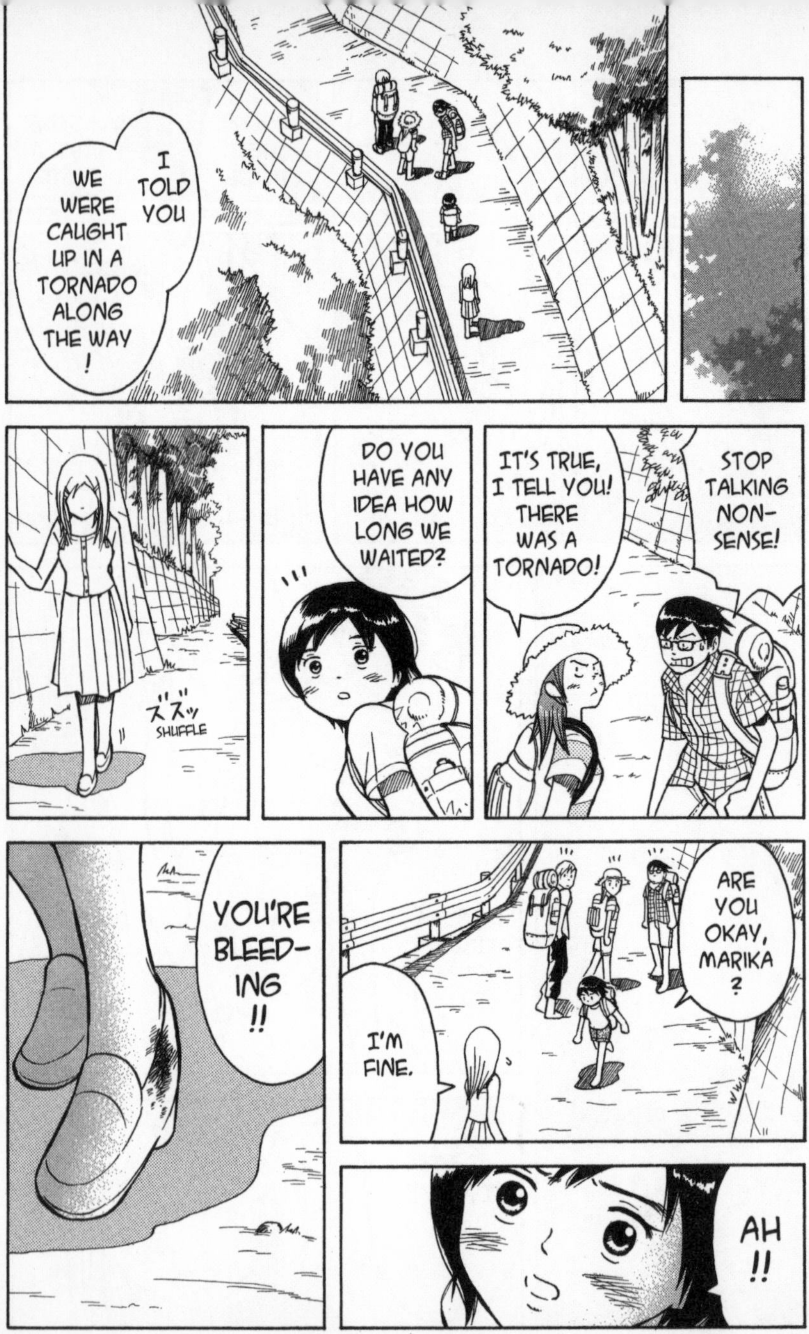
I TOLD YOU
WE WERE CAUGHT UP IN A TORNADO ALONG THE WAY!
STOP TALKING NON-SENSE!
IT'S TRUE, I TELL YOU! THERE WAS A TORNADO!
DO YOU HAVE ANY IDEA HOW LONG WE WAITED?
ズズッ
SHUFFLE
ARE YOU OKAY, MARIKA?
I'M FINE.
AH!!
YOU'RE BLEED-ING!!

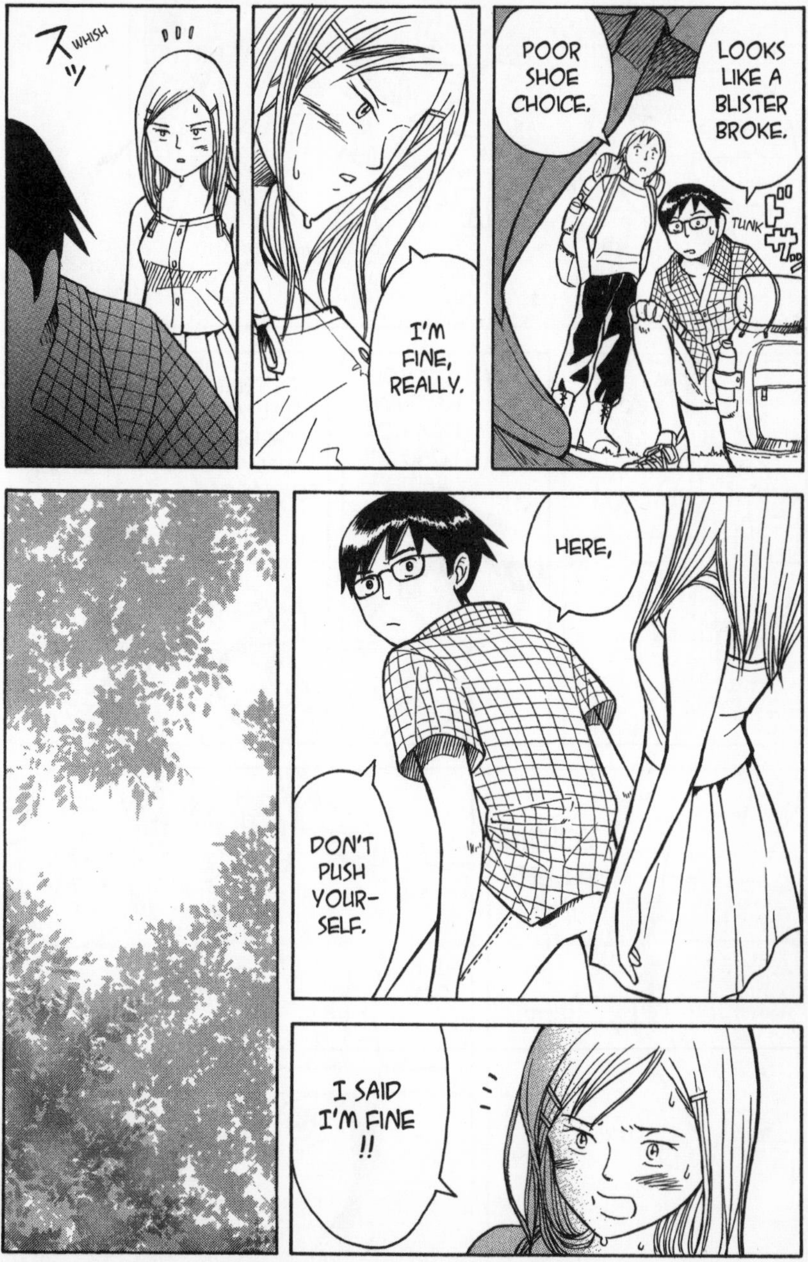
LOOKS LIKE A BLISTER BROKE.
POOR SHOE CHOICE.
TUNK
I'M FINE, REALLY.
スッ
WHISH
HERE,
DON'T PUSH YOURSELF.
I SAID I'M FINE !!

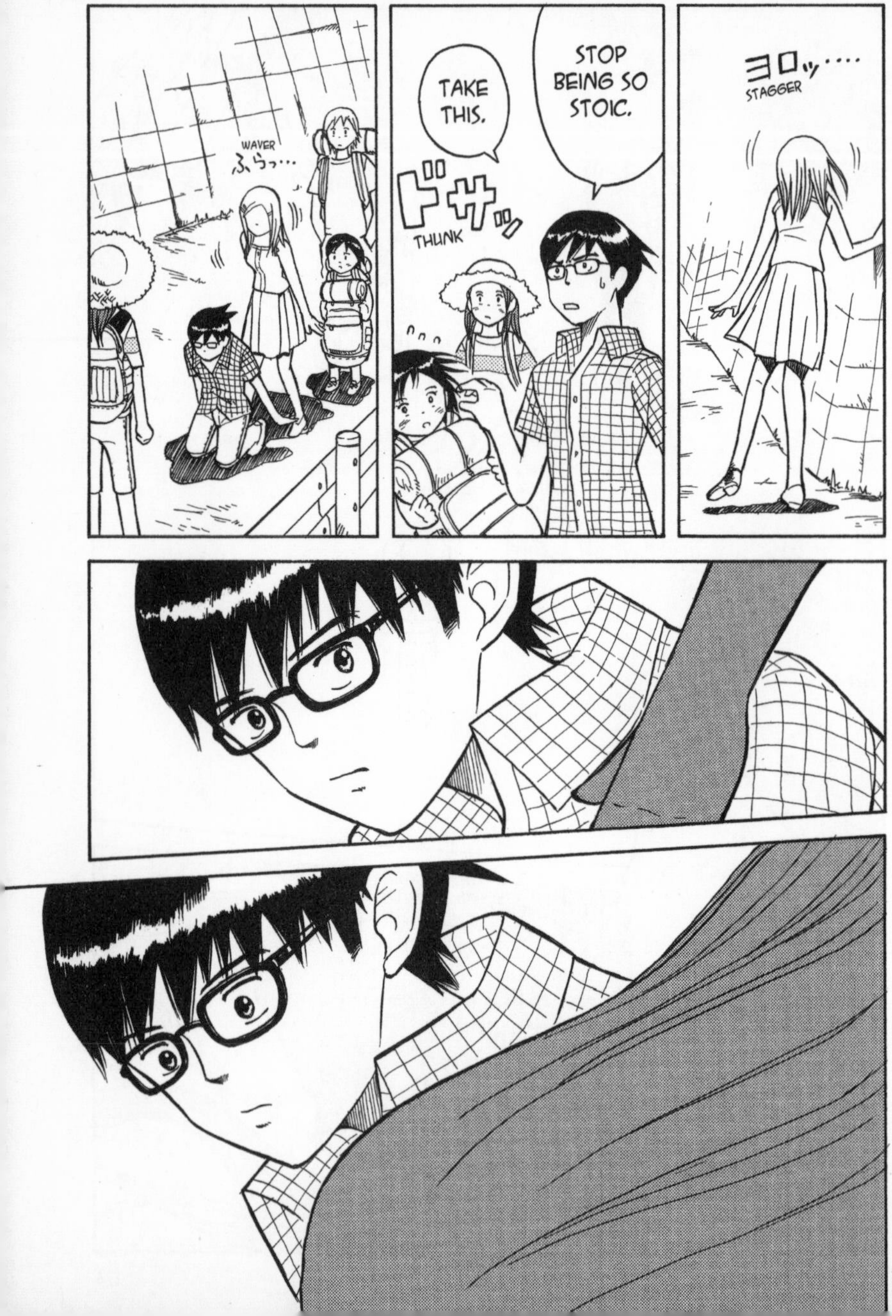
ヨロッ・・・・
STAGGER
STOP BEING SO STOIC.
TAKE THIS.
ドサッ
THUNK
WAVER
ふらっ・・・

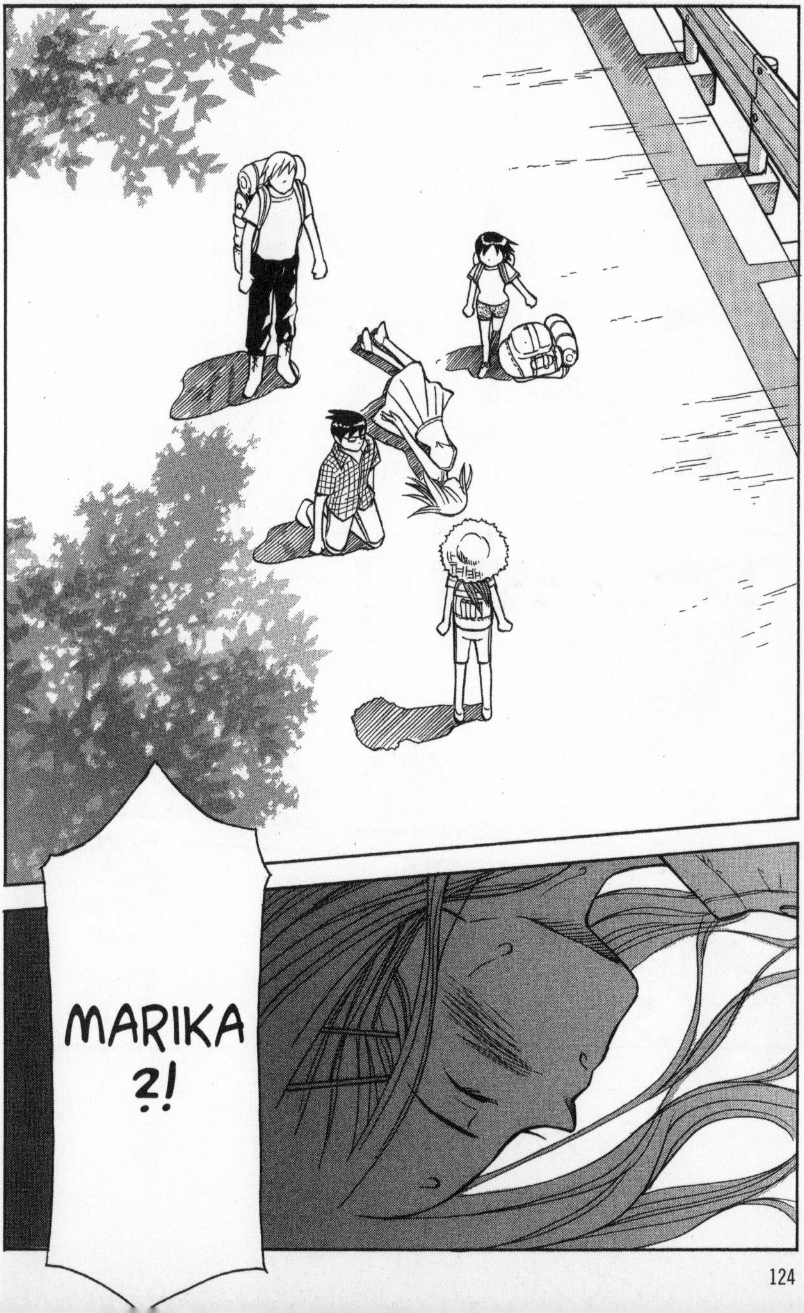
MARIKA ?!

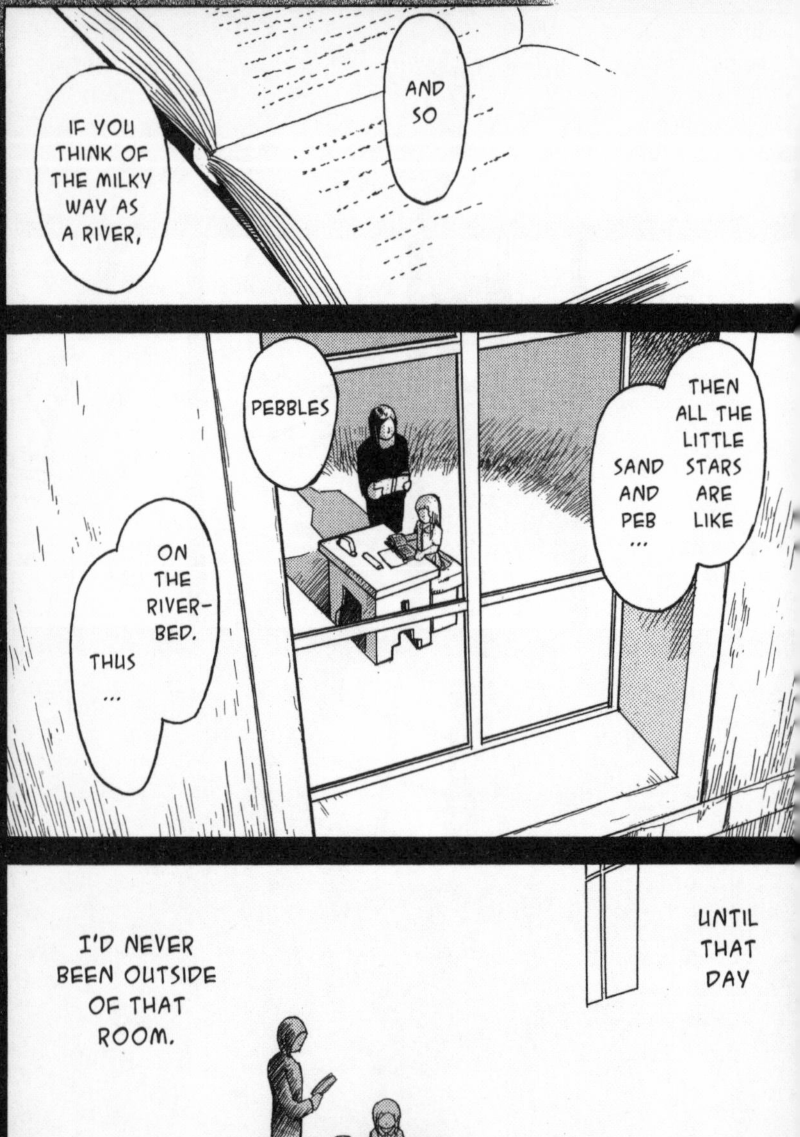
AND SO
IF YOU THINK OF THE MILKY WAY AS A RIVER,
THEN ALL THE LITTLE STARS ARE LIKE
SAND AND PEB...
PEBBLES
ON THE RIVER-BED.
THUS ...
UNTIL THAT DAY
I'D NEVER BEEN OUTSIDE OF THAT ROOM.

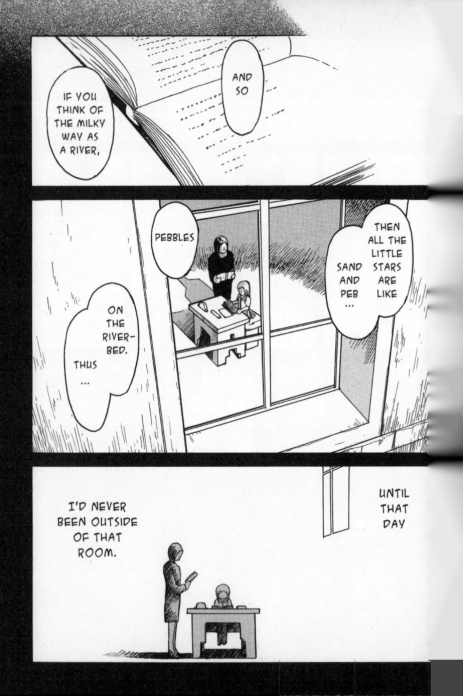

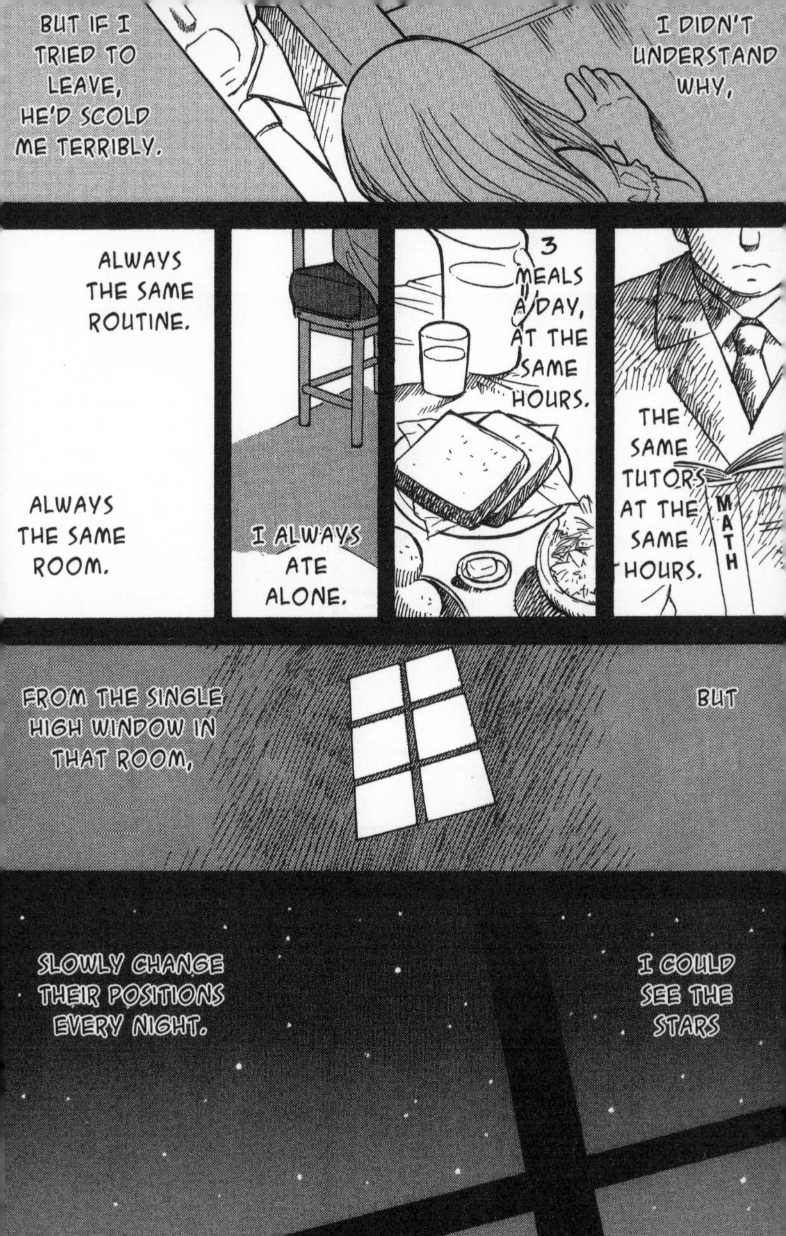
I DIDN'T UNDERSTAND WHY,
BUT IF I TRIED TO LEAVE, HE'D SCOLD ME TERRIBLY.
THE SAME TUTORS AT THE SAME HOURS.
MATH
3 MEALS A DAY, AT THE SAME HOURS.
I ALWAYS ATE ALONE.
ALWAYS THE SAME ROUTINE.
ALWAYS THE SAME ROOM.
BUT
FROM THE SINGLE HIGH WINDOW IN THAT ROOM,
I COULD SEE THE STARS
SLOWLY CHANGE THEIR POSITIONS EVERY NIGHT.

MISSION:13

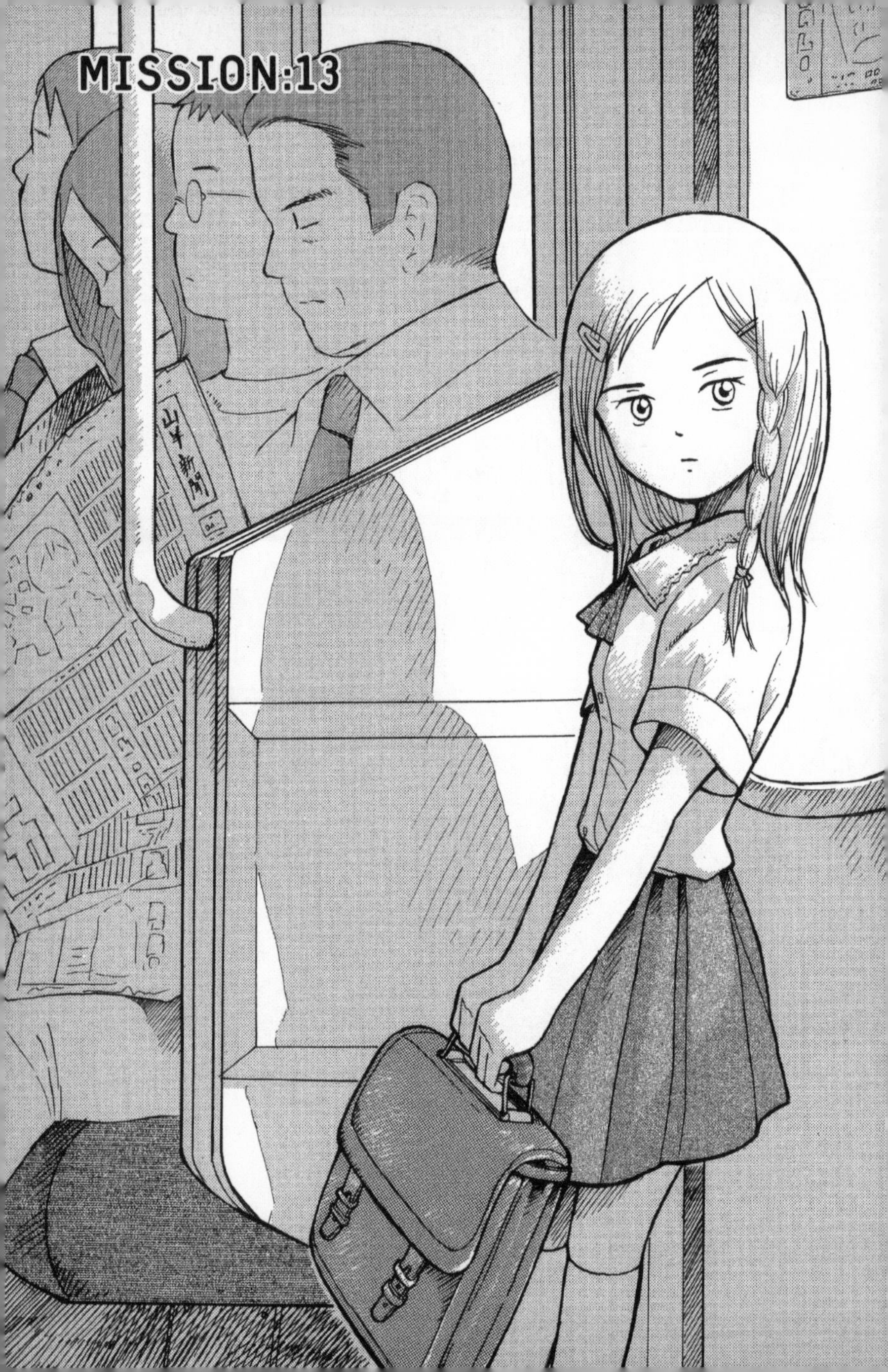

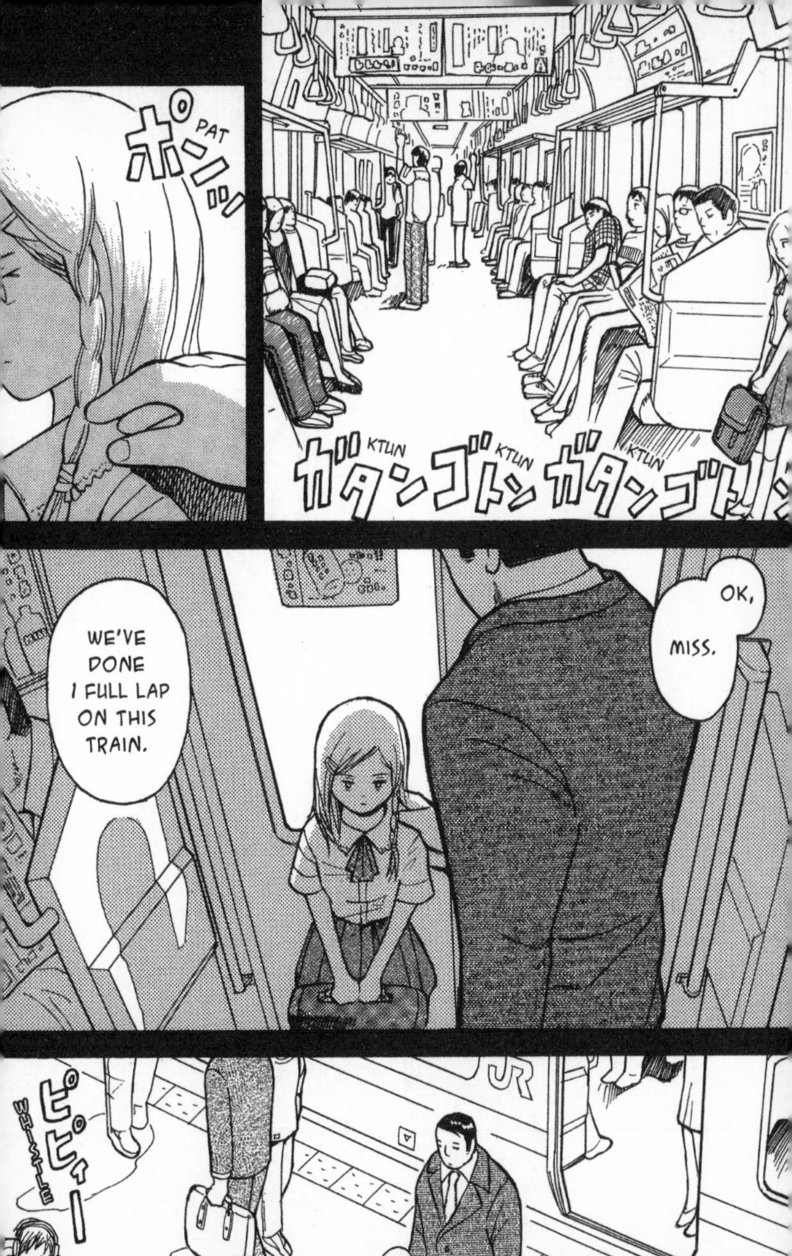
ガタンゴトンガタンゴトン
KTUN KTUN KTUN
ポーン
PAT
OK, MISS.
WE'VE DONE I FULL LAP ON THIS TRAIN.
ピピィー
WHISTLE

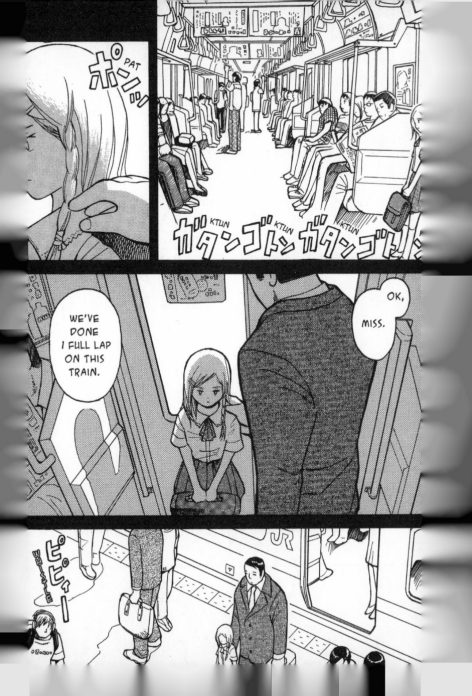

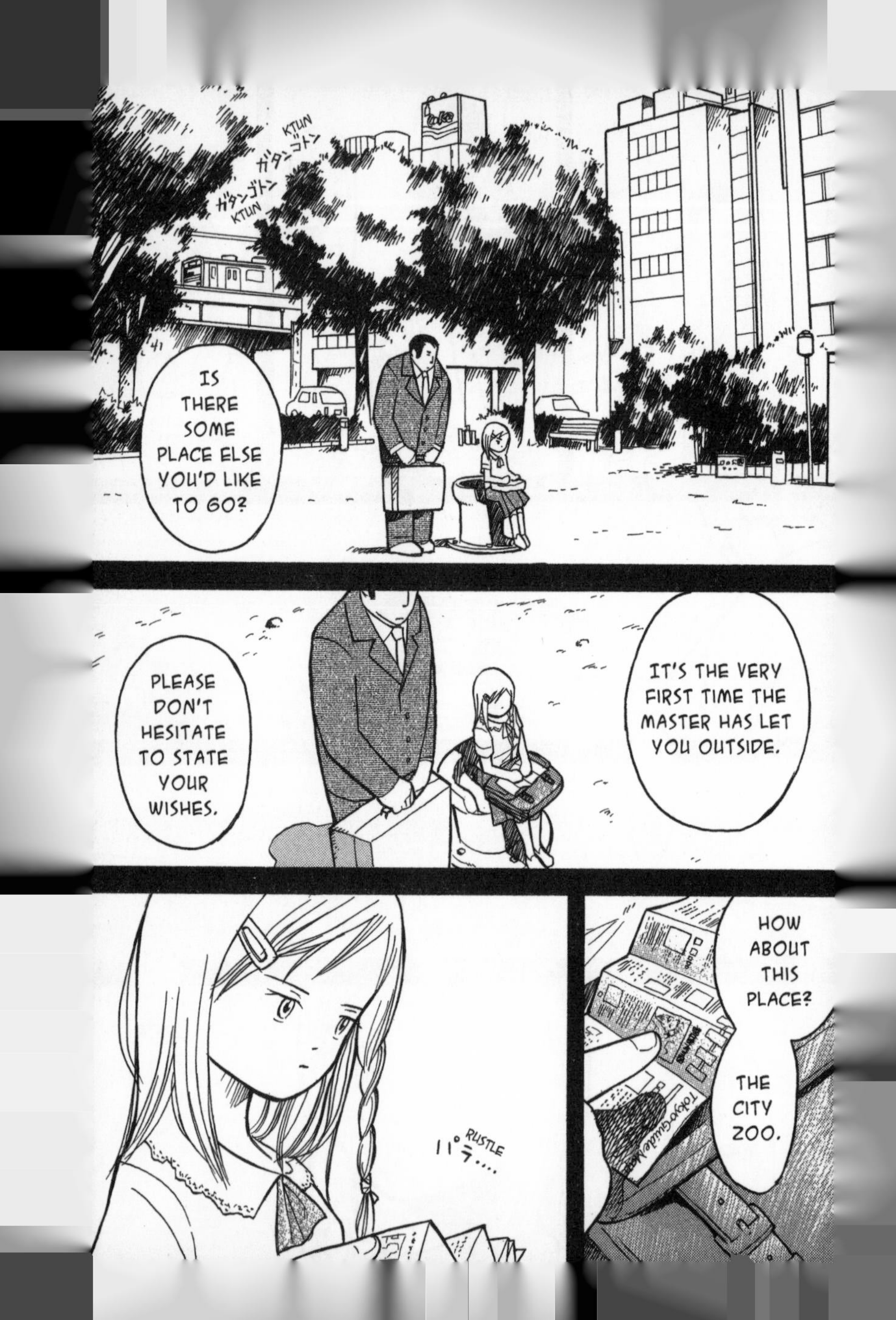

ガタンゴトン
KTUN
ガタンゴトン
KTUN
IS THERE SOME PLACE ELSE YOU'D LIKE TO GO?
IT'S THE VERY FIRST TIME THE MASTER HAS LET YOU OUTSIDE.
PLEASE DON'T HESITATE TO STATE YOUR WISHES.
HOW ABOUT THIS PLACE?
THE CITY ZOO.
Tokyo Guide Map
パラ....
RUSTLE

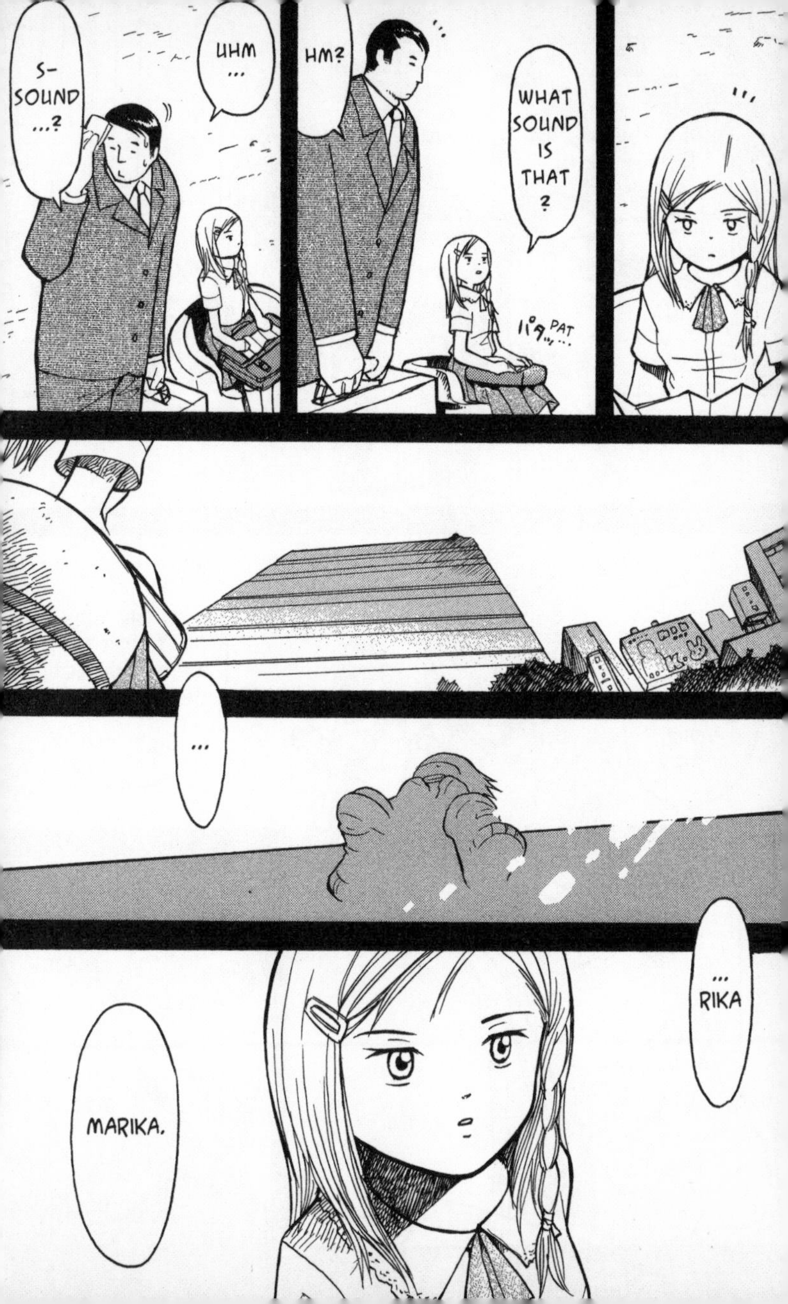

WHAT SOUND IS THAT?
HM?
パタ PAT...
UHM...
S-SOUND...?
...
...RIKA
MARIKA.

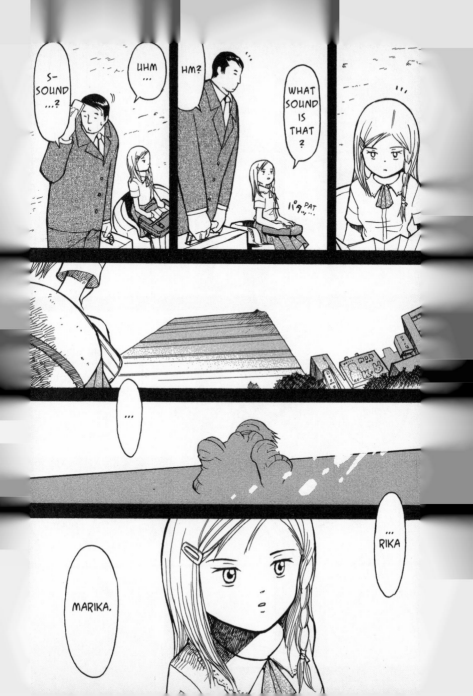

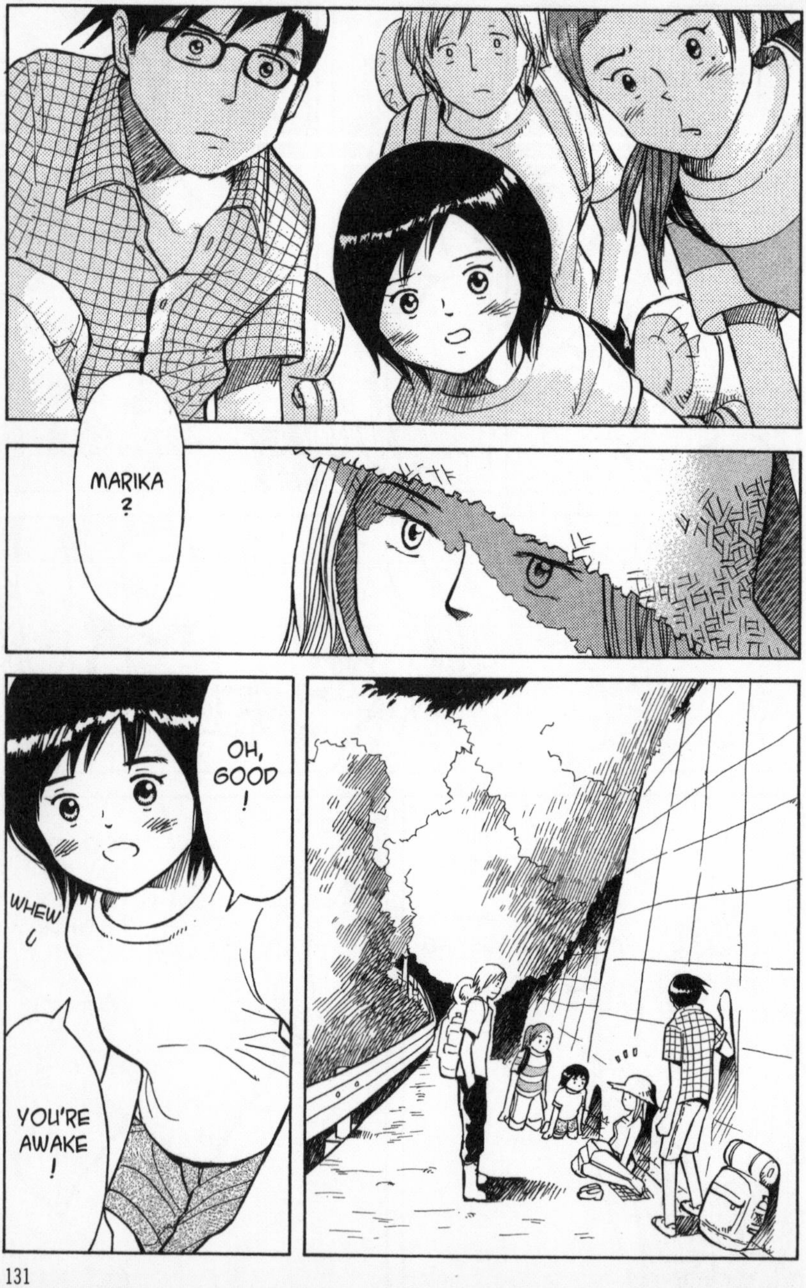
MARIKA?
OH, GOOD!
WHEW
YOU'RE AWAKE!

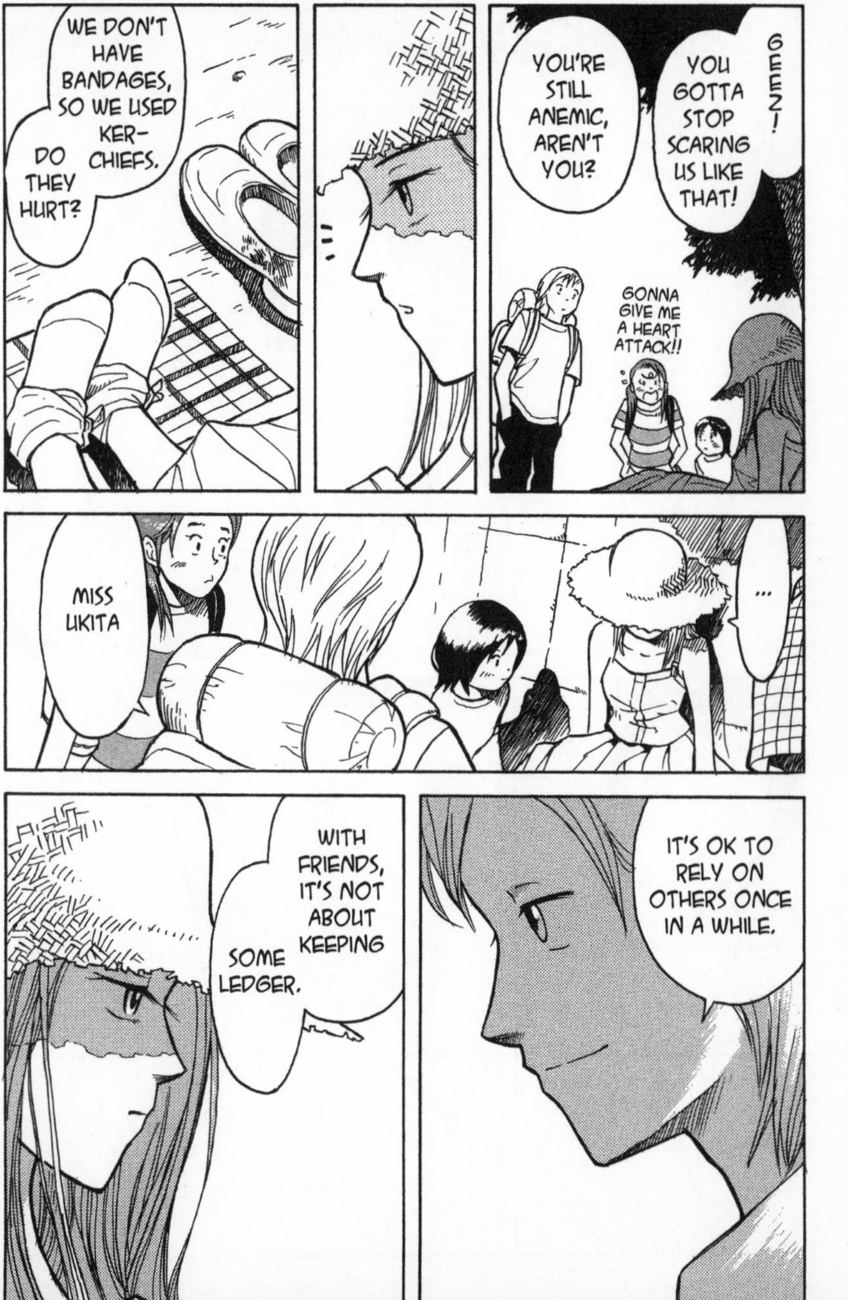
GEEZ!
YOU GOTTA STOP SCARING US LIKE THAT!
YOU'RE STILL ANEMIC, AREN'T YOU?
GONNA GIVE ME A HEART ATTACK!!
WE DON'T HAVE BANDAGES, SO WE USED KER-CHIEFS.
DO THEY HURT?
...
MISS UKITA
IT'S OK TO RELY ON OTHERS ONCE IN A WHILE.
WITH FRIENDS, IT'S NOT ABOUT KEEPING SOME LEDGER.

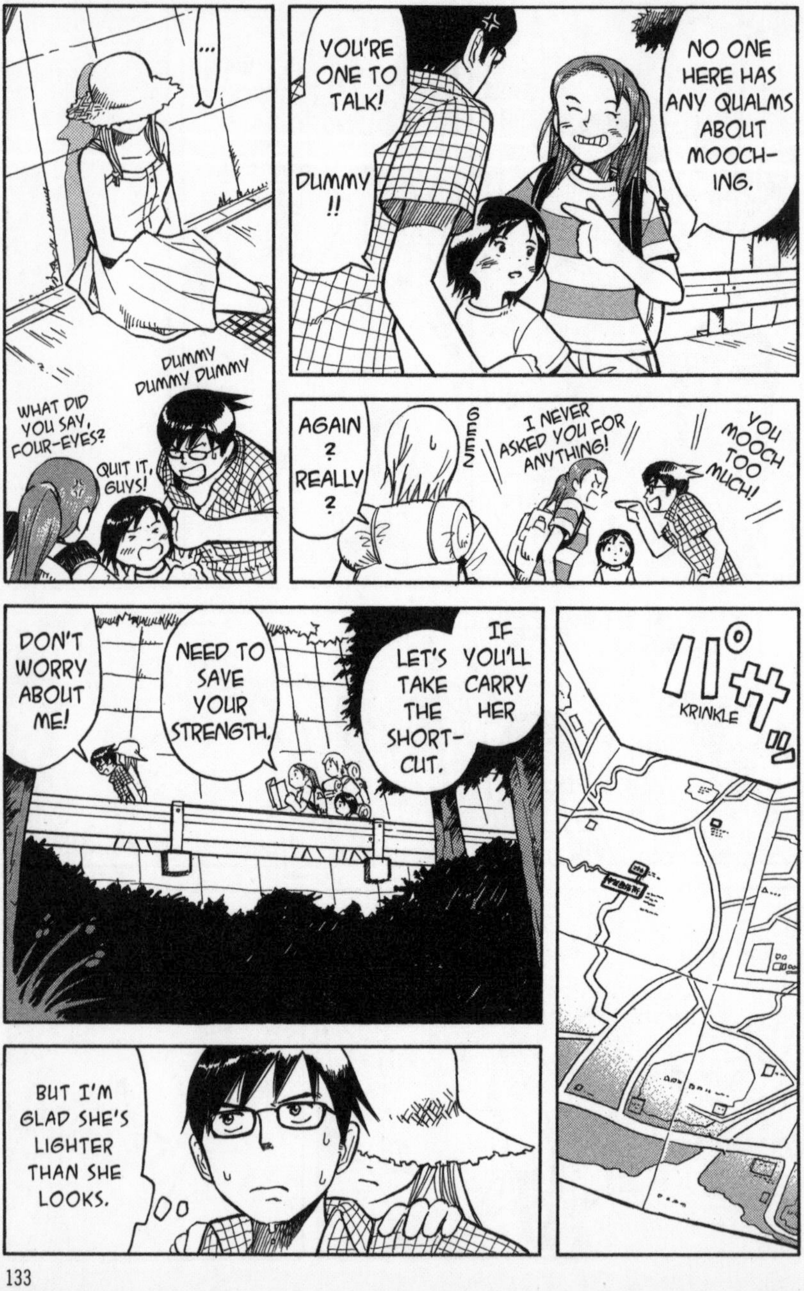
NO ONE HERE HAS ANY QUALMS ABOUT MOOCHING.
YOU'RE ONE TO TALK!
DUMMY !!
...
YOU MOOCH TOO MUCH!
I NEVER ASKED YOU FOR ANYTHING!
GEEZ
AGAIN? REALLY?
DUMMY DUMMY DUMMY
WHAT DID YOU SAY, FOUR-EYES?
QUIT IT, GUYS!
パサッ
KRINKLE
IF YOU'LL CARRY HER
LET'S TAKE THE SHORT-CUT.
NEED TO SAVE YOUR STRENGTH.
DON'T WORRY ABOUT ME!
BUT I'M GLAD SHE'S LIGHTER THAN SHE LOOKS.

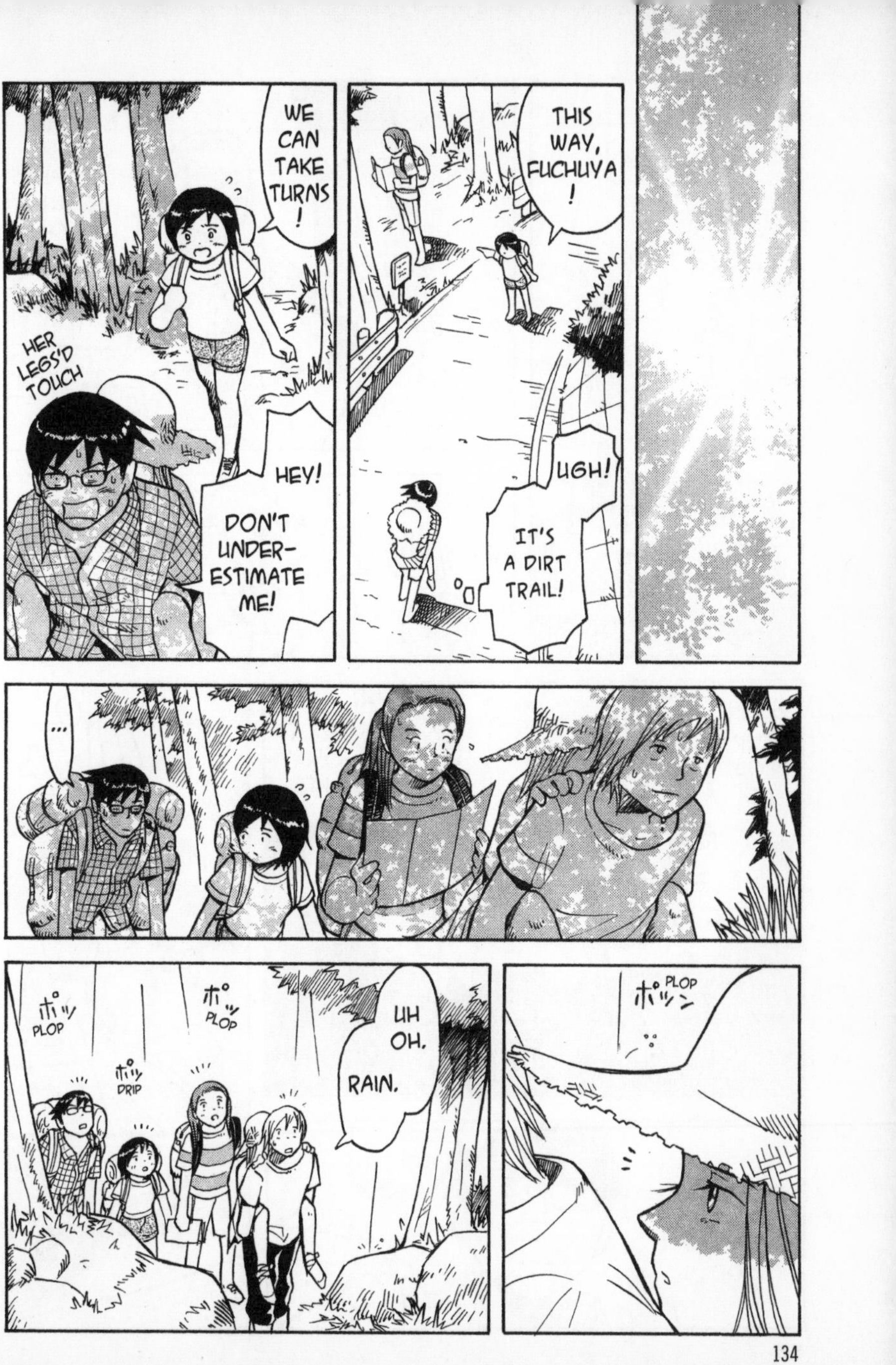
THIS WAY, FUCHUYA!
UGH!
IT'S A DIRT TRAIL!
WE CAN TAKE TURNS!
HEY!
DON'T UNDER-ESTIMATE ME!
HER LEGS'D TOUCH
...
ポツン PLOP
UH OH.
RAIN.
ポッ PLOP
ポッ PLOP
ポッ DRIP

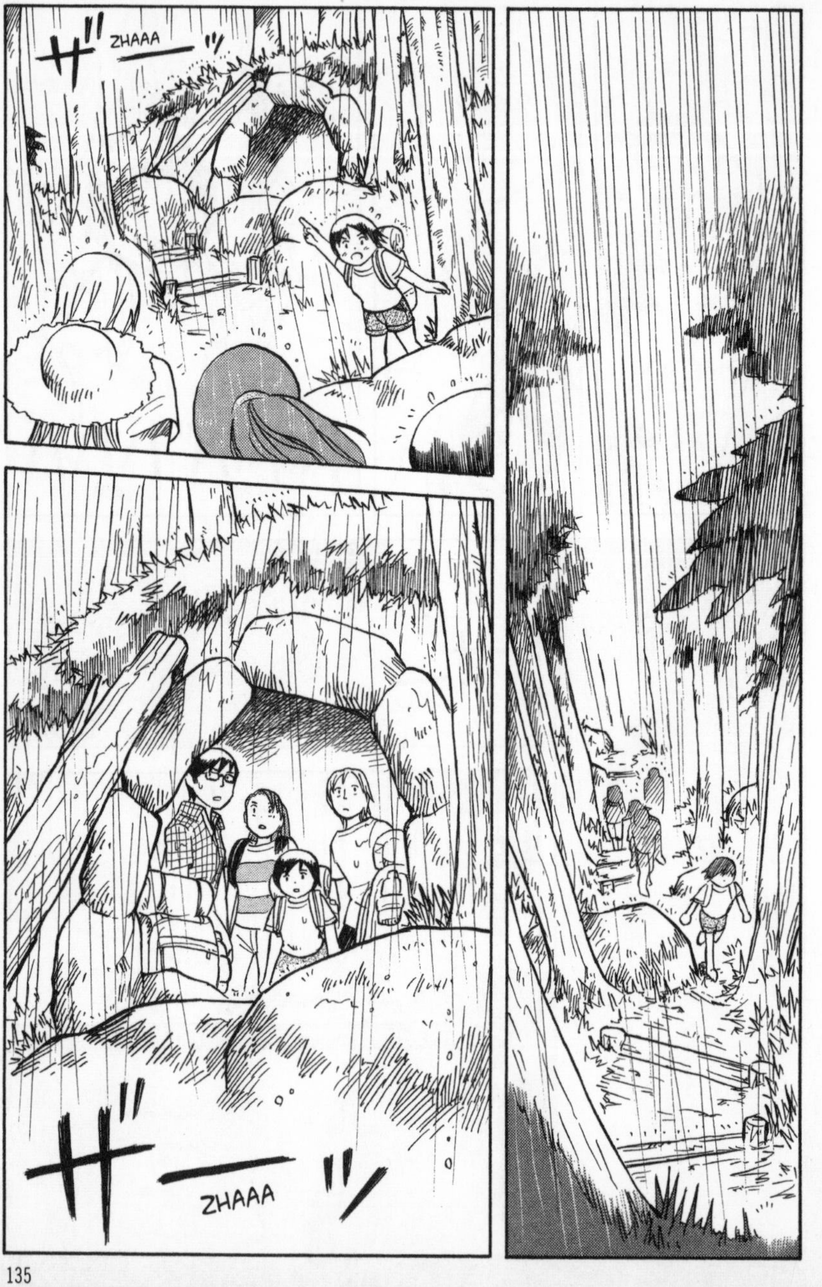
ザーッ
ZHAAA
ザーッ
ZHAAA

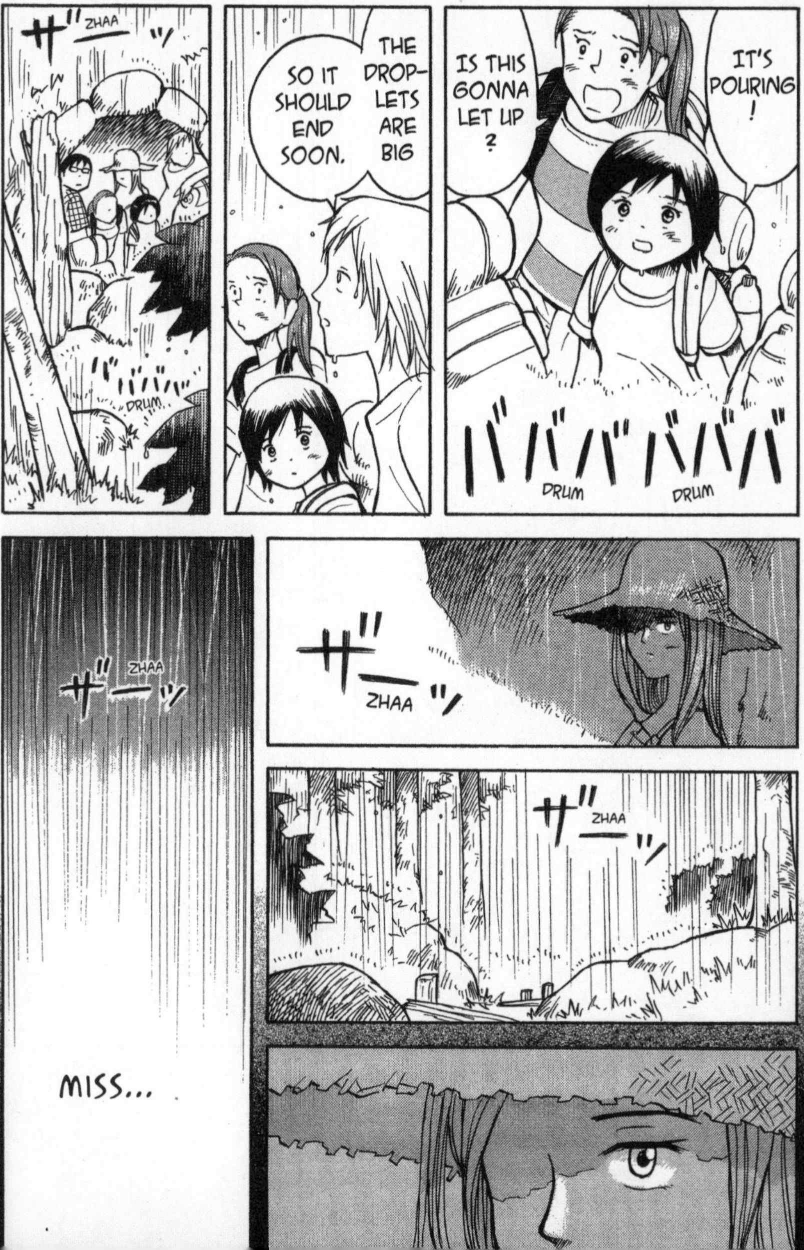
IT'S POURING!
IS THIS GONNA LET UP?
バババババ
DRUM
DRUM
THE DROP-LETS ARE BIG
SO IT SHOULD END SOON.
ザーッ
ZHAA
ババババ
DRUM
ザーッ
ZHAA
ザーッ
ZHAA
ザーッ
ZHAA
MISS...

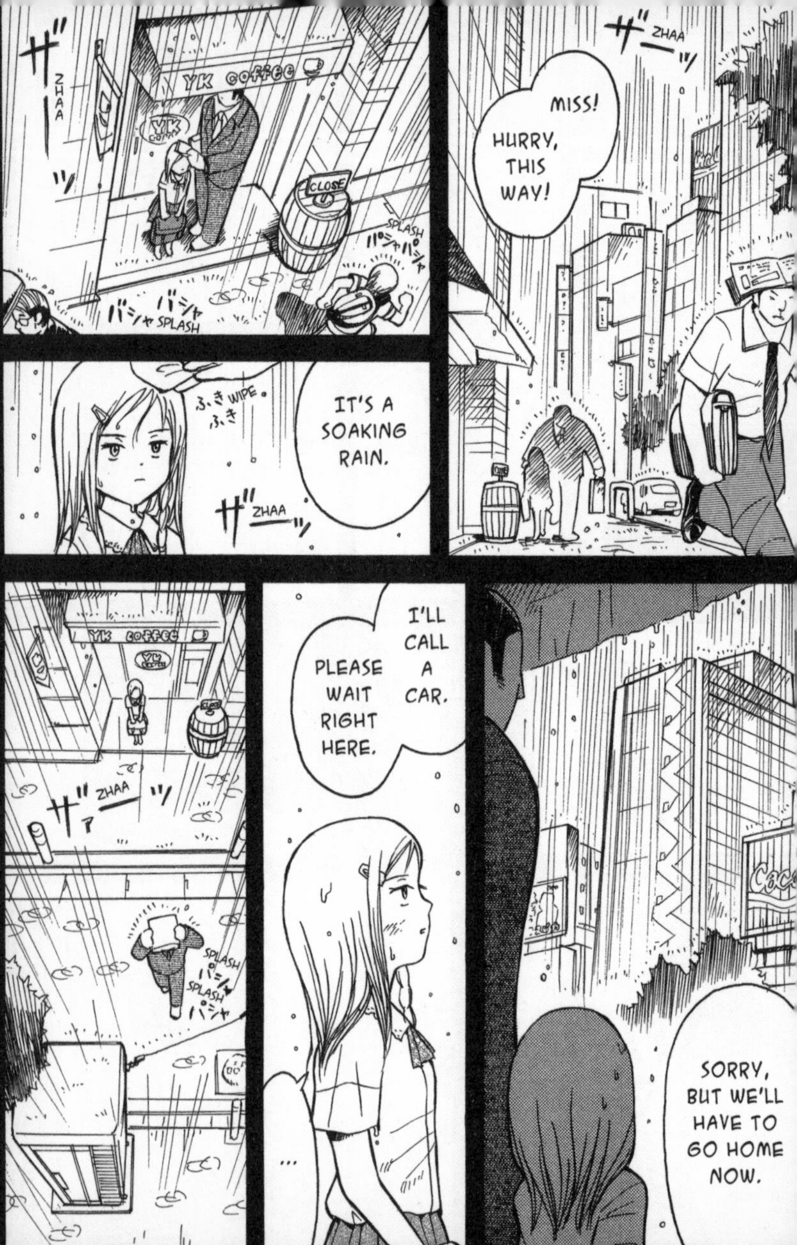
ザー ZHAA ッ
MISS!
HURRY, THIS WAY!
ザー ZHAA ッ
YK coffee
CLOSE
SPLASH
バシャ SPLASH
IT'S A SOAKING RAIN.
ふき WIPE ふき
ザー ZHAA ッ
SORRY, BUT WE'LL HAVE TO GO HOME NOW.
I'LL CALL A CAR.
PLEASE WAIT RIGHT HERE.
...
YK coffee
ザー ZHAA ッ
SPLASH
SPLASH

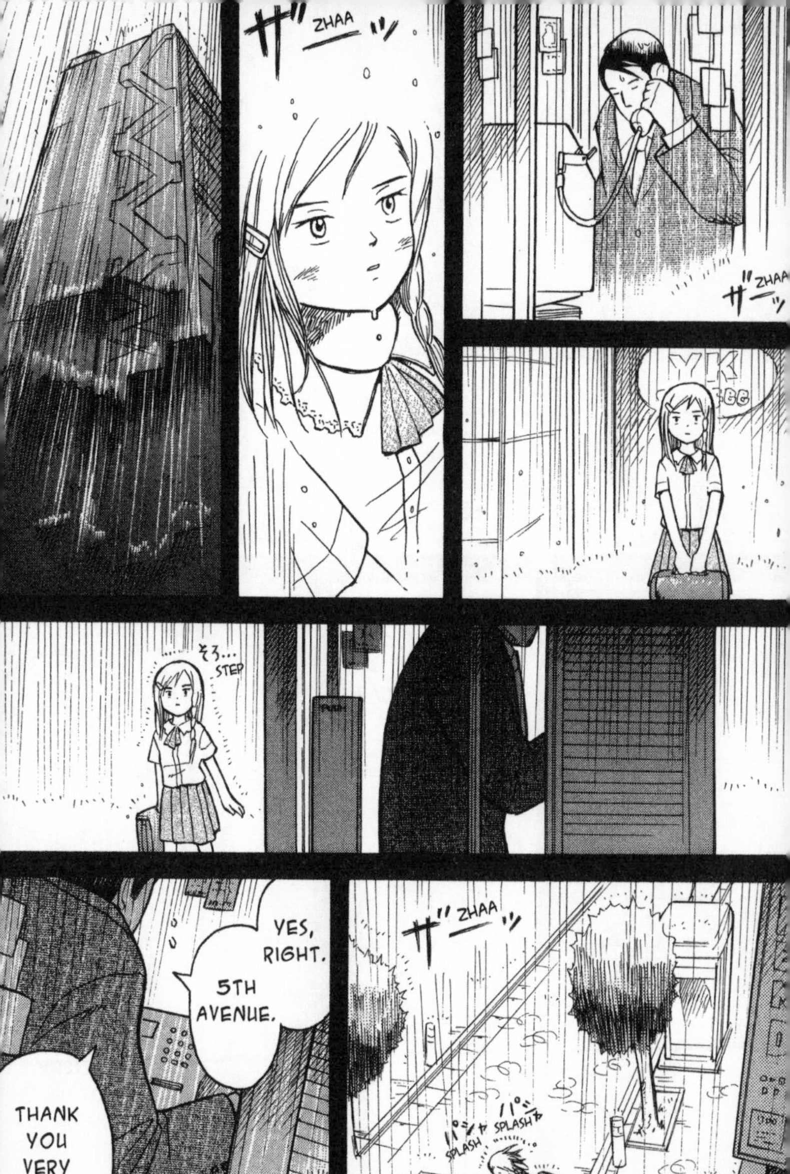

ザーッ ZHAA
YK
ザーッ ZHAA
そろ… STEP
ザーッ ZHAA
パシャ SPLASH
パシャ SPLASH
YES, RIGHT.
5TH AVENUE.
THANK YOU VERY MUCH.

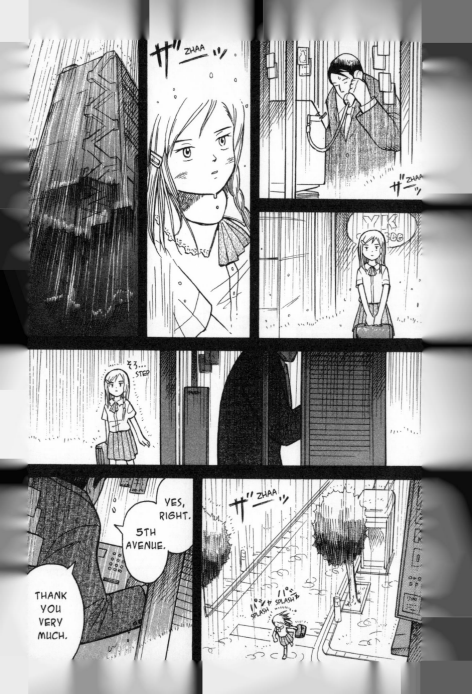

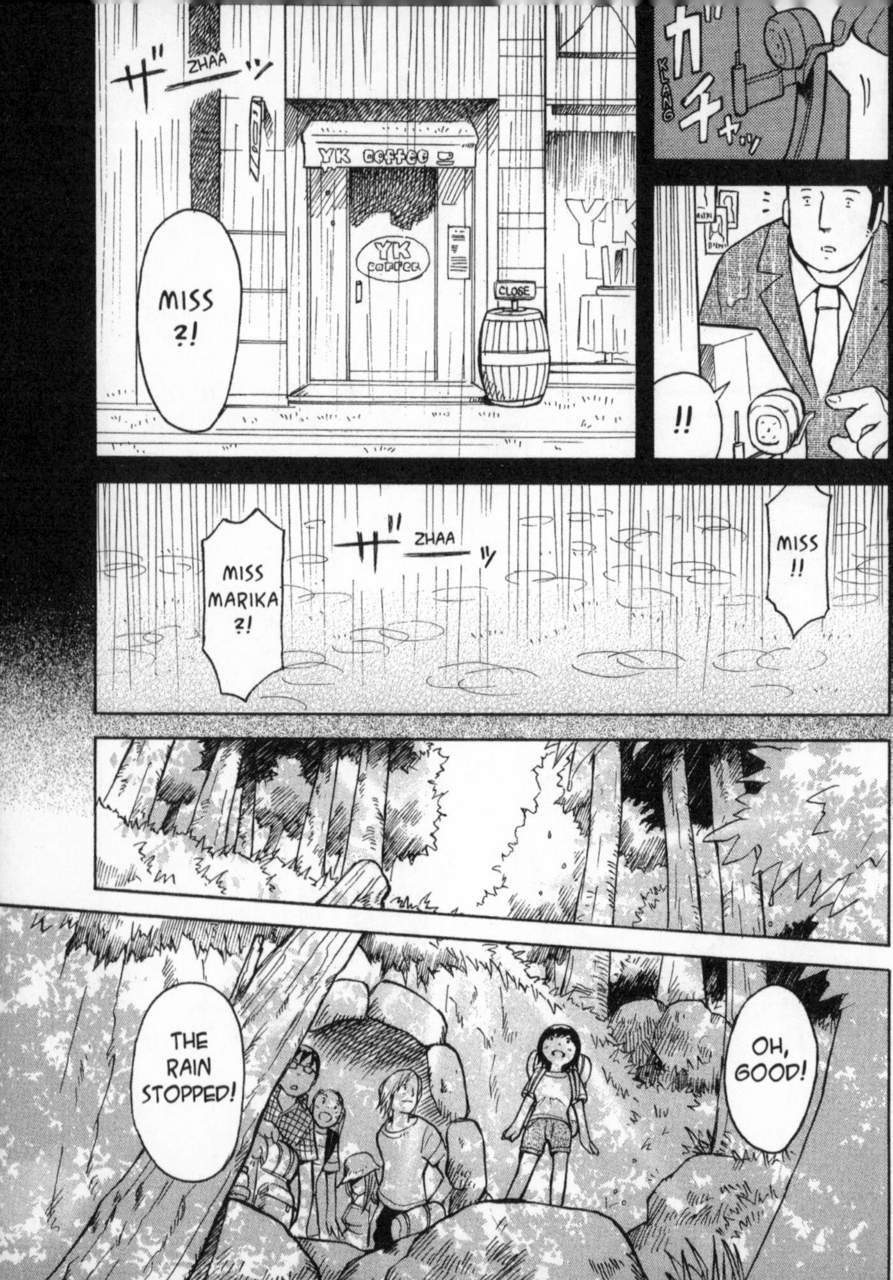
ガチャッ
KLANG
!!
ザーッ
ZHAA
MISS ?!
MISS !!
ザーッ
ZHAA
MISS MARIKA ?!
OH, GOOD!
THE RAIN STOPPED!

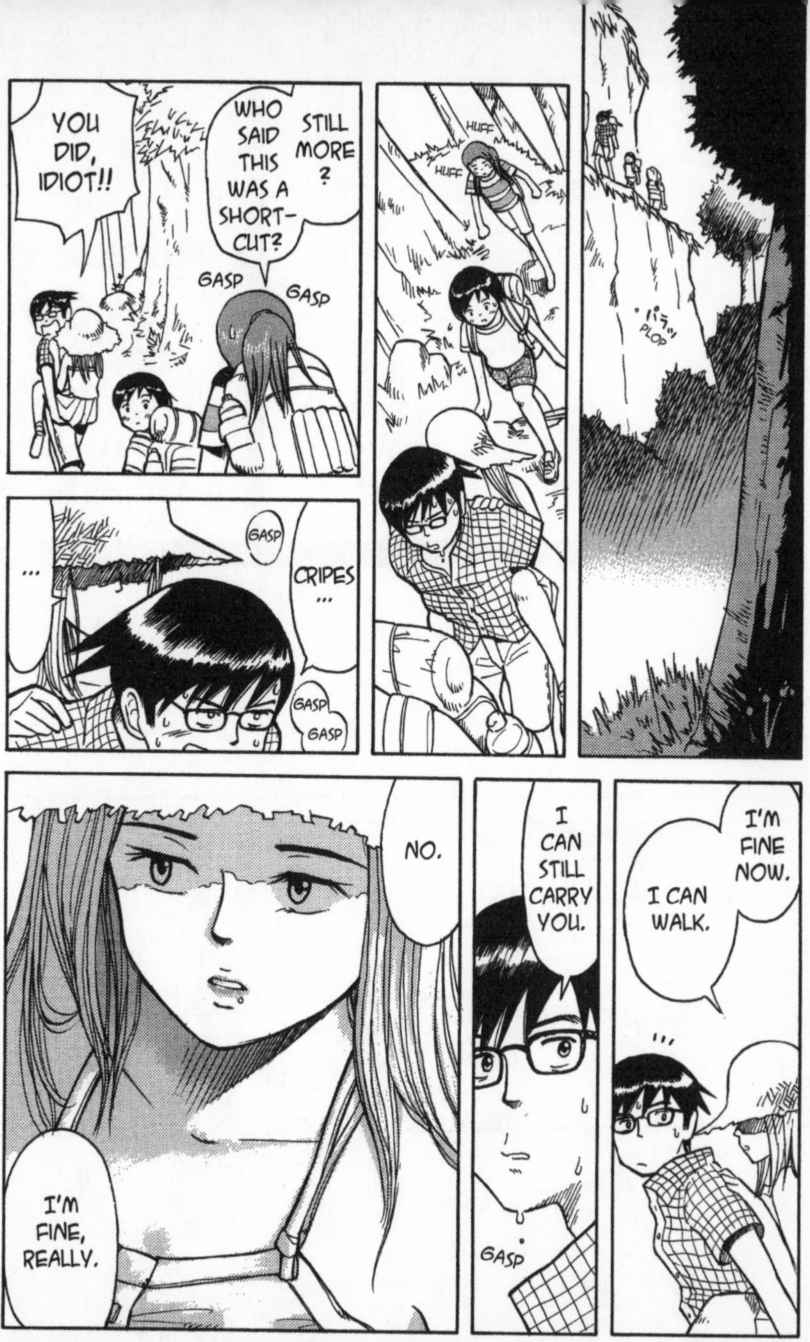
パラッ
PLOP
HUFF
HUFF
STILL MORE?
WHO SAID THIS WAS A SHORT-CUT?
YOU DID, IDIOT!!
GASP
GASP
GASP
CRIPES...
...
GASP
GASP
I'M FINE NOW.
I CAN WALK.
...
I CAN STILL CARRY YOU.
GASP
NO.
I'M FINE, REALLY.

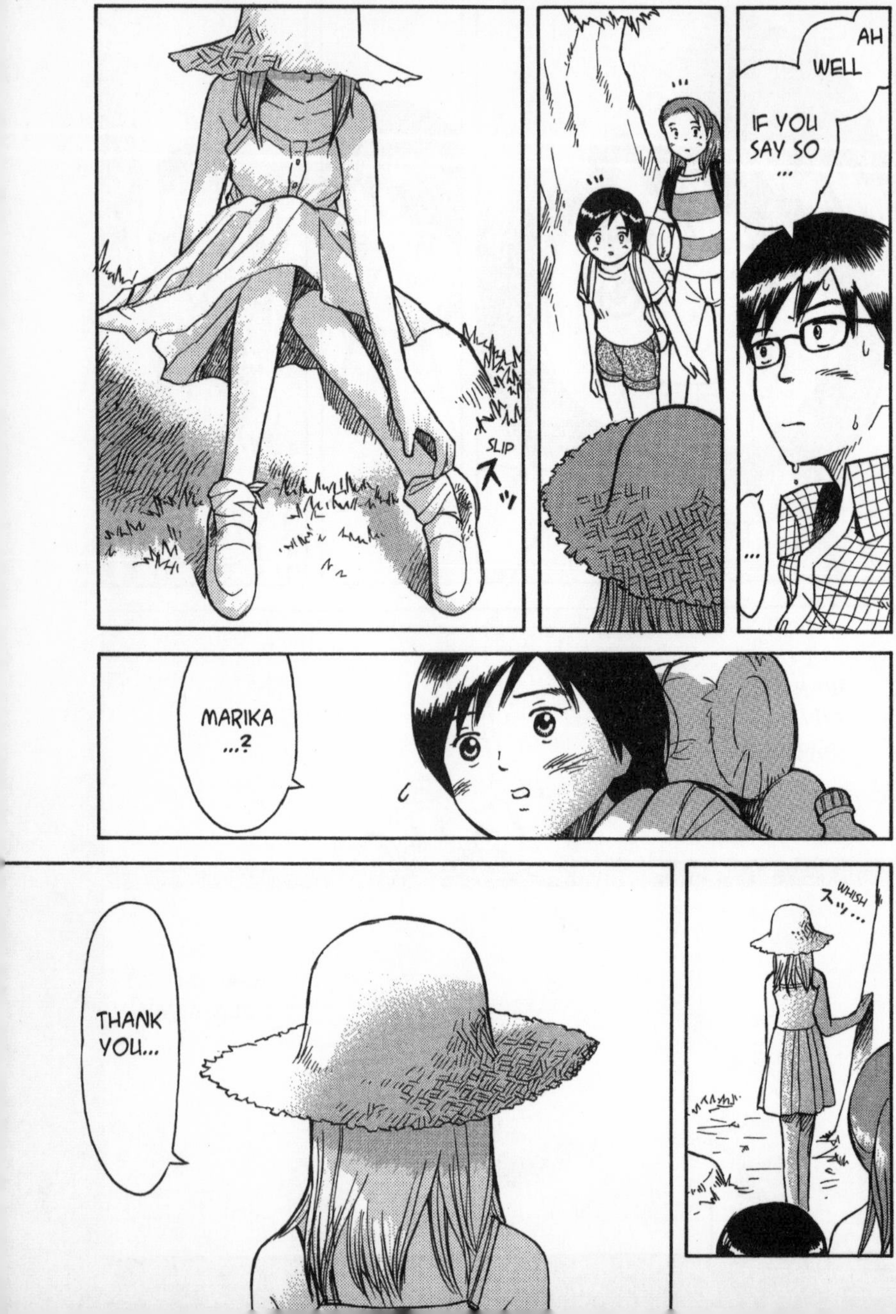
AH WELL
IF YOU SAY SO ...
...
SLIP
スッ
MARIKA ...?
WHISH
スッ...
THANK YOU...

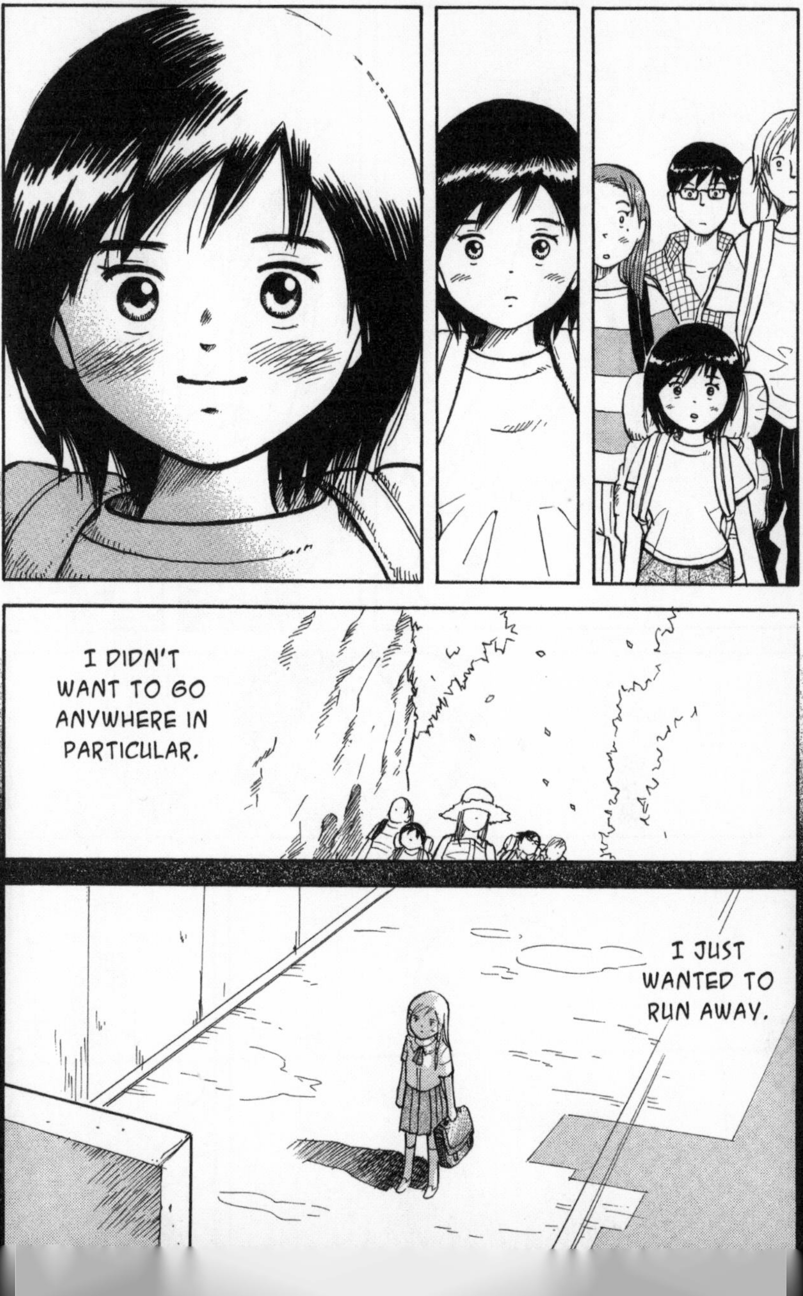
I DIDN'T WANT TO GO ANYWHERE IN PARTICULAR.
I JUST WANTED TO RUN AWAY.

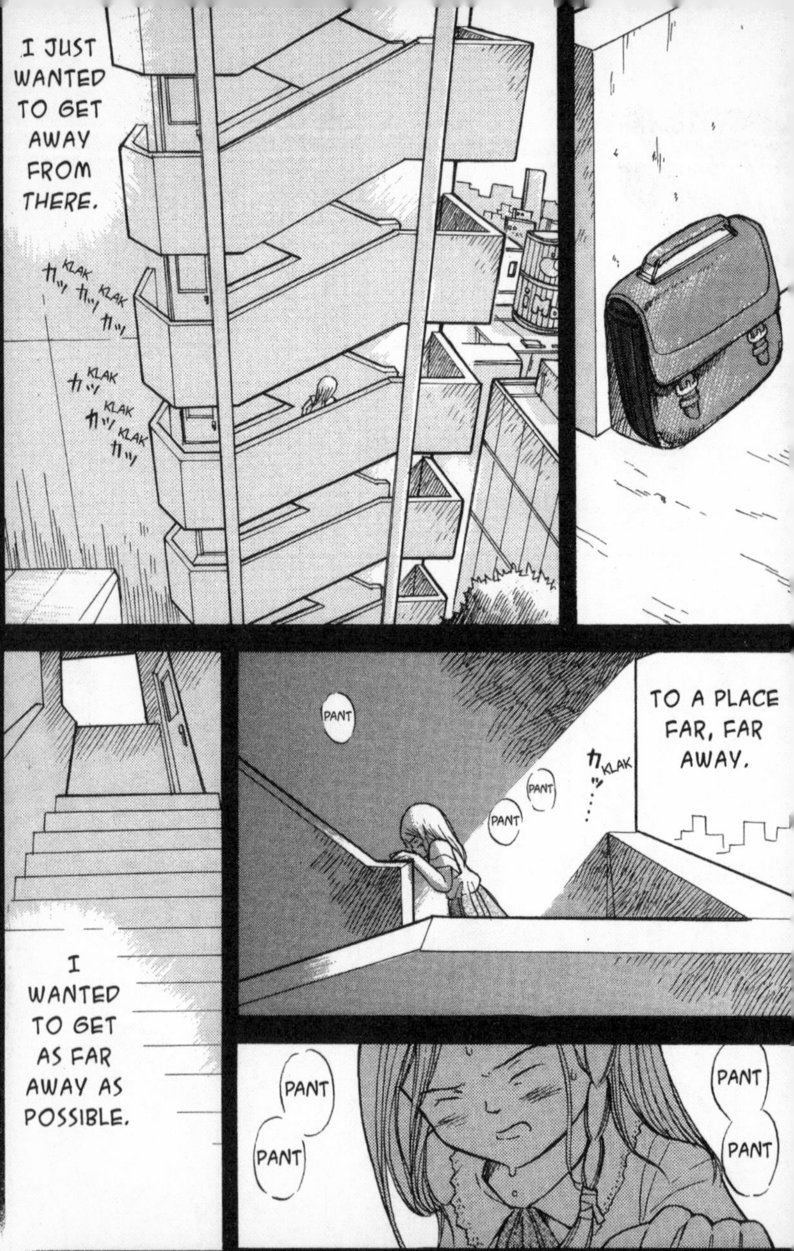
I JUST WANTED TO GET AWAY FROM THERE.
カッ KLAK
カッ KLAK
カッ
カッ KLAK
カッ KLAK
カッ KLAK
カッ
TO A PLACE FAR, FAR AWAY.
カッ KLAK
PANT
PANT
PANT
PANT
PANT
PANT
PANT
I WANTED TO GET AS FAR AWAY AS POSSIBLE.

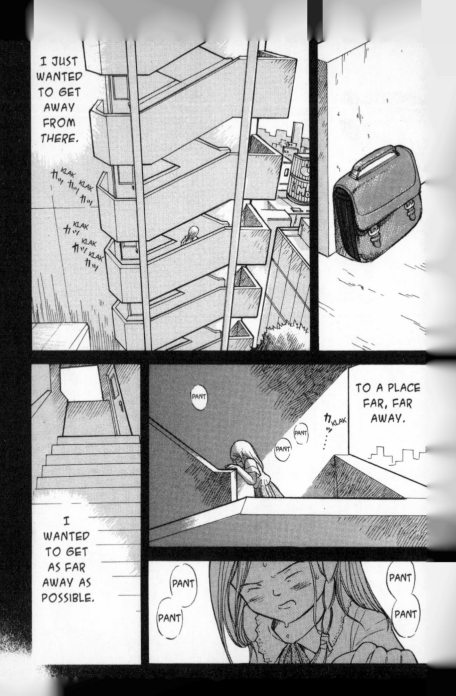

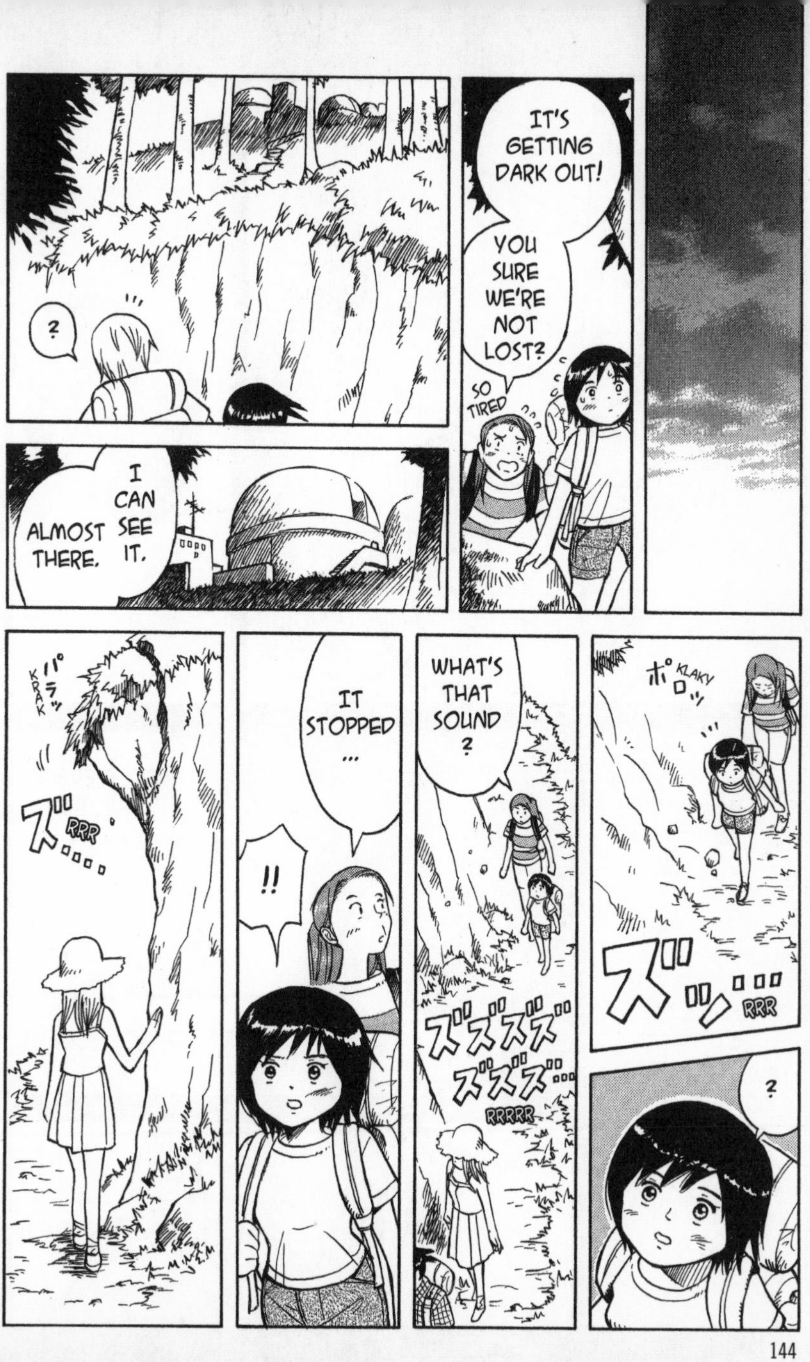
IT'S GETTING DARK OUT!
YOU SURE WE'RE NOT LOST?
SO TIRED
?
I CAN SEE IT.
ALMOST THERE.
KLAKY
RRR
?
WHAT'S THAT SOUND?
RRRRR
IT STOPPED...
!!
KRAK
RRR

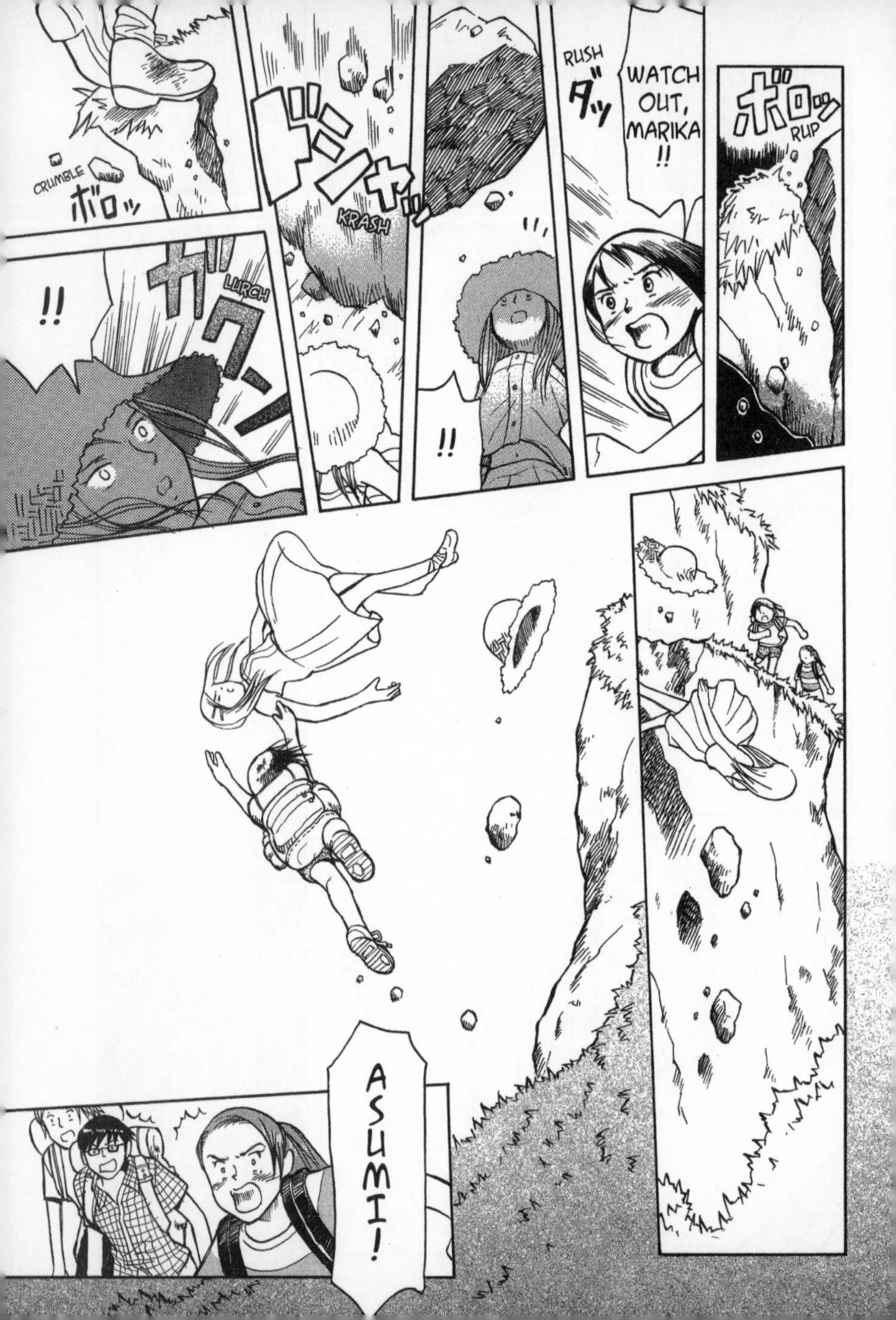
ボロッ
RUP
WATCH OUT, MARIKA !!
RUSH
ダッ
!!
ドシャッ
KRASH
CRUMBLE
ボロッ
ガクン
LURCH
!!
ASUMI!

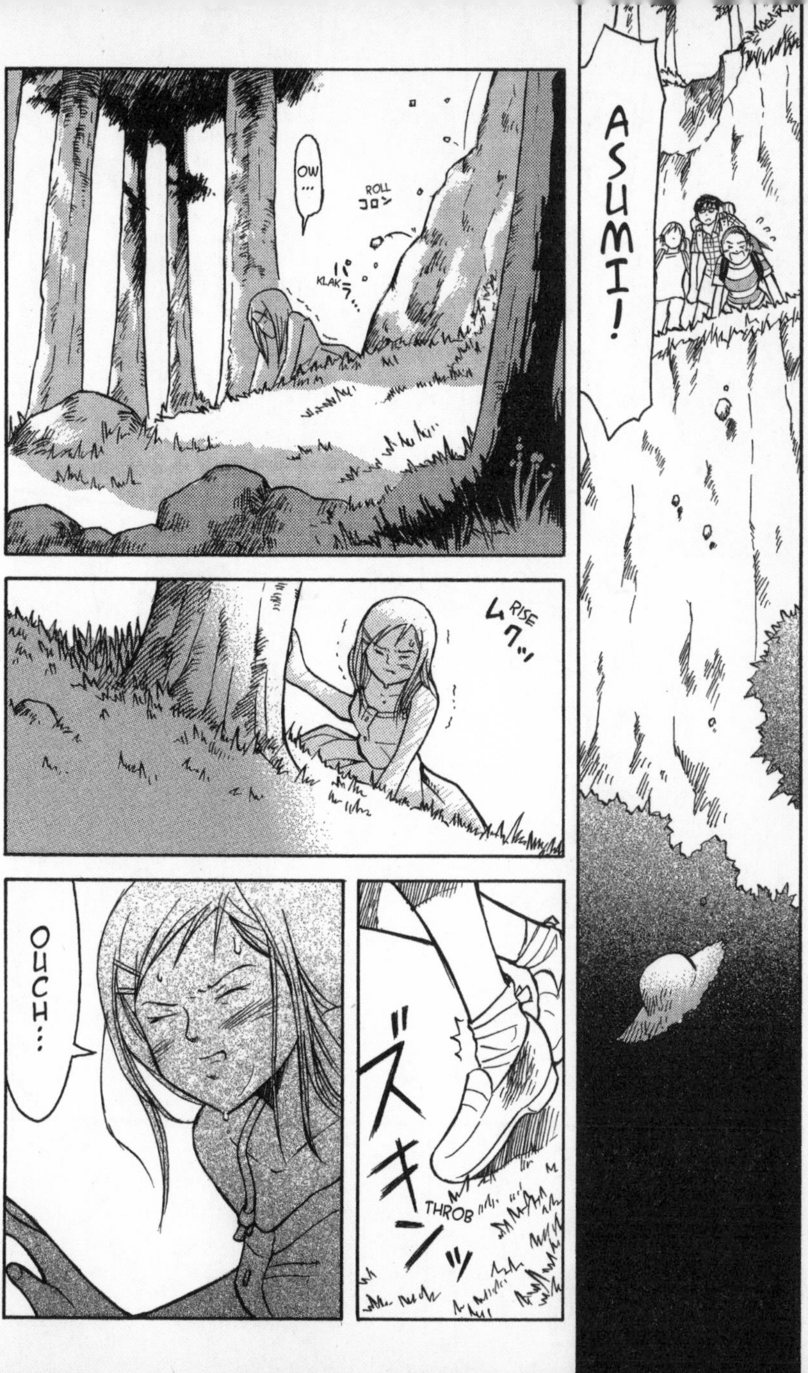
ASUMI!
OW...
ROLL
コロン
KLAK
パラ...
RISE
ムクッ
THROB
ズキーンッ
OUCH...

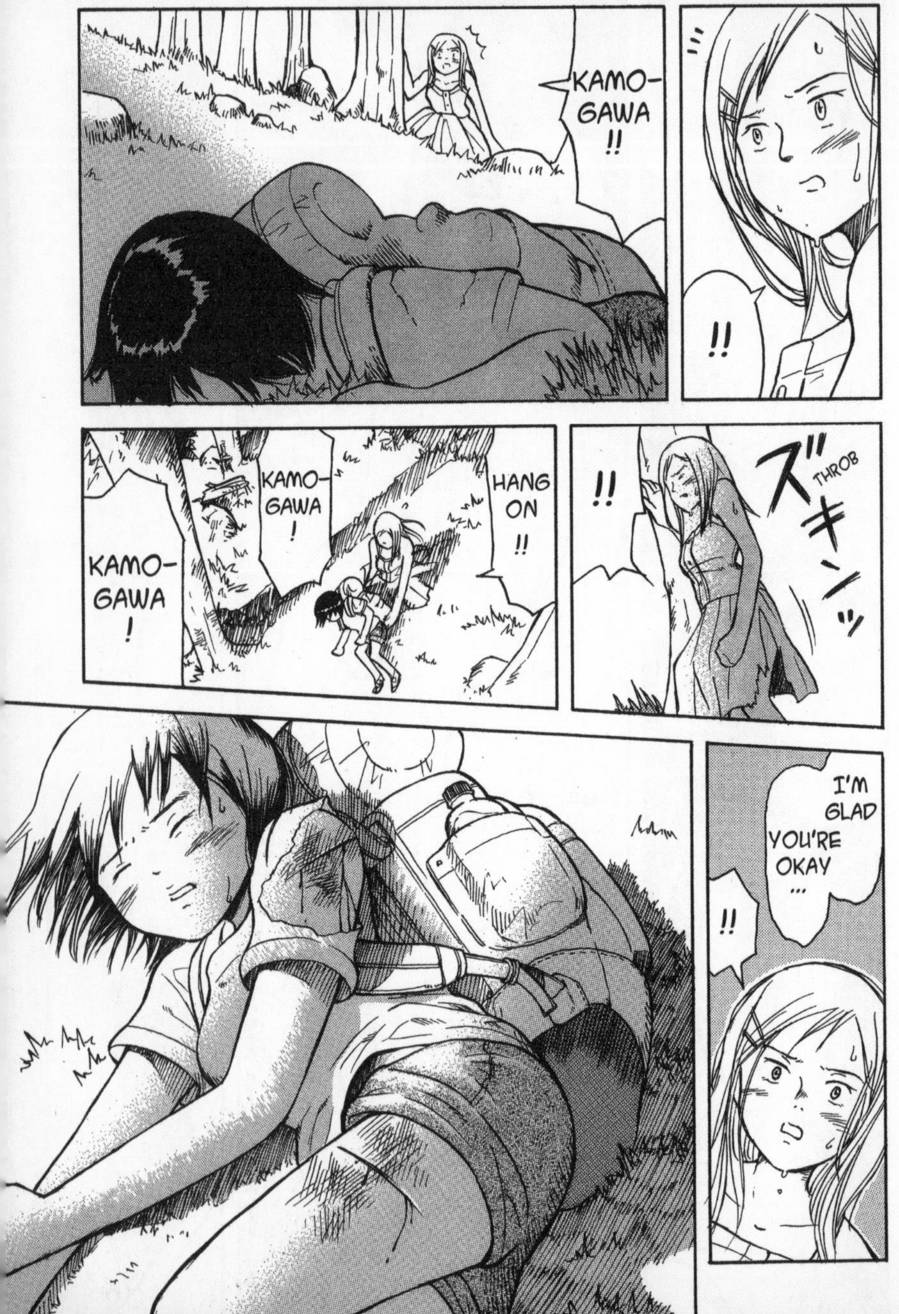
!!
KAMO-GAWA !!
!!
ズキンッ
THROB
HANG ON !!
KAMO-GAWA !
KAMO-GAWA !
I'M GLAD YOU'RE OKAY ...
!!

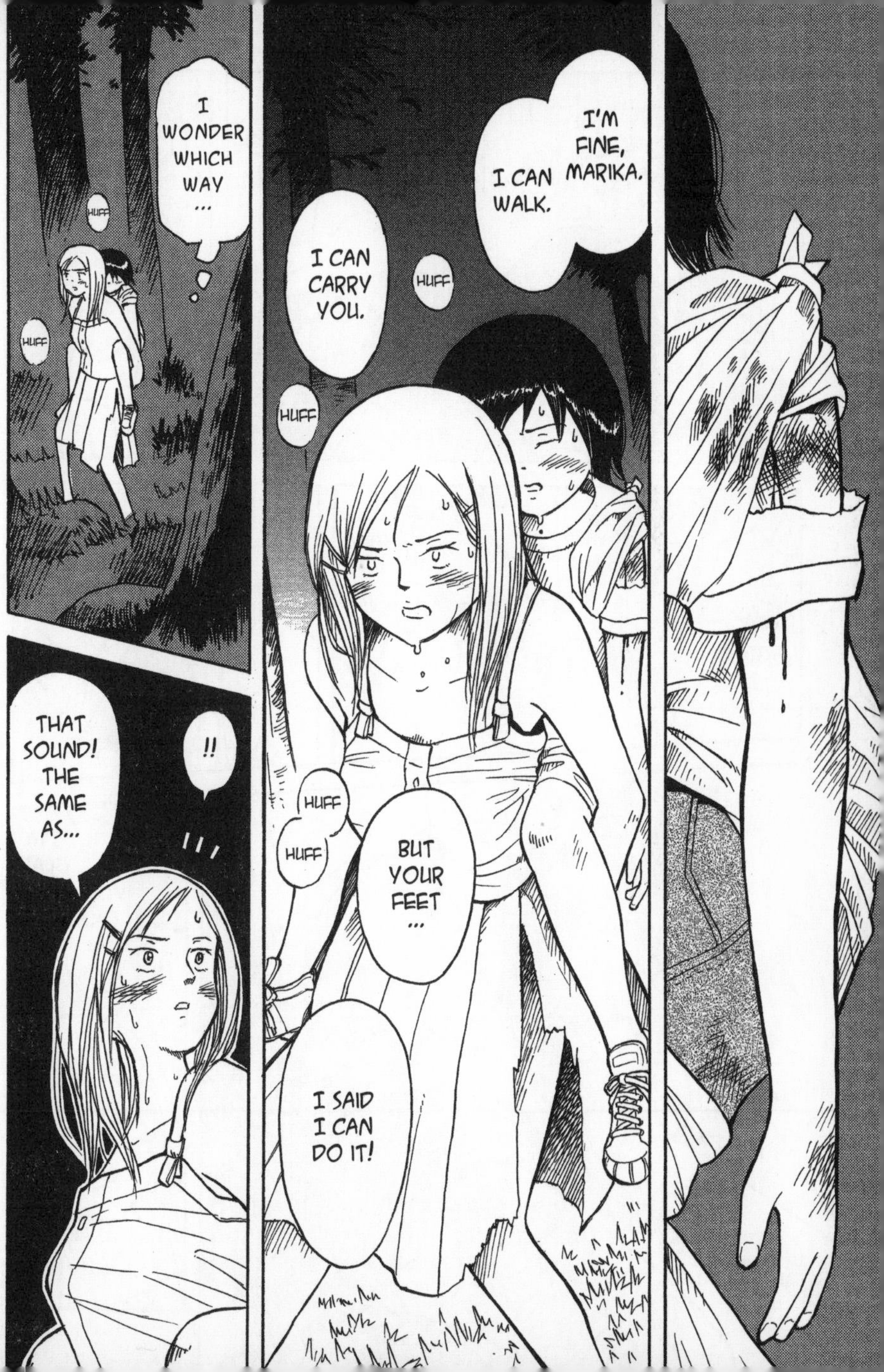
I'M FINE, MARIKA. I CAN WALK.
HUFF
I CAN CARRY YOU.
HUFF
HUFF
HUFF
BUT YOUR FEET ...
I SAID I CAN DO IT!
I WONDER WHICH WAY ...
HUFF
HUFF
!!
THAT SOUND! THE SAME AS...

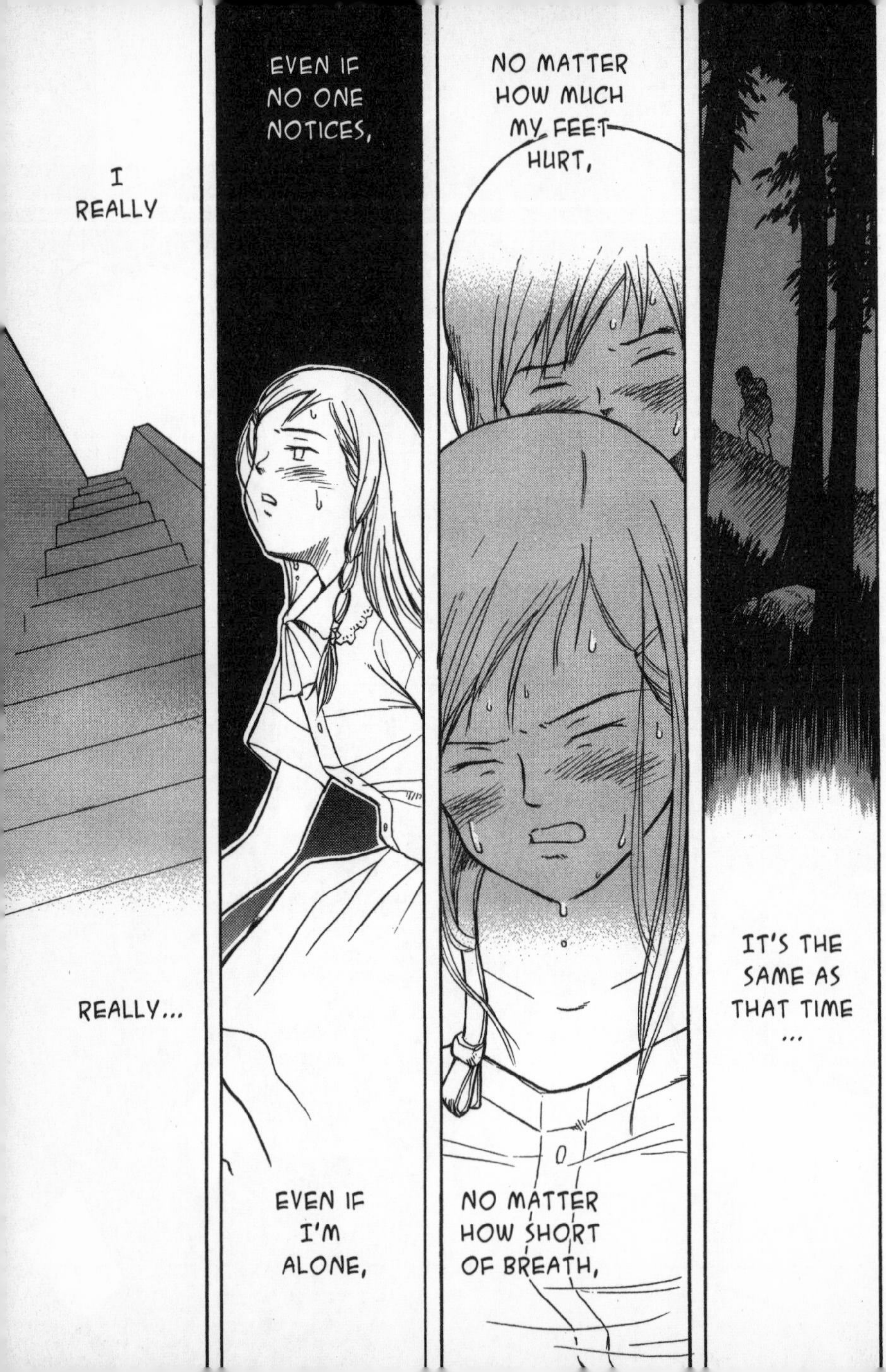
IT'S THE SAME AS THAT TIME ...
NO MATTER HOW MUCH MY FEET HURT,
NO MATTER HOW SHORT OF BREATH,
EVEN IF NO ONE NOTICES,
EVEN IF I'M ALONE,
I REALLY
REALLY...

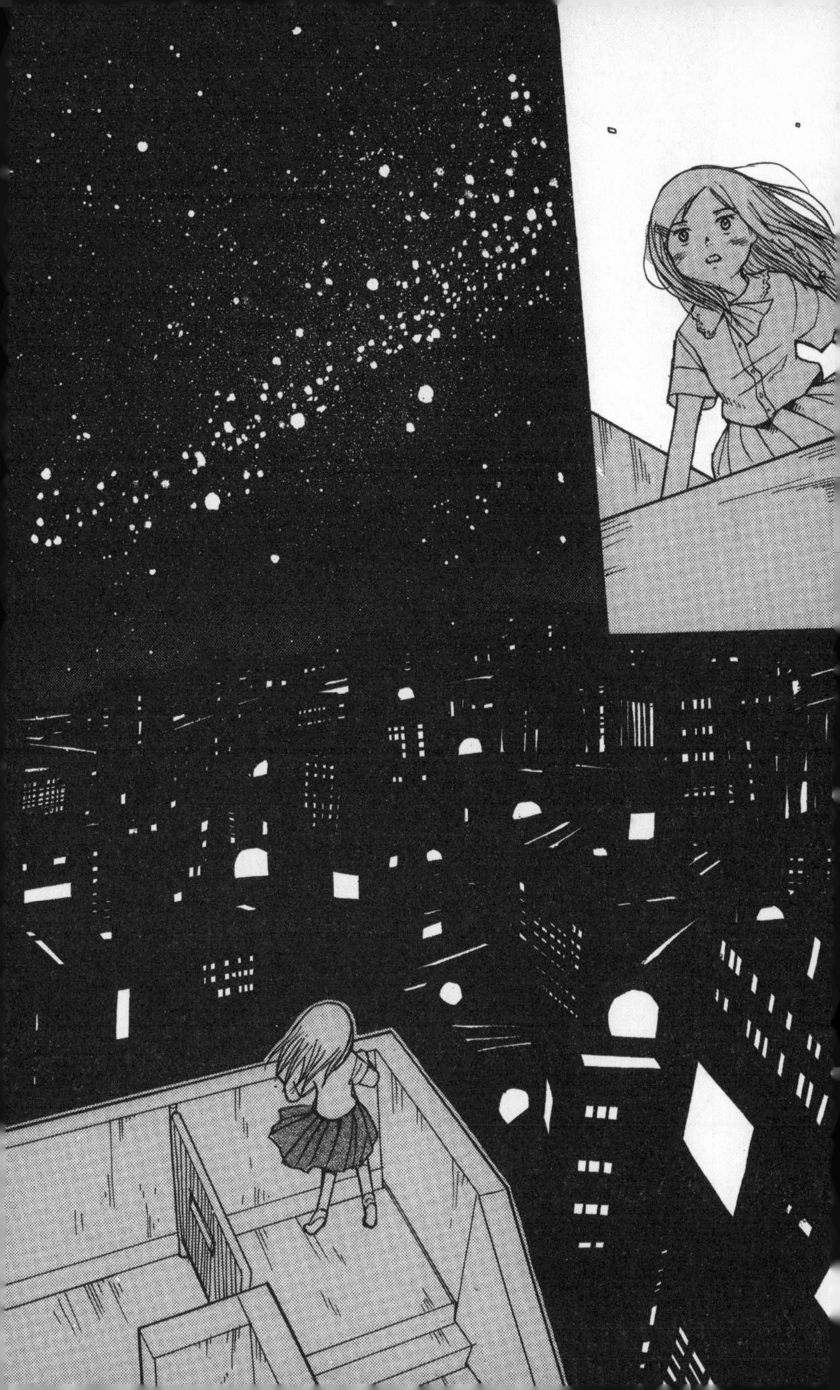

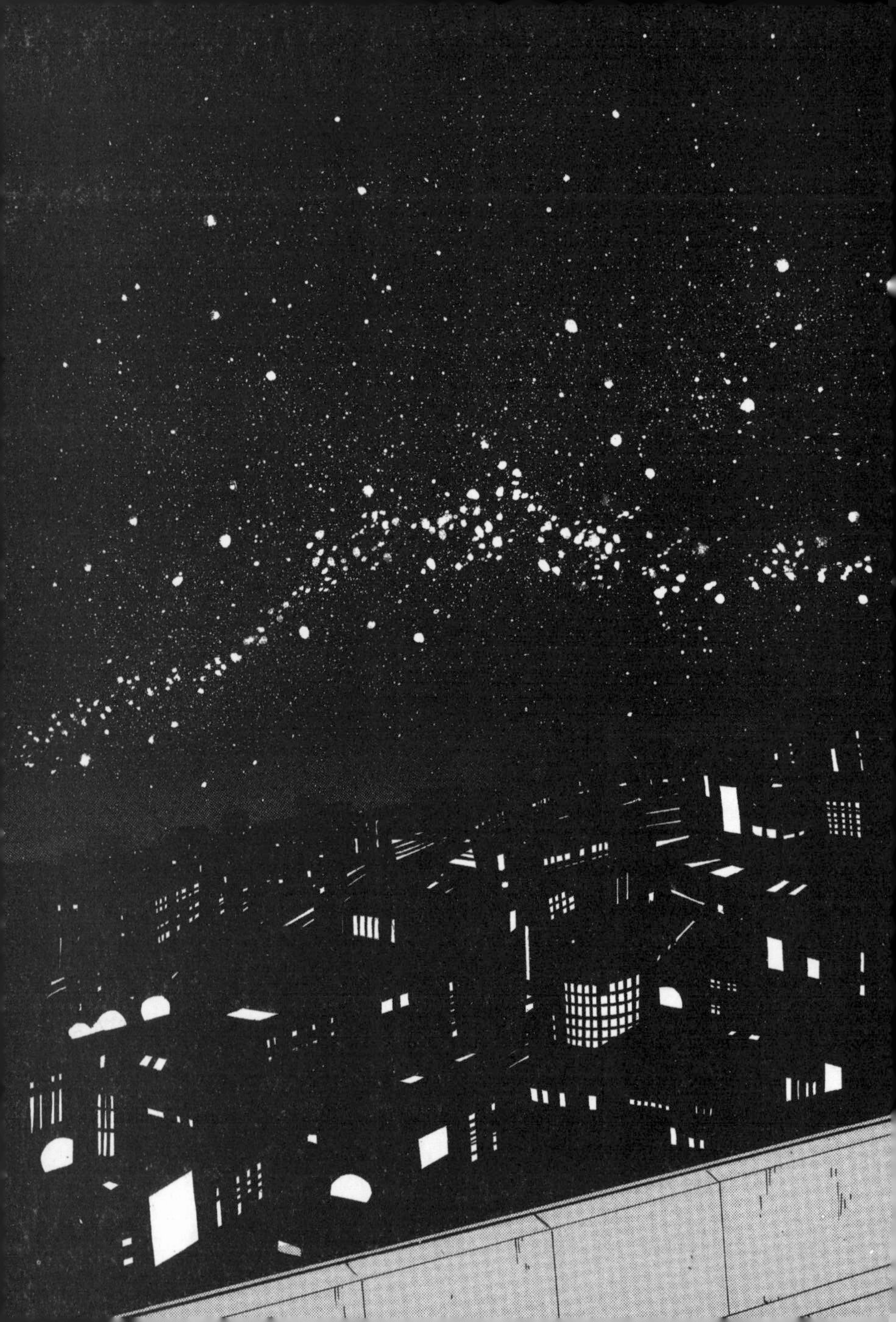

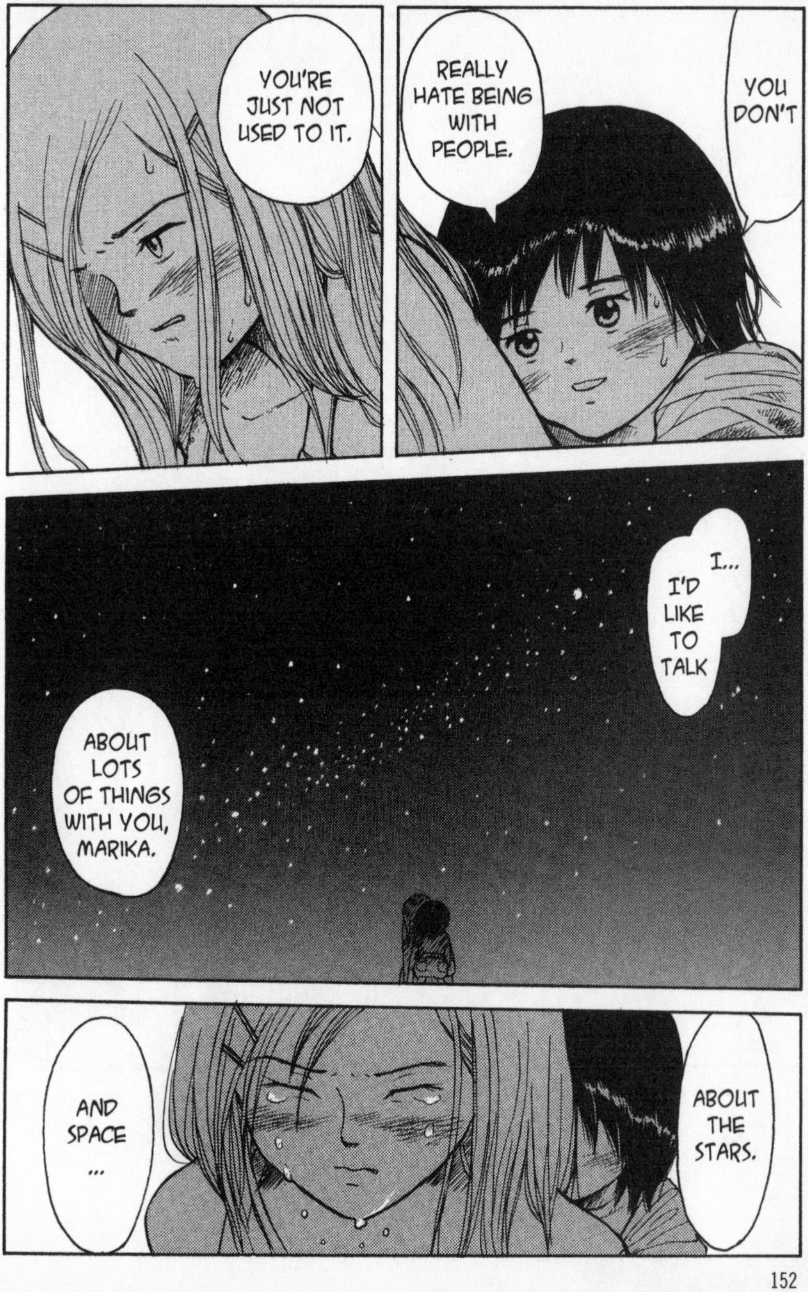
YOU DON'T
REALLY HATE BEING WITH PEOPLE.
YOU'RE JUST NOT USED TO IT.
I... I'D LIKE TO TALK
ABOUT LOTS OF THINGS WITH YOU, MARIKA.
ABOUT THE STARS.
AND SPACE ...

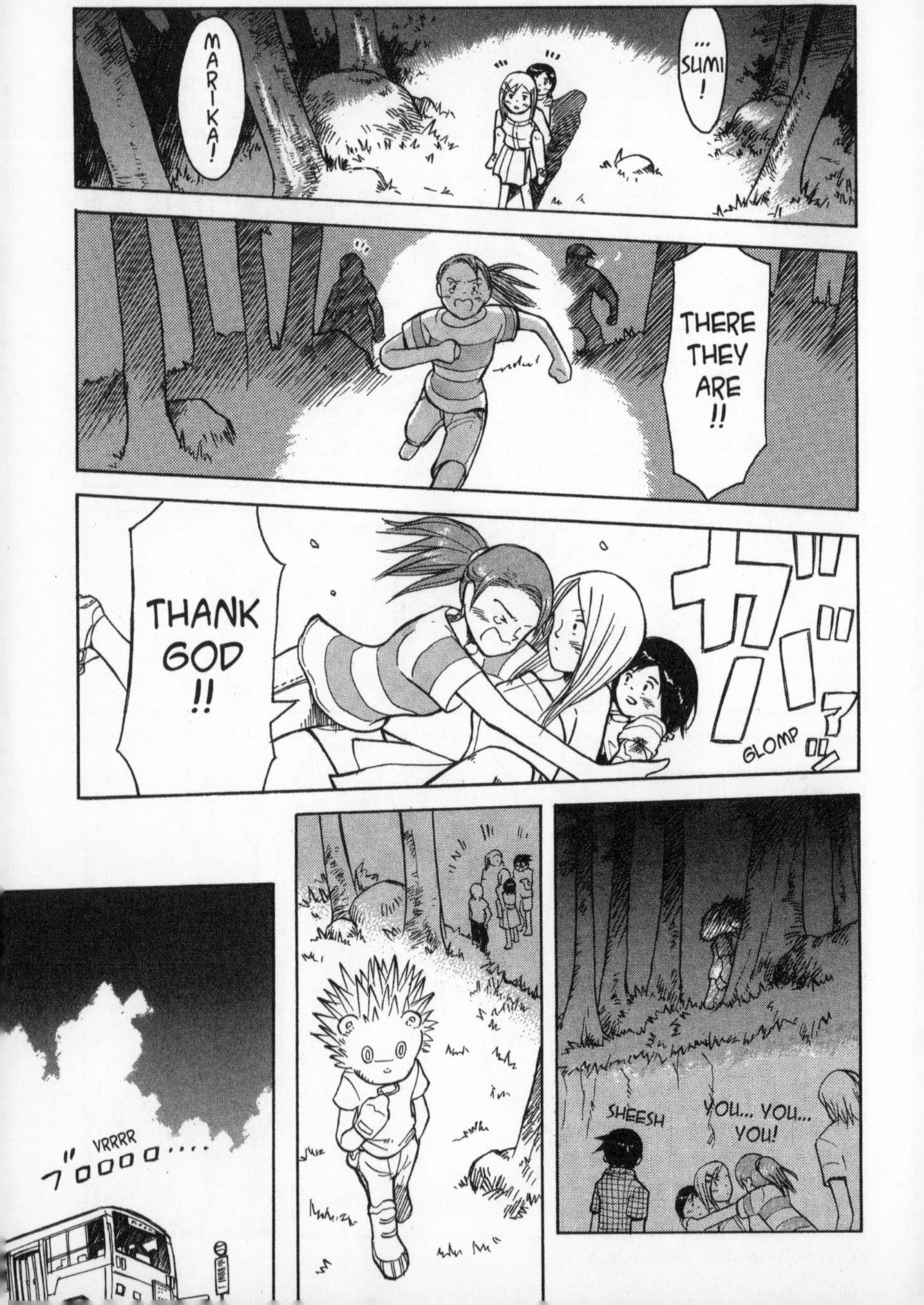
...SUMI!
MARIKA!
THERE THEY ARE!!
GLOMP
THANK GOD!!
YOU... YOU... YOU!
SHEESH
VRRRR

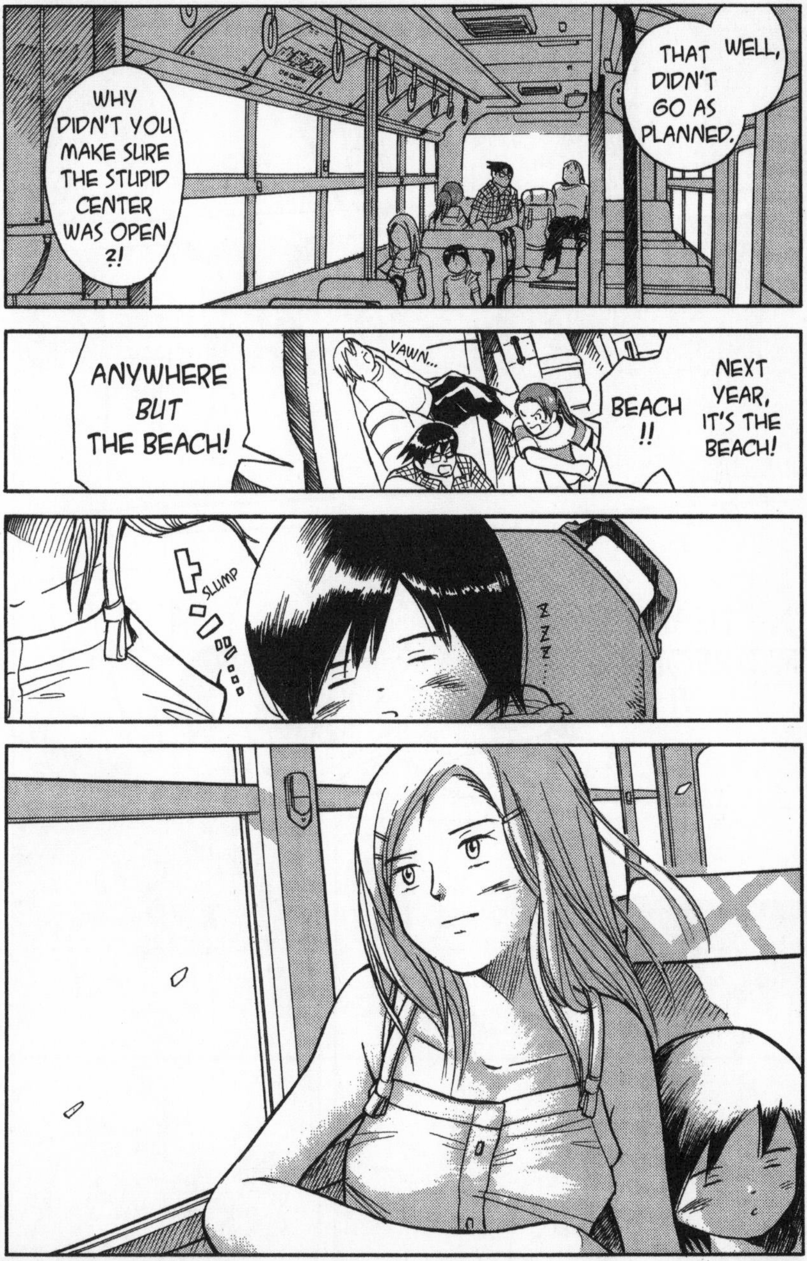
WELL, THAT DIDN'T GO AS PLANNED.
WHY DIDN'T YOU MAKE SURE THE STUPID CENTER WAS OPEN ?!
NEXT YEAR, IT'S THE BEACH!
BEACH !!
YAWN...
ANYWHERE BUT THE BEACH!
ZZZ...
SLUMP

CONTINUED IN TWIN SPICA VOL. 4

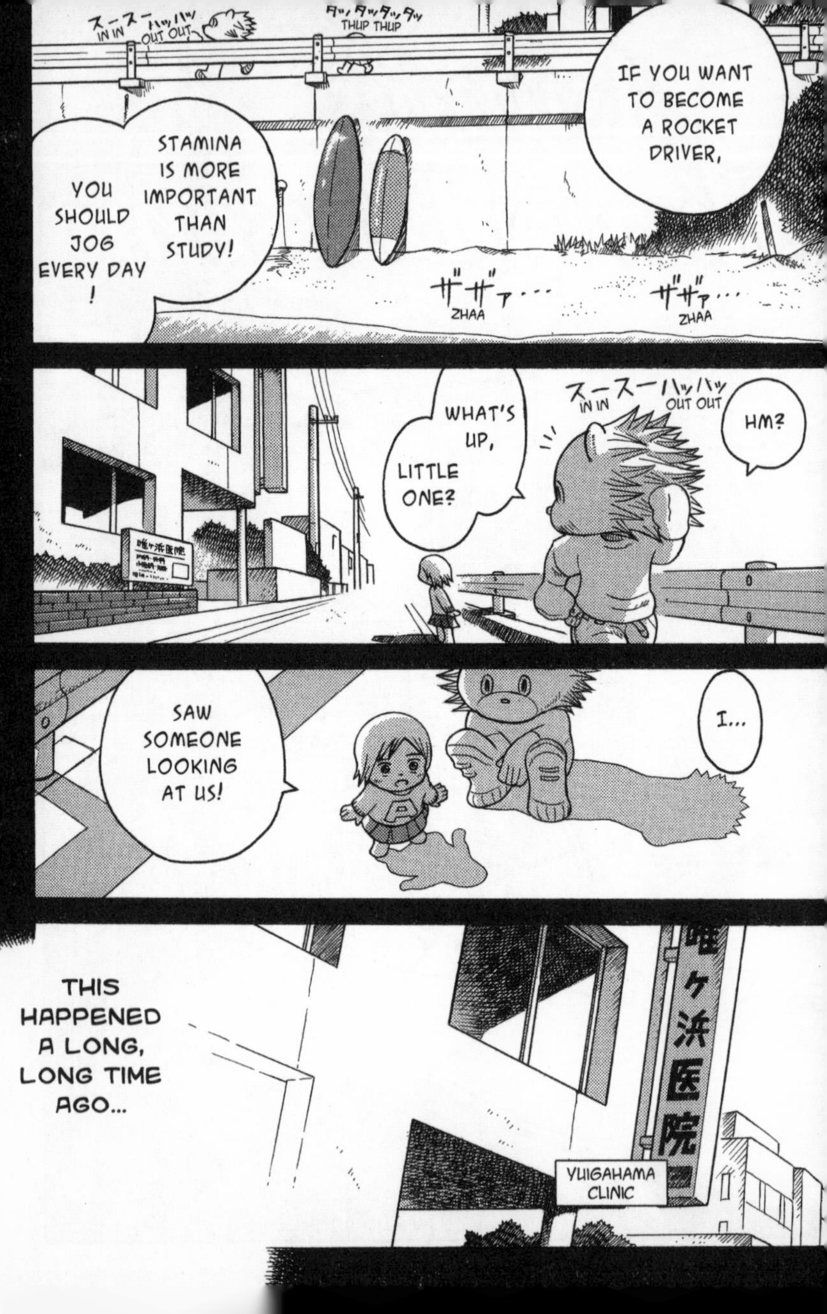
IF YOU WANT TO BECOME A ROCKET DRIVER,
タッタッタッタッ
THUP THUP
スースーハッハッ
IN IN OUT OUT
STAMINA IS MORE IMPORTANT THAN STUDY!
YOU SHOULD JOG EVERY DAY!
ザザァ…
ZHAA
ザザァ…
ZHAA
HM?
スースーハッハッ
IN IN OUT OUT
WHAT'S UP, LITTLE ONE?
I...
SAW SOMEONE LOOKING AT US!
唯ヶ浜医院
YUIGAHAMA CLINIC
THIS HAPPENED A LONG, LONG TIME AGO...

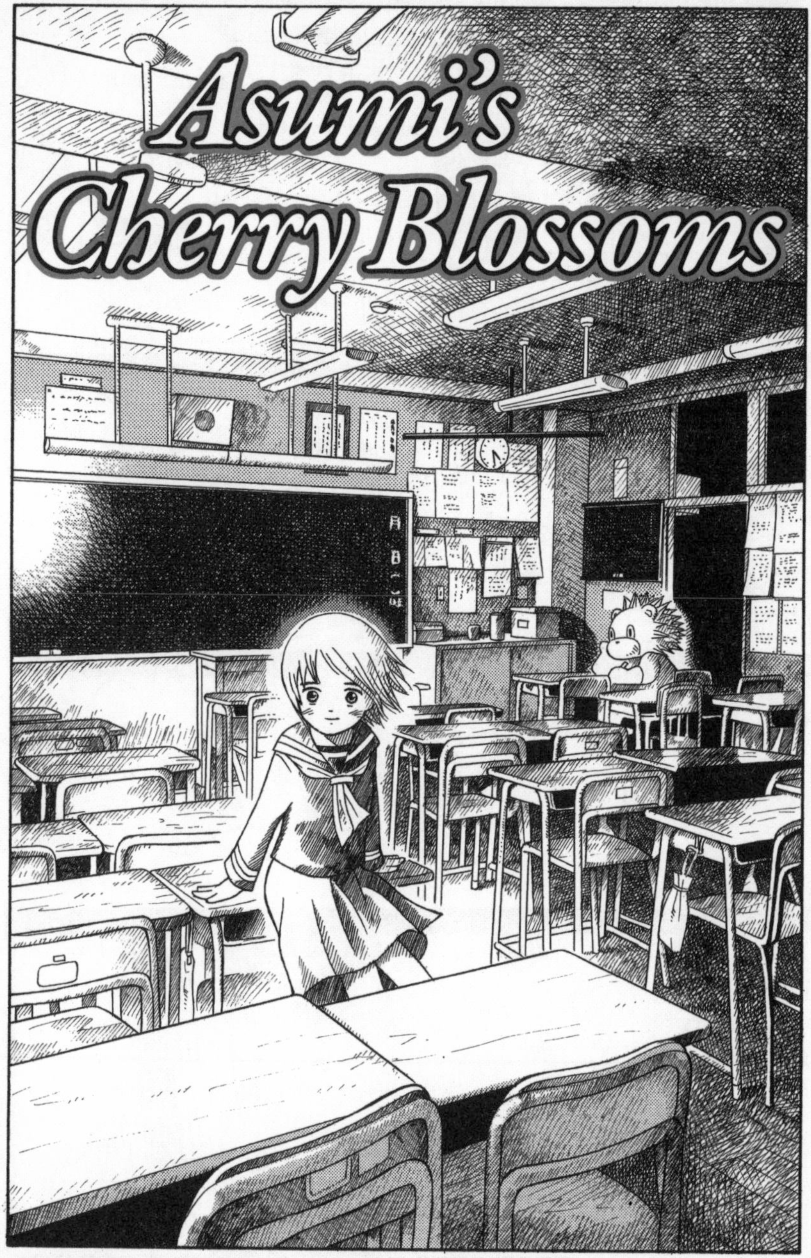
Asumi's
Cherry Blossoms

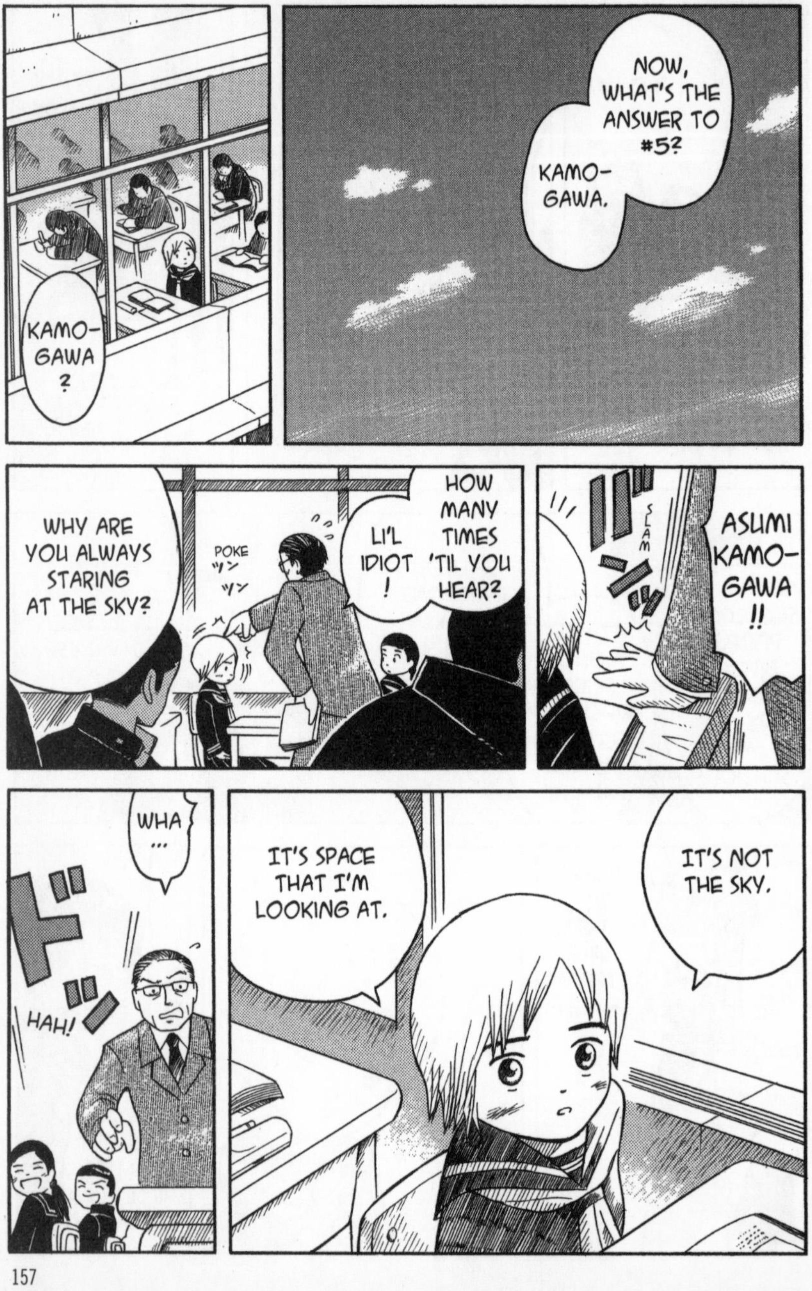
NOW, WHAT'S THE ANSWER TO #5?
KAMO-GAWA.
KAMO-GAWA?
SLAM
ASUMI KAMO-GAWA!!
HOW MANY TIMES 'TIL YOU HEAR?
LI'L IDIOT!
POKE ツン
ツン
WHY ARE YOU ALWAYS STARING AT THE SKY?
IT'S NOT THE SKY.
IT'S SPACE THAT I'M LOOKING AT.
WHA...
HAH!

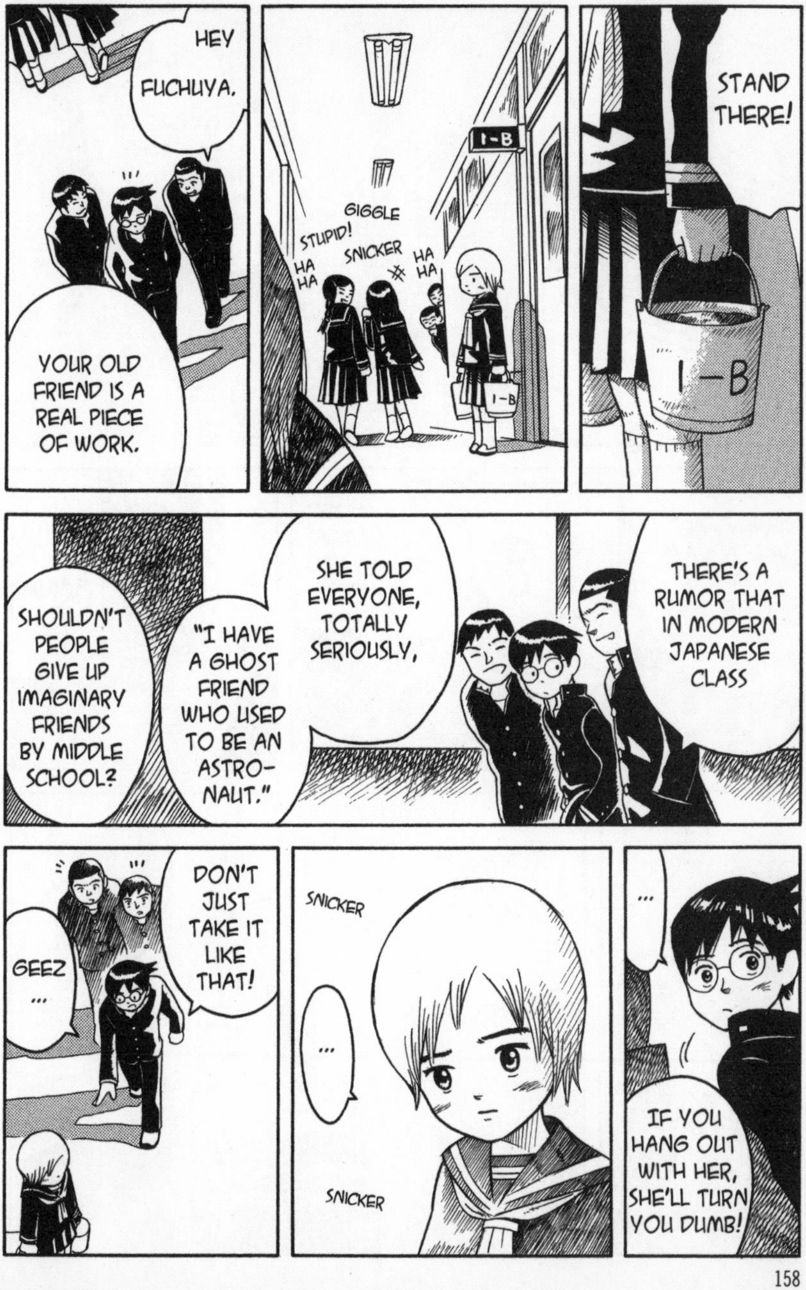
STAND THERE!
I-B
1-B
GIGGLE
STUPID!
SNICKER
HA HA
HA HA
I-B
HEY FUCHUYA.
YOUR OLD FRIEND IS A REAL PIECE OF WORK.
THERE'S A RUMOR THAT IN MODERN JAPANESE CLASS
SHE TOLD EVERYONE, TOTALLY SERIOUSLY,
"I HAVE A GHOST FRIEND WHO USED TO BE AN ASTRONAUT."
SHOULDN'T PEOPLE GIVE UP IMAGINARY FRIENDS BY MIDDLE SCHOOL?
...
IF YOU HANG OUT WITH HER, SHE'LL TURN YOU DUMB!
SNICKER
...
SNICKER
DON'T JUST TAKE IT LIKE THAT!
GEEZ ...

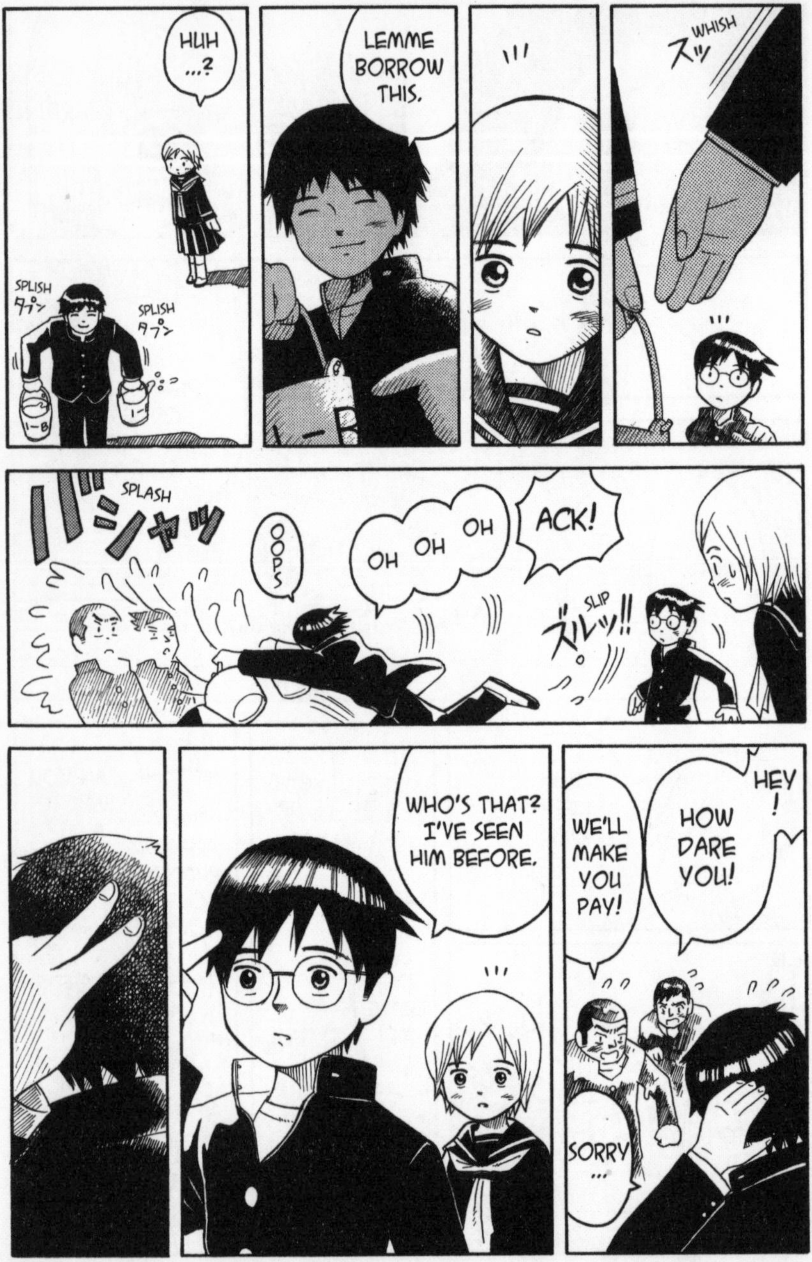
WHISH
ズッ
LEMME BORROW THIS.
HUH ...?
SPLISH
タプン
SPLISH
タプン
ACK!
SLIP
ズルッ!!
OH OH OH
OOPS
SPLASH
バシャッ
HEY!
HOW DARE YOU!
WE'LL MAKE YOU PAY!
SORRY...
WHO'S THAT? I'VE SEEN HIM BEFORE.

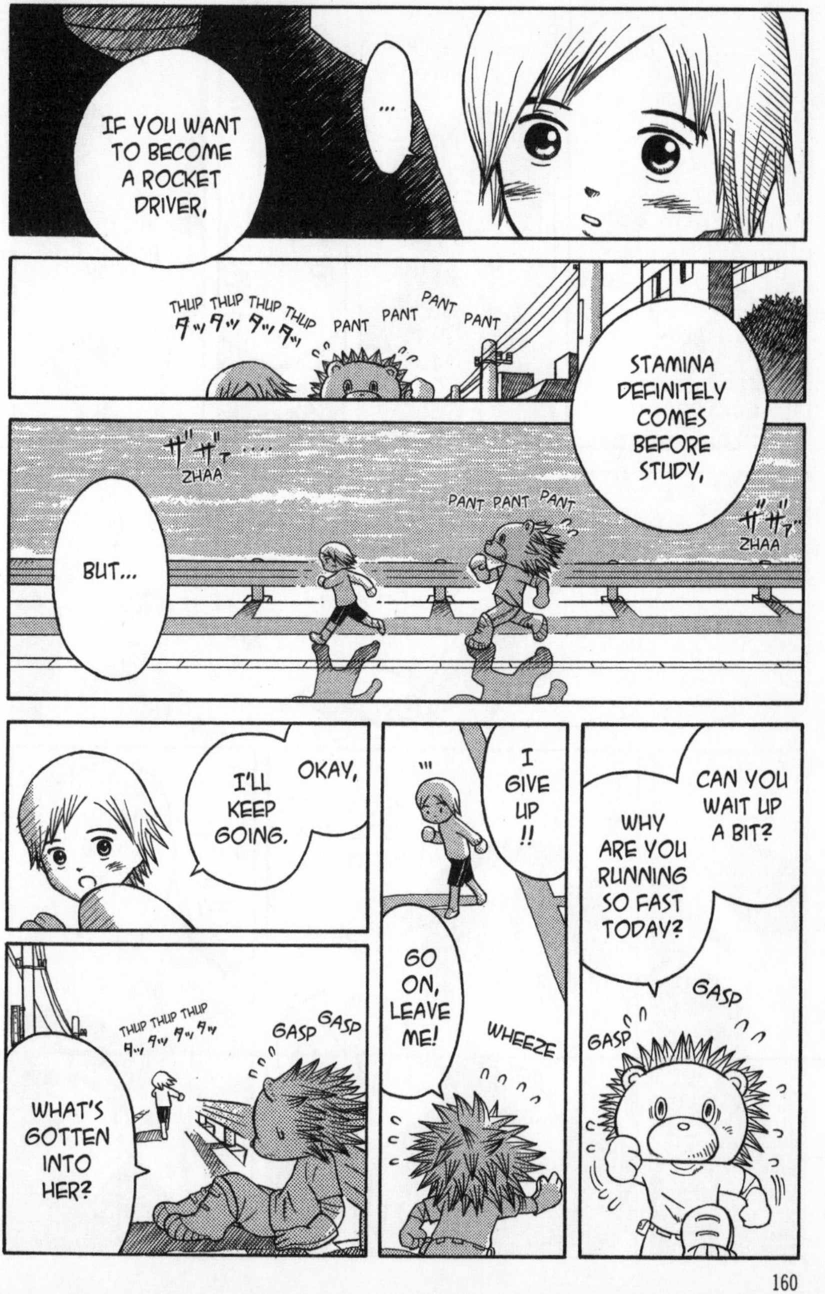
...
IF YOU WANT TO BECOME A ROCKET DRIVER,
THUP THUP THUP THUP
タッタッタッタッ
PANT PANT PANT PANT
STAMINA DEFINITELY COMES BEFORE STUDY,
ザザァ
ZHAA
ザザァ....
ZHAA
PANT PANT PANT
BUT...
CAN YOU WAIT UP A BIT?
WHY ARE YOU RUNNING SO FAST TODAY?
GASP
GASP
I GIVE UP!!
GO ON, LEAVE ME!
WHEEZE
OKAY,
I'LL KEEP GOING.
GASP GASP
THUP THUP THUP
タッタッタッ
WHAT'S GOTTEN INTO HER?

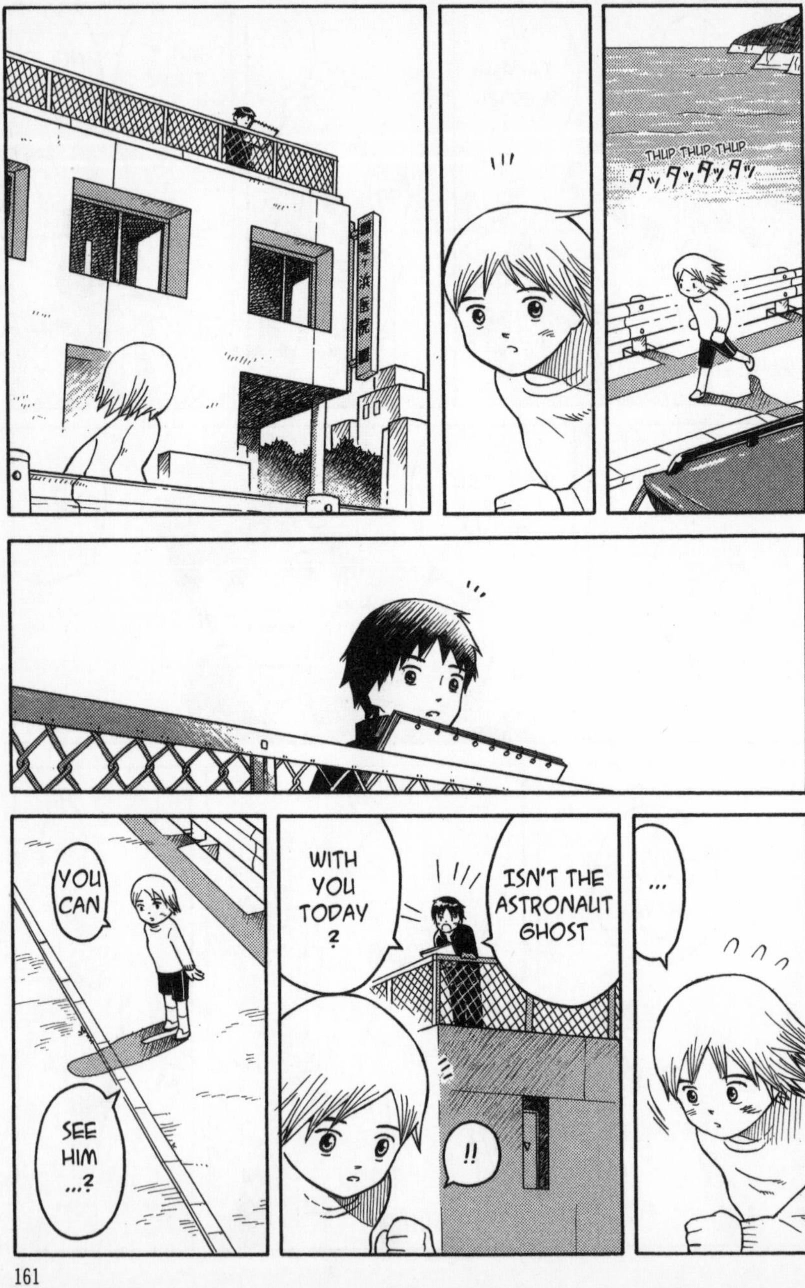
THUP THUP THUP
タッタッタッタッ
...
ISN'T THE ASTRONAUT GHOST
WITH YOU TODAY ?
!!
YOU CAN
SEE HIM ...?

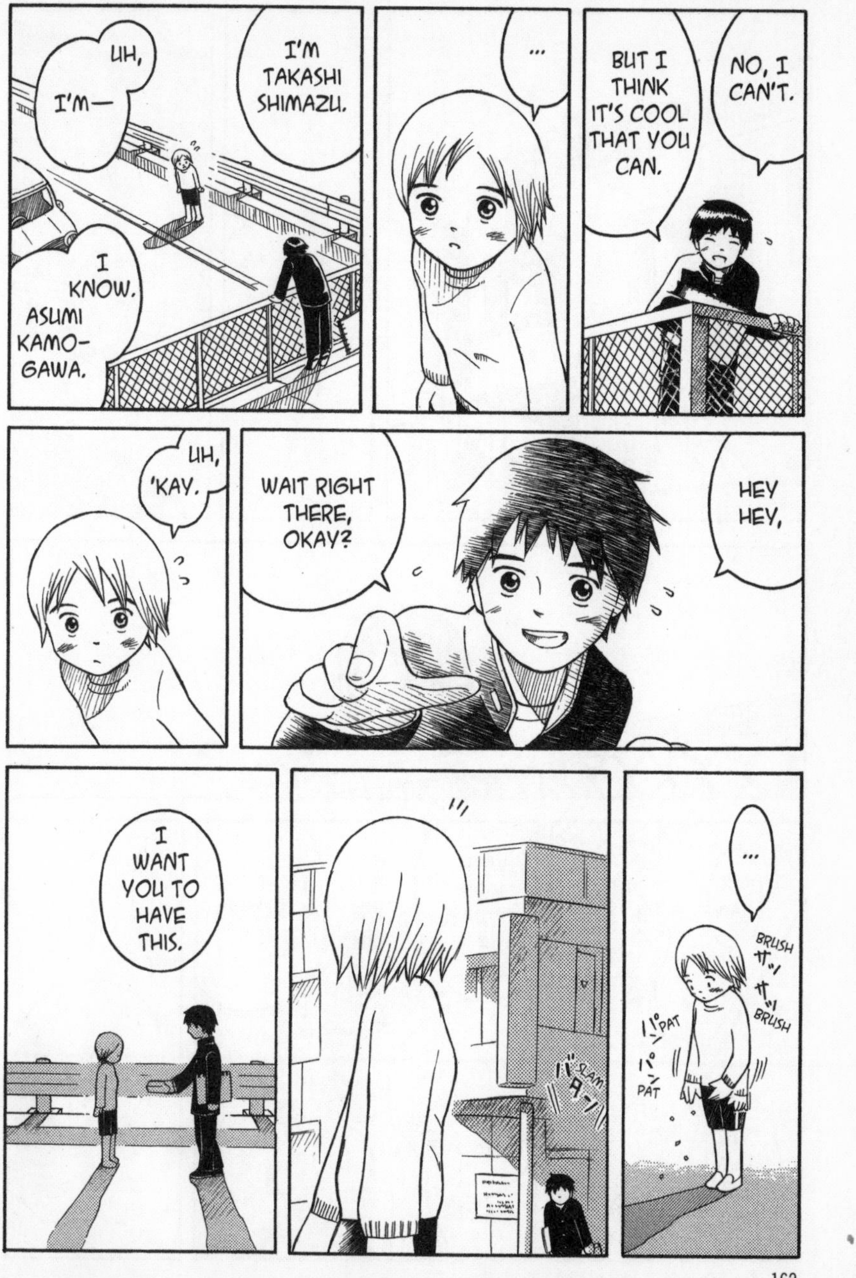

NO, I CAN'T.
BUT I THINK IT'S COOL THAT YOU CAN.
...
I'M TAKASHI SHIMAZU.
UH, I'M—
I KNOW. ASUMI KAMOGAWA.
HEY HEY,
WAIT RIGHT THERE, OKAY?
UH, 'KAY.
...
BRUSH
BRUSH
PAT
PAT
SLAM
I WANT YOU TO HAVE THIS.

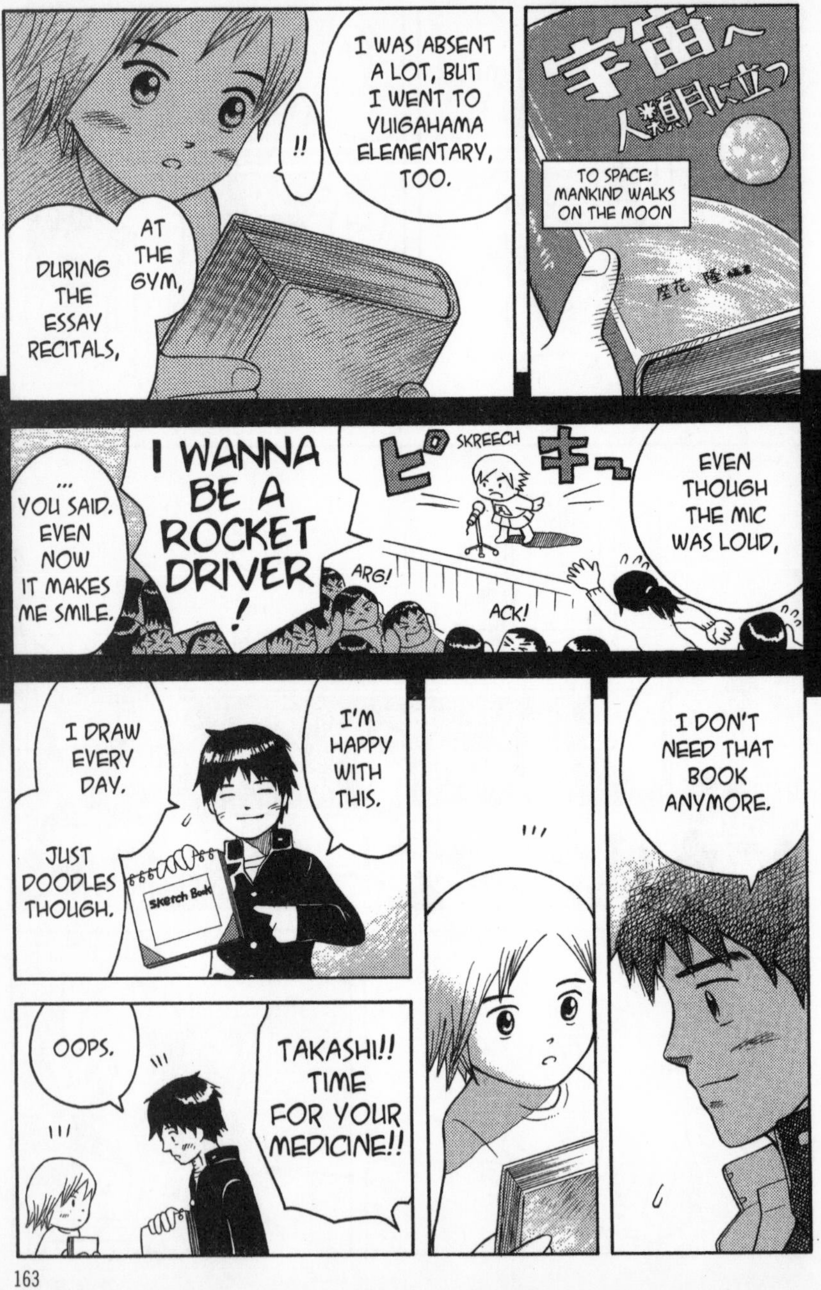
宇宙へ
人類月に立つ
TO SPACE: MANKIND WALKS ON THE MOON
I WAS ABSENT A LOT, BUT I WENT TO YUIGAHAMA ELEMENTARY, TOO.
!!
AT THE GYM,
DURING THE ESSAY RECITALS,
EVEN THOUGH THE MIC WAS LOUD,
ピキ~
SKREECH
ACK!
ARG!
I WANNA BE A ROCKET DRIVER!
... YOU SAID. EVEN NOW IT MAKES ME SMILE.
I DON'T NEED THAT BOOK ANYMORE.
...
I'M HAPPY WITH THIS.
I DRAW EVERY DAY.
JUST DOODLES THOUGH.
Sketch Book
TAKASHI!! TIME FOR YOUR MEDICINE!!
OOPS.

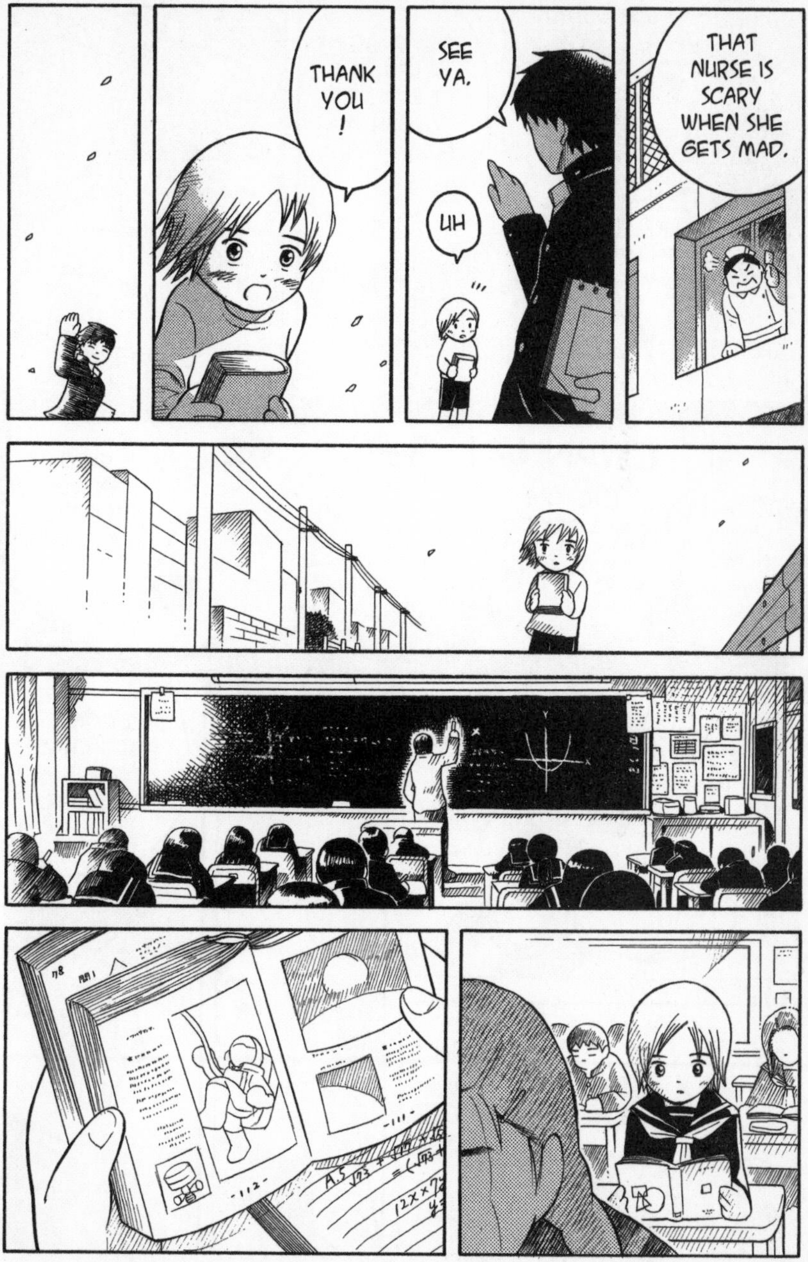
THAT NURSE IS SCARY WHEN SHE GETS MAD.
SEE YA.
UH
THANK YOU!

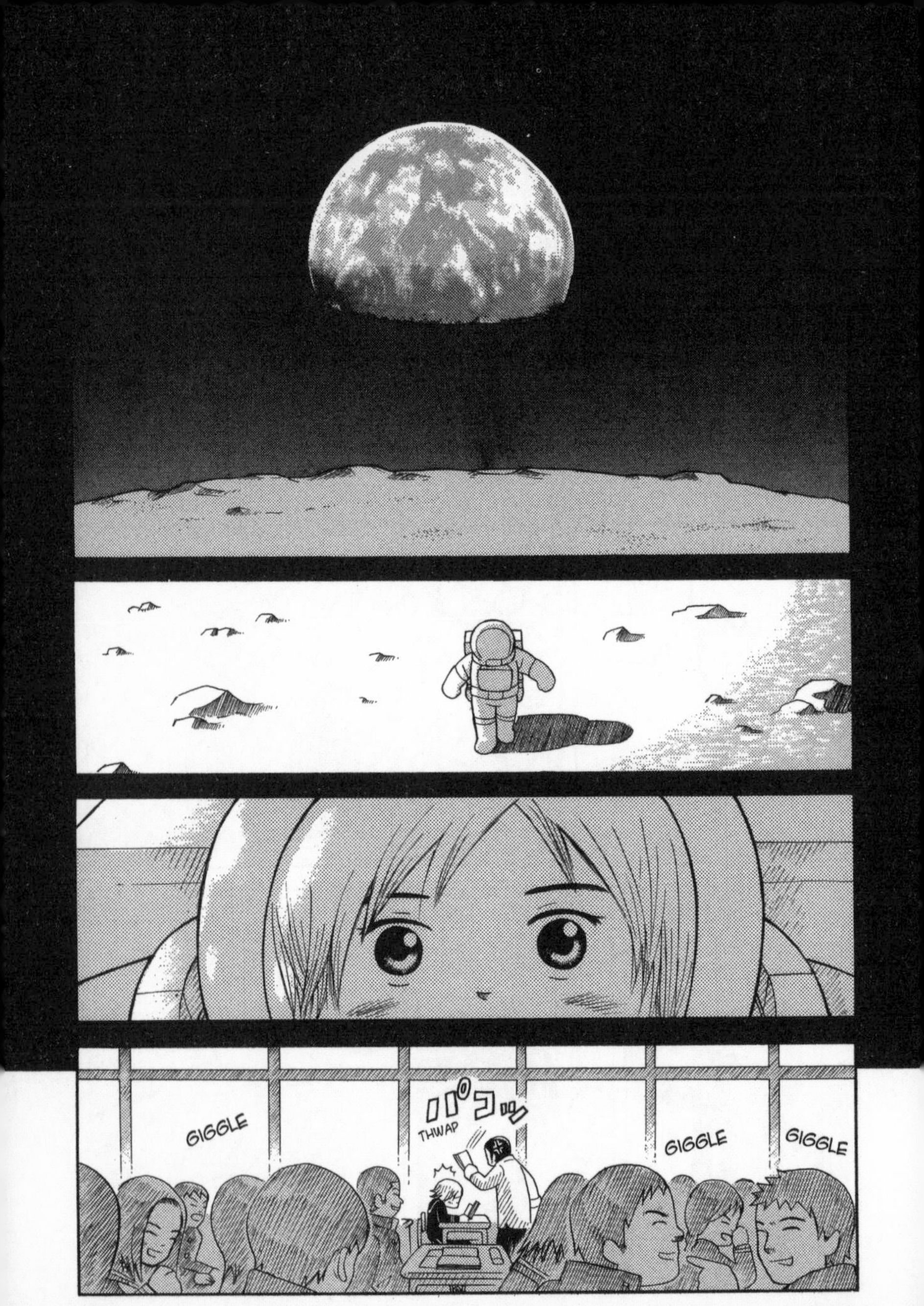
GIGGLE
GIGGLE
パコッ
THWAP
GIGGLE

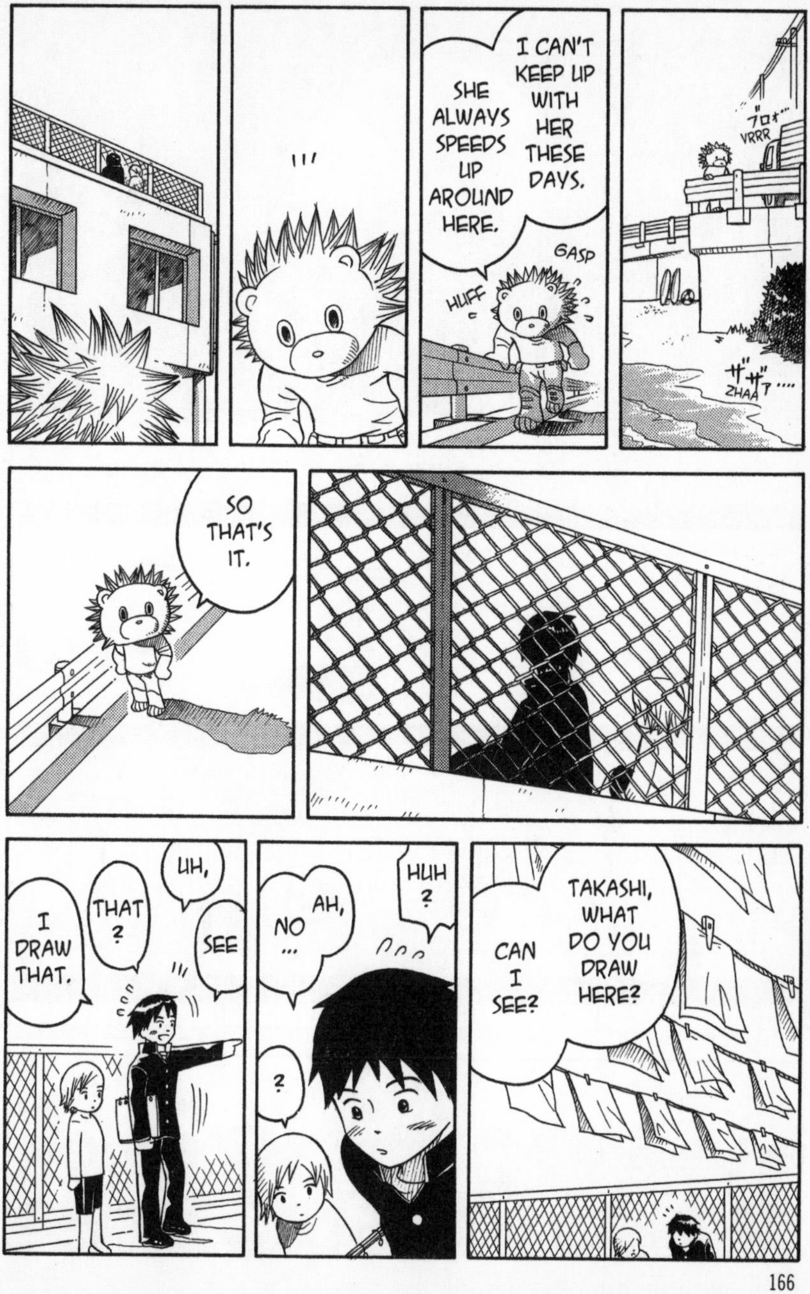
ブロォ
VRRR
ザザァ
ZHAA
I CAN'T KEEP UP WITH HER THESE DAYS.
SHE ALWAYS SPEEDS UP AROUND HERE.
GASP
HUFF
SO THAT'S IT.
TAKASHI, WHAT DO YOU DRAW HERE?
CAN I SEE?
HUH?
AH,
NO...
?
UH,
SEE
THAT?
I DRAW THAT.

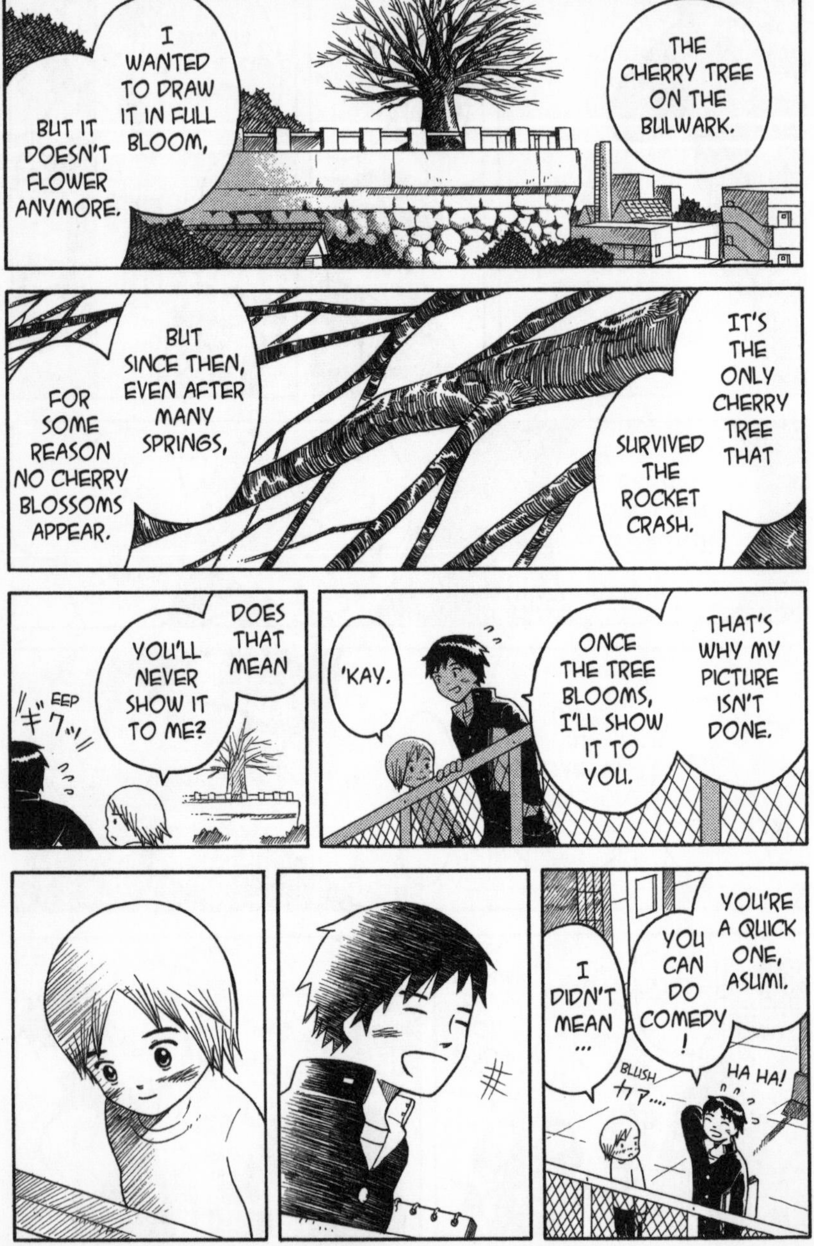
THE CHERRY TREE ON THE BULWARK.
I WANTED TO DRAW IT IN FULL BLOOM,
BUT IT DOESN'T FLOWER ANYMORE.
IT'S THE ONLY CHERRY TREE THAT
SURVIVED THE ROCKET CRASH.
BUT SINCE THEN, EVEN AFTER MANY SPRINGS,
FOR SOME REASON NO CHERRY BLOSSOMS APPEAR.
THAT'S WHY MY PICTURE ISN'T DONE.
ONCE THE TREE BLOOMS, I'LL SHOW IT TO YOU.
'KAY.
DOES THAT MEAN
YOU'LL NEVER SHOW IT TO ME?
EEP
ギクッ
YOU'RE A QUICK ONE, ASUMI.
YOU CAN DO COMEDY!
HA HA!
I DIDN'T MEAN...
BLUSH
カァ....

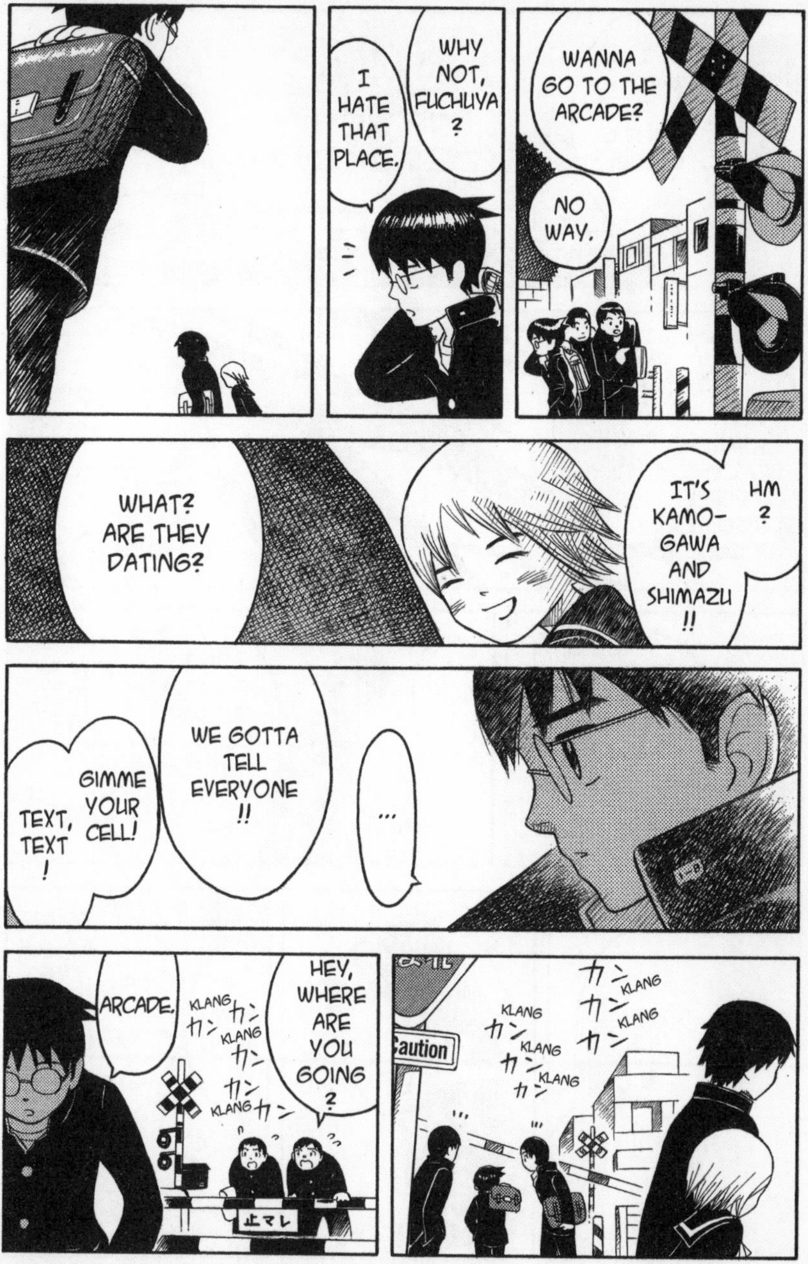
WANNA GO TO THE ARCADE?
NO WAY.
WHY NOT, FUCHUYA?
I HATE THAT PLACE.
HM?
IT'S KAMO-GAWA AND SHIMAZU!!
WHAT? ARE THEY DATING?
...
WE GOTTA TELL EVERYONE!!
GIMME YOUR CELL!
TEXT, TEXT!
カン KLANG
カン KLANG
カン KLANG
カン KLANG
カン KLANG
カン
Caution
HEY, WHERE ARE YOU GOING?
KLANG カン カン KLANG カン カン KLANG カン
ARCADE.
止マレ

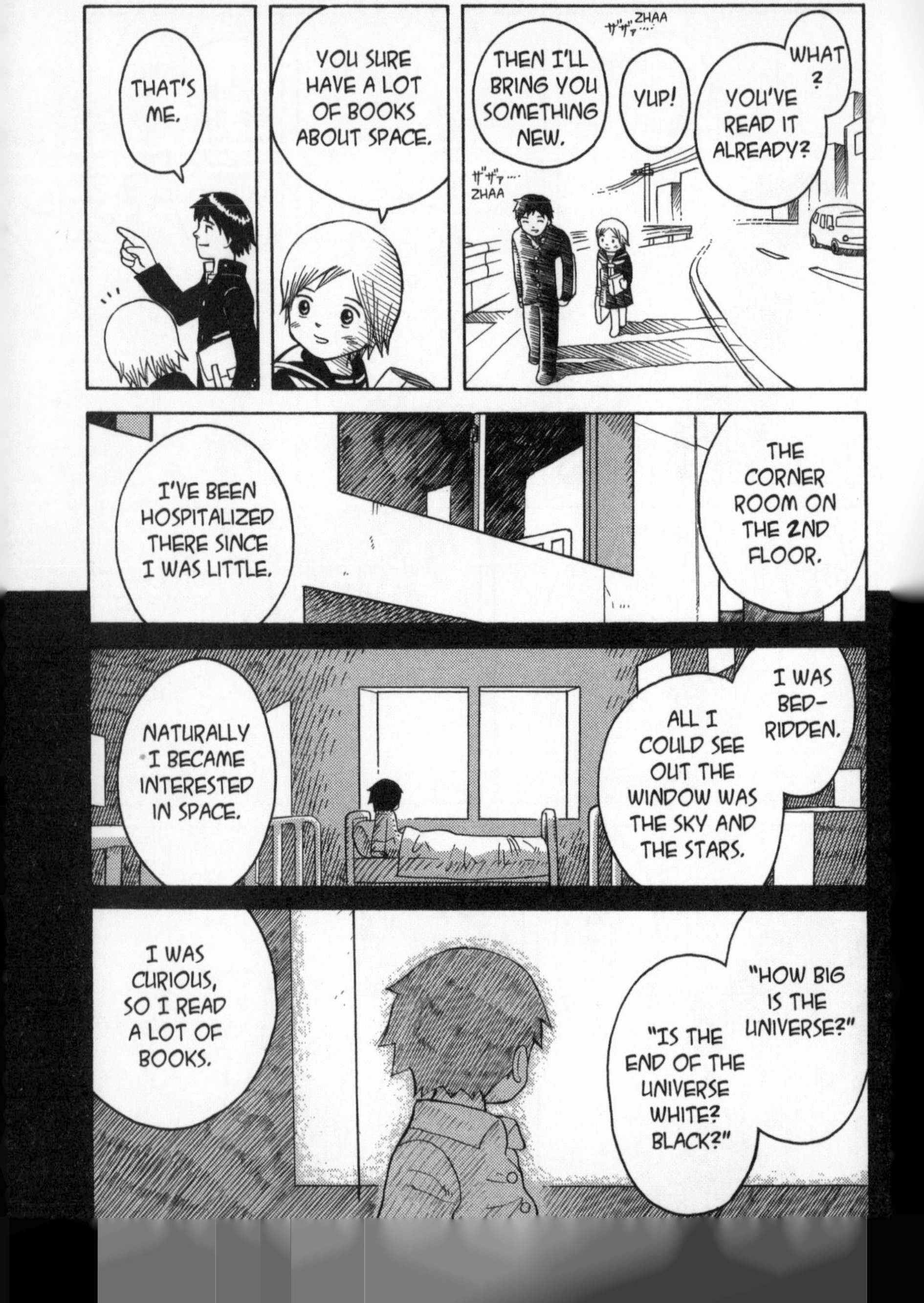

WHAT? YOU'VE READ IT ALREADY?
ザザァ… ZHAA
YUP!
THEN I'LL BRING YOU SOMETHING NEW.
ザザァ… ZHAA
YOU SURE HAVE A LOT OF BOOKS ABOUT SPACE.
THAT'S ME.
THE CORNER ROOM ON THE 2ND FLOOR.
I'VE BEEN HOSPITALIZED THERE SINCE I WAS LITTLE.
I WAS BED-RIDDEN.
ALL I COULD SEE OUT THE WINDOW WAS THE SKY AND THE STARS.
NATURALLY I BECAME INTERESTED IN SPACE.
"HOW BIG IS THE UNIVERSE?"
"IS THE END OF THE UNIVERSE WHITE? BLACK?"
I WAS CURIOUS, SO I READ A LOT OF BOOKS.

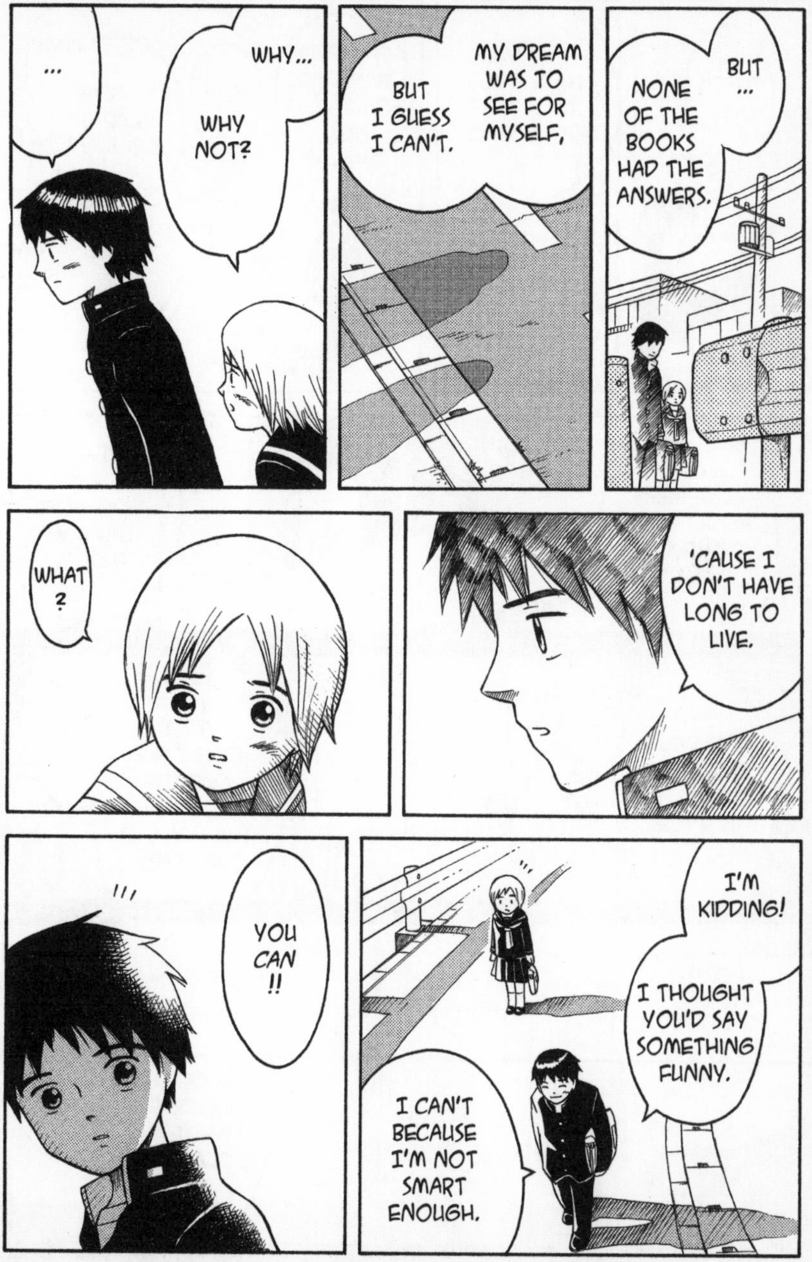
BUT ...
NONE OF THE BOOKS HAD THE ANSWERS.
MY DREAM WAS TO SEE FOR MYSELF,
BUT I GUESS I CAN'T.
WHY...
WHY NOT?
...
'CAUSE I DON'T HAVE LONG TO LIVE.
WHAT ?
I'M KIDDING!
I THOUGHT YOU'D SAY SOMETHING FUNNY.
I CAN'T BECAUSE I'M NOT SMART ENOUGH.
YOU CAN !!

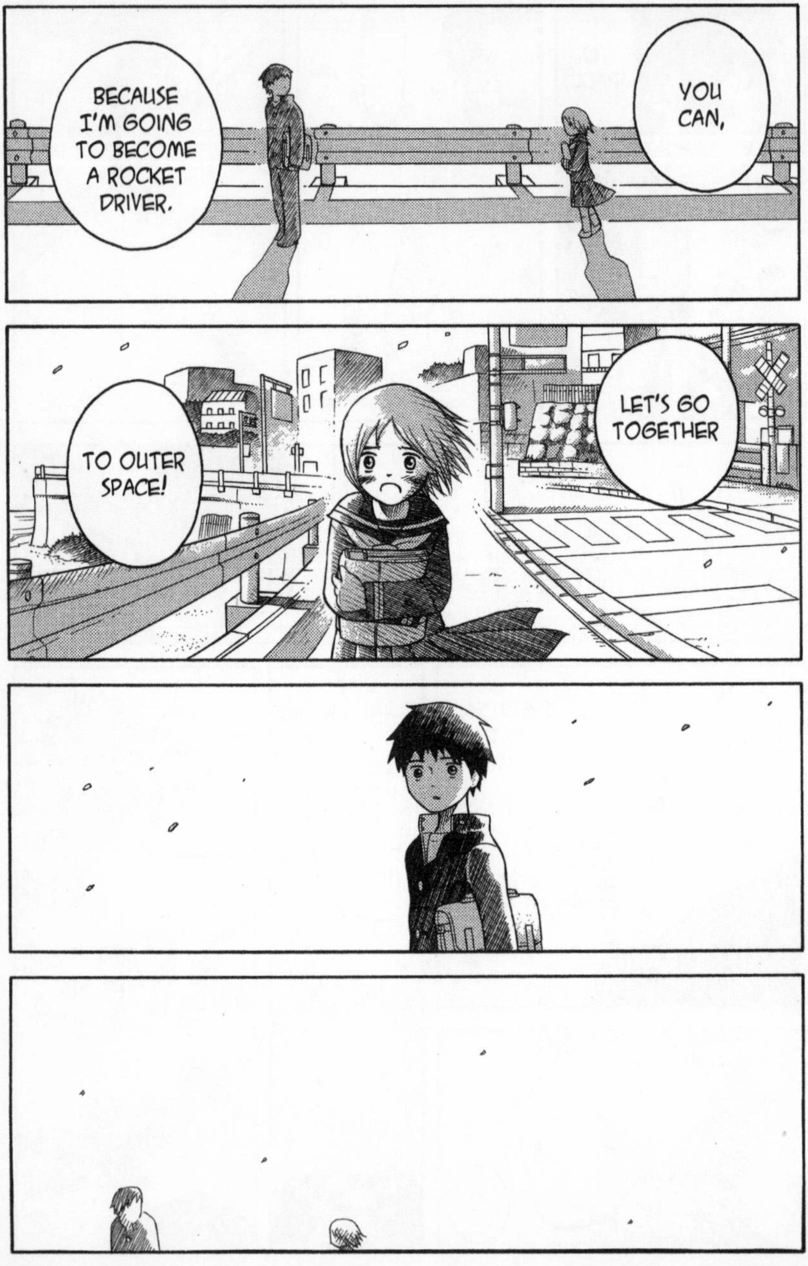
YOU CAN,
BECAUSE I'M GOING TO BECOME A ROCKET DRIVER.
LET'S GO TOGETHER
TO OUTER SPACE!

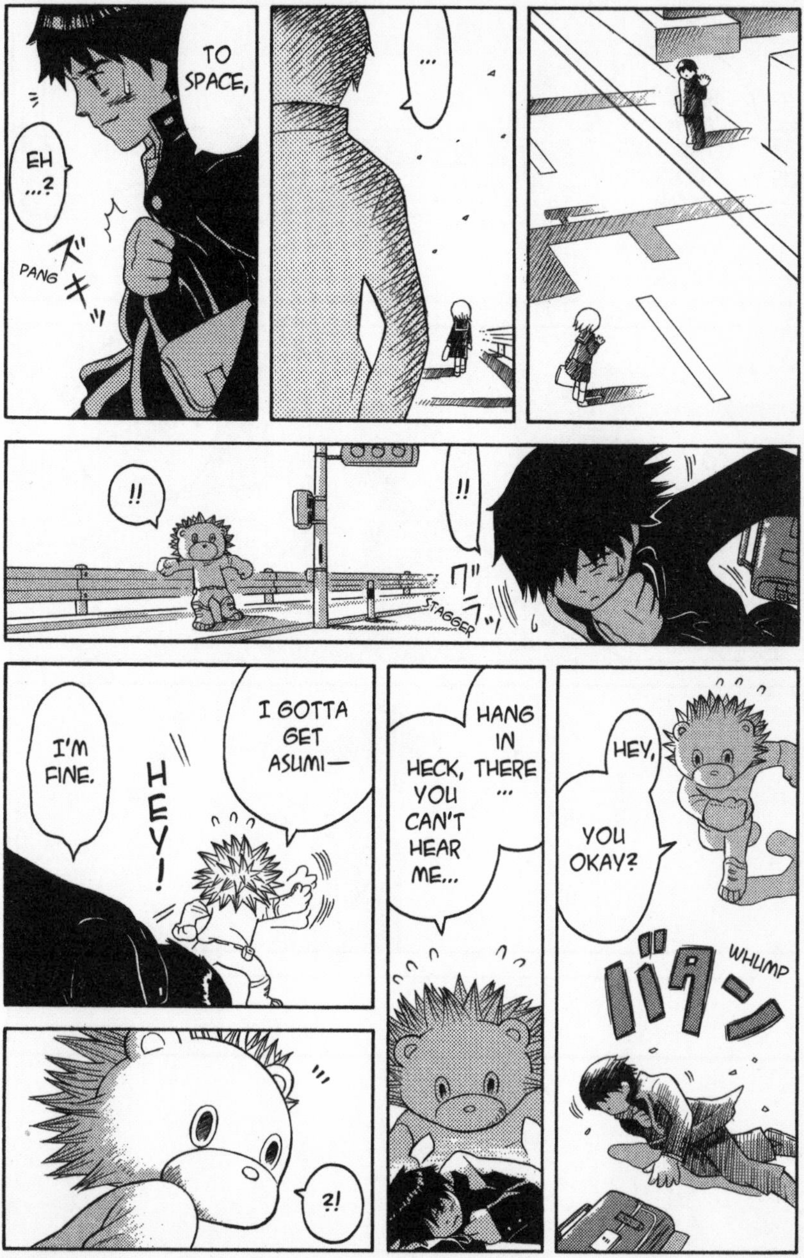
...
TO SPACE,
EH ...?
PANG
!!
STAGGER
!!
HEY,
YOU OKAY?
WHLUMP
HANG IN THERE ...
HECK, YOU CAN'T HEAR ME...
I GOTTA GET ASUMI—
HEY!
I'M FINE.
?!

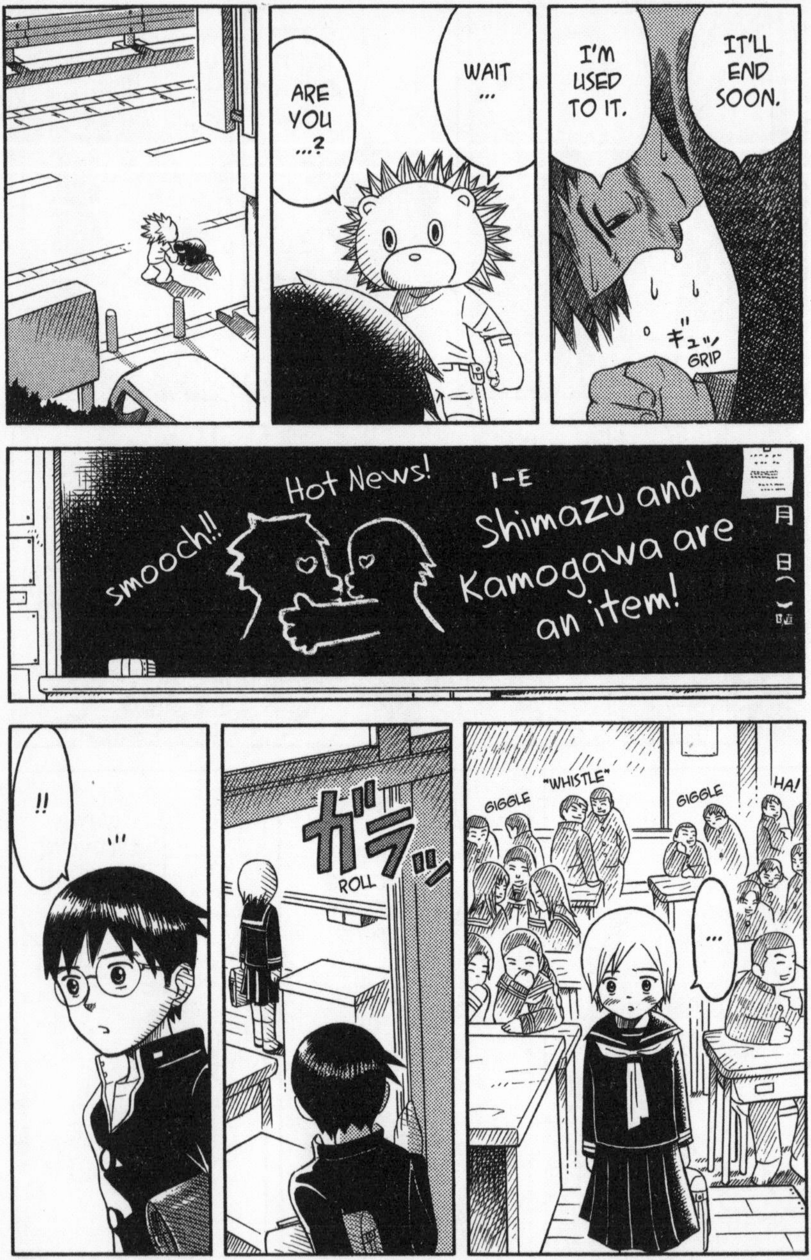
IT'LL END SOON.
I'M USED TO IT.
ギュッ
GRIP
WAIT ...
ARE YOU ...?
月
日
I-E
Shimazu and Kamogawa are an item!
Hot News!
smooch!!
HA!
GIGGLE
"WHISTLE"
GIGGLE
...
ガラッ
ROLL
!!

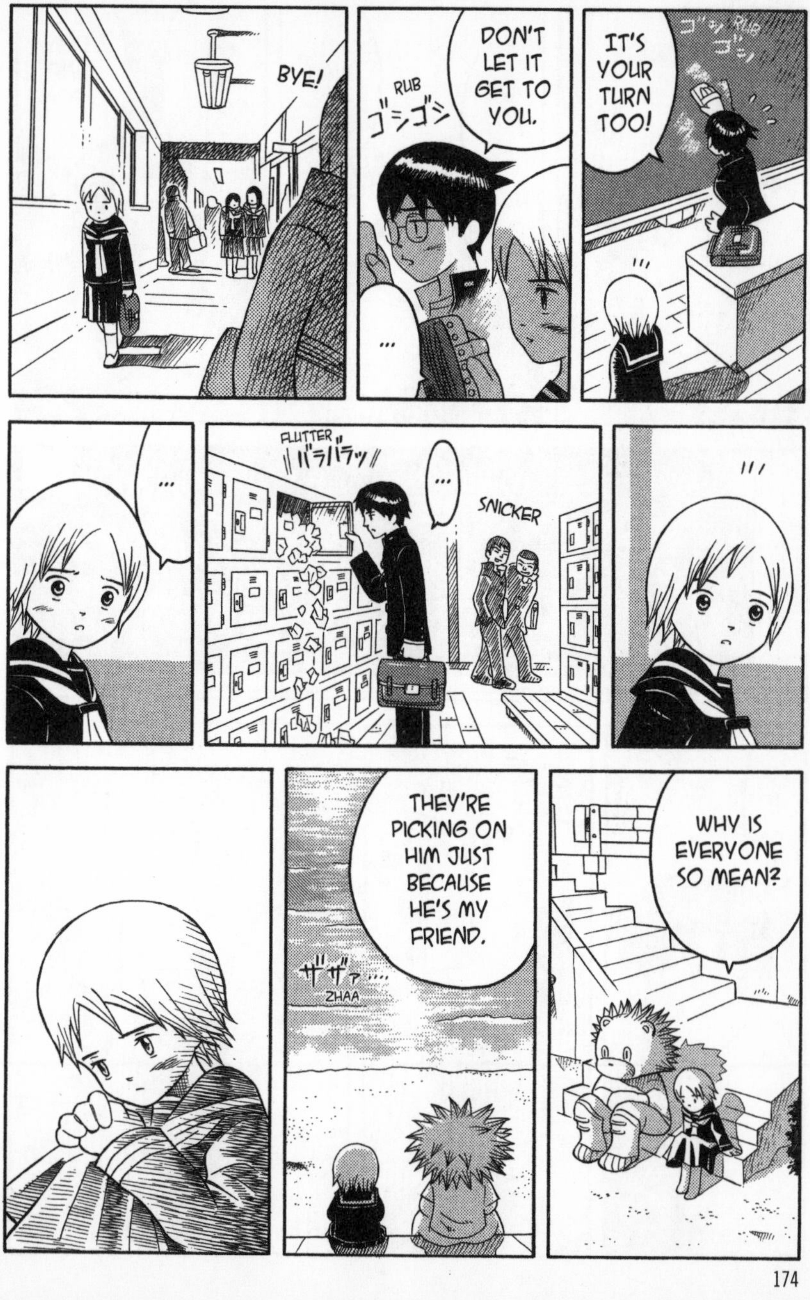
ゴシ RUB ゴシ
IT'S YOUR TURN TOO!
DON'T LET IT GET TO YOU.
RUB ゴシゴシ
...
BYE!
...
FLUTTER バラバラッ
SNICKER
...
WHY IS EVERYONE SO MEAN?
THEY'RE PICKING ON HIM JUST BECAUSE HE'S MY FRIEND.
ザザァ.... ZHAA

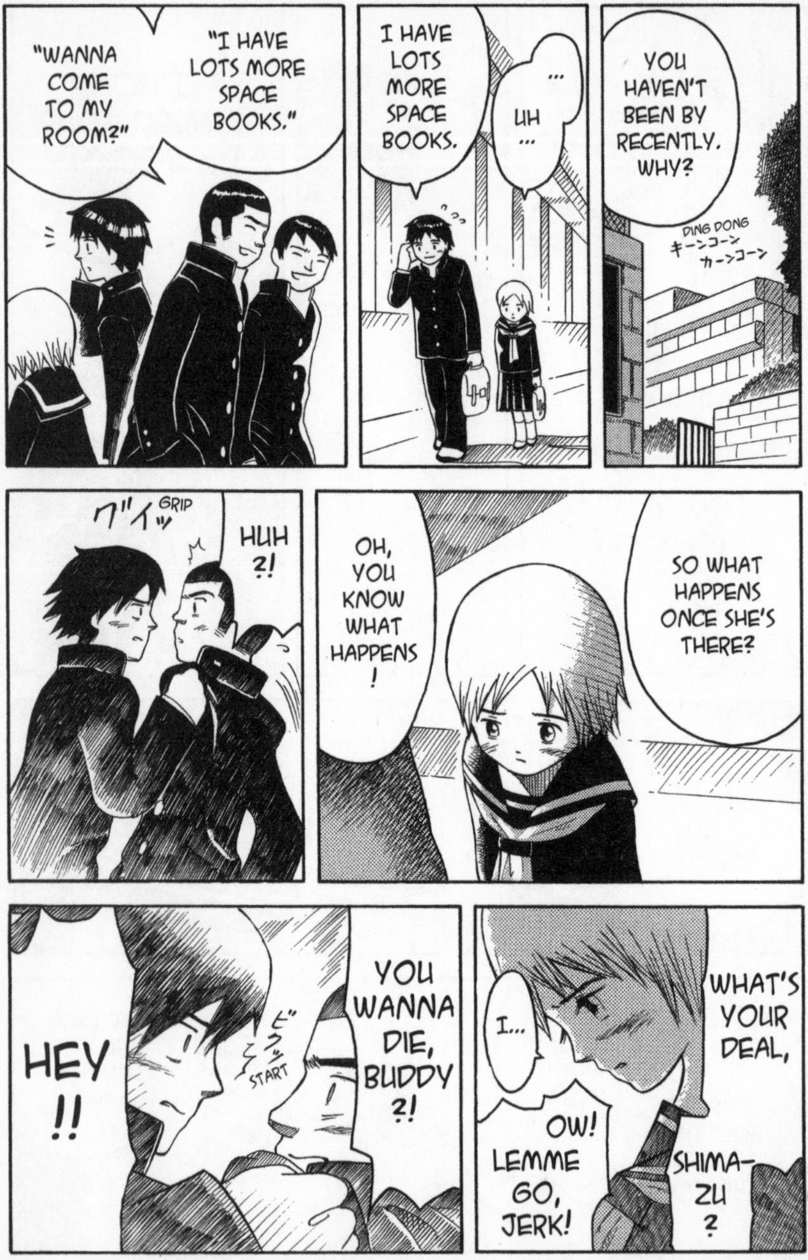
YOU HAVEN'T BEEN BY RECENTLY. WHY?
DING DONG
キーンコーン
カーンコーン
... UH ...
I HAVE LOTS MORE SPACE BOOKS.
"I HAVE LOTS MORE SPACE BOOKS."
"WANNA COME TO MY ROOM?"
SO WHAT HAPPENS ONCE SHE'S THERE?
OH, YOU KNOW WHAT HAPPENS!
HUH?!
GRIP
グイッ
WHAT'S YOUR DEAL,
I...
SHIMA-ZU?
OW! LEMME GO, JERK!
YOU WANNA DIE, BUDDY?!
ビクッ
START
HEY!!

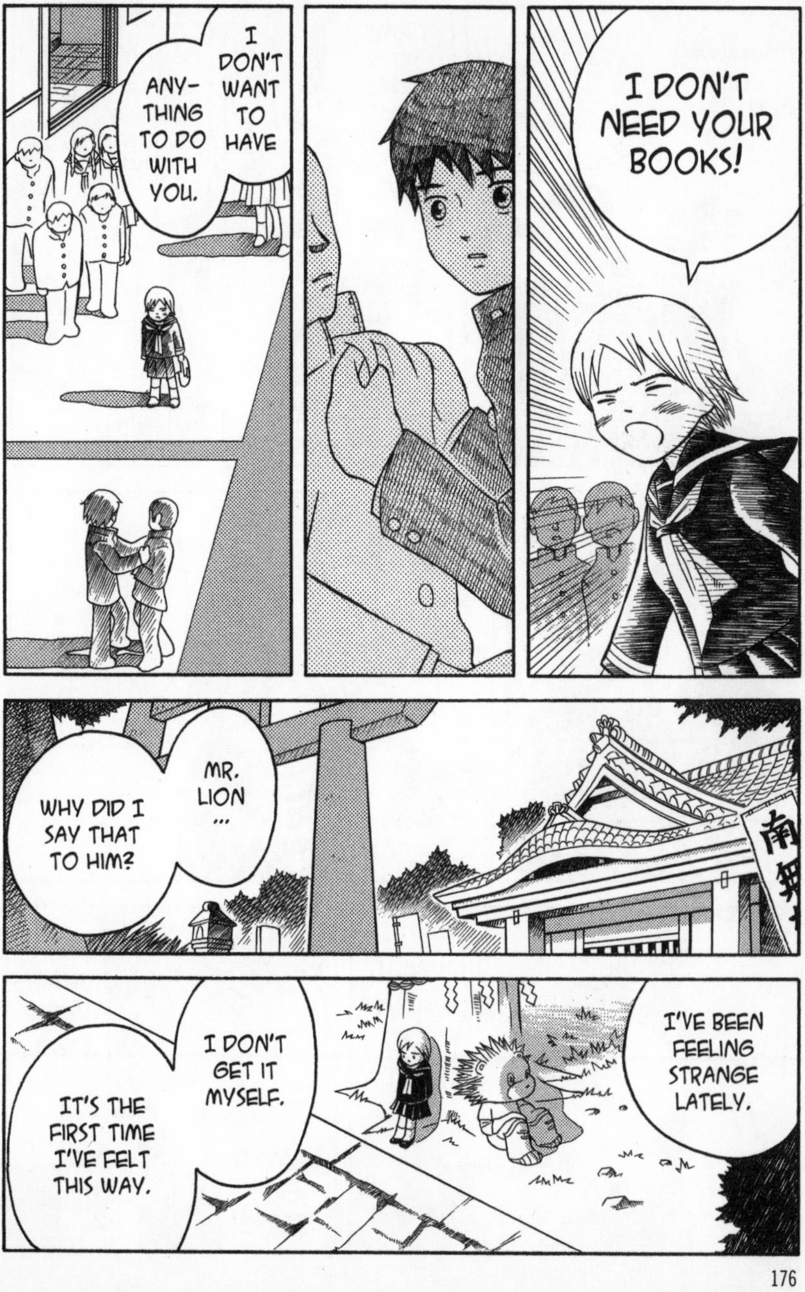
I DON'T NEED YOUR BOOKS!
I DON'T WANT TO HAVE ANYTHING TO DO WITH YOU.
MR. LION ...
WHY DID I SAY THAT TO HIM?
I'VE BEEN FEELING STRANGE LATELY.
I DON'T GET IT MYSELF.
IT'S THE FIRST TIME I'VE FELT THIS WAY.

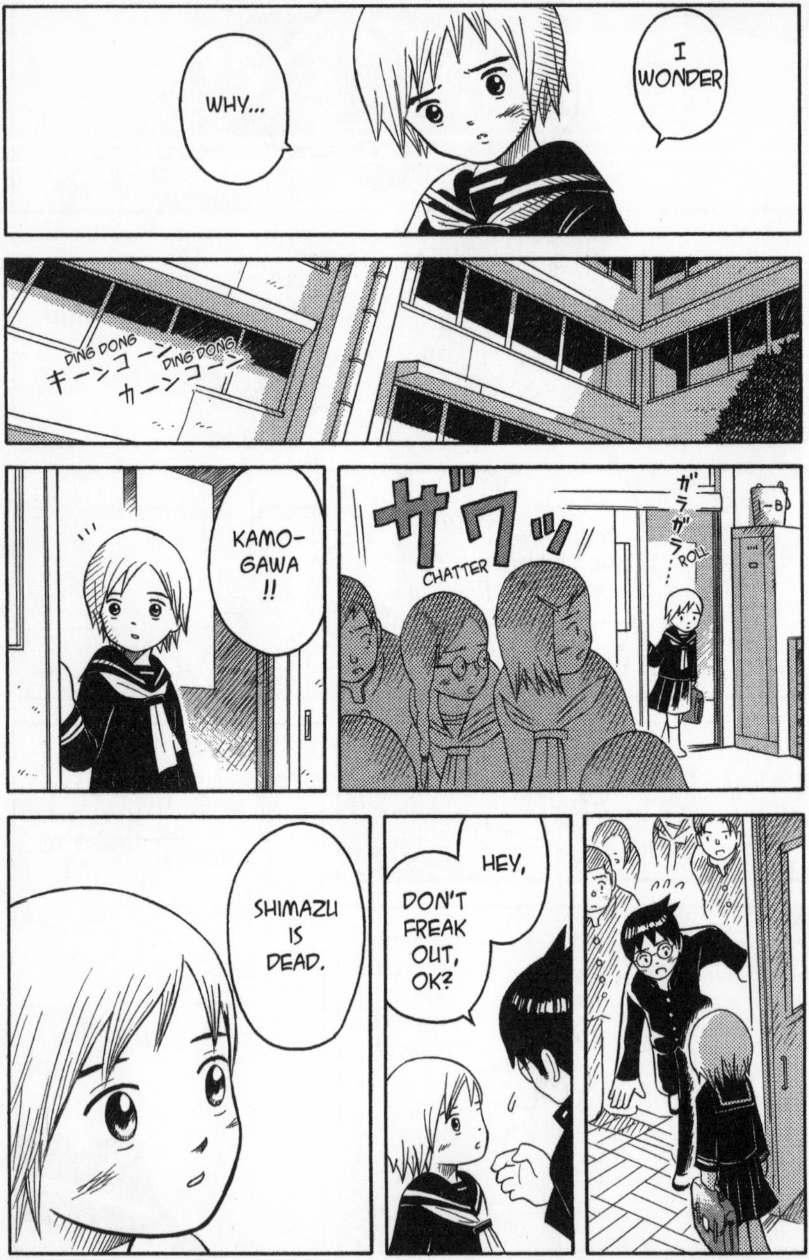
I WONDER
WHY...
DING DONG キーンコーン
DING DONG カーンコーン
ガラガラ ROLL
ザワッ CHATTER
KAMO-GAWA !!
HEY, DON'T FREAK OUT, OK?
SHIMAZU IS DEAD.

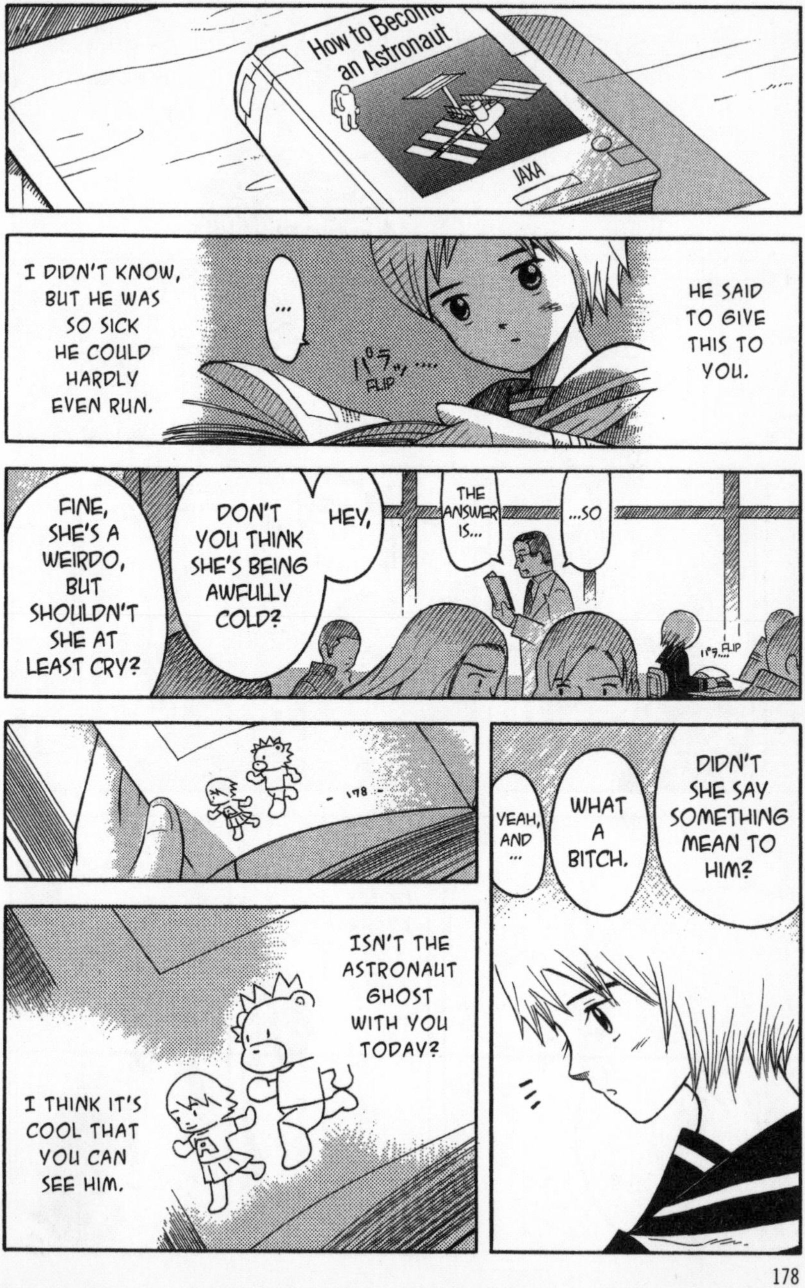
How to Become an Astronaut
JAXA
HE SAID TO GIVE THIS TO YOU.
...
FLIP
I DIDN'T KNOW, BUT HE WAS SO SICK HE COULD HARDLY EVEN RUN.
...SO
THE ANSWER IS...
HEY,
DON'T YOU THINK SHE'S BEING AWFULLY COLD?
FINE, SHE'S A WEIRDO, BUT SHOULDN'T SHE AT LEAST CRY?
FLIP
DIDN'T SHE SAY SOMETHING MEAN TO HIM?
WHAT A BITCH.
YEAH, AND ...
- 178 -
ISN'T THE ASTRONAUT GHOST WITH YOU TODAY?
I THINK IT'S COOL THAT YOU CAN SEE HIM.

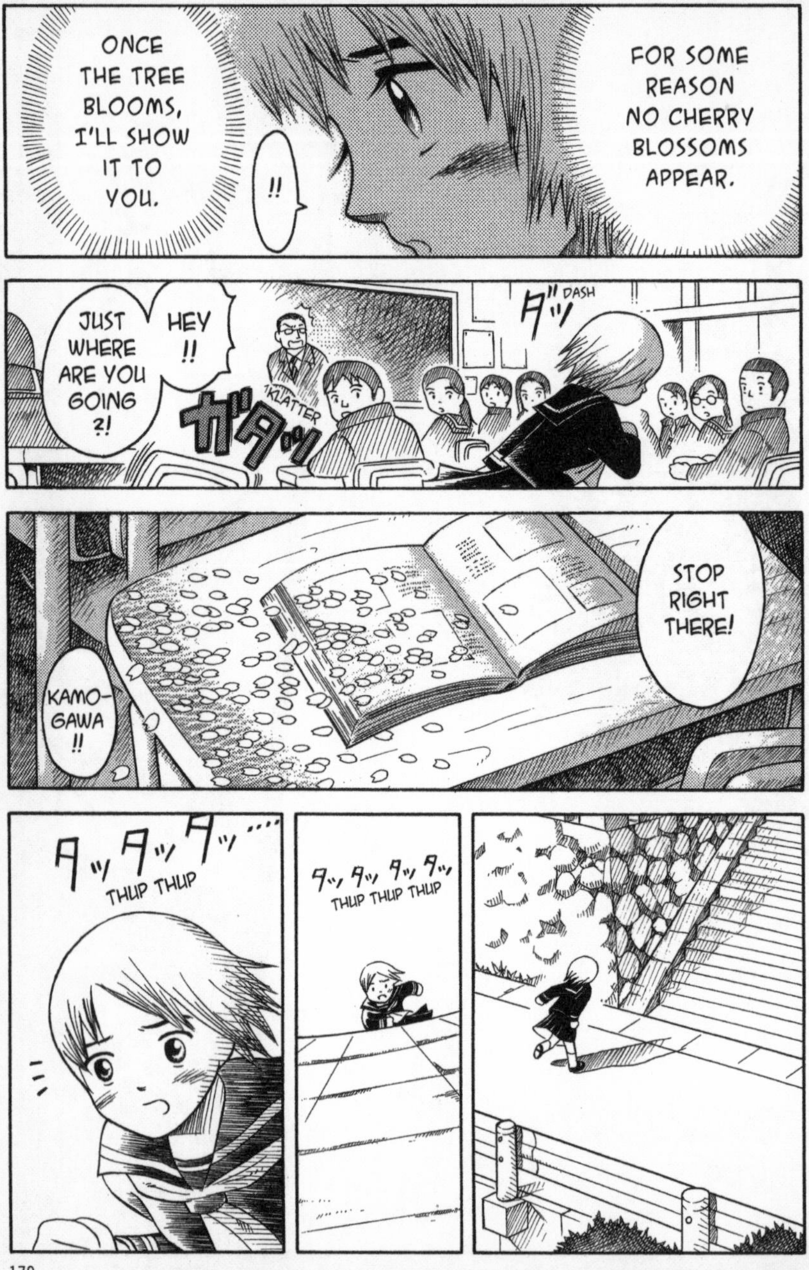
FOR SOME REASON NO CHERRY BLOSSOMS APPEAR.
!!
ONCE THE TREE BLOOMS, I'LL SHOW IT TO YOU.
ダッ DASH
HEY!!
JUST WHERE ARE YOU GOING?!
ガタッ KLATTER
STOP RIGHT THERE!
KAMO-GAWA!!
タッ タッ タッ タッ THUP THUP THUP
タッ タッ タッ… THUP THUP

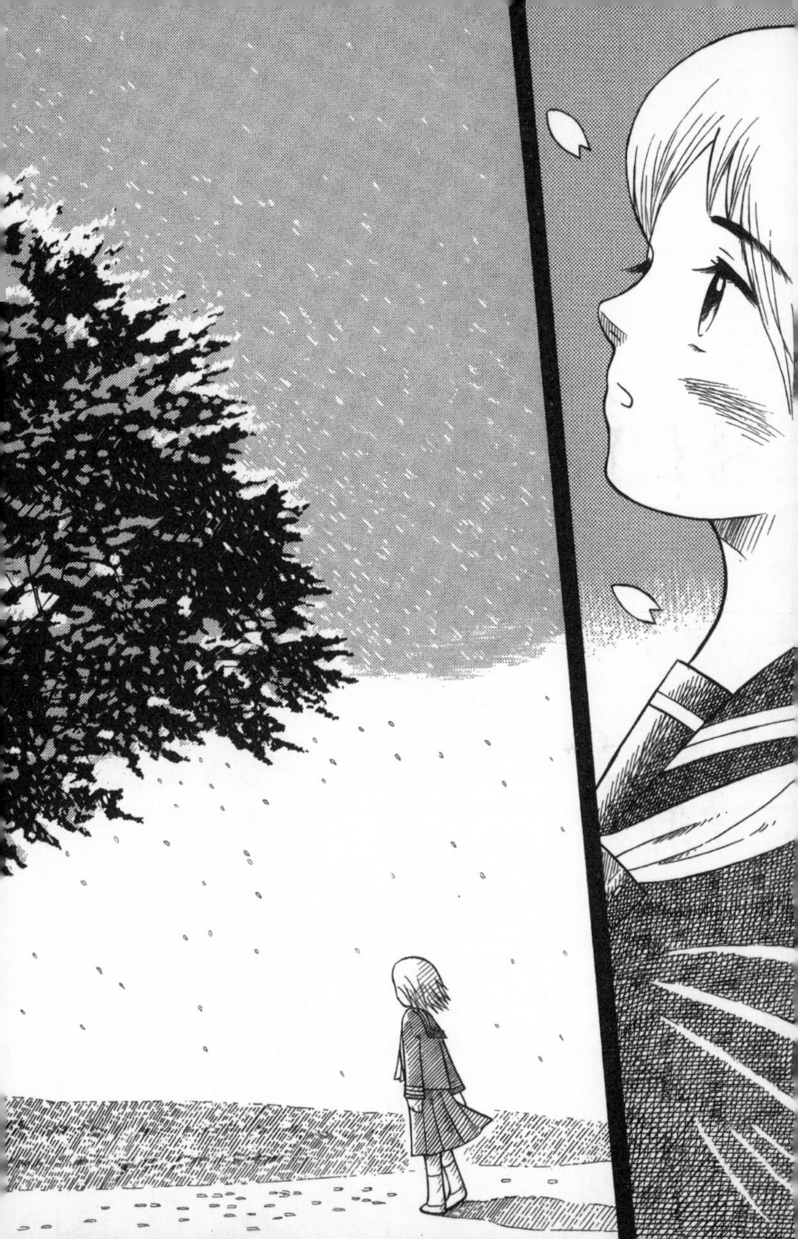

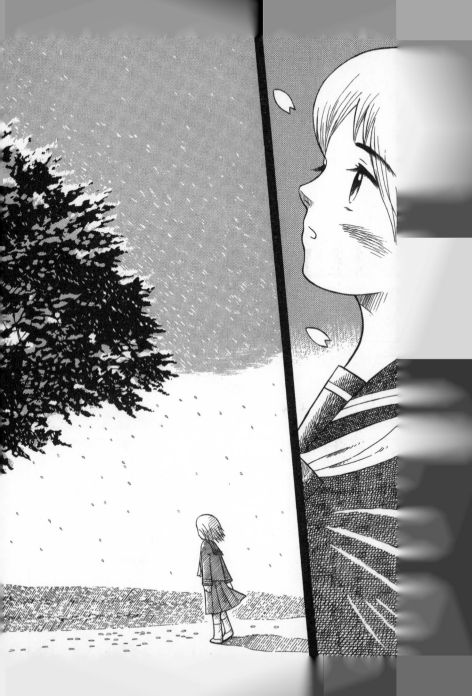

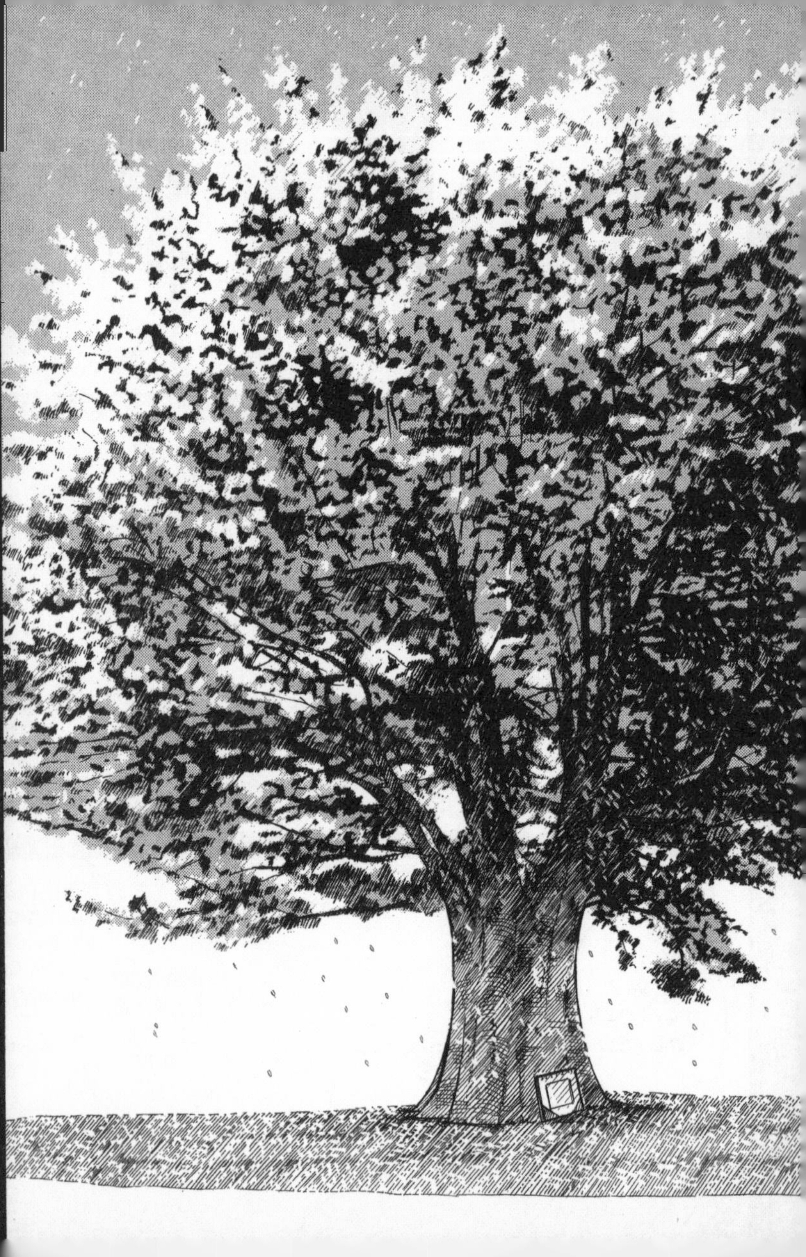

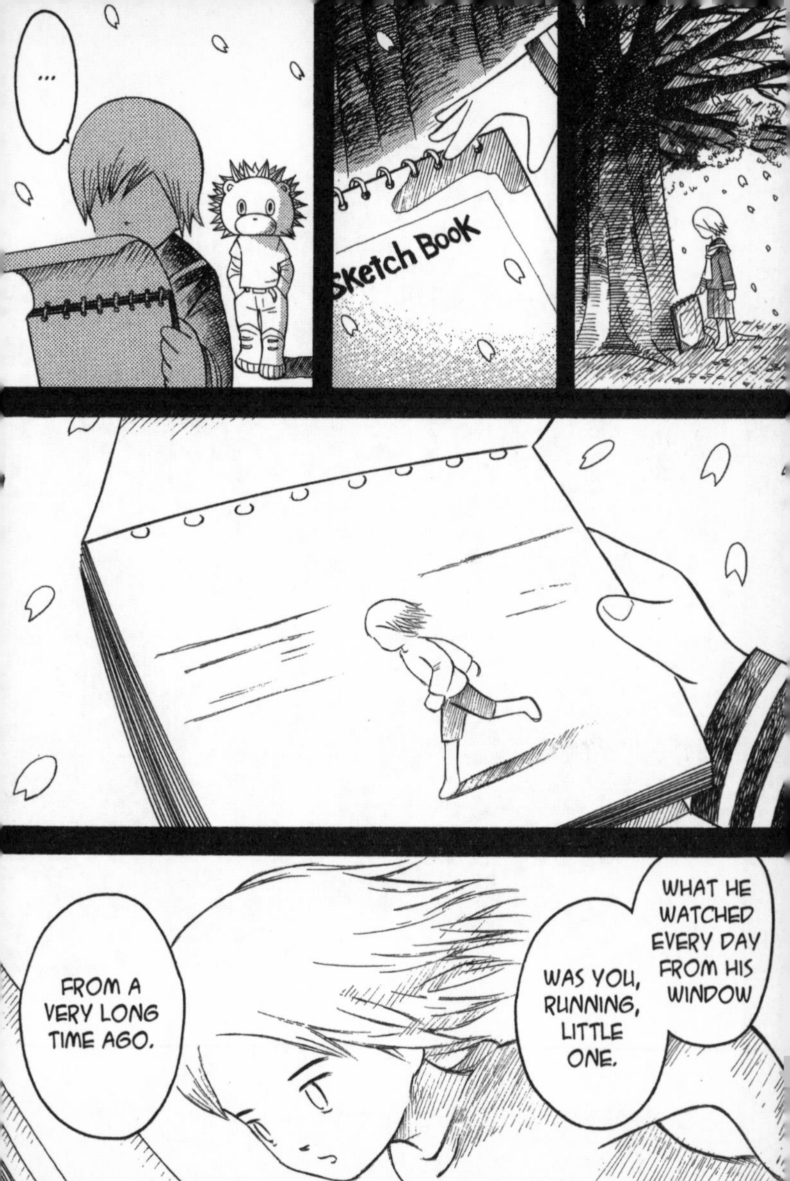
Sketch Book
...
WHAT HE WATCHED EVERY DAY FROM HIS WINDOW
WAS YOU, RUNNING, LITTLE ONE.
FROM A VERY LONG TIME AGO.

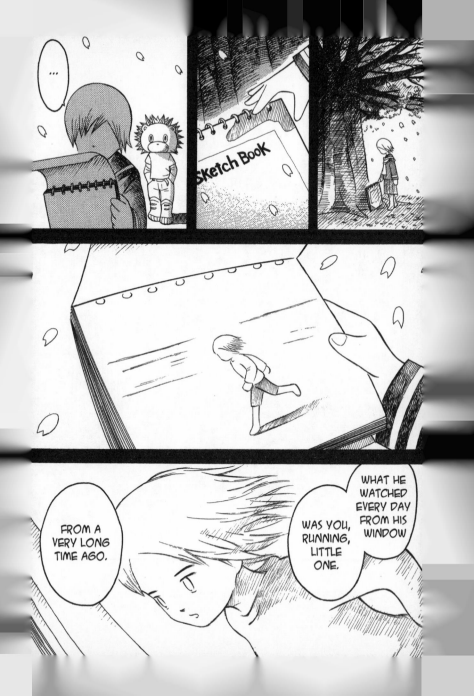

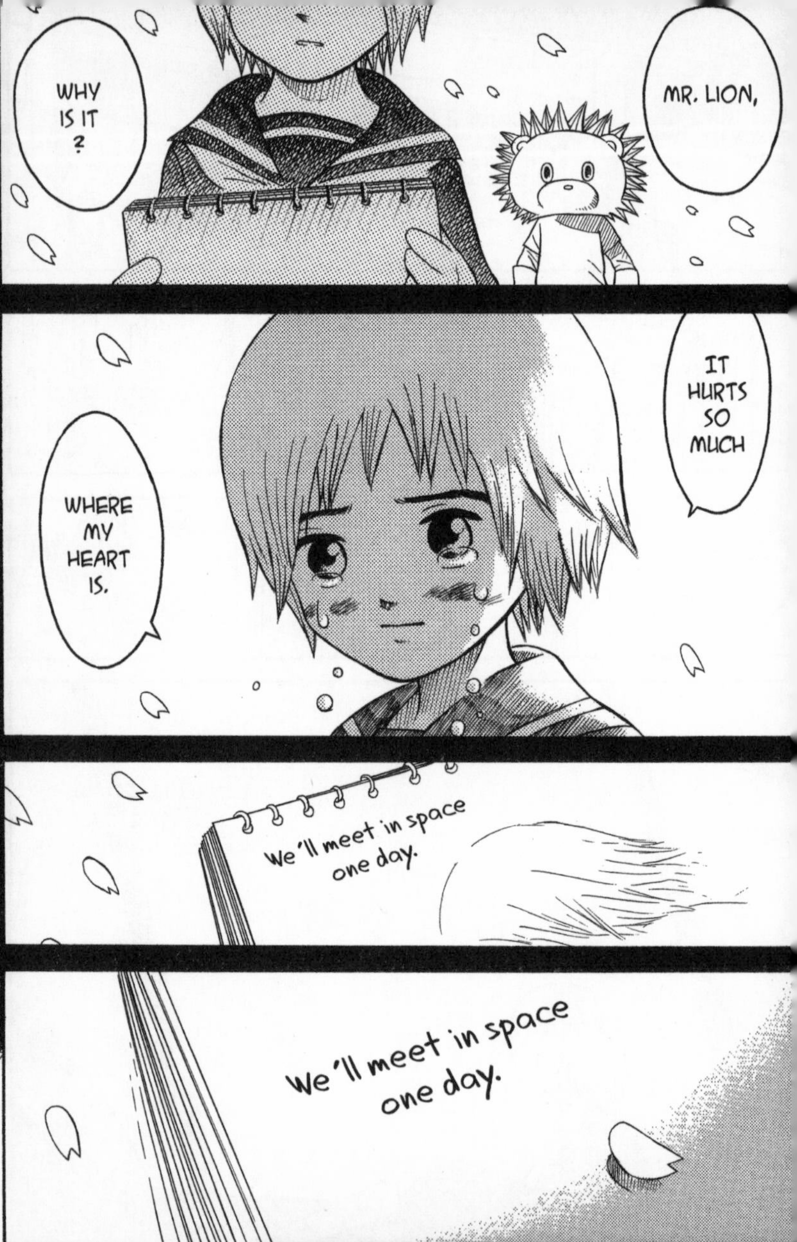

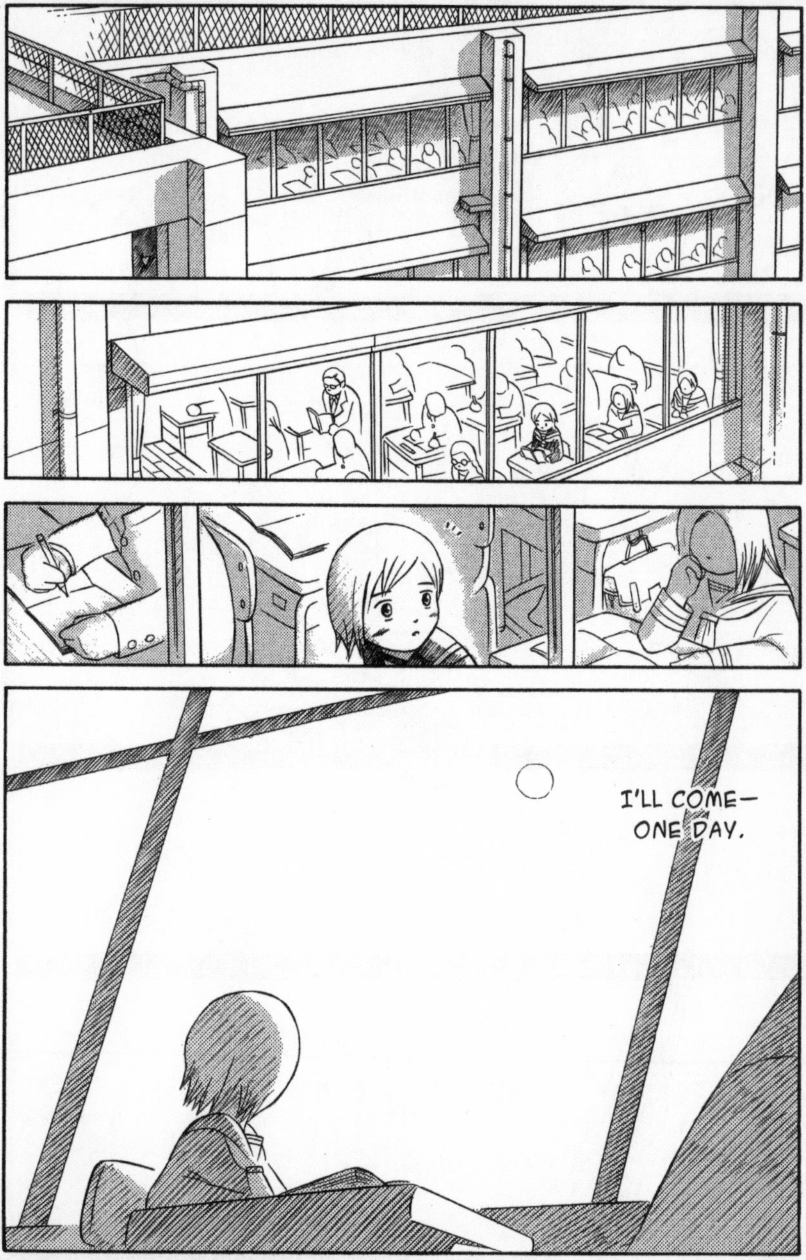
I'LL COME—
ONE DAY.

"ASUMI'S CHERRY BLOSSOMS" —THE END

ANOTHER SPICA

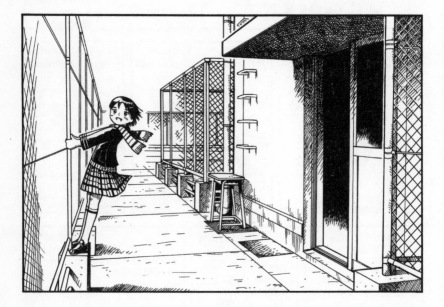

KOU YAGINUMA

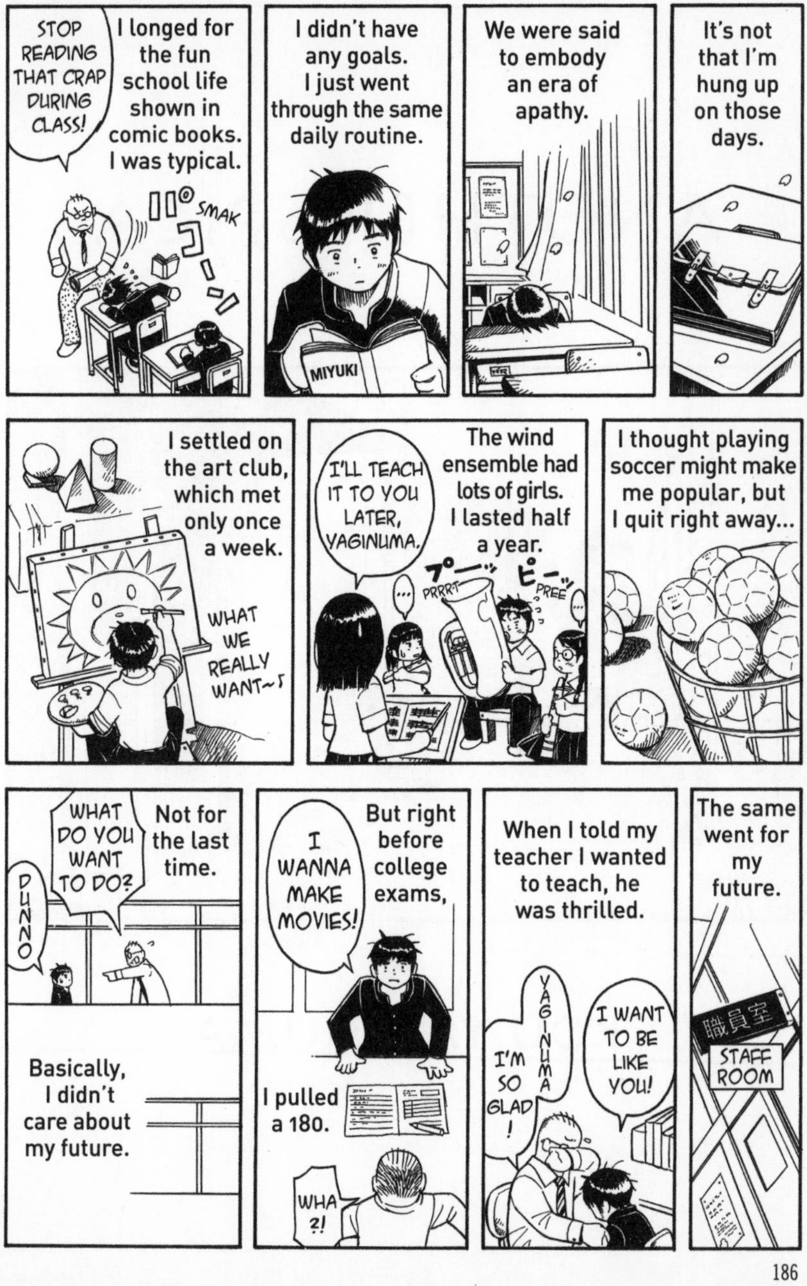
It's not that I'm hung up on those days.
We were said to embody an era of apathy.
I didn't have any goals. I just went through the same daily routine.
MIYUKI
I longed for the fun school life shown in comic books. I was typical.
STOP READING THAT CRAP DURING CLASS!
SMAK
I thought playing soccer might make me popular, but I quit right away...
The wind ensemble had lots of girls. I lasted half a year.
I'LL TEACH IT TO YOU LATER, YAGINUMA.
...
プーッ
PRRRT
ピーッ
PREE
...
I settled on the art club, which met only once a week.
WHAT WE REALLY WANT~♪
The same went for my future.
職員室
STAFF ROOM
When I told my teacher I wanted to teach, he was thrilled.
I WANT TO BE LIKE YOU!
YAGINUMA
I'M SO GLAD!
But right before college exams,
I WANNA MAKE MOVIES!
I pulled a 180.
WHA?!
Not for the last time.
WHAT DO YOU WANT TO DO?
DUNNO
Basically, I didn't care about my future.

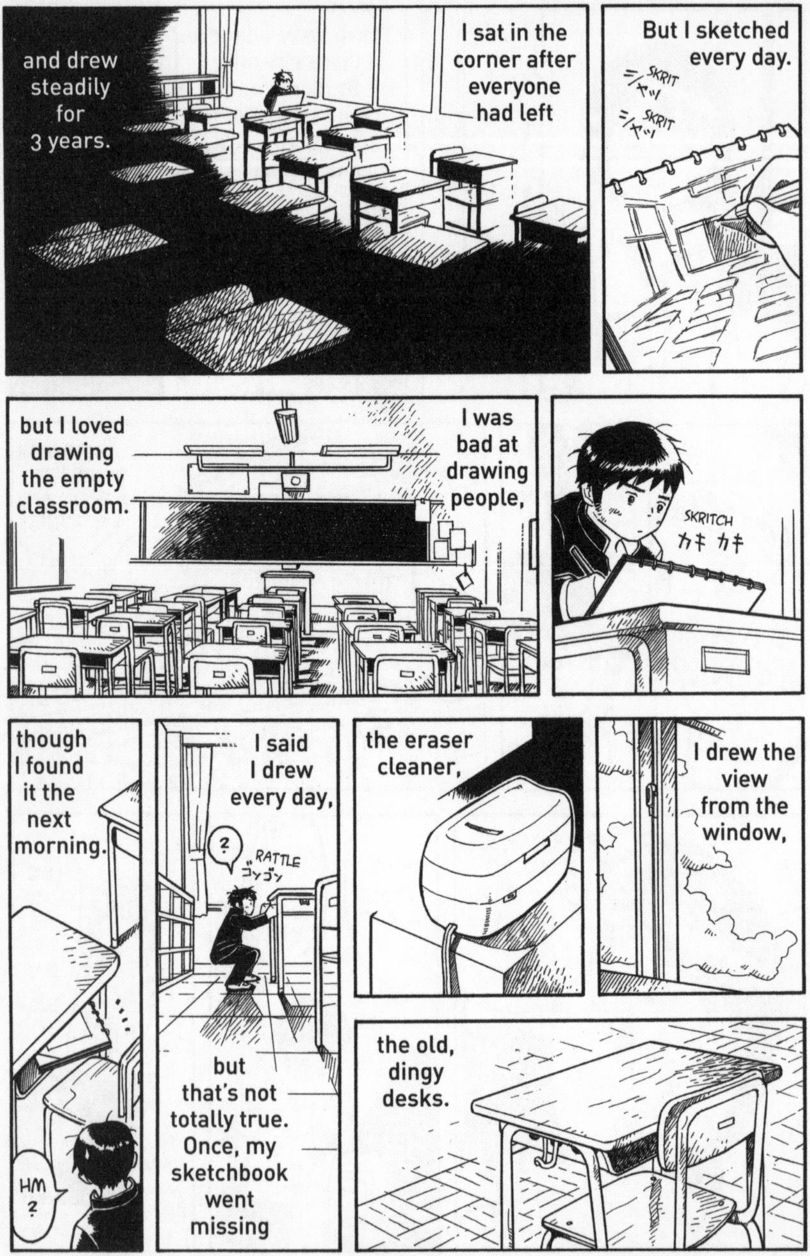
But I sketched every day.
SKRIT
シャッ
SKRIT
シャッ
I sat in the corner after everyone had left
and drew steadily for 3 years.
SKRITCH
カキ カキ
I was bad at drawing people,
but I loved drawing the empty classroom.
I drew the view from the window,
the eraser cleaner,
the old, dingy desks.
I said I drew every day,
?
RATTLE
ゴソゴソ
but that's not totally true. Once, my sketchbook went missing
though I found it the next morning.
...
HM ?

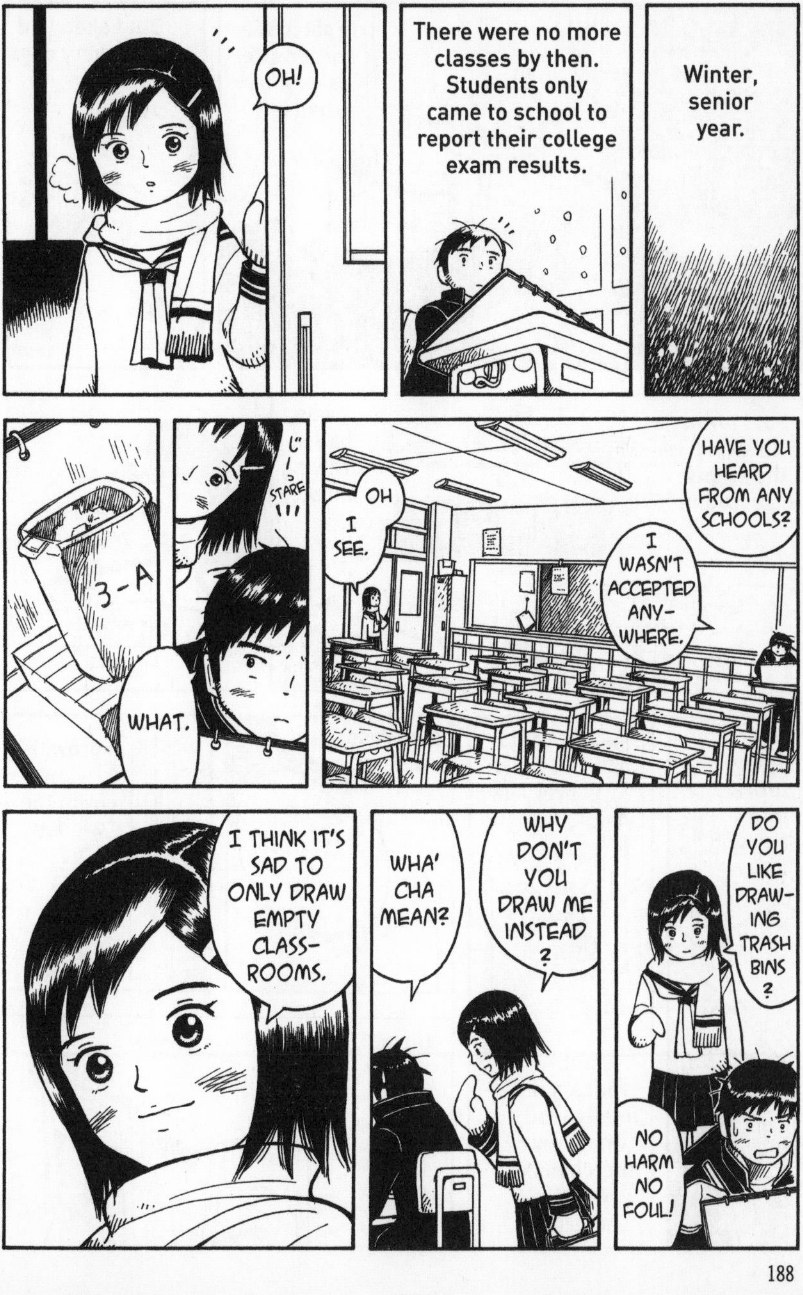

Winter, senior year.
There were no more classes by then. Students only came to school to report their college exam results.
OH!
HAVE YOU HEARD FROM ANY SCHOOLS?
I WASN'T ACCEPTED ANYWHERE.
OH I SEE.
じー
STARE
WHAT.
3-A
DO YOU LIKE DRAWING TRASH BINS?
NO HARM NO FOUL!
WHY DON'T YOU DRAW ME INSTEAD?
WHA'CHA MEAN?
I THINK IT'S SAD TO ONLY DRAW EMPTY CLASSROOMS.

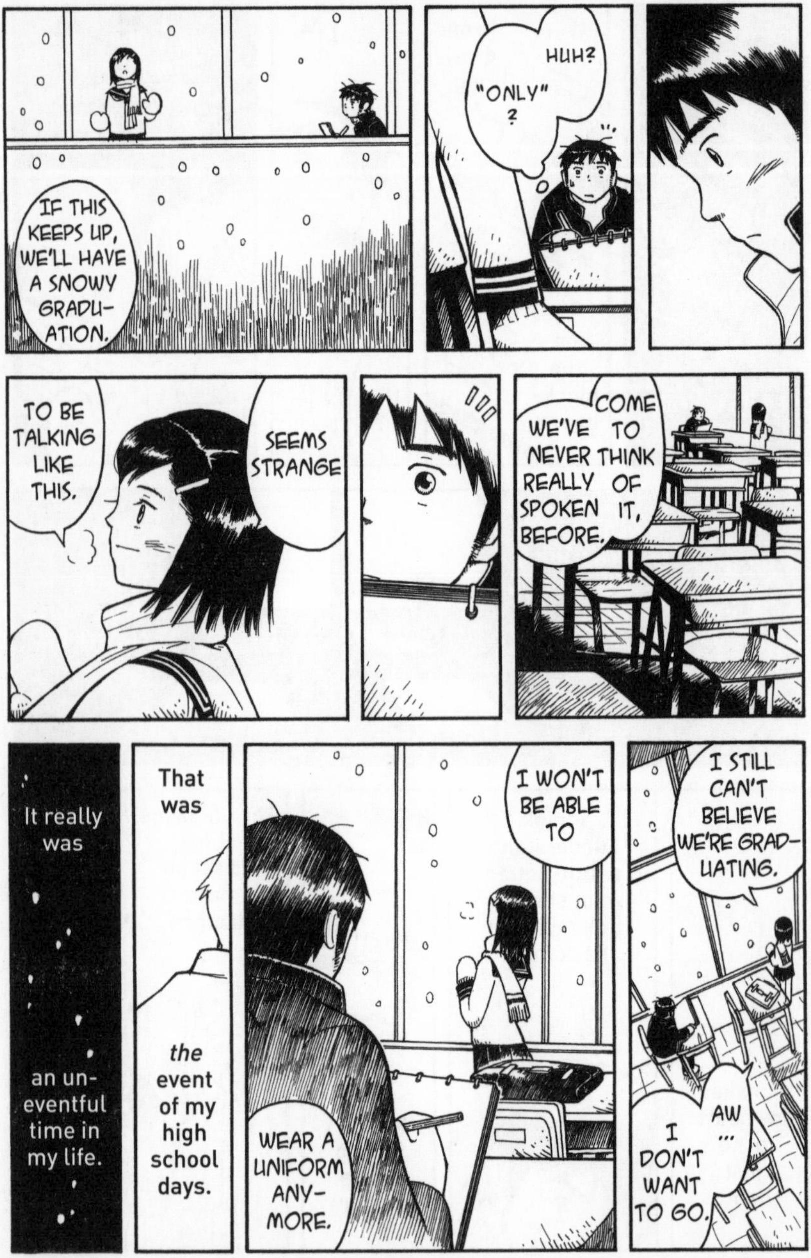
HUH? "ONLY" ?
IF THIS KEEPS UP, WE'LL HAVE A SNOWY GRADU-ATION.
COME TO THINK OF IT,
WE'VE NEVER REALLY SPOKEN BEFORE.
SEEMS STRANGE
TO BE TALKING LIKE THIS.
I STILL CAN'T BELIEVE WE'RE GRAD-UATING.
AW ...
I DON'T WANT TO GO.
I WON'T BE ABLE TO
WEAR A UNIFORM ANY-MORE.
That was
the event of my high school days.
It really was
an un-eventful time in my life.

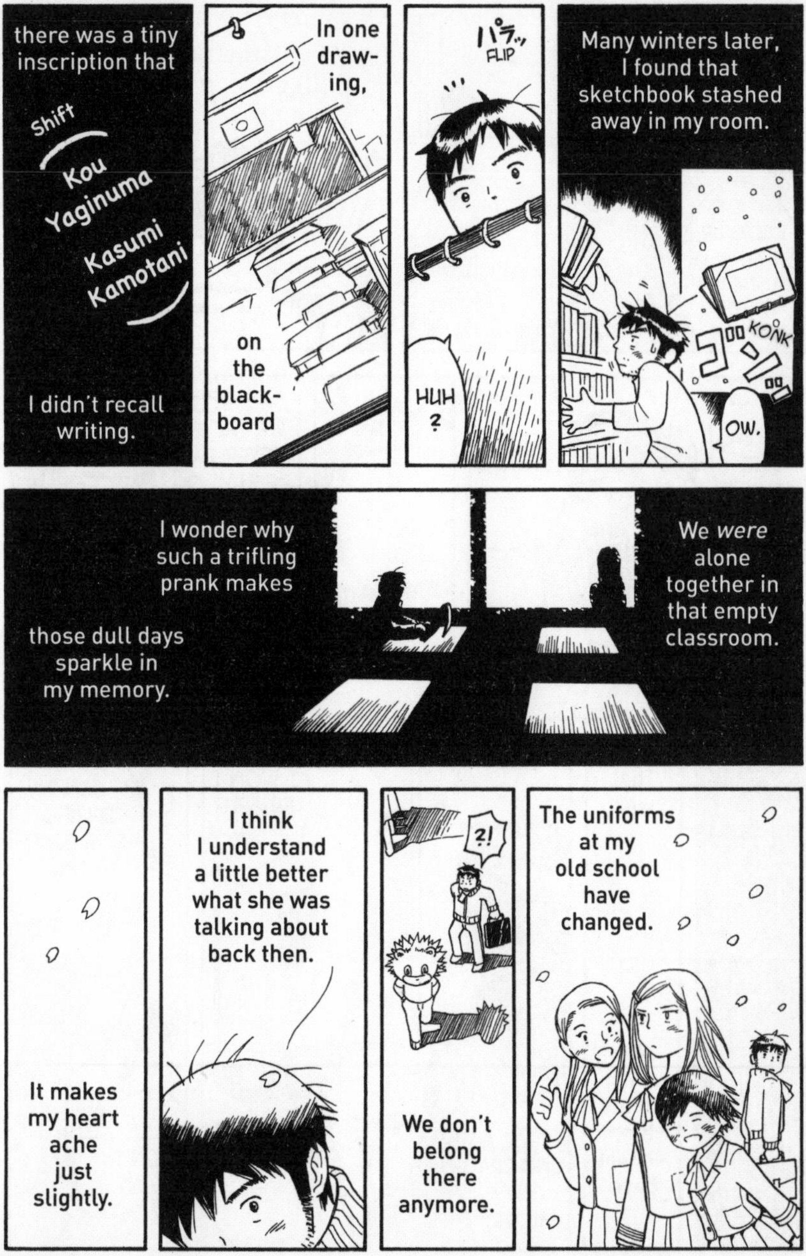
Many winters later, I found that sketchbook stashed away in my room.
KONK
OW.
パラッ
FLIP
HUH?
In one drawing,
on the blackboard
there was a tiny inscription that
Shift
Kou Yaginuma
Kasumi Kamotani
I didn't recall writing.
We *were* alone together in that empty classroom.
I wonder why such a trifling prank makes
those dull days sparkle in my memory.
The uniforms at my old school have changed.
?!
We don't belong there anymore.
I think I understand a little better what she was talking about back then.
It makes my heart ache just slightly.

THE END

Notes on the Translation

P. 23

The song "Look Up at the Stars at Night," from an eponymous musical, was covered in 1963 by Kyu Sakamoto of "Sukiyaki" fame. The song was chosen as the end theme of the animated TV series of *Twin Spica*.

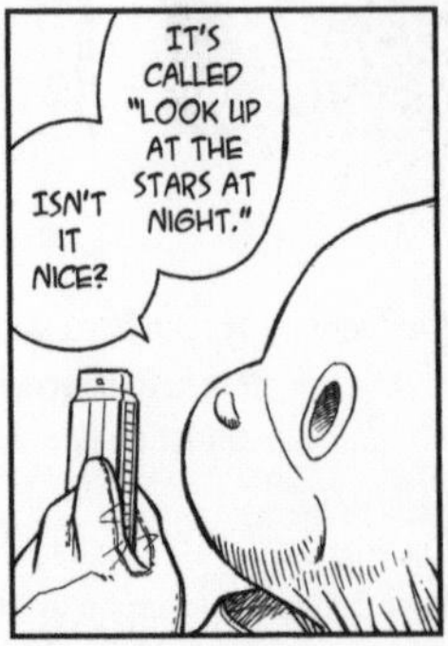
IT'S CALLED "LOOK UP AT THE STARS AT NIGHT."
ISN'T IT NICE?

P. 127

The name on display is *Yagi Shinbun*. The latter word means "newspaper"; the former plays on the first half of the author's surname but is written with the character for "goat"—an animal known for its taste for paper.

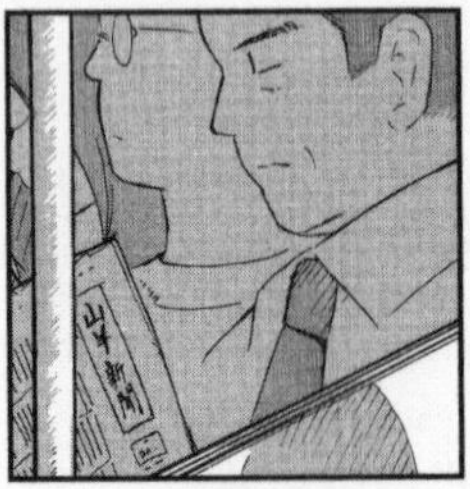

P. 163

The book is edited by a "Takashi Suwaribana," an allusion to leading journalist Takashi Tachibana (the character *tachi*, meaning "stand," has been replaced by the one for "sit"). He has authored acclaimed nonfiction books on astronauts, the cosmos, and numerous other subjects scientific and political.

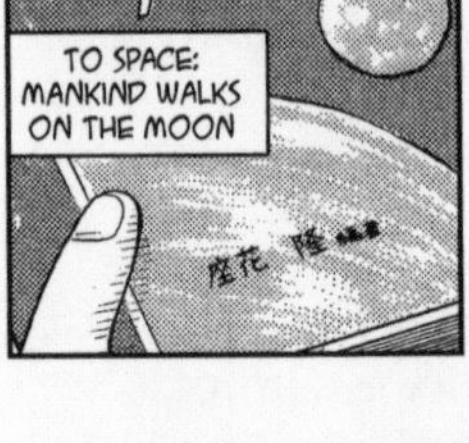
TO SPACE: MANKIND WALKS ON THE MOON

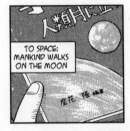

Production - Hiroko Mizuno
Maya Rosewood
Christine Lee

Originally published in Japanese as *Futatsu no Supika*
by MEDIA FACTORY, Inc., Tokyo 2002
Futatsu no Supika first serialized in Gekkan Comic Flapper,
MEDIA FACTORY, Inc., 2001-2009
"Asumi no Sakura" first published in Gekkan Comic Flapper,
MEDIA FACTORY, Inc., 2001

This is a work of fiction.

ISBN: 978-1-934287-90-3

Manufactured in Canada

First Edition

Vertical, Inc.
1185 Avenue of the Americas, 32nd Floor
New York, NY 10036
www.vertical-inc.com

A12005 719433